AF585418

MANNIX

ALSO BY BRENDA NIALL

Seven Little Billabongs: The World of Ethel Turner and Mary Grant Bruce

Australia through the Looking-glass: Children's Fiction 1830–1980 (with Frances O'Neill)

Martin Boyd: A Life

Georgiana: A Biography of Georgiana McCrae, Painter, Diarist, Pioneer

The Oxford Book of Australian Schooldays (with Ian Britain and Pamela Williams, eds.)

The Oxford Book of Australian Letters (with John Thompson, eds.)

The Boyds: A Family Biography

Brenda Niall on Arthur Boyd

Judy Cassab: A Portrait

Walking upon Ashes: The Footsteps of a Modern Biographer

Life Class: The Education of a Biographer

The Riddle of Father Hackett: A Life in Ireland and Australia

True North: The Story of Mary and Elizabeth Durack

MANNIX

BRENDA NIALL

TEXT PUBLISHING
MELBOURNE AUSTRALIA

Photographs reproduced with permission. The Australian War Memorial: formal portrait, 1919. © MDHC Catholic Archdiocese of Melbourne: Pro-Ireland demonstration; Raheen; newspaper clipping 'Jacob Children in O'Keefe Case'. Newman College by permission of the rector, William Uren SJ: country confirmation; Newman College (photographer John Kaufman); portrait by Clifton Pugh. Bob Mannix: Patrick Mannix. Michael Parer Papers: Ellen Mannix; Timothy Mannix; Deerpark; Maynooth Library; Queen Alexandra's visit to Maynooth; St Patrick's Day procession, 1920; conscription cartoon; Mannix in London, 1920; postcard, 1920; Mannix, 1930s; St Patrick's Day procession, 1941; Mozart Boys Choir; outside the catherdral, 1945; Little Sisters of the Poor soup kitchen; National Catholic Girls' Movement conference; Mannix, c. 1960; walking sticks; walking to the cathedral; burial at St Patrick's. Paul Santamaria: Bob Santamaria signing role. Wikicommons: St Patrick's College, Maynooth; Eamon de Valera.

textpublishing.com.au
The Text Publishing Company
Swann House, 22 William Street
Melbourne Victoria 3000 Australia

First published by The Text Publishing Company 2015

Design by W. H. Chong
Typeset by J&M Typesetting
Index by Nikki Davis
Jacket photo by Vincent Kelly, from MDHC Catholic Archdiocese of Melbourne
Jacket and endpaper pattern based on tile design of the central aisle, St Patrick's Cathedral, Melbourne
Printed and bound in Australia by Griffin Press, an Accredited ISO AS/NZS 14001:2004 Environmental Management System printer

National Library of Australia Cataloguing-in-Publication

Creator: Niall, Brenda, 1930–, author.
Title: Mannix / by Brenda Niall.
ISBN: 9781922182111 (hardback)
ISBN: 9781925095111 (ebook)
Subjects: Mannix, Daniel, 1864–1963.
Catholic Church—Bishops—Biography.
Bishops—Victoria—Melbourne—Biography.
Melbourne (Vic.)—History—20th century.

Dewey Number: 282.092

This project has been assisted by the Commonwealth Government through the Australia Council, its arts funding and advisory body.

CONTENTS

Introduction

IT TOOK THREE days to burn his private papers, so the legend has it. Not the letters Mannix himself had written—those went out to the world, and many were lost, or destroyed at his request—but those that had been sent to him. Letters came by sea from Ireland, Rome and the United States, later by air. If he kept the envelopes from his native Ireland, which in his absence fought and reversed seven hundred years of British colonial rule to become a republic, their stamps would have shown the red of empire yield to Eire's green, with an interregnum of the Irish Free State, which Mannix despised as an imperial compromise created by a flawed treaty with Britain. Evidence of his disdain for the monarchy survives on envelopes, addressed in Mannix's hand, with the stamp stuck on sideways: a schoolboyish gesture which persisted as late as 1939.[1]

Fifty years of correspondence, from 1913 to 1963: one can only guess at the numbers. Think of the famous guests who stayed at

Mannix's mansion Raheen: their letters of thanks must have been burned. In 1948 the formal rooms at Raheen were redecorated for the visit of two clerical celebrities, Cardina Spellman of New York and author and orator Bishop Fulton Sheen. Irish republican leader Eamon de Valera (later head of state) came to stay with his old ally. There is no knowing what they talked about or whether Mannix relaxed his rule of bedtime at 10 p.m. For a friend last seen in 1925, did he let the talk go on? De Valera, the 'Long Fellow', as tall and spare as Mannix himself, was never one to gush, but he must have sent some words of appreciation to his host, some recognition of their meeting.

The incoming letters would have dwindled over the years, as Mannix grew old and the human ties frayed and were broken. But during his early combative years, when he publicly opposed conscription and later gave strong support to the Irish nationalist movement, his letterbox would have been crammed. And as he always stressed (unconvincingly) that in political matters he spoke as a private citizen, he would have carried on much of the written argument himself, from his own house, rather than make it part of cathedral business.

In 1922, when the Irish were divided among themselves about the terms of their treaty with Britain, the anti-treaty leaders had no comfort from the bishops of Ireland. Even at the other end of the world, Mannix was their man; they wrote to him at Raheen so that he would know 'how things were' in the troubled country he had left. Robert Barton, one of those who signed the treaty with Britain but later repudiated it, sent Mannix a detailed personal account of the experience.[2] This historic document must be presumed lost. If Mannix didn't destroy it, for safety's sake, in the 1920s, it would have gone into the bonfire of his papers in 1963.

Who can guess what family letters there would have been? His father died three years before Mannix left for Australia, but others in the family must have written. How did his mother address him? What was the tone of letters from his sister? When he wrote to tell them about his new life twelve thousand miles from home, they might have sensed loneliness and responded to it. Was he Dan or Danny to old friends in Ireland, or did he turn into 'Your Grace'? It was rumoured that he was estranged from his two brothers. As an austere churchman who became a total abstainer, it must have been distressing to have one brother renounce his faith and the other become a heavy drinker who lost the family farm. Perhaps the brothers never wrote. And if there was estrangement, did it come from Daniel Mannix or from his brothers? His only sister, Mary, did keep in touch; and when their mother, Ellen Mannix, died in 1925 Mary would have sent the news to Melbourne, described the last illness and the funeral, expressed a shared grief. Nothing of this intimacy remains. A few letters from nieces and nephews show that there was contact and goodwill up to the mid-1950s; their everyday tone suggests that there were others. One of the nephews sent 'dear Uncle Dan' a message of support for his anti-treaty campaign.[3] Some letters may have been destroyed by Mannix himself, dropped into a wastepaper basket or burned in his study fireplace; but enough were left to keep the bonfire busy.

Letters from Ireland, where Mannix had spent his first half century, from powerful friends, bishops and priests, political leaders, professors, would have been revealing. So would responses to his first impressions of Australia in 1913. Mannix might have been discreet in writing about church matters, but such an intelligent and observant man must have had some thoughts on the new society, on landscape and climate, and on the grey Neo-Gothic cathedral of St Patrick in Melbourne which would become the centre of his daily life.

Mannix was a divisive figure, and the years would bring him many hostile letters; anger and disapproval would strain the polite forms of correspondence. Yet he had friends and allies in Ireland. To which of them did he write freely? Every letter is an episode in a relationship; its silences can be read, its tone of voice can be heard. But by ruling that all remaining personal papers be burned, Mannix imposed his will on subordinates, even beyond his death. He did not want to be interpreted. What survived would be the public voice of Daniel Mannix, the official letters over his signature, dictated and typed speeches, proofs corrected in his hand, published speeches and interviews. Hundreds of thousands of words, but not many in his own handwriting. Still less in the handwriting of others to express whatever personal relationships linked him to his birthplace in Charleville, County Cork, or to Maynooth, near Dublin, his home and place of work for more than thirty years.

Half a century after his death, Mannix still challenges biographers and historians. His long life has no parallel in Australia's history. No political leader, no matter how persistent, durable or charismatic, has commanded the stage to the end, as Mannix did. No other churchman has taken part in national debates with comparable effect. From the conscription debates of 1916 and 1917 to the ALP split in the mid-1950s, he was a dominant presence. His views on public questions mattered. Politicians watched him closely as the presumed deliverer of the Catholic vote. For his own Catholic people he represented stability in faith and morals, but he administered seismic shocks in matters of political and social policy that were felt nationally and internationally. A centre of unity in some ways, he was also a source of division.

Feeding the flames on three long summer days after the death of Daniel Mannix in November 1963 was a hot and thankless task. Each scrap of charred paper, each ember glowing in the incinerator at the close of day, confirmed the ending of an epoch. There, as anyone would have known, went fragments of half a century of history. Mannix had lived in the same house, Raheen, in Studley Park Road in the Melbourne suburb of Kew, since 1917, four years after his arrival from Ireland and very soon after he succeeded Thomas Carr as Archbishop of Melbourne. He had lived in the same way throughout that time, austerely yet with the dignity that went with his rank and sense of self. When he died at the age of ninety-nine, it was not so much the end of an era—the era Mannix represented had already ended—but a time to look back and reflect. But if anyone wanted imaginative entry into the private life of the powerful enigmatic Mannix, he had done his best to keep them out. As in life, so in death, he was untouchable.

It was vandalism to burn the Mannix papers, said one of his successors. Frank Little, the last Archbishop of Melbourne to live at Raheen, had heard the story from a reluctant vandal. May Saunders, housekeeper to Bishop Arthur Fox, was used to doing what she was told. So was Arthur Fox, auxiliary bishop to Daniel Mannix. Between them, they disposed of most of the Mannix papers, setting aside those that were clearly on diocesan matters. May Saunders didn't like it, but what could she do? Archbishop Frank Little, who told me the story in 2008, was still indignant, but he didn't blame May Saunders. And he understood Bishop Fox, who did his loyal and deplorable duty.[4]

Mannix's order to Fox is in keeping with his habitual reticence. Although he never shrank from the public gaze, where he performed magnificently, his whole life in Australia was disciplined, self-sufficient, answerable to no one and nothing except to God and the sense of mission to his people which expressed God's will.

It was said that his decision to have his papers burnt was a defence against biographers. He had read a life of one of the archbishops of Dublin, Dr William Walsh, and thought it a travesty of the man he had known. No one would do that to him; no one would analyse the mind and heart of Daniel Mannix. It would be bad enough if they got it wrong. And for him, it might have been almost as bad if they got it right. He knew what it was like to be misunderstood and, at least at the level of ideas and policies, he thrived on argument. Intrusion into his private world, his fortress, was another matter.

The three-day bonfire of 1963 was an ending. But the resolve to keep no private papers must go further back and have complex meanings. Other prelates have been just as discreet. The surviving papers of Archbishop Patrick Clune of Perth fit in a single archive box and those of Archbishop Andrew Killian of Adelaide are meagre. These three Irishmen must all have written to one another many times. In the days of the three-minute telephone call, most communication would have been by post. Besides, Mannix never used the telephone.

Here, as so often in Mannix's life, we have to remember the struggle in Ireland for independence from Britain. In 1920, Mannix was in Europe, paying his duty visit to the Pope. He had also planned to visit Ireland, but was arrested at sea by order of the British government. Landed in Penzance, he made his way to London and went on a series of provocative speaking tours in support of de Valera's radical nationalist Sinn Féin party while negotiating in secret with influential friends from Dublin and Rome.

When Mannix eventually returned to Australia, a network of friends and associates kept him in touch with Irish politics in a tragic, violent time. That was surely a time for secrecy. Living under British colonial rule, they had reason to be careful. Mannix was under surveillance and he knew it. During the First World War, his letters were read by the Australian censors, and their contents reported to the British government. His incoming mail during the Irish war of independence and civil war was intercepted and read before being delivered at Raheen.[5] Eamon de Valera sent letters by courier, marked 'Destroy immediately'.[6]

But politics alone cannot account for the obliteration of the private life, or the destruction of historic documents, after the turmoil of Ireland's civil war was over. Why not keep family letters and photographs, exchanges with friends, and other records of ordinary life? There must be something in Mannix's inner self to account for such ferocious privacy.

And yet on the question of biography, he did make a concession. In the late 1950s, Mannix agreed that an authorised life could be written by his disciple and friend B.A. Santamaria. If anyone was in a position to understand Mannix it should have been Santamaria, who by the mid-1950s was calling at Raheen two or three times a week. Their relationship had grown closer year by year, from its beginnings in 1937 when the awestruck twenty-two-year-old law graduate changed the course of his life because the archbishop asked him to. The Australian National Secretariat of Catholic Action, then little more than an idea in the making, needed a deputy for the director, Frank Maher. Santamaria's words—'so I said…"Yes", because I would have said yes to anything he asked'—echo down the years.[7] Was he still saying yes to the archbishop when the Australian Labor Party was divided and wrecked in 1954–55 over the question of communist influence? Or, by then, was it the archbishop who said yes?

When Santamaria asked to be his biographer, Mannix may have agreed out of habit as well as affection; he seldom rejected Bob Santamaria's ideas. He would also have trusted Santamaria not to come too near. Friendly and unassuming in manner, Santamaria was in his way as private a man as the aloof Mannix. He mistrusted 'psychologising' as he dismissively described any analysis of feelings. Inevitably, Santamaria's biography of Mannix would be narrative rather than reflective. He would not intrude on the private self of the man he admired beyond all others.

This is where I came in. In 1959, I was invited by Bob Santamaria to help with the Mannix biography. In my twenties and not yet focused on a career, I was tempted; it sounded more interesting than most possibilities open to a young woman with a degree in English Language and Literature who typed only with one finger. I was just back in Australia after a year overseas when he telephoned with his idea of a biography. I knew it might be a mistake to accept his offer. My first job, after graduation, had been as Santamaria's research assistant, and, although he was an easygoing employer, his office was an isolating place. Yet, Santamaria was persuasive, and when he spoke of the need to explore the archbishop's early life my imagination was caught. During my time in Europe, I had visited Ireland twice. Its landscapes were enchanting and it felt like home. I was astonished to find how easy it was to reconnect with the family of my emigrant great-grandfather, John Niall. I was made welcome by hospitable distant cousins in County Meath who knew everyone's place on the spreading family tree. Their house would have been the perfect base from which to seek out the Mannix family, if only the archbishop would allow it.

As it turned out, childhood and growing up in nineteenth-century Ireland interested me far more than it interested Santamaria. His sights were fixed on Mannix the leader, his own ally in the battles of church and state. His biography would be a tribute to the old man, a record of an unbroken alliance, and an explanation of the stormy history of Catholic interventions in Australian politics. I did not know how the archbishop would view the biography or my part in it, but I did hope it would open doors in Ireland and let me into his past.

Because Mannix was then ninety-five, it made sense for me to start with a series of interviews. So, some time in the autumn of 1959, I presented myself at Raheen with my little notebook and several sharpened pencils. It was a sunny afternoon, but the red-brick mansion was cool and dark. There was no small talk from the soft-voiced Jean Virgona, one of the two sisters who looked after the household. She led me silently from the front door, through the high-ceilinged library, to the study where Daniel Mannix sat in his usual corner, beside an unlit fire.

Of course, he was in charge from the beginning. I had in mind the usual questions: I would ask him about his parents, his sister and brothers, his childhood home in Charleville, County Cork, where he was born, in the unimaginably distant year of 1864, his schooling...But before I could ask about his family, he asked about mine. Not surprisingly, he had me placed. In 1935 my parents had built a house in Studley Park Road, a short walk from Raheen. As a presence (I wouldn't claim such a remote and magisterial being as a neighbour) Daniel Mannix was part of my childhood. He could be seen every day, anachronistically dressed in frock coat and top hat but magnificent in his bearing, taking his famous walk from Kew to St Patrick's Cathedral in East Melbourne. I had occasionally been sent on small errands to Raheen, carrying a letter from my school, Genazzano, whose Reverend Mother thought that delivery by hand was more polite than using the postal system. And, year by year, I was used to seeing the archbishop at our school concerts; wearily enduring, or perhaps covertly napping (head resting on hand, eyes half closed) during the familiar schoolgirl repertoire. From 'Nymphs and Shepherds' to 'God Save Ireland'—our tactful replacement, in Mannix's presence, for 'God Save the King'—he sat through it all.

Because he was such a familiar figure, I was not as awestruck as I might otherwise have been at the thought of asking him about himself. Yet any authority I might have had as interviewer soon slipped away. He asked about my mother; was she well? My younger brother and sisters; they must be growing up. He spoke of my father's early death in 1952, and the great debt the Catholic Church in Melbourne owed him as consultant physician to many priests and nuns. Although he didn't mention it, I was reminded of the day, soon after my father's death, when the archbishop asked my mother to come and see him. He offered to remit the school fees at Xavier and Genazzano for my younger brother and two sisters. She refused the offer because she didn't want her children to be made to feel grateful, but she was pleased at the archbishop's thoughtfulness. Looking back on that episode I realise that it expressed the Mannix style. He would not have consulted the Rector of Xavier nor Genazzano's Reverend Mother; they would simply have been told of His Grace's wish.

So from my family to his family, it was hard to reverse roles and start asking questions. For 'Did Your Grace have brothers and sisters?' I got the number of siblings, which I later found to be miscounted—could he have forgotten twins who died in infancy? 'Life on the family farm?' 'I don't remember that I ever did much work.' The old, weary voice trailed away. The best line of the session was from a question about schooldays. When the inspector came to choose those who were ready to move from the Sisters of Mercy to the Christian Brothers: 'I was such a big boy that the nuns hid me in a cupboard.' I wrote that down, pleased to have something in my notebook.

The low point of the afternoon came when the archbishop rang for tea. In it came, shining silver, fine china, stiff white linen napkins, homemade fruit cake: the whole ceremony, exquisitely prepared by the housekeeper. She poured my tea, but with an almost imperceptible signal the archbishop refused his cup, leaving me to deal with it all. The cup, saucer and plate, sugar tongs, milk jug, cake fork, could all have been small incendiary devices in my uncertain hands. And through it all, the archbishop leaned back in his chair, silently attentive, waiting for me to say something interesting. Or just waiting for it to be over, as he had waited at our school concerts for all those nymphs and shepherds to 'come, come, *come* away'.

I did another interview, perhaps two more, and fared a little better. This was because we had moved to the period of Mannix's public life, first as president of Ireland's major seminary, Maynooth College, and then as the newly arrived Coadjutor-Archbishop of Melbourne. But, as I became aware, with sinking spirits, he was telling me things I already knew. These were old stories, already published: the ones that began with the heat of the day in Adelaide in 1913 when he felt the pavement melt beneath his feet and thought: I'll never live a year in this climate. And yet this was not the repetitiousness of old age. Refusing to open up his past, I am certain, was a conscious decision. He gave me his time because he wanted to please Bob Santamaria. In the only spontaneous moment of our first session he asked me, quite eagerly, if I 'liked working for Mr Santamaria'. My reply, which I think was just a surprised 'Oh yes, Your Grace…', was probably less than he would have liked to hear, so he supplied words I hadn't spoken, surprising me even more with ' I think Mr Santamaria is the cleverest man I ever knew'. Cleverest? I left Raheen, puzzling over that oddly chosen word.

I can't remember how much more I contributed to the Santamaria biography, but most was from printed sources. I did, however, interview an Irish priest who had studied under Mannix at Maynooth, and who was old and indiscreet enough to say exactly what he thought. 'We loved him not—not at all—but he was a great man,' Father Morley Coyne summed up. He remembered high academic standards and strict, even unreasonable, rules. If you had toothache you had to write home to your own bishop for permission to see a dentist, and you might have a hard time while waiting for the letter of reply, or for the college dentist who came once a week. For me, the best of the Coyne interview was his comment on the aloofness of Mannix: 'He wasn't a man you could know…there was always a wall. You could go so far and then you might ask a question…you wouldn't get an answer.' Perhaps, I thought, it was not just because I was young, female and inexperienced that my Mannix interview failed. Others had faced that blank wall too.

I still have my badly typed notes of the Coyne interview. If I gave a copy to Santamaria, as I surely would have done, he would not have liked Coyne's sharpness of tone; at any rate he didn't use it. Uncharacteristically—for he was usually quick and decisive—he put the biography aside. I decided then to go back, belatedly, to the academic career which had been interrupted by my father's death. I couldn't afford to study overseas, as I had originally wanted to do, but by the early 1960s there was a good postgraduate school at the Australian National University. From there I moved on to the newly established Monash University, where I taught for the next thirty years in the Department of English, very happy to become part of a less-constricting world than Catholic Melbourne of that time. Perhaps it was coincidence that when I began to write seriously, I chose biography as the form that interested me most. Now, fifty years on, I can return to Daniel Mannix for a fresh look at the man and those distant times.

I kept in touch with Bob Santamaria and his family, but we never spoke of the Mannix biography. When it eventually appeared, twenty-five years after my Raheen visits, I felt a momentary pang, as if there was something I had missed. It strikes me now—much too late—that it was grudging of me never to have told Santamaria that I had read his book. Perhaps there was an element of resentment there. Father Coyne's remark about the man who put a wall between himself and others was a challenge I would like to have met. I had spent all that time for nothing. Was a full Mannix biography really an impossible task? By chance in the papers of the Irish Jesuit William Hackett, whose biography (*The Riddle of Father Hackett*) I completed in 2009, I found a new way of seeing Mannix, through the eyes of a candid friend. Hackett's comments, casual but shrewd, in letters to his sister in Ireland, rekindled my interest in the intractable subject.

I began to think about new ways of approach. I realised that, no matter how dutifully May Saunders had fed the Cathedral incinerator, she couldn't have destroyed the outward-going correspondence. Some letters written by Mannix had been found by his biographers; more searching might be done. Mannix in his own words could be found too in the records of his speeches. Week by week, for all but his last few years, he was followed by shorthand writers who took down every word. Even the abridged and edited versions would be revealing. The words he chose, the pauses, marked with 'applause' in the Catholic press, would be expressive.

In public, Mannix presented himself in the unvarying style of a century past. Top hat and frock coat outdoors, buckled shoes, soutane and biretta indoors: that was Mannix in 1913 when he first appeared in Melbourne. It was old-fashioned then, and by the 1960s it was an extraordinary statement of singularity. In any company Mannix stood out. In one way it was theatrical, but was it also a way to obscure, or defend, the private self? Portrait painters and photographers—how did they represent him? So often facing a camera, was he ever caught off guard?

Photographs show Mannix in company of various kinds. Men in clerical black predominate, and in those pre-Vatican II days, it's Roman collars by the hundred. What about the company he chose for himself? Could I look at Mannix through the prism of his closest relationships? Closeness came through shared enterprises; it might also come with an adversary. A way towards knowing Mannix might be through shared aims and ideas, but also in the interplay of temperament. In whose company was he most himself?

For the first fifty years, the record is thin. Mannix buried his Irish years so deep that I would struggle to retrieve any personal material. Some memories of the young Daniel and his family were recorded by earlier biographers. All agree that Daniel was a loner, silent and reserved. His most significant friendship began in 1920 when Mannix and the Irish republican leader Eamon de

Valera met in Omaha, Nebraska. Theirs was a political alliance, close and undeviating. What was it about de Valera that caught Mannix's imagination?

And the friendships of the Australian years: what can they reveal about Mannix? Irish Jesuit William Hackett, director of the Central Catholic Library, spent four to six weeks every summer as the chosen companion ('the court jester', Hackett said) when the archbishop took his seaside holiday. Another Irish Jesuit friend was Jeremiah Murphy, rector of Newman College, scholar and wit, at whose death in 1955 Mannix was desolate, as he had been when Hackett died the year before. Witty individualists who could make Mannix laugh, they were not overly deferential. Jesuit Bill Moloney, who taught at St Patrick's College, East Melbourne, had the same quality. Another Irishman, Francis Moynihan, edited the *Advocate,* which expressed Mannix's ideas, reported his speeches, published photographs of his doings. Moynihan must have had persuasive charm. 'Dr Mannix would sing sometimes. Father Moynihan could get him to sing', Father Coyne told me.[8]

Who else? Arthur Calwell, Labor Party leader, the man who might have been prime minister, was close to Mannix until Santamaria came along with his great adventure, the anti-communist campaign in the trade unions. A man of erratic judgment, Calwell was brave and forthright, with a gift for the telling phrase. He and Mannix were at one in their dedication to Irish freedom, and for many years Calwell felt welcome and valued at Raheen. But Mannix's support for Santamaria's political interventions was disastrous for Calwell. He was damaged too when Mannix openly criticised his rigid enforcement of the White Australia policy. Yet Calwell never blamed Mannix. By what magic did the archbishop hold his lasting affection?

In a list of Mannix's friends, the name of Prime Minister Hughes might be questioned. The two men were adversaries in the conscription debates, and in much else. Enemies can be close; mutual hostility may be a shaping and defining force. Without Hughes, Mannix would not so quickly have become a household name. Catholics learned to admire and love their new archbishop in 1917 because they saw him reviled by the Protestant Hughes. And when Mannix ridiculed Hughes, non-Catholics rallied to the harsh-voiced little Welshman who incongruously represented King and Empire. In the end, the two men came to like one another, as some late letters reveal.

In the last years of Mannix's life, Bob Santamaria is the dominant figure. Why Santamaria? Young enough to be Mannix's grandson, he became a protégé, an ally, almost at times a second self. Political activism united them, but there was affection too. And yet, as I later discovered, Mannix did not always support Santamaria; in some revealing ways he acted against his protégé's interests.

In 2010, with the present book in mind, I made my first visit to the Melbourne diocesan archives, not expecting much beyond official records of Mannix's reign. I was astonished to find eleven solidly packed document boxes from Raheen. The stacks of papers intended for Bishop Fox's bonfire had been raided by Bob Santamaria who, as Mannix's chosen biographer, took a considerable number of files from Raheen just after the archbishop's death.[9] More political than personal, some of these papers were cited in Santamaria's 1984 biography of Mannix, but their provenance and extent was not known until after Santamaria's death in 1998. His family brought them to the cathedral archives in 2001.

As well as the unexpected Santamaria retrievals, I found that the cathedral archives held the immensely valuable working papers of historian-priest James Murtagh, who in 1971 spent more than a year of travel in Mannix's footsteps, interviewing family members, friends and associates in Ireland. Close enough in time to tap into first-hand memories, Murtagh had the makings of a substantial biography. He died without writing more than a few pages. The Murtagh interviews are complemented by those done in Australia by Michael Gilchrist for his *Daniel Mannix* (1982, rev. 2002). The work of Michael Parer, academic and former priest, came to me as a generous gift; like Murtagh, Parer travelled in Ireland and gained insight into the Mannix family and the elusive early years. All these and more showed me that the bonfire of 1963 had not taken every trace of the life.

Of those close to Mannix, only two men outlived him. Calwell and Santamaria, political activists inside and outside the Australian Labor Party, grieved deeply but separately in November 1963 when the bells of St Patrick's Cathedral tolled ninety-nine times for the death of Daniel Mannix.

Before the bells rang out, Mannix's successor, Archbishop Justin Simonds, was called home from Rome, where he was attending the Second Vatican Council. Simonds, nearly blind, frail and exhausted from the long flight, needed all his failing strength to give the panegyric in St Patrick's Cathedral on 12 November 1963. 'A cedar of Lebanon has fallen,' he said. He stressed Mannix's achievements, his high intelligence, his dedication. An understated reference to the archbishop's 'political interventions' showed the strained relations between the two men, but it was not the time for reproaches. It was a day to celebrate Mannix's years in Melbourne; and in remembering that crowded history it was easy to forget that almost half of Daniel Mannix's life had been passed in Ireland where, in March 1864, this first son of a County Cork tenant farmer was born.

CHAPTER ONE

THE BIG HOUSE

'MILKING, YOUR GRACE?' My question about his childhood to the ninety-five-year-old Daniel Mannix seemed absurd: only desperation at my fast-failing interview prompted it. As I looked at the frail, fine-boned hands, the long fingers, and the jewelled episcopal ring that he wore, I couldn't imagine him helping out in the cowshed in 1870s Ireland. His reply was not quite a rejection: 'Milking…' He was always the master of the pause and there was a long silence before he added: 'I don't remember that I ever did much work.' Yet, as the eldest son of a tenant farmer, he must have helped to bring in the cows and feed them, done some of the milking, carried buckets to the house, cleaned out the shed, and taken part in the other daily chores of a dairy farm. If he did all this and more in the 1870s, he certainly didn't want to talk about it in 1959. Not, I think, because he was ashamed of his humdrum start in life, but because in his long years in Australia he had ceased to revisit in imagination the Charleville house of his childhood and the small farm that made the Mannix family a modest living.

In 2012, the Mannix farm, Deerpark, was up for sale. Dilapidated, with peeling paint on the window sills and a dank and dismal air of neglect, the farmhouse had never been promoted as the birthplace of the internationally famous archbishop. At its best it was a modestly respectable dwelling; a cut above the houses of most tenant farmers, it looks plain, solid, dull. The front door opens directly into the main room of a fair size. Three bedrooms upstairs: one for the parents Timothy and Ellen Mannix; one for their four sons Daniel, Patrick, Timothy and Michael; and the third, most likely, shared between the only daughter, Mary, and Aunt Lizzie Mannix who lived with the family.

If all the Mannix children had lived, the house would have been stretched to fit them in. But, like many mothers of her time and place, Ellen Mannix lost half the babies that she bore. First came two healthy sons, Daniel in March 1864 and Patrick in June 1865. The next four died in infancy: Timothy born in 1866, Margaret in 1867 and twins Mary and Joseph in 1868. Another daughter, also named Mary, born in 1869, survived, as did a second Timothy, born in 1873, and Michael, born in 1874. Margaret Josephine died in 1878, aged two. Miscarriages may account for the four-year gap between Mary and Timothy. Early childhood deaths at the time were commonplace, but that doesn't mean there was no grief. With nine siblings born in his first ten years, and five of them dying in infancy or soon after, Daniel would have felt more than he was capable of understanding or expressing, and Ellen Mannix's mothering would have been limited by her pregnancies and the series of little coffins.

Photographs of Ellen and Timothy used to hang on the wall

beside the staircase at Raheen. Passing them each night on his way to bed, how did the archbishop see them? Even now, faded with the years, these stiffly posed images give some sense of personality. Ellen looks formidable. Thin and upright with fine features, she has a look of intelligent alertness. Solidly built Timothy is more relaxed; there's humour in his gaze and although the photographer hasn't caught a smile there is a look of bonhomie about him. We know almost nothing about Daniel's feeling for his parents. To read that he wept uncontrollably at his father's funeral in May 1910 is startling, not just because it is the only testimony to their attachment, but because Daniel was then well on in his forties and his usual style was so restrained.[1]

As to the meaning of home for Daniel Mannix, who knows? A passionate love of Ireland, felt most in his Australian exile, and a romantic idealisation of life on the land, suggest that home meant a great deal. The fact that Timothy was a tenant might even make attachment stronger because of the heightened risk of loss. In his old age, when Mannix spoke to members of the National Catholic Rural Movement, his anger against the exploiting landlords of his boyhood still resonated, as did his image of what life on the land ought to be. 'The Irish farmers then were simply slaves,' he said. 'In Australia I hope there will be a peasantry satisfied to turn their backs on the glamour of the city and be satisfied with the simple but satisfactory life of the country.' Peasantry? That wasn't a word Australians wanted to hear. Mannix had second thoughts and deleted it from the galley proof of the Catholic weekly, the *Advocate*, but he cherished an idea of secure and simple rural happiness that he never knew.[2]

The Mannix family had lived in the Charleville district for three centuries. Timothy, born in 1826, and Ellen, five years younger, belonged to the generation liberated by the Catholic Emancipation Act of 1829, but shadowed by the horrors of the Great Famine of 1845–47. Their marriage in 1863, when Timothy was thirty-seven and Ellen thirty-two, is not unusually late for those times, but it may reflect a well-based fear. They were among the survivors of the famine, but they would have known many of the dead as well as many who had to migrate. Ellen told her children about the bodies she had seen on the roadside; reticent Timothy never spoke about them. One million dead from starvation, hundreds of thousands evicted by their landlords, and many forced to emigrate, their fates were burned into the collective memory of the survivors.

In the first decades after the Emancipation Act of 1829, the Catholic Church in Ireland had been growing in strength and number. Churches were built, and a middle class was emerging, but then the famine struck. As well as the intensity of suffering and loss, the famine brought a new level of anger against British rule which seemed at best indifferent to Irish suffering. Daniel Mannix was born into relative prosperity but not disregard of the past.

In the finely discriminated social and economic levels of 1860s Catholic Ireland, the Mannixes were somewhere in the middle. Timothy's 135 acres—not that they were his own—made him what was called a 'strong farmer'. Others in the Mannix family were shopkeepers in Charleville, while Ellen's brother and uncle had moved into the professional class; both were doctors. Her family, the Cagneys, came from Croom, an Irish-speaking district, but Ellen didn't teach her children their own language.[3] Perhaps this was because Timothy had no Irish; perhaps like many Irish of her time she thought of her native speech as the language of peasants. 'The Irish love their language but they love their children more', was a popular saying with a bitter truth in it. Without English, you couldn't get ahead. Above the Mannixes, and closer to the Protestant landholders, was the Carr family in Galway, who were Catholics and landlords too. Thomas Carr, who would precede Daniel Mannix as Archbishop of Melbourne, looked out through different windows from those of Deerpark.[4]

Well below the Mannix social level was the family of Daniel Mannix's future protégé and hero, Eamon de Valera, who grew up at Bruree, only seven miles from Charleville on the Limerick side. At the age of nineteen, his mother, Catherine Coll, had left her parents' mud-lined, one-roomed cabin to find work in New York, where she became pregnant to Spanish artist Vivion de Valera. No record of a marriage has been found. In 1884, she brought her two-year-old son Edward (later known as Eamon) home and left him at Bruree with her mother and her teenage sister and brother. The Colls had only half an acre and their two cows grazed illegally on common land beside the road.[5] De Valera followed the same paths to school as Daniel Mannix, but from a far greater distance, physically, socially and psychologically.

Daniel Mannix had left school before de Valera began his long walks from Bruree. The churchman and the political leader would not meet until both were well on in their separate but interlocking careers. Though eighteen years apart in age, they had the same initial education, the same passion for Ireland, and the same certainty that they spoke for their countrymen: 'Whenever I wanted to know what the Irish people wanted I had only to examine my own heart,' said de Valera.[6] And, even from distant Melbourne, Mannix was sure that he spoke for Irishmen everywhere.

Charleville was a small town, close to Cork's border with County Limerick. It was named after King Charles II of England in the late seventeenth century by Roger Boyle, first Earl of Cork and

Orrery. Having removed its 'heathenish' Irish name of Rathgoggan so as to make a respectful gesture to the newly restored English monarch, Boyle kept the lands he had occupied under Cromwell. In the 1860s Charleville had about four thousand people and good access by mailcoach, road and rail to Cork and Limerick. Though in some ways remote and rural, it had plenty of reminders that Ireland was ruled by the British. It was a garrison town in which a British army force gave employment to the local Irish. And, very close to Deerpark was the home of the Mannixes' landlord. One of the most beautiful houses in Cork, Charleville Park was owned by the Sanders family who had once been agents for the Earls of Cork and Orrery, and who by the mid-nineteenth century had large properties of their own.

Charleville Park, known as the Big House, was built for Christopher Sanders in the late eighteenth century, and had the classic grace of its period. Listed among the notable houses of Ireland, it earned its place for its architectural distinction more than its size.[7] It was an inescapable fact in Daniel Mannix's childhood. He could try to ignore its ownership but its beauty was inseparable from the way of life that it represented. Resentment was inevitable. As a young man Mannix was disgusted to see his cousin John Cagney take off his cap to Robert Sanders. 'I always do that to my superiors,' Cagney explained. 'Well, my advice to you is to go about bald-headed,' Daniel retorted.[8]

Just as important as the Big House was the parish church in Charleville, home of Father Thomas Croke. Tough and confident, Father Croke was a fearless nationalist. For the Mannixes at Deerpark and all those in the Charleville neighbourhood, a clash in November 1868, between Thomas Sanders and Father Croke, was a dramatic event. Church and state collided over a small matter but one that had larger implications. Not quite five years old, Daniel Mannix was too young to understand the drama, but for his parents, tenants of Sanders and parishioners of Croke, it was a hot issue in which their political and religious freedoms were under attack.

Sanders heard that Father Croke was planning a requiem mass for the Irish 'Manchester Martyrs', O'Brien, Allen and Larkin, hanged after a much-disputed trial for the murder of a prison guard during an attempt to rescue Fenian rebel prisoners.[9] In his role as Justice of the Peace, Sanders wrote to Croke, asking for an immediate assurance that the mass, which he judged more than likely to lead to an event of 'an illegal character', would not take place. As it happened, Croke, then nearly eighty-five, was too ill to celebrate the mass, but that did not stop him from robust defiance as soon as he was well enough to write back:

> *O tempora! O mores!* A Mass for the dead to assume an illegal character... This is my answer—dare question it. You are a magistrate, invested with Her Majesty's commission of the peace—an important trust—which may be used for good or ill. Its great object is to preserve the peace, not to disturb it—not to alarm, wound, terrify, domineer, put her Majesty's subjects in bodily fear, or provoke hostility. Your power of authority isn't supreme. It has its limits and when in excess of those limits it is to be resolutely resisted and treated with contempt.[10]

Father Croke's orphaned nephew and niece, Thomas and Isabella Croke, who grew up in the Charleville presbytery, had special importance to the Mannix family. Thomas, who became

Archbishop of Cashel, was a role model for Daniel Mannix. Isabella entered the Mercy order and, as Sister Joseph, was head of the convent in which the Mannix children began their schooling.

The great subject of debate in nineteenth-century Ireland was that of landlord and tenant relations. In the 1860s, Father Croke defended the right of the Irish to resist the exorbitant rents that forced many small farmers to leave the land and face destitution or emigration. Two decades later, his nephew, Archbishop Croke, backed the strategy named 'boycotting', after its landlord-victim, Captain Charles Boycott of County Mayo. Instead of resorting to violence, tenants were recommended to withhold rents and refuse labour to non-compliant landlords, and to ostracise anyone who bought or tried to buy a property whose tenants had been forced out.

Daniel Mannix grew up knowing the power of the Big House and the need for an equal power to contest it. His idea of priestly leadership began with Father Thomas Croke, and he learned his first political lesson close to home, with the Sanders family of the Big House.

Charleville Park's twenty rooms (the same number as Daniel Mannix's future home Raheen) would not have been too many for Thomas, his wife and their six sons and three daughters. They employed a staff of at least six indoor servants, all hired locally and all Catholics, except for Mrs Sanders' lady's maid who was a French Protestant. The Sanders' Dublin house in elegant Fitzwillliam Square was entirely staffed by Protestants. Employing Catholics in Charleville was a necessity, not a choice.[11]

Although the name of the Mannix house, Deerpark, has an affluent ring about it, it was of a quite different order from Charleville Park. It was so called because its land was once set aside by a former owner for the deer he bred for the very English sport of stalking and hunting. Timothy Mannix made a decent living for his family, but his 135 acres was a very small affair compared with the 2000 acres held by the Sanders family in Cork and Limerick, later augmented by an estate in Surrey, which maintained the Sanders' close link with England. Sanders, in turn, was nothing beside the absentee landlords of the English aristocracy like the Duke of Devonshire.

The Mannix children would have known, by sight at least, the sons and daughters of Thomas Sanders. Daniel Mannix and Robert Massey Dawson Sanders were much of an age. Both were the first-born sons in big families; both were clever. They might have been friends and perhaps they were, but the odds are against it. Land ownership and religion gave them separate places. Their expectations were quite different.

When Daniel Mannix and his brother Patrick started school at the Convent of the Sisters of Mercy in Charleville, a mile's walk from home, Robert and his brother Evelyn were sent to boarding school in England. The Sanders girls were taught by a governess. Before returning to Charleville to manage his father's property, Robert studied law at Trinity College in Dublin, as did Evelyn. Daniel Mannix seems always to have been destined for the priesthood, but if he had ever thought of a legal career, it would not have been easy. Trinity was off limits for Catholics, and would remain so for many years.

Daniel went on from the Mercy convent to the Christian Brothers' newly opened school in Charleville, where he stayed only three years; he was then sent to a small school in the village of Kilfinane, about twenty miles from home. There must have been some advantage to weigh against the need to board all the week with one of his many relatives in the district. The most likely reason is that the Kilfinane school taught Latin, which the Christian Brothers did not then think was needed for its mainly lower-class boys. The Mannixes were better off than most, but they could not afford boarding schools such as the Jesuits' Mungret College in County Limerick or Clongowes Wood College in County Kildare. These might, in any case, have smacked too much of 'West Briton' for the Mannix family, while the Christian Brothers in Charleville did not offer enough academic advantage to a boy of Daniel's ability. According to a senior member of the Christian Brothers order at that time, the study of classics 'properly belonged' to middle-class schools.[12] Many of Daniel's first classmates would have left school at twelve; he would not have had much competition from the few who stayed on.

After two years at Kilfinane, Daniel came back to Charleville. He and Patrick were enrolled in 1879 at another Latin school, this one run by Father Peter O'Leary, a classical scholar and pioneer in Irish language studies. Learning Latin was a signpost on the way to the priesthood, and at fifteen Daniel was probably thinking of a future in the church. If he had stayed with the Christian Brothers, he would have learned more Irish history and a more aggressive nationalism than he did at the two Latin schools, but his English language skills might not have been so subtly fostered.

O'Leary remembered Daniel Mannix as a natural stylist. When his class struggled with a difficult passage in Latin and O'Leary's own effort lacked something, he would say: 'Dan, will you try?' 'Out came the translation, as clear as crystal, and it fitted the text like a nightcap on a valetudinarian.'[13] Because there was almost nothing published in Irish, O'Leary's library was stocked with English classics, which he lent to Daniel Mannix, his best student. By then, the boy's feeling for language was affirmed. From

Shakespeare's plays, which O'Leary read aloud to his students, to the leaders in the London *Times*, which would later became Daniel Mannix's standard of well-shaped prose, the rhythms of the English language claimed the Irish schoolboy. He sometimes regretted that he could not speak or read Irish; its absence was a crack in his nationalist armour. His own phrasing, the tone and balance of his sentences, his characteristic understated humour, were very English. But his emotions—when he allowed them a voice—came from an Irish heart. Perhaps that tension is what made him a magical speaker when his feelings were released.

In 1879, while the Mannix boys were attending the O'Leary school, their father became directly involved in the land question. It was the wettest and coldest year of the century; crops failed for lack of a ripening sun and farm animals died. Even 'strong farmers' like Timothy Mannix on good land in County Cork were in trouble, while the small farmers on barren western lands like those of County Mayo faced starvation or eviction. Until the Irish owned the land that they farmed, they would never be secure. Nor would they achieve independence until they had their own parliament in Dublin. In October 1879, republican journalist and activist Michael Davitt, son of a Mayo farmer who had been forced to emigrate, formed an alliance with Charles Stewart Parnell, a Protestant landlord in County Wicklow with a seat in the House of Commons. Parnell won the leadership of the Home Rule Party, also known as the Irish Parliamentary Party, with the Fenian republicans' support rather than the more moderate parliamentarians. Parnell, Davitt and the Fenian John Devoy set the Land League in motion. The Fenians, who had previously refused a constitutional path to Irish independence, joined an uneasy alliance. Parnell, too, took a risk: as a Protestant he faced

Catholic Church misgivings or outright opposition. Nevertheless, the Irish National Land League of 1879 gained a strong following. It aimed in the short term to reduce rents and stop evictions. Its wider aim was to abolish the landlord system altogether; and with state-aided purchase turn the tenants into owners.

O'Leary encouraged his students, including the Mannix boys, to come to the meeting in Charleville that set up a local Land League branch. It was a tense occasion. With the Fenian reputation for violence in mind, the tenant farmers were afraid that they risked being taken for extremists and arrested. They gained confidence when they saw that some priests were ready to give public support to the Land League. Fifteen-year-old Daniel Mannix was watching the scene that O'Leary described:

> One thing I noticed that day I have never forgotten. When the people saw the crowd of priests on the platform, and each one speaking more boldly than the man before him, the sadness and fear and mistrust began to disappear from their faces.[14]

At sixteen Daniel left home for two years of boarding school at St Colman's, in Fermoy. In effect a diocesan seminary, with high academic standards, it had Archbishop Croke, a former president, as its patron. It prepared its students for St Patrick's College, Maynooth, where the intellectual elite of Ireland studied for the priesthood. As expected, Daniel did well; he won one of only three scholarships from St Colman's to attend Maynooth. His parents would have counted on his success and been proud to have a son a priest. And with three more sons to place in the world, it would have been a relief to be spared the Maynooth fees.

In some ways the two years at Fermoy, focused on learning and excelling, detached Daniel from home and family; he became used to self-reliance. The cloisters of Maynooth, which he entered in 1882, aged eighteen, gave structure, and measurable goals. As for the immeasurable distances of spiritual life, he was probably as well prepared as most.

Even before Daniel's place at Maynooth was settled, Timothy and Ellen Mannix had to consider their second son, Patrick, who left Father O'Leary's Latin school, aged seventeen, to enter medical school in October 1880. Catholic boys who wanted to enter the professions did not have a free or easy choice. There was a good medical school at Cork University College, but this 'godless' tertiary institution was banned for Catholics. Patrick could have gone to University College in Dublin, the Catholic alternative to Trinity College, but it would have been more expensive than staying near home. Whatever their reasons, the Mannixes sent Patrick to the forbidden place in Cork where he studied alongside his cousin Daniel Cagney and probably boarded with the Cagneys.[15] The bishop looked the other way, as many bishops did at that time.

Daniel and Patrick left Deerpark at a tense time, personally and politically. It must have taken courage for Timothy Mannix to align himself publicly with the Land League, and against his landlord Thomas Sanders, in the struggle for fairer rights to the land. The long association between the families went back to the time of Timothy Mannix's grandfather, who was employed by the Sanders of the day as land steward and rent collector. Earlier still, in 1697, William Sanders, the first of his family to live in Ireland, was a tenant to Lionel, Earl of Orrery. From Orrery to Sanders to Mannix: had the time come for a new power structure? After the miserable series of failed crops in the late 1870s, which roused fears of another famine, Timothy Mannix had emerged as a follower of Parnell, Devoy and Davitt.

By 1880 the Land League was well established in Charleville. The meeting on 26 September 1880, convened by Timothy Mannix, and attended by his sons Dan and Pat, drew 'not less than ten thousand persons'. Two days later, Timothy was in Fermoy as chairman of another inaugural meeting. His brother John Mannix, a local draper and farmer, chaired a second Fermoy meeting, while Timothy moved on to bigger things. In December 1880, as honorary secretary of the Land Leaguers in nearby Mitchelstown, Timothy organised a 'monster meeting' of twenty thousand people addressed by Michael Davitt.[16]

Holding its fragile alliance between men of differing beliefs and backgrounds, the Land League took a new direction for Irish nationalism. The main strands in the politics of the time were parliamentary action, agrarian agitation and defiance, and revolutionary conspiracy. Where in this spectrum of Irish nationalism did Timothy Mannix belong? A just solution to the land question may have come first; he is likely to have backed the Home Rule Party rather than open rebellion against the British. We can only look at his actions, think about the choices that his sons made in later years, and accept uncertainty.

Trouble in and around the Charleville district exploded in the winter of 1880–81. Several local landlords were chosen for the silent rebellion. Thomas Sanders' neighbours, the Townshends of Kilfinane, whose daughter married Evelyn Sanders, felt the impact. In spite of its comic tone, there is resentment and racist disdain in this account of Townshend's predicament:

> Not a blacksmith could be found to shoe his horse and not a living creature to cook his food…the good folk of Kilfinane eye us terribly askance, or, to be more literally exact, they either look at us as if we were panes of glass or suddenly become interested in their boots or finger nails, both of which would be better for more regular attention.[17]

Boycotting Sanders, whose house was so close to Deerpark, would have been a more personal act than giving the same treatment to one of the big absentee landowners like the Duke of Devonshire. The Sanders family had lived in Charleville for three centuries. Like Australian pastoralists who put the dispossessed Aborigines out of mind, they may have felt that they loved the land as well as any native Irishman. But for Timothy Mannix there had to be a breaking point. The tradition in which he had grown up was ending and, whether or not he counted himself a radical, it was evident that his four sons would face a very different Ireland.

Charleville, Kilfinane and Fermoy, the places Daniel Mannix knew best, were in turmoil during his last two years at school. The role of the Catholic Church was a key issue. How far would the Irish bishops go in backing—or denouncing—the Land League? The New Departure, as the League strategy was called, roused the Pope to send a stern warning against committing illegal acts. Because of their role in preparing young men for the seminary, Daniel's teachers at Fermoy would have been cautious. Yet they had a fearlessly nationalist model in Archbishop Croke of Cashel, who was president of the college in 1858 and a local hero in the district where he had grown up.

Most accounts of Daniel Mannix's life stress the formative role of his mother, and they may well be right. There was a strong physical likeness between the two. The image of the tall, erect figure of Ellen Mannix, walking the mile to mass in Charleville every day until her ninetieth year, has made comparison irresistible. Her habit of reading the daily newspaper carefully is remembered, and some family stories suggest a formidable quality: 'When Aunt Ellen was coming, you started to tidy the house two days before.'[18] Ellen's household was disciplined. Her children did not play the popular card games of the time. They came together in music. Each of them had a performance piece, which was sung without accompaniment. Dan's piece was the traditional Irish love song, 'The Snowy-breasted Pearl'.

Anecdotes of Daniel's attitude to his mother stop well short of reverence. As a small boy he cut short her circumlocutions about childbirth: 'Now, Mother, don't be telling us fairy stories. We know you carried us for nine months.' As a young man he was sardonic about what he saw as her spiritual complacency. Wanting reassurance about her progress in God's sight, she had prayed for guidance and a voice from heaven told her that she was doing everything just right. 'Can you beat that' Daniel remarked, 'for self-complacency and self-satisfaction? Nobody better than herself as spiritual director!'[19]

Ellen Mannix was proud of her brilliant son: 'My Dan, always head and shoulders above the rest'. But her brusque remark in old age, 'Dan never understood Ireland', shows that she didn't idealise him. Because Timothy Mannix died in 1910, before his son became famous enough to be talked about, their relationship has not had much attention, but the leadership he showed in the Land League foreshadows Daniel's public role.

Conflict with the Sanders family in Charleville smouldered on through the 1880s. In 1881 Thomas Sanders was burned in effigy, and his reputation as a landlord was attacked in the House of Commons by John Dillon, a Home Rule Party member of parliament.[20] Sanders made concessions, lowering some rents by amounts ranging between fifteen and twenty per cent. This was a big win for the Land League but it did not help Timothy Mannix, whose twenty-one-year lease, signed in 1858, put him in a different category from other tenants who rented from year to year. Rather than renew the lease on better terms, Sanders took Timothy to the Land Court in Cork in 1881. Judgment went against Timothy who was forced to sign a new lease at a higher rate for a further twenty-one years. If he had refused to comply, Deerpark would have been sold to the highest bidder. Timothy appealed to the Land Court in Dublin, where an out-of-court compromise was worked out in 1883, satisfying neither party.[21]

Thomas Sanders' last years at Charleville Park were marked by violence. He evicted ten families in 1886, and in the local rage that followed he risked assassination. Finally, Robert Sanders, who took over his father's role as landlord in 1892, decided to cut ties with Ireland. He took a pragmatic view. This is seen in a published work *A Practical Guide to the Irish Land Act*, in which he argued that Ireland was no longer a sound investment.[22] One might question whether three centuries of life in Ireland were so easily reduced to a balance sheet. The power and respect commanded by the Big House was no more measurable in figures than the outrage of having the scarecrow Sanders figure burnt. Daniel Mannix didn't forget. He had Robert Sanders' book on his shelves at Raheen more than half a century later.

Family stories never end. For a moment to pause in the Mannix story, 1890 is as good as any. That was the year of Daniel's ordination as a priest at Maynooth College—or, to use its official name, the Royal St Patrick's College at Maynooth, County Kildare. By 1890, Daniel's brother Patrick had qualified as a doctor and was working as a ship's surgeon.[23] He came home for his father's funeral in 1910 and again in 1925 when his mother was dying. Records show that he practised medicine in Lancaster from 1895 and made a late marriage in a Liverpool registry office in 1919. A clean break? Total rejection? Not quite. Patrick Mannix brought up his only son as an Englishman, but when the child was christened in an Anglican church in 1920 he was given his grandfather's name. Timothy Patrick Mannix sounds like a gesture of love, ten years after the death of the older Timothy.

Without Daniel, who came home only for short holidays after 1890, and without Patrick, Deerpark was depleted. Mary, who married a farmer, Edmond Wallis, lived close to Charleville. Michael, aged sixteen in 1890, looked to New York and a career in the law. That left Timothy, the third son, to inherit the farm as soon as he was ready to marry and found a family.

The times were still stormy. Parnell's career was ending in confusion and disgrace, with his leadership rejected by his own party and by the Irish bishops because of his liaison with the wife of one of his colleagues. When Parnell died in October 1891, the party he had led was split in two; the causes he had espoused, Home Rule and land reform, had lost momentum, and the fight had to resume under new and less charismatic leadership.

Although Daniel Mannix's commitment to a life in the priesthood had distanced him from public events, he had seen the responses of church and state to nationalist aspirations; and he had a model in Archbishop Croke's outspoken nationalism.

Anger at the obdurate British, personified in the Sanders father and son, might have to be subdued; priestly vows meant that duty to God and the church came before family ties, but seclusion at Maynooth did not mean letting go of Ireland, Deerpark and the places of his childhood.

CHAPTER TWO

MAYNOOTH

FOR AN eighteen-year-old country boy, Maynooth College was a revelation. It was the dominant presence in the little town of Maynooth, twenty-five kilometres west of Dublin. Daniel Mannix, who entered the college in 1882, had never seen anything so beautiful. He had once thought of becoming an architect; seeing Maynooth might have stirred that dream. Near its entrance gates, the ruins of the thirteenth-century castle of the Fitzgeralds evoked an Ireland beyond his imagining. The college itself was Georgian in style, serene and elegantly proportioned. Its oldest building, Stoyte House, once the home of the Duke of Leinster's steward, had housed Maynooth's first students in 1795. Later buildings had the same classic dignity. Only St Patrick's House, designed by Pugin, who also designed the library, was different, but its Neo-Gothic lines did not disturb the Palladian harmony.[1] The buildings were grouped to look inwards to formal gardens.

St Mary's Square and St Joseph's Square were made for quiet meditation.

Everything at Maynooth proclaimed order, as it was meant to do. Founded during the French Revolution, it was a British government attempt to keep the Irish Catholic Church away from seditious influences. Until the revolution, Irish priests were trained in continental seminaries; when these were closed by the new regime in France something new was needed at home. By naming the seminary the Royal College of St Patrick, the government looked both ways, with gestures to the nation's patron saint and the British throne. Students in the early years had to swear, after cross-examination, that they had not been involved in any way in the Irish rebellion of 1798. Later students took an oath of loyalty to the Crown.

The Maynooth establishment walked carefully where rebellions against the British were concerned. It condemned the Young Irelander rising of 1848 and was uncomfortable about the fact that a former president had seemed to support its leaders. But when Maynooth-trained priests were accused of inciting violence and using intemperate language at the time of the Great Famine, the Maynooth president responded sharply: those responsible for the 'wicked agrarian laws' had no right to judge:

> We may readily admit that some few priests said and did many things during these years of famine which it is impossible to defend. But it is also impossible for those who were not witnesses of the terrible scenes of cruelty and suffering which the priests daily witnessed to make due allowance for the provocation...They saw the abundant harvest of Irish grain daily carried off to England at the

> very time that their own people were dying in hundreds of starvation.
>
> They saw when outdoor relief was granted, that no man could get it no matter how wretched might be his condition, except he gave up his bit of land, for the Act of Parliament forbade the relief to be given to anyone who held more than a single half-acre...Then they saw the landlords come down like harpies on the poor tenants to snatch from them the price of their corn, or the corn itself; and when this could be had no longer, they saw them turned out to die by the roadsides or in the pestilential workhouse, or in the coffin ships that carried the poor emigrants over the ocean, only to bury them in its depths.[2]

Thirty years after the famine, Daniel Mannix was entering Maynooth at a time when his home town was convulsed with Land League conflicts and his family deeply involved in the struggle for justice. Whatever his own feelings were, they had to be put aside. The Maynooth regime was all-encompassing, spiritually and intellectually. It was an achievement to be there: Daniel had worked hard for his funded place in this expensive institution. It had more prestige than All Hallows, the alternative way to the diocesan priesthood, and its teaching standards were higher. Some Maynooth graduates went to the foreign missions, of which Australia was one. Some of those who stayed home and did parish work became bishops and archbishops.

Because of the decline in population after the famine of the 1840s, Ireland was oversupplied with priests and nuns. Some had entered religion for security as well as piety: 'The dollar or the collar'—or for young women the coif or bonnet—was a real and often painful choice. There were 1552 nuns in Ireland in 1851. The number had jumped to over eight thousand by 1901.[3] Many young women were pressured into the convent. If the alternative was a loveless marriage or dependence on a brother, it was an understandable choice. So too for young men. Only one son could make a living on his father's land. Jobs at home were hard to find. They could try New York, or even Australia, if they had the fare. But for a reasonably devout young man, the priesthood was a safe option; and it had status in an undereducated, impoverished Irish community. For many, it was the right choice, the way to a fulfilling life. Was it so for Mannix? We can only look at the record. As with everything else in his life, he was silent about his vocation.

Two years as a boarder at Fermoy didn't prepare Daniel Mannix for life at Maynooth. St Colman's was a small school, and there were Mannix and Cagney cousins in the neighbourhood. Maynooth was a vast, isolated place. Six hundred young men made a formidable array; so did the long line of professors at assemblies and feastday masses.[4] The students were segregated according to the stage they had reached in their studies, and housed in separate buildings. The first year intake of about one hundred would dwindle over the six or seven years with a few deaths, failures and expulsions. The regime was strict, with every moment accounted for, from the 6 p.m. rising through a day of prayer, lectures and study. On winter days, when the dark came early, the students read and wrote for hours by candlelight; then they blew out their candles in the dormitories at 10 p.m. sharp.

Maynooth had rules about everything, including recreation time. Even the forty-five minute breaks after breakfast and dinner were regulated. If you came from Cork, you had to walk with other Cork men. Dubliners spent the time with their own homefolk and men from Mayo did the same with theirs. Only after supper and after the midday lecture could students choose their companions. This limitation was thought to strengthen the bonds between men who would later work together, but it also reinforced provincial narrowness.[5] Most of the students were from rural backgrounds like that of Mannix. Thomas Carr, who preceded Mannix at Maynooth and as Archbishop of Melbourne, was an exception in being a landlord's son. Others were the sons of policemen, skilled workers and small-town shopkeepers. The few well-off Catholics—'strong farmers', doctors, and others in the middle class—were likely to send their sons to boarding schools run by religious orders. From these schools, the boys with vocations were encouraged to enter the order they knew rather than to go to the priesthood by way of Maynooth or All Hallows.

Alike in family background, the Maynooth students expressed their regional styles in distinctive accents. You didn't need a trained ear to know where they had grown up. Without the means to travel, and with no Radio Éireann to standardise the voices, local accents and habits persisted. The Dubliners, in novelist Francis Hackett's account of his Jesuit boarding school in the 1890s, were the most facile. Cork boys were 'farouche and clannish'. Connaught produced 'lantern-jawed saturnine peasants'. Kerry boys were gentler, as were the 'slow youths of the midlands'.[6] Whimsical as Hackett's divisions certainly were, they reflect the Irish passion for identifying local qualities, and for the solidarity that came from networking.

Worse than the diocesan clusters at Maynooth was the absolute separation between teaching staff and students. Three deans, a bursar and two 'spiritual fathers' had charge of everyday matters. Professors never spoke to students except in class. They never shared meals or joined in recreation. This strict divide narrowed the students' social and intellectual range and probably lowered the standard of their food. As to manners, many left much as they came; complaints about bad-mannered or uncouth priests in the parishes were not unusual.[7] In Mannix's time, students were allowed to go home at Christmas, though even then they were under the authority of their parish priest who was expected to report bad behaviour.[8] Discipline within the college was severe. To be caught smoking meant expulsion. Nothing in Maynooth's written charter spelt out sexual transgressions; but in this huge all-male establishment there must have been homosexual acts and secret relationships, as there were in the army and navy, but with an even heavier burden of guilt.

Women were invisible, although nuns and domestic servants came from their separate quarters to supervise, cook and clean, and look after the sick.[9] Family life was on the periphery wherever the estate gardeners and carpenters were housed, and there would be no reason for a student ever to speak to a child. Maynooth's numbers and its rigidly enforced stratification made it almost impossible for individualism to flourish, or individuals to be understood. The confessional might help a troubled student, but because the confessors came from the same system they were likely to reinforce it, with or without a sympathetic hearing. Dropping out was almost as bad as being expelled. To leave after ordination was an unimaginable disgrace. Once a priest, always a priest.

Like most of Maynooth's students, Daniel Mannix survived a tough system and met its expectations. Clever and hard working, he was a high achiever in all his classes: a *wunderkind*, as one of his classmates described him. With first place, again and again, throughout his time at Maynooth, and never lower than seventh, he was marked out for leadership. In his final year he was made head prefect. He accepted this role seriously but not unconditionally. At a time of unruly behaviour the college president reminded the assembled students that the head prefect would be reporting every lapse in discipline that he witnessed. Failure to report would mean losing his prefect's badge and status. The silent rebellion of Daniel Mannix was remembered by a classmate many years later:

> I can still see the stark figure of Daniel Mannix rise in his seat and proceed to the President's table where he removed the [prefect's] badge from his lapel and placed it on the President's table, and, with never a word, return to his seat.[10]

This scene shows Dan Mannix's instinct for the dramatic gesture and the telling use of silence. It also shows an attitude to authority that would appear in the older Mannix. No one could take his compliance for granted.

Authority at Maynooth came through the president, William Walsh, later Archbishop of Dublin, and his vice-president, Thomas Carr, later Archbishop of Melbourne. They took instructions from the bishops, which meant dealing with some changeable and arbitrary regulations. There was student unrest in the 1870s, under the enfeebled Dr Russell: 'unbecoming' behaviour in the refectory, and bread riots at Christmas 1881, just before Mannix's arrival. Walsh and Carr gradually created a more stable regime.

Because Mannix excelled in all his subjects, it's not possible to say which ones caught his imagination. Sacred Eloquence may have strengthened his love of the structure and rhythms of Latin and English. Future priests were taught to preach well, to watch for faults of pronunciation that came from Irish dialects, and not to imagine themselves better educated than men from Trinity, Oxford or Cambridge. There were practical lessons. The lecture notes of Thomas Carr, who taught Sacred Eloquence just before Mannix's time, stress the need for emphasis to be related to the meaning: no dramatic effects for the sake of drama.[11] Use the pause for clarity but take care: the rhetorical pause often leads to farce. These lessons Mannix learned well or knew by instinct. No one used the pause to better effect: in comic or dramatic mode, he had perfect timing.

Theology lectures made Mannix confront matters of justice arising from Ireland's troubled state: agrarian crime, boycotting, the withholding of rents, and other tactics associated with the Land League. The Pope's condemnation of the use of force meant cautious teaching at Maynooth.[12]

Lectures in Pastoral Theology, based on parish experience, dealt in an oblique way with sexual matters. Confessors were told to be strict in the matter of 'company keeping': if a penitent continues a relationship likely to lead to sin, the priest must be 'cruel in order to be kind'. Carr's lecture notes include advice on clerical etiquette. A Maynooth man, he said, might go on holiday to Dublin with his family, but he had better not be seen in public with any female members. Mother, sister, cousin, it was all the same. 'It is contrary to taste in clerical behaviour to walk with a lady in the street, no matter how near. The laity do not like it. It seems to them incongruous and it is so.'[13] The reasoning behind this is not just that female company means moral danger. The priest must be a man apart from human ties. That was clericalism, destructive then and ever since.

Carr moved on from Maynooth in 1882, just as Mannix entered the seminary, but as Bishop of Galway he came regularly to meetings until his posting to Melbourne in 1886. He would have heard about the prodigy from Charleville. If Mannix had been a nationalist firebrand, Carr would not have chosen him as his coadjutor in Melbourne. If he had not been gentlemanly and polite, Carr would have heard about it and crossed him off the list.

After seven years of study, Mannix was due for ordination in June 1889. In later life, he said, 'I should have been ordained in 1889, but I was not.' This gnomic statement has led to speculation: could there have been a crisis in faith, a misdemeanour, a family emergency or an illness? Eventually, in old age he volunteered the reason. A visiting Redemptorist priest at Raheen, Father Quillinan, prompted the memory of 1889.[14] Home at Deerpark for the Christmas holiday at the end of 1888, Mannix caught a chill which turned to pneumonia. On the way to recovery he was impatient at being told to rest. He got up and walked to the Charleville church where a Redemptorist priest was preaching. Redemptorists were famous for their hellfire sermons, and this one brought a long line of penitents to the confessional; Daniel waited in the unheated church, began to shiver and walked home again. Back in bed, and presumably rebuked by his mother, he was again seriously ill.

Altogether, this cost him so many weeks of his final year that he was not qualified for the 1889 ordination; and he then spent time in further study at the Dunboyne establishment for Maynooth's intellectual elite. The timing of this bout of pneumonia, on his last visit home before becoming a priest, might be linked with another bout, at another life-changing moment, just before he was due to leave Ireland for Australia.

Daniel Mannix was ordained at Maynooth in June 1890 by Archbishop William Walsh. He was then twenty-six. His was the first ordination in the newly completed college chapel which had been in the making since 1875. Mannix had watched its progress, which may have helped to form his architectural taste. Designed by J. J. McCarthy, the 'Irish Pugin', in a restrained French Gothic style, it is celebrated for its superb stained-glass windows. The ceiling panels were designed by Westlake of London and executed and installed by a Dublin artist named Robert Mannix.[15] The great rose window centres on Christ in glory; and a heavenly procession of angels and saints fills the ceiling panels in rich colours. Whether or not Robert Mannix was a kinsman, Daniel Mannix probably met the artist when he came to supervise the installation of his work.

With the opening of the chapel, and the 1890 ordination ceremony, William Walsh ended his ten years as president and took up his new post as Archbishop of Dublin. His contemporary and intellectual rival, Michael Logue, a Maynooth professor in the 1870s, became Bishop of Raphoe, coadjutor in Armagh, and finally Cardinal and Primate of All Ireland. Ambitious students, including Mannix, would have seen that success in teaching and administration at Maynooth paved the way to a bishopric at least. But some bishoprics were safer than others. Thomas Carr, happily settled as Bishop of Galway in 1882, was aghast when in 1885 he was told that Rome was sending him to Melbourne as coadjutor to Archbishop Goold. Just so, many years later, Daniel Mannix would have the same reaction to the same decree from Rome.

Mannix's academic success made him an obvious choice for a place on the Maynooth professorial staff. Staying on at the college distanced him from the storms of the final tragic period of Charles Stewart Parnell's leadership of the Home Rule Party, but even in the Maynooth common room he heard a great deal of argument.

Ex-president Walsh had barely left Maynooth for Dublin when the crisis came. Home Rule had seemed tantalisingly close and the land campaigns worth fighting, even though their aims were only partly attained. But, all through the 1880s, Parnell, the great leader, had been endangering the Irish cause for love of Katherine O'Shea, wife of one of his parliamentary colleagues. In 1890 the secret affair was out, with sleazy details involving Katherine's conniving husband. Three children, presumed to be O'Shea's, had been fathered by Parnell. Divorce proceedings were announced and friends and colleagues took sides, as did the Irish bishops and clergy. Parnell and Katherine married, but the personal and political damage was irreparable. The party split, in the famous meeting of 1 December 1890. A stopgap leader, Justin MacCarthy, was elected and Parnell was left with only a minority of his parliamentarians to follow him into certain electoral defeat.

The bishops entered the political game. Some thought that Parnell's power over the laity was too great: his being a Protestant meant that the church was bypassed in important ways. Cardinal Manning suggested to Archbishop Walsh that it was a good opportunity to reassert clerical control.[16] Walsh was cautious: it would be better not to intervene publicly. When he did speak out, a few weeks before Parnell contested the North Kilkenny by-election, Walsh stressed moral rather than political objections:

> If Parnell would not, or could not, give a public assurance that his honour was still unsullied, the party that takes him or retains him as its leader can no longer count on the support of the bishops of Ireland. In speaking as I have spoken, I confine myself almost exclusively to the moral aspect of the case.[17]

Walsh's 'almost', suggests preparedness to make some political move, and he did so by writing to Tim Healy, Parnell's chief opponent, to say that he regarded the party leadership as vacant.

The North Kilkenny by-election dramatised the split between clergy and laity. Not all the clergy deserted Parnell. Not all the laity continued to back him. But there were unedifying examples of direct clerical interference, even intimidation, in the voting. Kilkenny priests sat at the tables where the electoral rolls were checked: 'voters came in bodies with their priests [at] their head saying they were Catholics and would vote with their clergy.'[18] All but one of the bishops condemned Parnell as 'wholly unworthy of the confidence of Catholics'.[19] The dissenter Bishop Edward O'Dwyer of Limerick thought the 'politico-theologians' were imposing an absurd claim on the consciences of the people. It was a political matter, not a moral one. He didn't endorse adultery but everyone knew that the private lives of some of Parnell's opponents were no better. 'It is no sin to support Parnell,' O'Dwyer declared.[20]

Whatever the young Daniel Mannix thought of the controversy, he could not be indifferent to the result. It was a disaster for the Parnellites. When Parnell died in 1891, broken in health by scandal and political defeat, many blamed the Catholic bishops for deserting him. Home Rule receded while the party tried to mend itself. The crisis showed Mannix the damage done by clerical intervention in political matters and the fine lines between the moral and the political spheres. This party-political split would not be the last in his lifetime.

Mannix climbed the Maynooth ladder fast and easily. He was only twenty-nine when he was appointed Professor of Moral Theology. It was said that he 'fought' his way; there must have been stiff opposition.[21] His students praised the clarity of his teaching.

Plain language, soundly structured arguments and a spellbinding power of delivery made him an extraordinary performer.

But he was not liked, and he knew it. Cool, reserved, severe, he seems never to have risked being known. In 1901, when he was vice-president, he was blamed for refusing some concessions the students asked for. They made their resentment known on a formal occasion when the whole college was assembled. As the members of staff took their places on the stage of the great hall, each one was welcomed with a cheer from the students: 'nicely graded to our particular opinion'. Mannix entered last.

> Dan knew what was coming as well as we did...[he] stalked forward to the edge of the stage and stood there, daring us to do our worst...Tall, thin to emaciation, he looked as coldly aloof as one of El Greco's Spanish Grandees...His provocative gaze would have driven a convocation of nuns to demonstration. It drove us wild, and with a thousand heavy winter boots, we scraped the floor and stamped until the din deafened us all.
>
> Dr Mannix folded his arms, stood like a graven statue, contemptuous, supercilious, through it all. When we could do no more he turned quietly to his chair, swung the folds of his toga wide with his arms, and sat down at the President's right hand with malice aforethought. He had beaten us.[22]

As in the incident of the prefect's badge, Mannix used silence as a weapon and his sense of theatre kept the private self unreachable and almost unreadable.

Unpopularity didn't hold Mannix back; his power and influence within Maynooth grew steadily. Students valued his teaching. He never read aloud, or even brought a book into class; he answered questions in straightforward language, without patronising the questioner. His lecturing style was 'electric'. An inter-class football match was cancelled when it was known that Mannix was speaking on the temperance cause. Without raising his voice and with none of the obvious rhetorical flourishes of the revivalist preacher, he invited a student audience in the Great Hall in 1901 to take the Pioneer Total Abstinence pledge, as he himself had done several years before. One hundred and eighty men stepped forward. Drink, 'the curse of the Irish', was a high risk for the celibate parish priest in Ireland and even more risky for those sent to lonely posts in overseas missions. Mannix saw total abstinence as their best safeguard.

The political Mannix emerged discreetly in the Maynooth Union, a body formed in 1895 as a means of keeping college graduates together. Mannix became its secretary. Past students were invited back to Maynooth for an annual lecture on theological, scriptural or historical subjects. Mannix wanted the scholarly emphasis to be varied with discussions on urgent economic and social problems. His list of topics included the co-operative movement, the temperance movement, better housing for the poor, the management of workhouses and the care of the sick.[23] His own contribution, published in 1901, was: 'Have We Solved the Land Problem in Ireland?'[24] After discussing the many shortcomings of the Land Acts, he ended with a plea for retaining Ireland's traditional way of life as an agricultural nation. He thought that England had made a mistake in relying too heavily on manufactures; her 'virile, stalwart peasantry' was disappearing. Ireland should not go the same way.[25] Unexpectedly sentimental about England's past with its 'strong vigorous tillers of the fields' and her 'virile, healthy people', Mannix sounded a note that would be heard many years later in Australia when the National Catholic Rural Movement was created by B.A. Santamaria, under Mannix's active patronage.

To talk about the land problem was to be political. The old-fogey voice of Mannix's land problem essay, which ends with 'I am old fashioned enough to think…' suggests that he was trying to be moderate. It is a reminder too that in 1901 he had been almost twenty years at Maynooth. What did Rome have in mind for him? Would he be given the top job at Maynooth or be made a bishop? It was too late to make him a parish priest, even though parish experience was what he needed most. In good time, Maynooth's vice-president, Dr O'Dea, became Bishop of Clonfert, and Mannix moved up. The president, Dr Gargan, was old and frail at eighty-six—'tottering', according to Archbishop Walsh—but it was not the custom to resign. He tottered on for another six months. No one was surprised when the bishops chose Daniel Mannix for the presidency in December 1903. He was then nearly forty.

Part of Mannix's achievement was in modernising the buildings at Maynooth and creating a degree of civilised living. When he arrived as a student in 1880 he had to bring his own bed and bedding; ventilation in the dormitories was bad; the walls of the central corridor, which had no natural light, were dirty and the floors were stained with mud and boot blacking. As president, Mannix raised the money for electric lighting, better sanitation, a swimming pool and ten 'reclining baths'.[26] The 'rude plenty' of the meals—mostly meat and potatoes—was refined with vegetables grown in the college garden.[27] As a dairy farmer's son, Mannix noticed the poor standard of the butter, and had the purchase order changed so as to get the best quality from Cork. A primitive infirmary was replaced; nursing sisters were appointed; and the care of the sick came under the president's direct scrutiny. Mannix was known to sit all night at the bedside of students who were seriously ill or dying. Faced with extreme need, he dropped his reserve.

Except for a few short holidays in France and Spain and some visits home, Mannix scarcely left Maynooth. His only known recreation was an occasional day out with the local hunt club, which sometimes set off from Maynooth. 'I always got the best horse I could,' he said; believing that the horse had as much interest in safety as its rider, he let it decide what risks to take in jumping fences or ditches. He may have had some social life in Dublin, which was easily reached by train or in the president's brougham. His membership of the Household Club in London sounds like a courtesy that went with the president's office; he wasn't a clubman by temperament. He had a generous salary, but seems not to have spent much; he was able to help his brother Timothy through a number of financial crises.

As president of Maynooth, Mannix had public duties: he entertained visitors and appeared at church functions in Dublin and elsewhere. And because Maynooth came under government authority, he had occasionally to go to Dublin Castle, the seat and chief symbol of British rule. During his last months as vice-president, he had faced the politically loaded occasion of a royal visit.

In July 1903, Edward VII came to Ireland with Queen Alexandra. There were still bitter memories of Queen Victoria's Irish policies, as far back as the Great Famine. But King Edward saw himself as a peacemaker in Ireland as well as in Europe, and for the sake of Home Rule his visit was important to the Irish Parliamentary Party as well as the Catholic Church. Mannix took a diplomat's view. Writing to Archbishop Walsh, he spoke of the benefits of the visit, which he hoped would 'pass off without a hitch'.[28] 'God Save the King' was played, and the red, white and blue flag floated above the college entrance.

It has been said that rather than fly the Union Jack, Mannix welcomed the king with a display of the royal racing colours. The authority is Mannix himself, telling the story many years later.[29] Newspaper reports of the time, however, do not mention this strategy, and the records show that Maynooth paid all the usual courtesies of royal visits, Union Jacks included.[30] Shane Leslie's semi-autobiographical work, *Doomsland*, published in 1935, gives a vivid account of Mannix's preparations. These, according to Leslie, included the ingenious conversion of one of the parlours, which was set aside for the king and queen. Pictures of saints were taken down and replaced by photographs of the king's racehorses. Could Mannix in old age have remembered a fiction created by Leslie and believed it? More likely he did, in fact, deck a Maynooth parlour in racing style and preferred to forget that he also flew the Union Jack.[31] There was a second royal visit, in 1911, but the visitor was George V, who was not a racing man.[32] During both visits, Mannix must have stepped carefully. Photographs of smiling church leaders walking beside the King would have stirred memories of their desertion of Parnell. Edward VII's adulteries were well known. Yet this was a time of hope for Ireland, and if Archbishop Walsh of Dublin, a strong nationalist, could take part in welcoming the King, so too would Daniel Mannix have done.

Mannix's main achievement in his Maynooth years was in education. Within his lifetime, Catholics had made great progress in primary and secondary schooling, but at the tertiary level they still met obstacles. It was no accident that much of the leadership in the Irish nationalist movement came from Protestants like Parnell. Nor was it an accident that Parnell's defeat was brought about by the Catholic clergy. The parish priests who put pressure on illiterate or under-educated voters were often themselves poorly qualified to understand the economic, political or religious questions involved. Mannix worked inside and outside Maynooth to raise the level of education for Catholics. It was time for an educated middle class to prepare itself for Home Rule.

Along with Archbishop Walsh, a fellow member of the Education Board, Mannix worked towards the University Act of 1908, which gave Catholics equal access to the newly created National University of Ireland. That was a triumph, after a century of obstacles and failures: the Pope's condemnation of 'godless' colleges in 1852 and John Henry Newman's frustrations as he had tried to create an intellectually distinguished Catholic University of Ireland in 1857. Mannix had Maynooth accepted as a college of the National University, thereby lifting the academic standards of future priests. But in 1909 he was faced with another challenge: the highly emotive issue of the teaching of Irish.

Irish nationalism at the turn of the century was a tangled skein of aims and hopes. One strand was the Irish language movement. Irish declined throughout the nineteenth century and by 1901 it was spoken by only about fourteen per cent of the people.[33] English was the language of power, spoken by government officials, landlords and policemen. There were few books in Irish, and no newspapers. Parents who wanted their children to get on in the world did not pass on the language, which many saw as a marker of peasant ignorance. Daniel Mannix spoke and wrote English with such precision and flair that he couldn't fail to love it. It seems that he knew no Irish. That may have been a reflection of his family's ambition. Timothy Mannix did not speak Irish, and Ellen Mannix's failure to teach the language to her clever children is unremarkable in the context of the time; it was not valued enough.

There was an explosion of enthusiasm for the language in the 1890s, in which the strongest voice was that of Douglas Hyde, son of a Church of Ireland clergyman. He was co-founder of the Gaelic League in 1893, which aimed to encourage pride in Irish culture, to restore the spoken language and to create a new literature with books and newspapers in Irish. An important early contribution came from Maynooth in 1892 when the professor of Irish, Eugene Growney (later O'Growney), wrote *Simple Lessons in Irish*. This textbook helped to build up Irish teaching circles across the country. In 1899 the Gaelic League started a newspaper, which was edited by the poet and future Easter Rising leader Pádraig Pearse. Eamon de Valera, a then unknown mathematics teacher, signed up for lessons in 1908, fell in love with his teacher Sinéad Flanagan and married her two years later. The League grew quickly to about seventy-five thousand members. It persuaded the Post Office to accept letters addressed in Irish and lobbied successfully for the right of shopkeepers to display their names in the Irish form.

The Gaelic League had an important win in 1909, after lobbying to make Irish a prerequisite for entry into the new National University. The further demand, that it should be compulsory within the degree structure, was rejected. Mannix was on the No side. Unluckily for him, because it led to coolness between them, Archbishop Walsh voted Yes.[34] Because the decision applied to Maynooth, now a constituent college of the university, Mannix also faced hostility on his home ground.

Irish had been taught at Maynooth for decades, and some former students, including Cardinal Logue, were notable scholars in the field. Eugene O'Growney, who entered Maynooth in the same year as Mannix, became a dedicated leader in the Irish language movement before returning to Maynooth as Professor of Irish in 1895. He had scarcely time to re-establish the subject when his health broke down. He was sent to the warmth of Arizona, but he died there of tuberculosis in 1899. Four years later, in a remarkable gesture of friendship and admiration, Mannix arranged to have O'Growney's body brought back for reburial at Maynooth. He travelled to Queenstown to meet the coffin, and he and Douglas Hyde spoke to a large crowd at the wharf. On to Dublin, where Pádraig Pearse gave the panegyric, and then to Maynooth, where the coffin was placed in the grounds. A little replica of the church of St Kevin at Glendalough was later built as his memorial. O'Growney's welcome home, just over two months after the visit of the British king and queen, should have restored Mannix's nationalist credentials, but a new test was on the way.

Although the O'Growney welcome placed him as a supporter of Irish, Mannix did not apply all the Gaelic League policies to Maynooth. He was intent on lifting academic standards overall; and because few students came well-prepared for formal Irish language studies, he preferred Irish to be voluntary. He disliked compulsion, and his nationalist priorities placed Irish language and literature below the land problem and the need to give every Maynooth priest a broad education and a university degree. The fact that he did not himself speak Irish may have been a factor. He questioned the usefulness of Irish for the many priests who would spend their working lives in overseas missions like Australia. In October 1904, the Maynooth trustees ruled that although Irish would remain a subject for university entrance, bishops might dispense students in individual cases. In practice this meant the end of compulsory Irish. The decision infuriated O'Growney's successor as professor of Irish, Dr Michael O'Hickey. O'Hickey leaked details of the bishops' debates to the press. Anger was fuelled by the Gaelic League and by the paper *Sinn Féin*. Archbishop Healy of Tuam was denounced as a 'bully' and 'an archbishop rampant'.[35]

There was a good case against compulsion. The Gaelic League leader Eoin MacNeill worried about its effect: could a love of the language come from enforced learning? O'Hickey had no doubts. In 1908 he gave an inflammatory lecture, which he also published. He called for a blacklist of all those who had voted against compulsory Irish, so that 'in after times all men may know who were the false and vile, in a supreme crisis in Ireland's history'. Among the clerical members of the board, only Archbishop Walsh was exempt from condemnation. 'For the rest, I shall say nothing further than to commend them to your prayers.'[36]

O'Hickey's 'false and vile' would have been more than enough, but he also described Mannix and the bishops who had opposed compulsory Irish as a 'worthless faction', guilty of 'squalid and foolish apostasy'.[37] Moreover, he spoke openly and angrily to Maynooth students. Mannix was entitled to see this as a breach of discipline. His letters to a friend in Rome show anger at O'Hickey's disloyalty in leaking the story to the press, his breach of staff solidarity in denigrating colleagues and bishops, and his incendiary words to the students.[38] The Archbishop of Tuam threatened to withdraw his students from Maynooth as long as O'Hickey remained on the staff. Others might follow. After discussion with the trustees, Mannix sacked O'Hickey. It is hard to see what else he could have done, but it made O'Hickey a victim and Mannix an enemy of 'true Irishmen'. Pádraig Pearse's anger against Mannix and Maynooth, eloquently expressed, would not easily be forgotten:

> Maynooth belongs to the Irish people. It is endowed by the money of the Irish public. The church for whose ministry it is educating the students is voluntarily supported by the Irish public...The Irish public is no impertinent outsider in this matter as its president would seem to suggest. It wants to know how its money is being spent, how its sons are being educated, how its vital interests are being controlled. The young men at Maynooth are our own—our brothers, our cousins, our sons. It is we who sent them to Maynooth; it is we who pay Maynooth to educate them; it is amongst us they will work. Their spiritual education we are content and shall always be content to entrust to the hands of those whose special function it is to direct such things; but their secular education is a matter on which we claim to have a voice—a claim which we intend to make good against all who impeach it.[39]

One of the Maynooth professors, Walter McDonald, who was a habitual stirrer, took up O'Hickey's cause and helped to raise the money for an appeal to Rome against wrongful dismissal. There was no open rebellion against Mannix among his students, but lapses in discipline made his authority less certain. The rule against smoking, which he rigidly enforced, became a serious problem during the period of the O'Hickey case: Mannix expelled nine students in 1911. Instead of basking in the success of his academic program, Mannix felt coolness among some of his colleagues. His reforms, which had included many practical measures for student health and well being, were obscured. A colleague, Dean Cornelius Healy, noted for anti-authoritarianism, later summed up the Mannix legacy as 'generous and progressive'.[40] Nevertheless,

Mannix was damaged by the language controversy. Was he, as Pearse and others said, out of touch with the Irish people? Had he been too long at Maynooth?

O'Hickey went to Rome to put his case. The miserable business dragged on for years, with Rome taking no great trouble to give its verdict. When it came, in 1914, it was against O'Hickey.[41] He died in 1916, depressed, bankrupt and jobless, at the age of fifty-five. His supporters blamed Mannix. But by that time, Mannix was twelve thousand miles away, playing a part in Irish politics from distant Melbourne that would have astonished Pearse and O'Hickey and all those who thought of him as a West Briton cleric, the 'consecrated ramrod' of Maynooth.

The call to Melbourne was not unexpected. There had been rumours in Rome and Dublin since 1911 that Thomas Carr wanted Mannix as his coadjutor. It was anyone's guess how Rome would respond. Writing to Carr in March 1912, Monsignor O'Riordan, rector of the Irish College in Rome, said that if any nomination were pushed too hard, 'it is almost sure to make [the Pope] set it aside':

> Yet, if reports are true, you all are so strong for Dr Mannix that he will very likely be sent. He will be a great loss to Maynooth, however; and especially at a very critical time in its history. They need a *clear, cool, strong* man there; and Dr Mannix is all that; and a spiritual man also.[42]

From Mannix's point of view it was time for a move. After thirty years in the same institution he was in danger of being fossilised, but at his level of seniority there were not many places to go. There would have been a nice symmetry in his replacing the Archbishop of Dublin, William Walsh, whose career pattern was much like his own. Clerical watchers, alert to birthdays and health reports, wondered about Walsh who was seventy-one in 1911. But Walsh was not about to retire—bishops didn't retire, any more than popes—and if he had wanted a coadjutor, Mannix would have been a bad choice. Apart from their differences over the Irish language question, Mannix was too strong-willed to be his deputy.

Melbourne was not a bad posting, nor necessarily a sign of disfavour in Rome. Ten years later, another intellectual star from Maynooth, Michael Sheehan, was made Coadjutor-Archbishop of Sydney, with no suggestion that he was being sidelined. But Mannix did not want to leave Ireland. He could have refused, but that was risky: something worse might have been produced. Carr had resisted his own Melbourne posting in 1885 without success; resistance from Mannix would probably have failed too. Was Melbourne a life sentence? Thomas Croke had been recalled from Auckland, after only three years, to be Archbishop of Cashel. There was a fair chance that if Mannix succeeded Carr, and did well in Melbourne, he might be called back when Walsh died. Walsh, who had a slight stroke in 1912, kept his options open by appointing an auxiliary bishop without right of succession, rather than a coadjutor. Steady, hard-working Edward Byrne served only a year before being rewarded on Walsh's death in 1921 with the job that seemed made for Mannix.

Mannix took the news of his exile in his usual inscrutable style. During a week with his family in the late summer of 1912, he refused to talk about it. He was going, 'and there's an end to it', he said. He refused the official farewell and testimonial offered by the Charleville parish priest, saying that he wanted just to 'get away quietly'.[43] In the absence of Archbishop Walsh, who was ill, he was consecrated archbishop in the Maynooth College chapel on 6 October by the seventy-one-year-old Archbishop Healy of Tuam who, like Walsh, was getting near the end of his active life. The spectre of vacant thrones prompted the question: why was Mannix, in his prime at forty-nine, being sent far away at a crucial time in Ireland's history?

He would have liked to get the parting over quickly, but a severe bout of pneumonia, like the one that had delayed his ordination, kept him from sailing for Australia for several months. Bulletins about his progress were issued; there was concern about his survival. 'The Archbishop passed a good night', was reported in December 1912. His farewells to his family were almost wordless. He met big occasions with aplomb. In intimate moments he became 'as silent as a ghost'.[44]

One curious postscript to the Mannix farewell to Maynooth has never been explained. Just two days before being consecrated as archbishop, near the end of his nine-day retreat of prayer and silence, he wrote a short note inviting an underqualified, obscure young teacher, whom he had never met, to apply for a part-time job lecturing in mathematics at Maynooth.[45] Mannix could have left it to his successor to find a candidate for this minor post. Why did he want to help Eamon de Valera? In 1912, de Valera, a father of three, was struggling to get by with bits and pieces of teaching in secondary schools. The Maynooth connection would be an immense asset to a future political leader, but in 1912 de Valera hadn't entered politics. All he had done was to get a disappointing pass degree in mathematics, learn Irish, and become secretary of a branch of the Gaelic League. Was Mannix trying to atone for the O'Hickey case? Whatever his reasons, he brought the future Sinn Féin leader, like a Trojan horse, into the clerical fortress of Maynooth.

CHAPTER THREE

MANNIX IN MELBOURNE

WHEN THE OVERNIGHT train from Adelaide drew in at Melbourne's Spencer Street station on Easter Sunday morning in March 1913, Daniel Mannix confronted his future. He had left the *Orama* at Adelaide instead of sailing on to enter Melbourne from Port Phillip Bay, giving himself a few days to recover from the voyage. He had been seasick most of the way, and the choppy waters between Fremantle and Adelaide were the worst of all. Adelaide wasn't restful. There was no escaping official hospitality from Archbishop O'Reilly and other churchmen and laity. His cousin Daniel Foley, then returning to his post as parish priest at Terang in country Victoria, had been a familiar, friendly presence on the voyage. Now, Mannix had to face an official welcoming party from Melbourne. Archbishop Carr sent two senior priests and a layman, Dr Leo Kenny, to share the train journey and tell Mannix whatever he needed to know about Melbourne.

Mannix's first impressions of Australia were dismal. He had never felt anything like the Adelaide heat. As the pavements bubbled and melted under his feet, he thought, I'll never live a year in this climate. Those who saw him first were inclined to agree. 'He looked a very sick man like a consumptive. Tall, thin, gaunt.'[1]

The welcome on the Melbourne platform from the priests and people of Melbourne was Adelaide all over again, only bigger.[2] By chance, however, Mannix's future as a political figure in this new setting was foreshadowed. The prime minister, Andrew Fisher, happened to be at Spencer Street that morning, and the two men were introduced.[3] A Labor man who needed to watch the Catholic vote, Fisher would have been pleased at the chance to make himself agreeable to the new archbishop.

Among those on the platform, eager to see the archbishop, was sixteen-year-old Arthur Calwell, newly employed in the public service. His friendship with Mannix would help to make, and later to undermine, his career. Another observer Michael Chamberlin, a twenty-one-year-old junior public servant from a working-class background, was to become a financial adviser to Mannix, and a lifelong friend. That evening, about five thousand people came to St Patrick's Cathedral to see Carr's coadjutor. By 7 p.m. there was standing room only for Mannix's first speech in Melbourne. He performed gracefully. Regrets for leaving Ireland ('my own dear country and my own kindred') were balanced by his sense of the youth and hope and buoyancy of the new country. He was a 'true believer in the great future of Australia'.[4] Following Dr Kenny's introductory speech, in which the unequal treatment of Catholic schools was mentioned, Mannix spoke of 'one great stain' on the statute books, but in the context of so much that was positive in his speech he did not upset the daily papers in which, next morning, he could read all about himself. For a man who had lived so quietly at Maynooth, it was a shock to find himself a Monday-morning celebrity. The *Age* was impressed with his looks and his voice, and so was the *Argus*:

> Standing up towards 6' in height with a clean-cut, even-featured face and strong searching eyes, the Coadjutor Archbishop made a commanding and striking figure. He speaks with the clear enunciation and ready eloquence of his race, and uses his clear, pleasant-toned voice with practised effect.[5]

When first told of his appointment to Melbourne, Mannix summed up pungently: all that he knew of Australia was that it was on the wrong side of the equator and too close to it. He had plenty of time to learn more before he left Ireland; bishops home on leave and priests who had served in Australia were not hard to find. Everyone at Maynooth knew Carr, their former vice-president, and liked him. It was well known too that Melbourne was a flourishing diocese. It could be seen as a good career move for Mannix, except for the risk that there would be no return. There were precedents either way. Archbishop Croke had been called back to Ireland after three years in Auckland, but the case of Archbishop Moran showed Rome's unpredictability. Summoned from Sydney in 1885 with a well-founded expectation of becoming Archbishop of Dublin, he was met by embarrassed clerics. Pope Leo XIII had changed his mind. He had prayed at the tomb of St Peter for guidance, got up from his knees and said 'Valsh'. The next day Cardinal Simeoni, who had the list of appointments, politely corrected him: 'Moran, Your Holiness?' 'No, we mean Valsh.' And Walsh it was.[6] Moran went back to Sydney in a huff, not appeased by the consolation prize of a cardinal's hat.

Because of their disagreement over the Irish language question, it is likely that Archbishop Walsh was happy to see Mannix off to the Antipodes. If he had wanted Mannix to succeed him in Dublin, Walsh could have made him coadjutor. By appointing moderate, well-liked Edward Byrne as auxiliary bishop, Walsh kept his authority to the end. Some coadjutor archbishops were given a hard time by the old man whom they were to replace: only the dull jobs were passed on and there was no sharing of ideas or visions of the future. That was true of Cardinal Moran, whose downtrodden deputy Michael Kelly waited ten years for the top job in Sydney. Then, after ten years as archbishop in his own right, Kelly was given his own coadjutor, whom he proceeded to harass so effectively that unlucky next-in-line Michael Sheehan was soon pleading for release. But Thomas Carr, by all accounts, gave Mannix a share in all the big projects. As Carr's choice, Mannix was allowed—even expected—to take a prominent place in church matters and to be seen in the wider Catholic community.

As the seat of federal government while Canberra was still a paddock, Melbourne in 1913 put Mannix immediately in touch with national politics. On his first evening, looking at the handsome Cathedral designed by William Wardell, he saw also the confident Italianate façade of Parliament House, so close that anyone could hear a speech and say a prayer with barely a five minute walk between the two buildings. Carr used to drop in to Parliament House for morning tea with one or two parliamentary friends.

Catholic politicians in need of pastoral counsel could slip out at question time and scarcely be missed.

Mannix's new home, St Mary's in West Melbourne, was a brisk thirty-five minute walk from St Patrick's. Carr had done his coadjutor proud with this well-proportioned Neo-Gothic structure, so big that it could have been a cathedral. The presbytery beside it was equally spacious and handsome. This was to be Mannix's base for the next four years, and it introduced him to the people of Melbourne. Because Maynooth had claimed him early he lacked parish experience to an unusual degree. Carr had been a lowly curate for two years at Westport in County Mayo in the west of Ireland and taught at St Jarlath's College, Tuam, before returning to Maynooth as vice-president. He had been Bishop of Galway for a little more than three years when the summons to Melbourne disrupted a contented life.

Few clerics would have been as ignorant as Mannix was about ordinary lives, family happiness and sorrows, social pleasures, jobs, babies, housing problems, bills. Apart from his own Charleville family with its vast number of female cousins (many of them nuns) he had had almost nothing to do with women or children, and although he was presented as an authority on education he knew nothing about classrooms or playgrounds.

Now, belatedly, Mannix was a parish priest with nearly everything to learn. He was used to speaking to big audiences at Maynooth, where at a full college assembly he would face six hundred young men, all in clerical black, as uniform as an army battalion. The pews at St Mary's, however, were filled by family groups. There were a few middle class families but most parishioners came from the respectable poor. Shabby suits, the 'best hat' that had to last for years, hand-knitted baby clothes that had shrunk in the washing, and faded hand-me-downs for children: that was Dr Mannix's Sunday morning congregation.

The splendour of St Mary's church belied the realities of life in West and North Melbourne. St Mary's was designed in French Gothic style in 1882: a spacious building in brick faced with sandstone, and limestone dressings, with a tower and turrets, an elaborate interior and a magnificent rose window. A bishop's throne was made for Mannix in 1913. Although the design reflected the confidence of the Marvellous Melbourne decade, St Mary's depended on working-class parishioners whose members struggled to contribute to the building fund during the depression years of the 1890s. Against the odds, it opened in 1900. The district was hit hard by depression. Historian John Rickard traces its struggles:

> The 1890s saw Melbourne's population shrink, and North Melbourne lost 2877 people, most of them men. Clearly the exodus to the West Australian goldfields was having an effect. The number of inhabited dwellings fell from 3981 to 3640. Some houses were empty; others perhaps giving way to industry. For the first time, Anglicans were outnumbered by Roman Catholics in North Melbourne, which became the only municipality in Melbourne to boast a Catholic majority.[7]

As a Catholic parish, St Mary's, Star of the Sea, dated from 1854, when the first mass was said in a tent on the Victoria Street site. Because there was an earlier St Mary's, in North Melbourne, founded by the Anglicans in December 1853, the Catholics chose the title Star of the Sea to define their church. It welcomed migrants with the refrain of the wistful hymn: 'Virgin most pure/ Star of the Sea/ Pray for the wanderer/ Pray for me'. It was a parish for displaced people: Irish-Australians in the nineteenth century, and Italians and Maltese a century later. Many found work at the Victoria Market, the Newmarket saleyards, the North Melbourne meat market, the abattoirs, the Spencer Street railway station, the Flemington racecourse.[8]

Anglicans, Presbyterians, Wesleyans and Catholics all held services in North Melbourne from the late 1850s. By the time Mannix arrived, more than half a century later, all four denominations were well established. They kept to their own corners in contained suspiciousness. There is no evidence that Mannix and his counterpart at the other St Mary's talked to each other.

Some of Mannix's parishioners had bitter memories of the railway strike of 1902, in which many families suffered and no gains were made. Walking to work at the Cathedral every day, as he chose to do, Mannix could see the children on their way to their separate schools. Some were neat and tidy, others barefoot and bedraggled. Mannix did not need to be told that the Catholic community was straining to pay for its own schools; poverty was all around him in West and North Melbourne. When he spoke at a fundraising fete, as he often did on a Saturday afternoon in parishes all over Melbourne, he would see the exchange of hard-earned pennies and halfpennies for small items, many of them second-hand. A new hair-ribbon was a luxury, so was a new pair of bootlaces, a handkerchief or a little bag of boiled lollies. Mannix saw his parish in its Sunday best, but he learned the realities of its struggles.

In a speech given within weeks of his arrival Mannix showed his awareness of social inequity. Dismayed at the level of unemployment, he called for a broad national policy to ensure that profits were divided between labour and capital. This sounded like socialism. As historian Patrick Morgan points out, Mannix 'wasn't so much church centred as society centred'.

> He didn't in his early years as archbishop publicly ponder much on such questions as salvation outside the church, or mixed marriages, or other staples of the sermons of Catholic moralists…nor did he emphasise the nineteenth century devotional practices of Jansenist piety…He identified with his people, speaking on their behalf to the public rather than blaming them, which made them warm to him.[9]

Perhaps because he had been cocooned at Maynooth for the whole of his adult life, Mannix was more shocked and indignant at the evidence of economic injustice than the average parish priest would have been. In 1891, the papal encyclical *Rerum Novarum* called Catholics to amend the social order. Mannix was then a teacher and administrator whose public voice was limited to the education issue. Now, he was part of a community. A man of rational intelligence at Maynooth, he developed emotional intelligence at St Mary's. Using homely terms that any listener could understand, he allowed himself a degree of emotion that did not often come from the pulpit. His identification with the Melbourne working class began at St Mary's. Without it, he would not have held the sometimes strained affection of most of Melbourne's Catholics through three generations. Even in the 1950s, when he was blamed, with some justice, for splitting the Australian Labor Party, its members found it hard to turn away from him.

The tone and language of Mannix's response to the seamen's strike of 1919 were not very different from those of a labour leader. He took the point of view of the families of the strikers. His contempt for employers who complained about having to eat cold meals during the strike was stirred by direct knowledge of 'families who had to be thankful if they got any kind of breakfast, cold or hot'.[10]

Australian Catholics had been arguing the case for state aid to their schools since the 1872 government decision for 'free, secular and compulsory' education. Their grievances were not fully understood, and many of the non-Catholic majority had stopped listening. Memories of religious and cultural indoctrination in Irish national schools resonated. When he chose his coadjutor, Carr hoped that experience in Ireland's educational policy and administration would pay dividends, but he probably did not expect the sharp edge of Mannix's indignation, nor his readiness to apply political pressure.

The financial burden of the Catholic schools system was the big disappointment of Carr's thirty years in Melbourne. Given Mannix's energy and intellect, gains might finally be made and that burden might be eased. The next stage of Catholic education—the tertiary level—could then be tackled. So far, Carr's efforts and those of some prominent Catholic laymen had made no headway. The Australian Catholic Federation, a pressure group that lobbied politicians on the education issue, had been operating since 1911 without success.[11] Carr had tried to bring the Catholic vote into play, but his conciliatory style was ineffectual. While political leaders were pleased to be seen at Catholic functions looking friendly, they were wary of actually doing anything about the touchy issue of the Catholic schools. State aid to Catholic schools would be costly, and it would exacerbate sectarian tensions.

Hugh Mahon, a sharp-tongued Irish-born member of the

federal parliament, who had been imprisoned with Parnell for Land League activities, accused his Labor colleagues of thinking that they could keep the Catholic voters 'sweet' merely by appearing at a St Patrick's Day function or a communion breakfast.[12] Even though Labor had been in power on and off since 1904, Carr was not at home with its men. In 1915, after the governor-general, Sir Ronald Munro-Ferguson, and Lady Munro-Ferguson had accepted his invitation to the St Patrick's Night concert, Carr wrote diffidently to Mahon, asking him to come and to bring his Labor colleagues: 'I am anxious that you and Mrs Mahon should be present. If you think well of it, I should like that you would invite in my name some of the other federal ministers and their wives.'[13]

Mannix did not think much of this tentative approach; he made it clear to the Catholic Federation members that they would have to try harder. Reason was not enough; they had to use their votes. There was a striking contrast between Carr's measured words and Mannix's electric style. When they shared a public occasion, Carr, who always spoke first, was gentle and reasonable. Mannix roused his hearers; they went home amused, exhilarated, even stirred to action by his directness and the comic edge of his rhetoric. 'To reason with the average politician,' Mannix said, 'unless you vote against him also, is about as useful as throwing confetti at a rhinoceros.'[14] Because reasoning was Carr's style, this was not tactful, but Mannix could never resist a pithy phrase.

The years at St Mary's, Mannix said, were the happiest of his life. Why this should be so is hard to explain. They seem in retrospect to be filled with strife. Perhaps after the sameness of thirty years at Maynooth he liked the unexpectedness of Australian life. After so long as a functionary at Maynooth, though an influential one, he was free to make his own rules. He found a voice of his own, capable of stirring big crowds. But this had not come easily; he spent hours on Saturday afternoons with Jesuit orator William Lockington, learning how to throw his voice from the cathedral pulpit or across an open space. His days were balanced between the formal and the improvised. He went to the cathedral every weekday, and he could be alone in the evenings if he pleased. His household was quite small; his three assistant priests did most of the parish work. And, although his habit of reclusiveness did not change much, he was making some friends and even visiting a few neighbours in North Melbourne.

Ireland was a bond; a number of Melbourne's Catholic intellectuals were deeply involved in the Home Rule movement. Mannix used to go for long walks with Irish-born Morgan Jageurs, a builder and stonemason and a founding member of the Celtic Club. Nicholas O'Donnell, who had a medical practice in Victoria Street, near St Mary's, was a Home Ruler and, like Jageurs, spoke fluent Irish.[15] The Brennan family were leaders in political and legal circles. Mannix was the celebrant when Frank Brennan, the Labor member for Batman, married O'Donnell's daughter Cecilia in December 1913. Brennan's journalist brother Tom wrote for the Catholic weekly paper, the *Advocate*, which was owned by a strong Home Rule supporter Joseph Winter. A complex interweaving of clubs and societies kept these men together. They met at the Celtic Club, read Irish news in the *Advocate*, and in 1913 they were all hopeful that an independent Ireland would soon emerge under the leadership of John Redmond, who had visited Melbourne and counted them among his friends.[16]

Before Mannix left Ireland, Redmond's Home Rule Party had made important gains. The Third Home Rule Bill, introduced in the House of Commons in April 1912, had proposed to set up an Irish parliament to deal with internal Irish affairs excluding taxation and the police. Other matters—the Crown, foreign affairs, trade—would be dealt with in the Westminster Parliament, to which Ireland would continue to send its elected members. The provisions of the Bill fell short of Irish aspirations for a republic but it was generally well received in nationalist circles. Although it was certain to be vigorously resisted by the unionists of the northern counties of Ireland, the Bill had enough votes in Westminster, from the Liberal, Labour and Irish parties, to ensure its passing. Then, after a two-year delay in the House of Lords, it was due to become law in 1914.

The outbreak of the First World War weakened the resolve of the British government to give Ireland this modest measure of Home Rule. It had been evident that the northern unionists would not let Home Rule go through without a fight. Well-drilled and armed men had been appearing at unionist demonstrations since 1911. These Ulster Volunteers were matched by Irish Volunteers who also armed themselves. Gun-running, on both sides, threatened violence at a time when Britain needed all its strength for the war with Germany. Faced with the possibility of civil war in Ireland, the British government decided that the Home Rule Bill should be put aside until the war with Germany was over. Redmond and the Ulster leader, Sir Edward Carson, pledged support for the war. Carson accepted a place in the government as attorney-general. Redmond kept his pledge of independent opposition and refused to join, thereby putting himself outside the centre of power. His leadership was damaged by concessions to Ulster by which he appeared to accept partition.

Everything changed with the Easter Rising in Dublin on

23 April 1916. A dedicated group of Irish nationalists—men and women, poets, academics and revolutionary socialists—took action. They no longer believed that Britain would keep its promises. British concessions to Ulster and Redmond's perceived weakness fed the republicans' flame. Inadequately armed and poorly prepared, they occupied Dublin, seized the General Post Office as headquarters, and proclaimed Ireland a republic. Plans to make this the centre of a national rising went awry; contradictory orders and a last-minute change of mind made failure inevitable. Yet it was a powerful failure. The GPO as command post was a bad choice tactically (the well-provisioned Shelbourne Hotel would have been better) but it was a splendid site for unfurling the new national flag, the green, white and orange tricolour in which the white, signifying peace, came between the traditional enmities of nationalists and Ulster loyalists.

Only a few startled Dubliners were close enough to hear Pádraig Pearse read the Proclamation of the Irish Republic on that Easter Sunday morning. It summoned Irishmen and Irishwomen 'in the name of God and of the dead generations' to bring freedom to their land. A provisional government proclaimed a sovereign state. It guaranteed 'religious and civil liberty, equal rights and opportunities for all its citizens'.[17]

There was only a brief time of rejoicing. Within a few days the Post Office was a smoking ruin, the inner city a wasteland in which doctors, nurses and ordinary citizens tried to save the wounded and bring in the dead.

Perhaps because the British were caught unprepared, and because the European war was first priority, their response was swift, brutal and arbitrary. Martial law was proclaimed across Ireland. Searches and arrests without warrant were common, and shootings were often based on mistaken identity or deliberate carelessness.

Within days of the uprising Pádraig Pearse surrendered. He was shot at dawn on 3 May in the yard of Kilmainham Gaol, along with Thomas MacDonagh and Tom Clarke. Day by day, the leaders were executed. The cruellest death was that of James Connolly, who had been so badly wounded that he had to be propped up and tied to a chair to face the firing squad. Willie Pearse was executed for no better reason than his being Pádraig Pearse's brother. Others who had fought in the Rising were rounded up and sent to gaol; by mid-May there were more than two thousand Irish prisoners in England.[18] Some escaped; others died on hunger strike. Many would emerge from prison more radical than before. Eamon de Valera and Michael Collins were young and untried when they fought in the Easter Rising. De Valera, aged thirty-three, was teaching maths and working for the Gaelic League. He was given command of a battalion. Michael Collins, then a twenty-seven-year-old bookkeeper, played a minor part in the Rising and, without trial or sentence, was shipped off in a batch of six hundred men in a cattle boat to Frongoch gaol in Wales. De Valera and Collins, leaders in the next stage of the campaign for Irish independence, would become friends and allies, rivals and finally adversaries. Their single-minded ambition, the heroic aura of the Rising, and the prison terms that they served, brought these two men out of obscurity to become national figures.

Australian Catholics, nearly all Irish by birth or descent, were in accord with most other Australians in supporting Britain's war against Germany. Irish-Australian nationalists had taken their lead from John Redmond when he offered 'Ireland's sword' to the cause. The most prominent Melbourne Catholic laymen, like

Carr and the other Australian Catholic archbishops and bishops, believed that the war was just. Although Mannix expressed doubts about the war, the Catholic community had no reason to worry about his basic loyalty in 1914 and 1915.

At first, Mannix, like the other Australian archbishops and bishops, thought that the Easter Rising was deplorable folly. Archbishop Carr called it 'an outburst of madness, an anachronism, a crime'. All agreed that the rebels who proclaimed an Irish republic were wrong to take violent action with no hope of success. The Rising was seen by many as a self-destructive breach of the British parliamentary process which was trusted to bring Home Rule eventually. Mannix, however, shifted the blame to the British for bad faith. Ulster Protestant Sir Edward Carson, who had threatened armed force against the parliamentary decision to give Home Rule, was rewarded with a place in the British Cabinet. Pádraig Pearse was shot.

> People must expect to reap what they sow...I am quite clear in my own mind that the British Government by its failure to deal with the treason of the Carsonites and by its shifty policy in regard to Home Rule has, unwittingly I suppose, led to the result which we must all deplore.[19]

Mannix's early comments on the Rising were not inflammatory. He deplored and regretted; he did not praise or condemn. But when he read newspaper reports that the British had condemned all the leaders to death, his mood changed. 'Michael, they've shot some of them!' he exclaimed, weeping as he broke the news to the St Mary's handyman. In shock and grief, he condemned the reprisals. Ireland would never be given Home Rule, he concluded.

The British government's brutality had proved the rebels right.

Mannix knew some of those who faced the firing squad. Pádraig Pearse had berated him over the O'Hickey affair, calling him a traitor to Ireland. Thomas MacDonagh, a writer and a lecturer at University College in Dublin, was a champion of the Irish language who also loved English literature. In his final class at UCD, as one of his students remembered, MacDonagh 'simply closed his copy of *Pride and Prejudice* and sighed: "Ah, lads, there's nobody like Jane!" He was shot by soldiers from Jane Austen's England. The British officer-in-command said that "they all died nobly but MacDonagh died like a prince."'[20] Eamon de Valera's death sentence was commuted because he was American-born, and because the British commander-in-chief did not think he sounded important. Countess Constance Markievicz who, like de Valera, had served as a commandant, went to gaol because the British would not execute a woman.

Something in Daniel Mannix was released in the aftermath of the Easter Rising. Alone among the Australian archbishops and bishops, he took the side of the rebels. It was a sudden shift from his attitude during the O'Hickey case, when he had been inflexible in the matter of the Irish language. He had followed the majority view of the Irish bishops then. Now he was taking the same side as the maverick Bishop Edward O'Dwyer of Limerick, who denounced the British commander-in-chief, General Maxwell, for 'wantonly cruel and oppressive' actions that outraged the conscience of the country. These included the deportation without trial of thousands of young men.[21]

Late in 1916, Mannix heard that Michael O'Hickey had died at the age of fifty-five, having spent years in Rome waiting for a response to his appeal against his dismissal from Maynooth. Rome upheld Mannix's authority. Friends said that O'Hickey died of heartbreak; they blamed Mannix.[22] Perhaps the ghost of Michael O'Hickey played a part in Mannix's change of heart.

Mannix had to wait for news of Eamon de Valera, whom he had helped to find a job at Maynooth in 1912. After the Rising, de Valera served little more than a year in gaol before being released in an amnesty in 1917. He then began his political career. He would carry the legend of romantic Ireland through years of struggle and several more gaol terms. And, almost overnight it seemed, Daniel Mannix, Maynooth's cool pragmatist, became as fiercely romantic as any of the men of the Easter Rising.

CHAPTER FOUR

DUELLING WITH THE PRIME MINISTER

THEY CREATED ONE another as public figures: they owed each other fame. Without Mannix, Prime Minister Hughes might never have captured the King and Empire vote; he was not a natural leader of conservative Australians. Welsh, working class, self-educated, Billy Hughes belonged to Labor, and when he changed allegiances in 1916 to lead the National Party, he took the risk of being left without a secure power base.

In many ways, the sudden appearance of Daniel Mannix on the political scene shaped Hughes as a public figure. The two men were contrasts in appearance, voice and personal style. Tall and strikingly handsome, Mannix moved across the stage as if he owned it. He spoke softly, sometimes seeming deliberately to drop his voice so as to make the audience strain to catch every word.

His accent had nothing of the stage Irish about it; there was wit and mischief, but no blarney. You could have taken him for an expatriate Irish intellectual like George Bernard Shaw.

Hughes was quick, fierce, abrasive. Short in stature—Mannix had the advantage of him by almost a head—Hughes made up for his lack of inches by his intensity of feeling and his natural eloquence. They were fire and ice. 'Mr Hughes called me a liar, a traitor or rebel', Mannix said. 'But I always called him Mr Morris Hughes.'[1]

Mannix never needed to shout. His measured tone, with a touch of *hauteur*, worked perfectly against the voluble prime minister. Passion was tempered with comedy in a style that delighted many, though not all, of his Catholic listeners. For the descendants of the Irish underclass it was exhilarating to have so fearless a leader. The disdain with which Mannix spoke of the Australian establishment was heady stuff for an underprivileged people with little education, low self-esteem and a long history of resentful submission. With his aristocratic bearing and his beautifully modulated voice, Mannix could have passed for the most privileged of 'Them'. By 1916 it was clear that he was one of 'Us'. In 1917, under direct attack from the prime minister, he won the hearts of many Australian Catholics.

There were some who had reservations. A small number of talented Catholic men had broken through to affluence and status. For many in this group Mannix was too much the stirrer, too aggressive, too Irish. He made a few friends among them, most notably Dr Leo Kenny, one of his escorts on arrival from Adelaide to Melbourne. Others were wary or disapproving. In his time at West Melbourne Mannix visited a few families but he was never gregarious. After 1917, when he became Archbishop of Melbourne in his own right, Mannix made it known that he never visited private houses. This was a way of keeping independence. It was also self-protection for a shy man who coped more easily with a massive audience than an intimate group. He seldom broke his rule. When he consented to join the Kenny family for supper one Sunday evening, the boiled egg that they gave him was talked about for years.[2]

The early life of William Morris Hughes was a complete contrast with that of Mannix. There was one bond, however; they were both Celts, and it could be said that Celtic passion informed their politics. They were also close in age: Hughes was born in 1862, two years before Mannix. But their backgrounds were vastly different. From Charleville to Maynooth, up to the age of forty-nine, Mannix was tightly held within the structure of the family and the Catholic Church. It was only after he left Ireland that his individuality appeared. Even then, his maverick self was expressed within the system. Order and dignity were maintained, in public at least. Behind the scenes it was different; Vatican officials and the heads of state in Britain and Australia tried their best to restrain Mannix, but it was not easy to silence an archbishop, especially one who was a natural leader.

Hughes lived in chaos, and thrived on it. London-born, with Welsh parents and a childhood divided between working-class Pimlico and semi-rural North Wales, William Morris Hughes learned self-reliance early. He was an only child. His mother died when he was seven, and he was sent to live with his father's sister who ran a boarding house in Llandudno. Aged twelve, he was back in London for two years' schooling, followed by five years as a pupil-teacher. Unlike Mannix who never talked about his childhood, Hughes was a prodigious spinner of tales about his early years, many of them contradictory.[3] He left gaps in the narratives:

he never mentioned his father, who is thought to have been a carpenter and a deacon in the Welsh Baptist church in Pimlico. Hughes knew his Bible well, and some of his eloquence may have stemmed from Welsh pulpit oratory. He was an independent battler with limitless ambitions. Short and spindly, with the big nose and ears that would delight future cartoonists, he started life with no advantages except his intelligence, quick wit and courage. He liked to say that on a dull day in London he tossed a coin and it came up 'Heads, Australia'. In 1884, aged twenty-two, he left for Australia, apparently alone and with no friends or family to join. True or not, it fits the pattern of an improvised life, dependent only on the strength of the self.

Once landed, Hughes did whatever came his way. From a roving life as swagman, stockman, boundary rider and rural labourer in Queensland, he took ship to Sydney. Again he worked at anything he could find, took lodgings in what were then the slums of East Sydney, and from about 1886 or 1887 lived permanently with his landlady's daughter, Elizabeth Cutts, whom he seems not to have married. Elizabeth, who took in washing and ironing, had a son from an earlier relationship. Between about 1890 and 1906 she and Hughes had six children together. Hughes opened a shop in Balmain, where he did all kinds of work; as umbrella mender, knife grinder, locksmith, seller of second-hand books, he was endlessly versatile.[4] At the same time he was finding his way into the Australian labour movement, which was then a work in progress. His political career began in the 1890s depression years. He took part in the Maritime Union strike of 1890, and made his name as a negotiator and orator.

From union organiser on, it was a straight path for Hughes. He travelled widely, winning support for the Labor Electoral League, from which emerged the Australian Labor Party. He qualified for the bar in 1903 and in 1894 won the seat of Lang in the New South Wales Parliament.[5] Elizabeth died in 1906. Her plaintive letters to Hughes show that he neglected her and their children. He moved from state to federal politics; and his centre, after Federation in 1901, became Melbourne, where in these pre-Canberra years the parliament met. He married Mary Campbell, a former nurse, in 1911. It sounds a marriage of convenience rather than one based on any strong feeling. Hughes had risen far beyond the social level of Elizabeth Cutts. Mary (Dame Mary in 1922) liked being the prime minister's wife; she was not intimidated by Buckingham Palace visits, and she nursed Hughes in his many bouts of ill health. Together, they settled in Cotham Road, Kew, in a house that Mannix passed many times after he too made his home in Kew. In August 1915 the only child of Hughes and Mary was born: a beautiful, clever, confident girl named Helen, to whom Hughes gave unconditional love.

When Mannix arrived in Melbourne in March 1913, Billy Hughes was the member for Bendigo and attorney-general in the Labor government of Andrew Fisher. As one of the founding fathers of the Australian Labor Party, Hughes had a sound electoral base in the working class. Many of his people were Catholics. He and Mannix could have formed some kind of alliance on social justice problems. At any rate they need not have been violently opposed, nor would they have been, if the Home Rule Bill, for which the Irish had been waiting so long, had not been set aside by the British government in 1914.

Before 1916, most of the Australian people, including those of Irish birth or descent, gave their support to the war. On 17 March, 1916, the St Patrick's Day procession stopped outside Parliament

House to play 'God Save the King'. Then came the Easter Rising in Dublin, which nearly everyone thought was foolish, or worse. Within weeks, the brutal executions of the Irish leaders changed the general mood. In a speech made some weeks after the executions, Mannix's passionate denunciation carried a reminder that it was British guns that murdered the Irish rebels:

> Men said to be innocent were put against a wall in a Dublin barrack yard and, without trial by judge and jury, were shot in cold blood and sent before their Maker. These outrages will rankle in the minds of men and they are not likely to bring a blessing upon British arms.[6]

By using the conventional notion of 'bringing a blessing', so often heard by Catholic children when good behaviour was being judged, Mannix was quietly reminding his listeners of ceremonies in which Anglican bishops blessed the guns of Allied troops, and of sermons from Protestant church leaders in which the sanctity of the war was upheld.[7]

While Irish-Australian public feeling towards the war was shifting in the aftermath of the Easter Rising, Hughes was in England. The news he heard most clearly was that of terrible losses in France. In close touch with the British War Cabinet, he resolved to send more Australian troops to help. As soon as he came back to Australia he announced a referendum on conscription to be held in October 1916. This shook the traditional beliefs of his Australian Labor parliamentary party as well as its rank-and-file members. Conscription threatened civil liberties and economic stability. In this context, the Irish struggle for independence from Britain and the growing popularity of Mannix became increasingly important.

In other circumstances, Catholic working-class people might not have taken to this cool, ascetic archbishop. But from the first Mannix took their side. He gave a voice to their grievances in the matter of education; and by refusing to defer to anyone in government or vice-regal circles, he gave Catholics a new sense of confidence. And when it came to the debates over the conscription issue, it was a tonic to watch him undermine the prime minister's certainty.

Cartoonists loved the two leaders. From his top hat, or purple biretta, to his buckled shoes, Mannix obliged by always presenting in costume. The cartoonists' extras—an Irish harp, a shamrock or a shillelagh—were scarcely needed. Hughes, 'the Little Digger', was defined by small stature, big ears and frenetic activity.

Mannix and Hughes did not emerge as a warring duo until after the first conscription referendum. During that first campaign, Mannix confined himself to two statements, neither of them especially fierce. The first, however, was crisply phrased and telling. Rather than an instant inflammatory effect, it invited thought:

> I am as anxious as anyone can be for a successful issue and for an honourable peace. I hope and believe that peace can be secured without conscription. For conscription is a hateful thing, and it is almost certain to bring evil in its train...
>
> The Prime Minister has very wisely avoided evil counsels and allowed the people to decide for themselves... We can only give both sides a patient hearing and then vote according to our judgment. There will be differences among Catholics, for Catholics do not think or vote in platoons, and on most questions there is room for divergence of opinion. But for myself it will take a good deal to convince me that

> conscription in Australia would not cause more evil than it would avert. I honestly believe that Australia has done her full share, and more, and she cannot reasonably be expected to bear the financial strain, and the drain upon her manhood, that conscription would involve.[8]

Mannix noted that certain Anglican prelates gave public support to conscription, as was their right. The other Catholic archbishops made their views known too. Kelly, who had joined the pro-conscription Universal Service League, vacillated after the Easter Rising. Clune of Perth openly advocated conscription. Duhig of Brisbane said it was a matter for individual voters. It is impossible to be sure how much influence these prelates had. The 1916 Yes vote won in Mannix's Victoria, and in Tasmania and Western Australia. New South Wales, South Australia and Queensland said No, and the overall vote was No.[9] It is likely that Mannix won No votes outside Victoria; he was widely reported and talked about in all the other states. He may also have contributed to the Yes vote by offending members of the other churches.

Hughes did not mention Mannix during the 1916 referendum campaign. His reproaches, when the No vote prevailed, were scattered around the community: he spoke of 'the selfish vote, and the shirker vote and the Irish vote'.[10] He saw an unholy alliance between left and right: between the IWW (International Workers of the World) and conservatives, farmers and businessmen.

By November 1916, Hughes faced an Australian Labor Party caucus bitterly divided over conscription. At a caucus meeting on 14 November, he was under such fierce attack that he saw no point in waiting to be expelled from the party he had helped to found.

'Enough of this', he said. 'Let those who think with me follow me.' And out he strode, 'leaving behind a scene of confusion and air blue with tobacco smoke'. Twenty-four men followed him. He was afterwards to say that he had never left the Labor Party; it had left him.[11] Hughes and his pro-conscription colleagues were able to stay in office with the support of the opposition; and in 1917 a new organisation, the Nationalist Party, emerged under Hughes' leadership to fight the next election. The Australian Labor Party, fatally weakened, regrouped under the leadership of the uninspiring Frank Tudor.

Beset by hostility from former allies and suspicion from former opponents, Billy Hughes pressed on undaunted. During the 1917 election campaign, he announced that a second conscription referendum would be held 'if national safety demands it'. His Nationalist Party easily defeated the Australian Labor Party in the House of Representatives and the Senate, but the win left Billy Hughes with the character of a Labor 'rat', a class traitor. A demoralised left wing, without effective leadership, looked to Daniel Mannix for a champion.

The Easter Rising and its aftermath had fatally weakened the Irish Parliamentary Party and brought the radical republican Sinn Féin Party to the fore. Mannix declared himself a Sinn Féiner, giving Hughes a new weapon. Hughes told the British prime minister, Lloyd George, that Ireland and Mannix were at the bottom of his government's difficulties:

> They—the Irish—have captured the political machinery of the Labor organisations—assisted by the syndicalists and I.W.W. [International Workers of the World] people. The Church is secretly against recruiting. Its influence killed conscription.

> One of their archbishops—Mannix—is a Sinn Féiner. And I am trying to make up my mind whether I should prosecute him for statements hindering recruiting or deport him.[12]

In November 1917 Hughes described Mannix as 'a man to whom every German in the country looks...if you follow him you range yourself under the banner of the deadly enemies of Australia.'[13] Calling on Keith Murdoch, then a journalist based in London, to rally support from Lloyd George, Hughes said that 'the bulk of Irish people led by Archbishop Mannix...are attacking me with a venomous personal campaign...'[14]

Mannix took a less obviously aggressive tone. His 1917 speeches were a rich blend of fierce irony, reasoned argument and comic belittlement of his opponents. He addressed his audience directly, identifying himself with the working class who, he said, would pay the highest price in the war and be forgotten by the wealthy. He used homely images: ants running about with their eggs when their anthill is disturbed; leaders with no more backbone than a stick of boiled asparagus.

Mannix scored points for logic. If it was disloyal to vote No against conscription, why was Hughes offering the nation the chance to do so? When he said that Catholics were doing their fair share of the fighting, he was on solid ground, as may be seen in the high number of volunteers from the working-class suburb of Richmond.[15] 'I understand that not enough nuns are enlisting', was one of many droll lines with which Mannix parried the charge of disloyalty.[16] He put comedy aside when, like other parish priests and ministers of religion, he was charged by the Commonwealth authorities with the grim duty of taking the news of a serviceman's death to his bereaved family. It is not known how many of these visits Mannix took on himself, but it would be unlike him to have left them all to his assistant priests in West Melbourne. Parish visiting of the normal kind became almost impossible by 1917: the approach of a clergyman brought such terror to the families of serving soldiers.

Hughes matched Mannix in vigour and quick repartee, but he didn't show the comic sense that made Sundays such wonderful entertainment for Melbourne's Catholics. The usual functions—opening parish fetes, laying foundation stones—stopped being dull and predictable. Mannix never made political speeches from the pulpit. That was a matter of principle. But his claim that on public occasions in the community he spoke only as an ordinary citizen was belied by his appearance in full clerical dress, with an entourage of priests.

Both men drew huge crowds. Hughes reacted with such fury to an egg-throwing incident in the town of Warwick in Queensland that it became a brawl, in which he joined vigorously.[17] By contrast, Mannix used stillness and mockery, only occasionally releasing passionate emotion.

'What has *he* been saying today?' Every Sunday evening Archbishop Carr asked about his coadjutor's doings, even though the news was likely to upset him. The young priests at St Patrick's Cathedral had to be tactful. But no matter how they dodged his question, Carr would find the answer next morning, often as front page news.

For Carr, 1916 had been bad enough. The easy relations he had built with the community, both Catholic and non-Catholic, were being fractured. But 1917 was worse. The news from Ireland, after the Easter Rising, was heartbreaking for him, as for any Irishman.

And, having identified himself with his new country and his people in Melbourne for thirty years, Carr read the lengthening casualty lists in black type on the front pages of the newspapers and felt the daily tragedies of the war in Europe.

Monday was a day of reckoning for Mannix too. He would scan the pages of the *Argus* with special care. That was where he was most likely to be misrepresented. Reporters who followed him on his Sunday excursions might get it wrong; and they would in any case choose the emphasis and often supply an inflammatory headline. The main Catholic newspaper, the weekly *Advocate*, was then still owned by the Winter family, as it had been since its foundation in 1868. Under the editorship of Joseph Winter, always a Home Rule man, it had a strong Irish flavour, and as a matter of course it gave plenty of space to Mannix's speeches. But, as Mannix was well aware, Winter was in favour of conscription. When Winter died in December 1915, his wife, Delia, and their daughter Mary, who became office manager, carried on the paper for several years with conservative Tom Brennan as editor. They knew that eventually Mannix would pounce, as he did in 1919, with an offer they could not refuse; after that the *Advocate* was Mannix's second voice.[18]

In February 1917 Carr was asked to receive a deputation of Catholic laymen, headed by lawyer Vincent Nolan, who wanted to protest against Mannix's political statements; these, they said, were 'opposed to the interests of the Catholic Church, alien to Australian sentiment and their expression was ill-timed in the extreme'. Consenting to see the deputation, Carr asked that it be small in number, and he warned in advance that 'in regard to political matters the coadjutor is perfectly independent of his chief'.[19] By then Carr was so frail that the protesters knew he could not help them. The real power had already passed to Mannix.

By mid-April, it was known that Carr was dying of cancer. Writing to Archbishop Kelly in Sydney, Mannix reported that although the old archbishop was too weak to say his daily mass, 'his mental faculties are as keen and active as ever'.[20] Did they talk, during the old archbishop's last weeks, about the future? Carr was never one for confrontation, so it is unlikely that he expressed his worries about the massive changes that the coming of Mannix had brought about. On the evening of Sunday 6 May, Carr said that he wanted his people around him; the priests on the cathedral staff and the sacristan Hubert Cooney came to his bedside. Someone asked, 'Should we call Dr Mannix?' 'Not yet,' Carr replied, and again, 'Not yet.' Later, still fully conscious, Carr said, 'Now, you may send for the coadjutor.' A message was sent to St Mary's, just too late. Without knowing it, Mannix became the new Archbishop of Melbourne as he made his way to Carr's bedside.[21]

While Carr lay dying, on Saturday 5 May, the Australian people were casting their votes in the federal election. Billy Hughes's Nationalist Party defeated the Australian Labor Party by a comfortable majority. Hughes had foreshadowed a second referendum on conscription. His win meant that Mannix was facing another conscription campaign, more bitter than the first, just at the moment of succeeding the old archbishop.

Archbishop Carr's body lay in state at St Patrick's Cathedral for six days before being carried through the streets with an escort of mounted troopers. A crowd of a hundred thousand lined the way. The Anglican archbishop, seated in his carriage with two archdeacons beside him, joined the long procession. Daniel Mannix, the new archbishop, marched alone, ahead of the four black horses that drew the hearse. As he walked, he could hear the sound of weeping from the crowd. A woman shouted, 'Mannix, you will never be half the man he was'. Later, one of the priests said, 'Take no notice, Your Grace, she is drunk.' Telling the story years later, Mannix added: 'Unfortunately, I do not think she was.'[22] He took it as the clearest demonstration that Carr was loved as he would never be.

Four weeks later Mannix paid homage to Carr. He spoke from the Cathedral pulpit with extraordinary grace and feeling in a panegyric that did justice to Carr's qualities of heart and mind. It was so moving, so well wrought, that it was easy to miss a subtext that revealed a good deal about Mannix himself. In speaking about Carr's style of leadership, Mannix set it against that of Cardinal Moran of Sydney, who had died seven years earlier. These two, Mannix said, were linked even by their contrasts:

> They were not more unlike in appearance than they were in temperament. The one was quick, impetuous, almost fierce in his energy, not easily brooking rebuff or opposition, successful, triumphant, wherever intense earnestness could carry big ideas to a happy issue. The other was calm, restrained, tactful, firm, slow to act but rarely needing to turn back, and always succeeding wherever a wisdom that often seemed more than natural could provide against failure. The one might sometimes seem to court opposition in order to override it. The other, by tact and delicate handling, often disarmed opposition which, had it hardened and taken shape, he might not have had the energy and power to overcome.[23]

In the context of an hour-long speech, in which Carr's personal qualities and achievements took the foreground, Mannix's reservations about the old archbishop's leadership could have been overlooked. His carefully crafted words, however, show self-awareness. In his four years as coadjutor, his quickness to oppose was balanced by Carr's tact and restraint. Now, in stormy 1917, Mannix was choosing to continue with the energy and 'big ideas' that had made him so controversial.

In a piquant turn of events, Carr's death meant that Mannix became Chaplain-General of the Australian armed forces. This horrified many non-Catholics. The memoirs of architect and academic Brian Lewis, a schoolboy at Scotch College in 1917, recall the sectarian feeling in middle-class Melbourne: 'Once, the Irish Catholics had ranked about equal with the Jews on our social scale; now they had dropped well below…'

According to Lewis, the bitterness was felt most sharply in eastern Victoria, near Sale, where Irish-Australian numbers were high. Fights as well as verbal abuse were common. Because his Christian name sounded Irish, Lewis was mistakenly given a job on a farm owned by Catholics. 'The business arrangements of generations were scrapped. No Protestant would trade at a Catholic store and vice versa, and neither party would meet the other socially.'[24]

Mannix and Hughes were not the only actors in the theatre of 1917 and 1918. Mannix's supporting cast included Father Maurice O'Reilly, the portly rector of St John's College, Sydney, and Bishop Phelan of Sale, who both joined vigorously in the anti-conscription debate. Most of Melbourne's prominent citizens followed the prime minister. His most vigorous supporter was Herbert Brookes, businessman, pastoralist, and son-in-law to former prime minister, Alfred Deakin. 'Let the Sinn Féin stand shoulder to shoulder with the Hun and the hosts of Satan,' Brookes thundered. A few days after the 1918 St Patrick's Day procession, in which Mannix had refused to raise his biretta for a provocative rendering of 'God Save the King', Brookes led an angry crowd of Empire loyalist demonstrators from the Town Hall to Parliament House. Standing on the roof of a car, he demanded the prosecution of Archbishop Mannix for sedition. The crowd roared approval. A flustered Billy Hughes appeared and gave a non-committal reply.[25]

Dr Alex Leeper of Trinity College, University of Melbourne, held Mannix responsible for the defeat of conscription. Leeper admired the archbishop's 'courage and candour', but saw him as a threat to stability in Australia: 'No other man in the Commonwealth at present commands equal influence with the proletariat.'[26]

A subplot in the drama came from within the Catholic Church. Mannix might be, as Leeper believed, the idol of the proletariat, but many middle-class Catholics deplored his forays into politics, and were angered by his attitude to the war. Some, like Dr Leo Kenny, Supreme Court Justice Leo Cussen and Father O'Dwyer of Xavier College, dissented quietly. Although it was true (as Mannix himself had said) that Catholics did not 'vote in platoons', opposition was cautious and muted; with few exceptions the traditional solidarity was maintained in public.

The sharpest attack came from Sydney Catholics, Lord Mayor Sir Thomas Hughes, Judge Heydon of the Arbitration Court, and a former Catholic, Sir Frank Madden. Hughes and Haydon complained to the apostolic delegate, Archbishop Cattaneo, that Mannix was damaging the Australian Catholic Church. Non-Catholics, they said, were unable to distinguish between the utterances of Mannix the man and Mannix the archbishop. Cattaneo listened and promised to take advice on the matter. As always Rome was slow to respond, and its reprimand, sent through the Australian Bishops' Conference, did not reach Mannix until the following year. As the referendum vote came closer Judge Heydon lost patience. He sent a letter to the daily papers denouncing Mannix for disloyalty to the Empire and for being untrue to the teachings of the church.[27]

Mannix's reply turned up the heat. These so-called leaders of the Sydney Catholic community, he said, had no more followers than would comfortably 'fit in a lolly shop'.[28] To this childish and obviously untrue statement, he added something more hurtful: that these men had attained social rank only by denying either their faith or their Irish origins. This appalling insult was made worse by the fact that Thomas Hughes had two sons on active service, one of whom would be killed in action.

The results of the 1917 referendum on conscription brought a defeat for Prime Minister Hughes and a win for Mannix. But there were gains and losses in reputation for them both. In Mannix's own state, where there had been a narrow victory for Yes in 1916, the No vote prevailed. The divisions expressed in the conscription debates had far-reaching effects. One was a shift in the composition of the Australian Labor Party. Those who followed Hughes into the new Nationalist Party were predominantly non-Catholic.[29] Thus, although the Labor Party was weakened by the split, it had a stronger Catholic presence thereafter. Many years later, in the ALP split of 1955, Mannix contemplated the ironies of a similar situation, but one in which the Catholic presence declined.

When the war in Europe ended in November 1918, Mannix had reached new heights of popularity. He was disliked by some Catholics, especially those whose professional or material success was giving them status equal with non-Catholics and with it a new insight into the evils of sectarianism, whichever way it was directed. But most of his people admired him extravagantly; they followed him as fervently as others followed the British royal family. Soon the cult of the Hollywood film star would catch popular attention, but in 1919 Mannix was, for many, the most exciting presence on show. That is not to forget the devotion owed to a church leader as God's representative, but if Mannix had been six inches shorter, as rotund as Archbishop Kelly and had a squeaky voice, he would never have commanded such a following.

When the armistice came in November 1918 Mannix was not invited to the celebration at Government House. No surprise there; he and Hughes would have had to shake hands. And although Mannix rejoiced at the end of the slaughter in Europe, his mind was on Ireland where British rule was being enforced with unparalleled brutality. When Mannix had declared himself for Sinn Féin and an Irish republic, he was taken by many within and outside the church to be the spokesman for Australian Catholics. Australians who still put their faith in the Home Rule policy, were awkwardly placed, with no comparable leader and limited access to publicity in the *Advocate*, which Mannix would soon own.[30]

In 1919, Mannix's control of Irish-Australian politics was affirmed when he convened the Australasian Irish Race Convention in Melbourne. Archbishop Kelly wanted Sydney to be the host: '*We* think the meeting should be held in Sydney.' Mannix ignored him and used the occasion for an unequivocal demonstration of support for a republic. Eamon de Valera, released from gaol in June 1917, united the various anti–Home Rule groups in a remodelled version of the Sinn Féin party of 1908, with himself as president. It was an amalgam of groups with different aims and methods, but there was agreement on what then seemed the main issues. Sinn

Féin (translated as 'We Ourselves' or 'Ourselves Alone') aimed at winning international recognition of an independent Irish republic. Members elected to the British parliament, as de Valera was when he won the seat of East Clare in October 1917, were pledged never to take their seats at Westminster. The party advocated passive resistance to British rule. Questions about armed resistance in the event of failure of peaceful means were not discussed at the 1917 meeting; they would emerge later.[31]

Those Irish-Australians who had for years been fighting for Home Rule within the Empire were angry and bitter at being sidelined in this way. Writing to John Dillon in Ireland, Morgan Jageurs admitted defeat:

> Weakened by desertions, one by one, of our colleagues, a mere handful of survivors received its death blow from Dr Mannix yesterday when the largest Irish convention ever held in Australasia took place in the city. Dr Mannix, assisted by nearly all the Archbishops and Bishops of Australasia, usurped control of the Irish National Movement and promulgated the doctrine of Republicanism coupled with recognition of de Valera as leader of the Irish race and as President of the Irish Republic.[32]

The fallout from the Irish convention helped Hughes to win the federal election in December 1919. The convention, as Morgan Jageurs said, created an 'awful rumpus', and the anti-Irish feeling it aroused was a factor in Labor's poor performance.[33] Once more, and not for the last time, Mannix was seen as a divisive influence in Australian political affairs, and a dubious asset to the Australian Labor Party.

Billy Hughes and others kept stirring the sectarian pot. Given a choice between the Kaiser and Mannix, Hughes remarked, he would prefer the Kaiser. During the epidemic of Spanish influenza in 1919, Mannix offered to send the Sisters of Charity from St Vincent's Hospital to nurse the sick and dying in the improvised wards in the nearby Exhibition Building. The offer was refused. The sight of a nun at the bedside, so it was said, would bring such terror to the patient that relapse or even death would follow. Medical students, who had no nursing skills, were called to help in the emergency.[34]

Turning to matters of social justice, Mannix backed the workers in the seamen's strike of 1919 with a swinging attack on the employers:

> Would any of the sneering critics undertake to balance the family budget on the strikers' wages and at the present cost of living? Would they live in the conditions, in the holds, or in the slums, on sea or land, in which the strikers have been living? . . . The sooner people realise that the worker must get, not merely a living wage, but a fair share of the wealth he produces the better. The sooner people realise that men and women and children count for more, and are more sacred, than property, the better it will be for the community.'[35]

This speech and others in support of strikers endeared Mannix to trade unionists. But, at a time when anything with even a whiff of socialism brought the Russian Revolution to mind, it seemed dangerously radical to others. Add to that his vigorous commitment to an Irish republic, and his declaration for 'Australia first, the

Empire second', and it is easy to see why he was demonised by Hughes in the early postwar period.[36] Uneasily placed in the party he had created in 1916, derided by his former ALP associates as a turncoat, Hughes found the 'Rasputin of Australia', as Mannix was called by some, a ready target.[37]

Hughes was returned to office in 1919 with a reduced majority but with his 'Little Digger' status enhanced. Mannix's popularity with his people grew, as did his image as the bogeyman of Protestant Australia. Historian Patrick O'Farrell argues that the nature of the anti-conscription movement 'had the general effect of integrating Irish Catholics much more firmly into the labour movement. And, crucially, into the Labor Party.'[38]

If there was no clear winner in the Mannix–Hughes conflicts of the war years, it was Hughes who spoke the most poignant line. Representing Australia in the peace talks at Versailles, he was brushed aside by the American president, Woodrow Wilson. 'But after all you speak for only five million people,' Wilson said. Hughes retorted: 'I speak for sixty thousand dead. For how many do you speak, Mr President?'

Fast forward to 1937. Against the odds, Mannix and Hughes became friends. Twenty years after the bitter strife of 1917, both men were still powerful: loved and hated by many but so much part of the landscape that they both commanded respect. They met at Mannix's house, Raheen, in the wake of the great tragedy of Hughes' life.

In a long tempestuous career, Hughes neglected his family; his three older daughters and his three sons never had his full attention, nor was he a generous or loving husband. He and Dame Mary got along just well enough to make a suitable impression in public. The one exception in an arid private life was their daughter, Helen.

Hughes pruned his personal papers but he kept Helen's teasing, loving letters to 'Darling Daddy'. He would have wanted to read them again and again, to prove that he had been loved. As the prime minister's daughter, taken everywhere by her parents from babyhood, Helen Hughes grew up in the bright light of celebrity. In 1934, when she danced with the Duke of Gloucester at the State Ball at Parliament House, people commented on the Duke's attentiveness. She was in demand to model clothes at charity functions; she was noticed and admired wherever she went. Sure of her father's love, she told a reporter that 'if Daddy is cross with me I just pick him up, for he is very little'.

In January 1937 Helen sailed for London. Interviewed at Fremantle she smiled for the cameras as she always did.[39] It was said that she was on her way to the coronation of George VI, and after arrival in London she was once again in the news, dancing with the Duke of Gloucester. For the next few months she appeared in occasional press reports, travelling in Europe, skiing, enjoying herself in the London social round. Then came the shock announcement of her death on 9 August in a London nursing home. The cause of death, evasively described as 'complications after abdominal surgery', roused talk about a possible abortion. Her body was brought back to Sydney for burial. Her funeral ceremony, at which her stricken parents were present, was a public occasion. The truth about her death remained a secret.

Until her death certificate was traced in 2004 the cause of Helen Hughes' death was known only to a few. She had been pregnant when she left Australia, and had somehow kept her secret. Admitted to a London nursing home she endured a twenty-four-hour labour before giving birth to a son by caesarean section. She died from septicaemia. Vincent Duffy, a Catholic who was acting secretary to the Australian High Commission in London, took charge of the baby. The identity of the father is still not known, nor is it clear how Helen kept her secret in London. After her death Hughes changed his will. He left £5000 to David Evans Hughes, then nine months old, and another £5000 to Vincent Duffy who appears to have fostered the child. This unacknowledged grandson of Billy and Mary Hughes, who grew up in Sydney under an assumed name, has never agreed to make himself known.[40]

Among the hundreds of letters of sympathy sent to Billy Hughes, one had a special impact. In Melbourne some time later, Hughes astonished his secretary by asking her to drive him to Raheen. Waiting in the car, she watched the tall, gaunt figure in the doorway put a brotherly arm around Hughes and draw him into the house. The front door closed. No one knows what was said.[41]

One reason for this extraordinary reconciliation may be that Mannix knew the truth about Helen's death, and perhaps had played some part in its aftermath. If so, the two men could meet without the strain of concealment. There would be no need for the evasive words that must have added to the pain of Hughes' loss. But how could Mannix have known? Prime Minister Lyons, whom Mannix knew well, would have directed the Australian High Commission, through Vincent Duffy, to help Hughes with the birth and death certificates and the care of the newborn child. And where better than a convent to keep Helen's child discreetly until his future was decided? If anyone could call in a favour from a Reverend Mother in London, Mannix could. The substantial legacy to Duffy in Hughes' will, matching the sum left to his grandson, is another clue to a possible Catholic intervention in the Hughes tragedy.

Some day the truth may be known. All that is certain about the Mannix–Hughes meeting of 1937 is that it was not their last. From then on, Hughes visited Mannix, and the two men exchanged birthday greetings. One of Hughes' last letters was a friendly note to Mannix, announcing a visit he did not live to make.

Politically, Mannix and Hughes came closer over the years, but the timing of their reconciliation and its emotional expression make the occasion wholly personal. Mannix's letter of sympathy to Dame Mary after Billy Hughes died, aged ninety, in October 1952 has the tone of genuine regret. The letter about Helen's death has been lost. Whatever the words Daniel Mannix chose to comfort his old adversary, they were the right ones.[42]

CHAPTER FIVE

PLAYING POKER WITH THE JESUITS

ELEVEN UNUSED ACRES in the grounds of Melbourne University: a reminder that Catholics couldn't afford to claim their proper place in public education. In 1913, more than sixty years after the founding of the University of Melbourne, this corner still looked rural. The land, set aside by a secular university for a Catholic residential college, was waiting until the church found the money to build on it. The Church of England had Trinity College; the Presbyterians had Ormond; the Methodists had Queen's—all up and running by the 1880s. For Catholic students there was nothing. A few country boys won scholarships to Ormond. Others found lodgings, and the majority, who were city boys, studied at home.

It was different in Sydney, though not necessarily better. St John's College had a history of troubles. In 1885 Cardinal

Moran dismissed the rector, Father Barry, for reasons that included 'levity of conduct with young ladies' as well as low enrolments.[1] Looking for someone else to run the college, the cardinal ruled out 'two types': Englishmen and Jesuits. Englishmen were debarred because of their nationality and Jesuits because they were 'a law unto themselves'.[2] Archbishop Carr thought differently, and when he had the means to found a college he chose the Jesuit order for its experience in education and its intellectual prestige.

The vacant land at the university had been an irritant to Archbishop Carr ever since he came to Melbourne. Because of the costs of the Catholic primary and secondary schools he hadn't been able to look at the tertiary education of his people. That they were admitted to the secular university was a welcome contrast to the exclusion policy he had known in Ireland, though a breakthrough there had come in Mannix's time at Maynooth when the National University of Ireland accepted Catholic students on equal terms. Mannix had played a part in resolving this ancient grievance, so it made sense that he should turn his mind to Melbourne University and give Catholic students in Victoria the chance to live on campus in an institution that would sustain and broaden their faith.

Some Catholics thought it would be better to bypass the secular university and build a university of their own. Neither Carr nor Mannix wanted to go that way. Mannix made his views clear on his first day in Melbourne. Responding to his official welcome to St Patrick's Cathedral, he asserted the right of Catholics to take their share of the good things of private and public life and their duty to act as a 'leavening' element in the thoughts and ideals of the secular university.[3] He didn't quite squash an idea he was never to favour, but before any Catholic university was considered,

Mannix said, a college should be built so as to put Catholics 'on a footing similar to that of other denominations.'[4]

The idea of a college had been floated in 1910 when Archbishop Carr welcomed the Newman Society, an association for students and graduates at the University of Melbourne. The first purposeful moves, in early 1914, were halted by the outbreak of war, but in May 1915, an extraordinary offer came to Archbishop Carr. A wealthy Sydney businessman, Thomas Donovan, had been nourishing a dream of a Catholic college, to be endowed from his life savings. In the normal course of events he would have spent his money on St John's College within the University of Sydney. When Archbishop Kelly failed to meet his conditions, Donovan tried Brisbane, again without success. Donovan then looked to Melbourne, and offered Carr the astonishing sum of £30,000 to fund bursaries. The Melbourne archdiocese had to match Donovan, pound for pound in cash, and secure promises for a further £10,000. As well as the cash and the promise, Donovan wanted quick action. At first he wanted a building contract to be signed within six months, but when this was shown to be impossible he extended the date until 1 April 1916. Carr took up Donovan's challenge and deputed Mannix to run the campaign.

Just three weeks after the agreement was signed, the political climate changed abruptly. The Easter Rising in Dublin, on 23 April, with its aftermath of brutal reprisals, turned Mannix the moderate Irish nationalist into a passionate fighter for Irish independence. Billy Hughes was then in England, absorbing news of Allied losses in the war. It was on his return in August 1916 that he and Mannix took centre stage as opponents in the conscription debate.

Raising money for the college could never have been easy. Why would the Catholic people—most of them working class—donate hard-earned cash so that privileged young men could live in an expensive college on the edge of the university campus? Mannix's words about equality would have had the strongest appeal: if Anglicans, Methodists and Presbyterians had colleges, we should have one too. Harder to accept was Mannix's belief in Catholics as a leavening element in the secular mix. Catholics were used to hearing about the evils of secular education in government schools. Many thought that going into a secular place spelled danger to their faith. Founding a college was pointless, according to Melbourne's richest Catholic, John Wren, who gave generously to church causes. Not this one. He had done very well without tertiary education. Instead, he wrote Mannix a cheque for the Catholic primary-school fund.[5]

Throughout 1916, while the conscription campaign raged. Mannix gave the college project his close though sometimes irascible attention. Getting the money was the easiest part. He sent several persuasive priests out to the parishes of city and country Victoria; and he made the cause part of his own continuing campaign for Catholic education.[6] The success of the fund-raising probably owed a good deal to Mannix's embattled position on conscription and to his identification with Ireland after the Easter Rising.

These two public controversies created Mannix as leader. Being seen in single combat with the prime minister gave him a status that no other churchman attained. If there had been no war in Europe, and if Home Rule had come in quietly to Ireland, would Mannix have been a hero to his people? A priest who had known him at Maynooth thought not. Mannix was not loved until he was reviled, said Father Morley Coyne.[7] Out of the hatred roused in the war years came a strong bond with the people. An unlikely alliance between the austere intellectual and the working-class Catholics was formed in 1916. That was one element in the Newman College campaign. It also brought the university closer to the aspirations of working-class Catholic parents. A Catholic college might open a door to privilege. 'My son the lawyer', 'my son the doctor...': these were better dreams than 'my son at the front'.

So, against the odds, the money came in. In January 1916 Mannix thanked the donors, rich and poor, for the £40,000 that would guarantee Donovan's bounty. From then on, the project moved fast. By contrast with Trinity College, which took eighteen years from foundation stone to opening day, Newman would be ready for students two years later. Archbishop Carr laid the foundation stone on 11 June 1916. Archbishop Mannix celebrated its completion in March 1918 when the first students were admitted.

Those two years of planning and building were stormy. The everyday Mannix was as formidable and strong-willed in committee as he was on the public stage at weekend gatherings. There were two crucial decisions to make: the choice of an architect and the appointment of a religious order to staff the college. The team of advisers included Dr Leo Kenny, by now established as a good friend to Mannix, Michael Mornane, legal consultant to the archdiocese, Justice Leo Cussen of the Supreme Court, Father James O'Dwyer, rector of Xavier College, and stonemason Morgan Jageurs, best known as a spokesman for Irish Home Rule and the maker of Celtic crosses for many Irish-Australian graves in Melbourne.

Kenny was a natural diplomat; he took care of much of the correspondence on Mannix's behalf and calmed many tempests. On conscription and the Irish question he differed politely but publicly from his leader. Cussen, who had two sons fighting in France, gently urged Mannix to consider the feelings of Catholics who differed from him on conscription. Jageurs was chosen for his experience of building, but he brought his politics with him. When his son was killed in action at Pozières in July 1916 he could not forgive Mannix's comments on the war, and he deplored Mannix's radical policy on Ireland.[8]

The Jesuits, Carr's choice for the college, were well established in secondary education in Melbourne. Their boarding school, Xavier College, had many of the country students who were most in need of a base at the university. But all through the planning period Mannix gave the Jesuits a hard time. He had two Jesuit leaders to deal with: the head of the Irish mission in Australia, Father John Ryan, and Father James O'Dwyer. Both were shrewd and tough. Both wanted the new college, but were wary of giving way to Mannix at the expense of the order. Negotiations were kept quiet. It was thought that parish priests in the diocese would not be happy to give to the Newman appeal if they thought the Jesuits would benefit. O'Dwyer advised 'the most absolute secrecy': 'We cannot expect PPs [parish priests] to pinch themselves by £500 to build a College for the Jesuits.'[9] Mannix agreed: 'one never knows what naïve views [about Jesuits] will be started even among Catholics themselves.'[10]

In fact, it was the Jesuits who were pinched. An agreement made between Carr and Ryan in August 1915 was almost immediately vetoed by Mannix. Ryan wanted a guaranteed salary for a college staff that was to comprise three highly educated and experienced Jesuit priests. Mannix refused: there should be no salaries until the college could fund them from the profits. Ryan was appalled. Why should the order take the risk of going into debt, perhaps for years to come, when the profits, if ever there *were* profits, were to be reinvested in a college that the order did not own? Mannix appeared to see no difficulty. The order funded Xavier College: why not Newman? 'I must say I was quite amazed,' Ryan wrote, 'at the coolness with which [Mannix] made these statements.'[11] Mannix brushed aside the crucial distinction between Xavier, which belonged to the Jesuits, and Newman College, which they were being asked to staff for the archdiocese.

The question of the Jesuit salaries was still unresolved in May 1917, when Mannix succeeded Carr. Ryan thought that £500 a year was reasonable: it was the salary given to the Rector of St John's in Sydney. Mannix countered with the niggardly offer of £200, while stressing the need to get first-class scholars. Worse than that, Mannix insisted that the college had to pay its own way from the start. Any losses would be at the expense of the Jesuits, while the profits, if any, would go into the college funds. Ryan protested: how could he be sure that the college would be a success? Mannix was terse:

> You will have to see to that. I am not going to make myself responsible for it. You are getting a College fully furnished & equipped & you should be able to make it pay...These are my terms and I am not prepared to discuss them further.[12]

At that point Ryan thought it was all over. 'Dr M. understood my position very well and seemed most annoyed with me but neither of us spoke and the short interview ended abruptly.' Yet, somehow, the negotiations resumed. Bishop Phelan of Sale told Mannix that he had a duty to those who had given money to build the college; he could not drop the Jesuits at this late stage. He urged a guarantee of £500 a year for five years for Jesuit salaries.[13]

In fact, Mannix was keen to draw on the Jesuits' intellectual assets. So as to give the college 'scientific status and distinction', he wanted to set up an observatory at Newman with the distinguished Jesuit Father Edward Pigott, then in Sydney, to run it. Father Pigott, then happily running the observatory at the Jesuits' Sydney school, Riverview, was appalled at the idea of leaving it and moving to Melbourne—and even more resistant to the thought of working for Mannix. Pigott, who came from an Anglo-Irish establishment family, abhorred Mannix's politics. Although he was willing to believe that Mannix 'might be as charming as some people said', working for him was out of the question. His fellow Jesuits were startled at Pigott's resoluteness: he was normally so gentle. Father Ryan smoothed things over by telling Mannix that Pigott had commitments with the New South Wales government. He then reassured Pigott, adding his own candid comments about Mannix:

> I am afraid we shall have considerable difficulty with him. His terms are most exacting...He practically wants us to train & supply a staff of 'highly distinguished university graduates' & 'take up the whole management of the new College' & all we are getting is *board and residence*. I had great difficulty in getting him to exonerate us from responsibility for *debts*.[14]

Ryan's diaries and letters of 1917 show a tense situation. As well as dealing with Mannix, Ryan had to negotiate with the head of the Jesuit order, the father-general, based in Europe, and with his deputy in Dublin, the Irish provincial, to whom the Australian Jesuits were directly responsible. Without agreement on the salary question from the father-general and approval for staffing from Dublin, the Australian Jesuits could not commit themselves. Six months before the college was due to open, the wrangling over Jesuit salaries was still unresolved. 'His Grace seemed in an angry mood', Ryan wrote in early October 1917.[15]

Eventually, there was a breakthrough when the other Victorian bishops—whom Mannix seldom took into account—decided to assert themselves; it was their college too.[16] Urged by Bishop Phelan, Mannix conceded the £500 a year for salaries to go to the Jesuit order.[17] That done, he made life hard for Father Ryan over the choice of staff. The Jesuits had been canvassing that question from the beginning. They were worried that a man 'straight from home' might be appointed to the senior post in the unknown territory of the University of Melbourne. 'They might just send us a crank,' O'Dwyer said.[18] The obvious choice for the post of rector was O'Dwyer himself. He had been in charge of Xavier College since 1908, and had proved his competence in preparing boys for university entrance. But politics came between O'Dwyer and Mannix with the Easter Rising and the conscription debate. O'Dwyer was a King-and-Empire man. Although he was Irish-born, like most of the Jesuits in the Australian mission of the time, he had an idealised view of British colonialism. On the outbreak of war he told a gathering of Old Xaverians that 'in the story of Empire there has been nothing so unselfish as the relation of the Motherland to her Colonies.'[19] Unselfish? Even before the Easter Rising, that word would have affronted Mannix.

Under James O'Dwyer's rectorship, Xavier had been enjoying its status as one of the six members of the Association of Public Schools (APS) in Victoria. After Mannix's inflammatory words in the conscription debates, a 'regrettable incident' between Xavier and Scotch College footballers led to the cancellation of the remaining public school matches of 1917.[20] O'Dwyer was proud of Xavier's wartime record. With a high proportion of enlistments—about seventy-five per cent of those eligible volunteered—his former students could not be called disloyal. By the end of the war, fifty-two Xaverian volunteers had been killed and many wounded. O'Dwyer saw the war as right and noble: Mannix had called it 'an ordinary trade war.'[21] And O'Dwyer must have felt injured when Mannix insisted that the Irish provincial send him the classical scholar Father Albert Power. 'Power or nobody,' Mannix cabled to Dublin.

The fact that O'Dwyer lacked scholarly credentials would have weighed with Mannix. Albert Power was sure to command intellectual respect in the university community. Whether he was the right choice for Newman may be doubted. Known as the Mighty Atom, Power was small in stature and his sensitive, even tremulous, piety would not appeal to rowdy eighteen-year-old school leavers, and still less to the war-damaged returned servicemen of 1919. But Mannix insisted, and as soon as he could be released from his duties as rector of Milltown Park theological college, Power sailed for Melbourne. Meanwhile, James O'Dwyer would take charge as acting rector for 1918.

John Ryan and James O'Dwyer had to be polite at the negotiating table, but their frustration with Mannix was known within the order, and shared. How much did they want the college after all? Father Wilfrid Ryan, a scholarly Jesuit then based in Sydney, was sceptical: 'From the tone of Dr Mannix's remarks one would think that he was conferring a favour,' Ryan wrote. He added that St John's College within the University of Sydney had been described by its former vice-rector as 'a horror and a waste of energy and with very little or no good coming from it'.[22] Wilfrid Ryan's scepticism would be tested: he was one of the first three Jesuits appointed to the Newman staff.

For all their grumblings the Australian Jesuits were bound to accept the charge of the new college. They got little comfort from Ireland or from their father-general in Europe. A university college was seen as a good thing and so was a harmonious relationship with the archbishop. And even without the top job, Father O'Dwyer was prepared to work for Newman's success.

The Jesuit wrangle was only one of Mannix's problems with the Newman College venture. He had to choose an architect, work out costs and approve draft plans. This had to be done quickly, to meet the conditions of the most important patron, Thomas Donovan. In return for his massive donation of £30,000, Donovan expected to be consulted at every stage.

Donovan dreamed of endowing a college like those he had seen in his travels in Europe. He assumed that Newman would be built in traditional Gothic style. He also assumed—as did most of the other donors—that a Catholic architect would be given the job. Almost automatically in this period of sectarian divisions, Catholics employed their own.

For once, that rule was broken. By an extraordinary combination of luck, good judgment, and the stubborn support of Mannix, an outsider was chosen. Walter Burley Griffin, the gifted and controversial winner of the competition to design the national capital, was in Australia, waiting for the Canberra work to go ahead. He needed other commissions; and the idea of a university college appealed to his imagination and that of his wife and professional partner, Marion Mahony Griffin.

It happened that Burley Griffin was renting an office in Melbourne in the same building as Augustus Fritsch, a Catholic architect, educated at Xavier, who had travelled and studied in the United States. It seems likely that Fritsch, then working on the design of Our Lady of Victories Church, in the Melbourne suburb of Camberwell, backed Burley Griffin, whose ideas he would have understood. Eventually, Fritsch joined Burley Griffin in the Newman project as associate builder and architect, but he had no part in the designs that reached Mannix and his committee in 1915. These were a dazzlingly innovative expression of the Griffins' style. And they were nothing like the college that Donovan envisaged.

Just as stubborn with Donovan as with the Jesuits, Mannix backed Burley Griffin's plan. He never liked being predictable and it would have pleased him to have the Catholic college, a latecomer to the University of Melbourne, make such a strong statement of individuality. Choosing between adventurous modernism and predictable Neo-Gothic, Mannix would take the risk of the new, even at the cost of antagonising his main donor. Thomas Donovan had been recommending 'all that is attractive and soul-subduing in the stately shrines of Oxford'. Talk of a flat roof upset him. Even before he saw Griffin's drawings, he was suspicious: 'Mr Griffin is American and perhaps Mr Fritsch is German.'[23]

Donovan was appalled by almost everything in the Newman College design. Ease of access was a risk; students could get out as readily as burglars could get in. There was moral danger in the arrangement of its sets of rooms. A bedroom and a study for each student (these were later to be shared between two) was an insidiously corrupting luxury. A swimming pool would bring sin and disease. The Donovan ideal was something externally grand but spartan indoors, a place where deserving young scholars would live simply. With Burley Griffin's plan, he predicted horrors:

> Our poor boys taken from their squalid homes will be plunged into a vortex of luxury which is bound to turn

> their heads to evil: two rooms each, sunken baths, hot water in their [bed]rooms, electric fans, pneumatic fans and whatnot…[24]

Another horror, which seemed suspiciously American, even socialist in feeling, was the circular dining room. No humble approach to High Table, no dignity, nothing to signal the authority of the rector: what was Archbishop Mannix thinking of? Burley Griffin's aim, Donovan believed, was to 'enforce equality'.[25] That was the sort of thing Americans did. As well as sending furious letters to the college planning committee, Donovan confronted Burley Griffin who was in Sydney for much of 1915. But the architect was as stubborn in defence of his design as Mannix was in having it carried out.

Marion Mahony Griffin's 'gaudy drawings' for the college gave Donovan another line of attack. He was suspicious of the woman's hand in the design. She, however, was grateful for the archbishop's steadfastness: 'Dr Mannix was a power to lean on and could grasp things beyond the custom.'[26] Mannix's support went beyond the Newman venture. In April 1916, when Burley Griffin's Canberra plan was being attacked, he lobbied federal member Hugh Mahon, urging him to do all that he could in defence of the design.[27]

To his great credit, Donovan did not withdraw his funding. Bitterly disappointed at his lost Gothic dream, he refused ever to look at Walter Burley Griffin's college. He was not the only one to dislike the building. For some the dome looked Moorish; for others the whole design was a freak, a circus, a tram shed. Some Australian architects resented Burley Griffin's winning the Canberra competition and turned their rage on the Newman building.

The Jesuits' commitment to the idea of the college did not mean that they liked the design. After all, they had to run it, and it did have practical defects. George O'Neill SJ listed some of them:

> It is odd rather than beautiful. The low pitch calls attention to the flat situation; it would have better suited a hilltop. It centres on a grandiose refectory which was at first unaccompanied by a separate kitchen, so that dishes or cups had to be washed in places intended for the Muses. There was neither a grand hall, nor a common room for tutors, nor a chapel...The ground floor rooms are very dark; the cloister is too low; all the ceilings are very low. About a hundred windows are available for furtive exits and entrances, so that burglaries have become rather a commonplace.[28]

More than one thousand people came to see Newman College when it was officially opened on 24 March 1918.[29] Its completion was a victory for Mannix: so was the enduring Donovan endowment and the installation of the Jesuits. There it was, Walter Burley Griffin's creation: a serenely beautiful building, quite unlike the other colleges, destined to be seen as a major architectural achievement, a national treasure.

Mannix didn't make a rousing triumphalist speech at the Newman opening. Perhaps after the passion of his anti-conscription campaign he was ready to be circumspect. Yet by inviting a speech from Father Maurice O'Reilly, the republican firebrand rector of Sydney's St John's College, he made sure that a political point would be made. O'Reilly conflated religious and political duty by deploring the fact that 'not a single [Catholic] man at the University of Sydney had taken up the cause of liberty' against conscription in the referendum campaign. He hoped that Newman students would never forget that they were Australians and democrats:

> When they came out of [Newman] the students should be prepared to take their place by the side of their great Archbishop as champions of the faith. If the young men were going to apologise for the magnificent Church to which they belonged...all the money expended upon Newman College would have been in vain.[30]

Newman College was a high-risk venture for Mannix. A last-minute withdrawal of Donovan's £30,000 or a strategic retreat by the Jesuits would have made him look foolish. By snubbing Father O'Dwyer in the matter of the rectorship, he risked losing essential backing. O'Dwyer played a key role in promoting the college among Xavier students. Donovan's dream of bringing poor boys from 'squalid homes' to the University of Melbourne did not allow for the dearth of country high schools or Catholic secondary schools that taught to university entrance level.

O'Dwyer was popular and persuasive, well placed to convince students that Newman would be good for them. Because of the speed of the building project, Catholic parents had not much time to get used to the idea of sending their sons to the new college. Finding the first fifty students, at short notice, when so many young men were away on war service, would have been hard.

Father O'Dwyer used his influence as rector of Xavier to Newman's advantage.[31] Of the sixty-five students in that first crucial year of 1918, the majority came from Xavier, with no fewer than ten first year medical students among them.[32] A scattering of older students, already well established at the university, gave a useful balance of experience. O'Dwyer would have seen the perils of supervising a college made up entirely of freshers, some exuberant, some bewildered, even if he could have found them. Students from the Christian Brothers' school, St Patrick's College, in Ballarat, helped make up the numbers. Mannix's cousin and friend, Dr Daniel Foley, the Bishop of Ballarat, probably promoted the college.

Some of the young men who came to Newman in 1918 were from prominent and well-off families: Alan Cussen, son of Justice Leo Cussen, Gilbert Boileau whose father was a baronet, Kevin O'Day, from a wealthy Ballarat manufacturing family with a seaside house in St Kilda. It would take time to reach the boys that Thomas Donovan had in mind, but on the 1918 list the name of William Fazio stands out. Fazio, who came from an Italian migrant family, was a thirteen-year-old cabinetmaker's apprentice when, after an industrial accident, he had one arm amputated.[33] He was given a free place at Xavier where he did well at secondary level. With Father O'Dwyer's backing, Fazio won a Donovan bursary, studied Arts–Law and went on to become a successful Melbourne barrister. When the college opened, miraculously on time for the academic year of 1918, and with students in every room, Dr Mannix owed a great deal to O'Dwyer's initiative in bringing in Fazio and others from Xavier.

It is hard to understand why Mannix was so tough with the Jesuits on the matter of salaries. Their predictions of a financial shortfall were realistic, and they lamented the loss of Archbishop Carr, with his 'far more liberal views on how to deal with us'.[34] After his first year as rector, Albert Power wrote in dismay that 'we have *not* covered expenses...we have *nothing* to pay the [Jesuit] Society'.[35]

Mannix was equally stubborn, though more courteous, with Donovan, but one can understand his being so enthralled by Griffin's design that he couldn't surrender to second-rate Neo-Gothic. Did he feel that in this first encounter with an order known for its independence, he had to exert his authority? His lack of sympathy with O'Dwyer's views on King and Empire may have been a factor, but it scarcely seems enough. Perhaps in a year when Mannix was being assailed from outside and inside his Church over the conscription issue, the Jesuits took the punishment.

By the time Mannix's choice as rector, Albert Power, arrived from Ireland, O'Dwyer had Newman in good shape. Mannix said that Newman was like the new model cars, a self-starter. But as Jesuit scholar Brian Fleming argues, it was 'a felicitous combination...an experienced, capable and amenable Rector [O'Dwyer] and a co-operative, energetic and productive body of students'.[36]

Albert Power's imprint is fainter. He seems not to have understood the difference between a university college and a school or seminary; his attempts to exert authority in small matters led to unnecessary confrontations. When he arrived from Ireland in 1919, Power had the special problem of trying to impose discipline on returned servicemen, some of them traumatised by war, all experienced beyond their years.[37] Mannix did not have to admit his mistake in insisting on 'Power or no one.' In early 1923 he sent Power to head the newly created diocesan seminary, Corpus Christi, in Werribee.

Whatever the gifts to Newman of this gentle scholar, they were eclipsed by his successor, Jeremiah Murphy SJ, who ruled Newman for thirty-one years. Unusual among Jesuits, who were seldom left in high office for more than six years, Murphy owed his tenure at Newman to his friendship with Mannix as well as his own remarkable qualities. As long as Mannix wanted Murphy at Newman, Murphy's superiors hesitated to move him on. They got round the difficulty by declaring Newman part of St Patrick's College in East Melbourne—which meant that Murphy was not really a rector at all. This creative fiction kept him in place rather longer than was good for anyone.

Jeremiah Murphy (Jerry to friends, but not to Mannix who was always formal) was thirty-seven when he came to Melbourne in 1920. He taught classics for three years at Xavier before taking the job that he was surely meant for. Because Murphy had studied at postgraduate level at Oxford he was better prepared than most of the Irish Jesuits to understand the tightly held academic world of Melbourne University, in which Catholics were few and, after Mannix's wartime stirring, Irish-Australians were under suspicion. Murphy was a brilliant success at Newman. He did much to dispel the idea held by academics and college heads that Newman was a Mannix stronghold, 'a kind of Catholic fortress, located in the university and directed *against* them'.[38] So soon after the bitter wartime clashes between Mannix and Dr Leeper, Master of Trinity College, Murphy's friendly relations with the heads of Trinity, Ormond and Queen's were a huge achievement. He was on good terms with academic staff; he served on many committees with sound judgment, quickness to see essentials, and a wit that relaxed tense moments.

Murphy's Oxford lessons, in understanding how Ireland looked from an English viewpoint, served him well. He did not make political statements and, although his friendship with Mannix would have been known, it does not seem to have damaged him in university circles. His relationship with Thomas Donovan, who kept a sharp eye on the awarding of bursaries, was a diplomatic triumph. Because Donovan refused to look at the 'horror' that was Newman, Murphy went to Sydney where he found the college patron 'very gracious and reasonable'.[39]

Murphy also visited St John's College at Sydney University. Reporting to Mannix, he said that the new 'Ladies College' was very beautiful, but he sympathised with the rector of St John's for its being so close: 'I should not care (nor should our students) to have our Ladies quite so near us.'[40] Albert Power, who held the same view, had found that 'women could not be excluded' from the tutorial system at Newman because of 'usage in the other colleges'.[41] A note on tutorial enrolments, '*puellae* admitted', sounds grudging.[42] In fact, Power's tutorials in classical and modern languages would have scarcely been viable without women students.

It now seems obvious that Mannix's efforts for equality in tertiary education failed the young women of 1918 and later years. James O'Dwyer claimed that Griffin's 'tram-shed style' left no room for a women's hostel.[43] In fact there was plenty of room, as the present St Mary's College, adjoining Newman, has shown. If a women's college (or hostel, as O'Dwyer and the heads of the other colleges described accommodation for female students) was wanted, it could have been done. Marion Mahony Griffin's drawings provided for a separate wing on the Carlton site, with space for twenty-three women students and a female supervisor.

But as late as February 1917 Mannix had made no decision about how best to include women in the college. Places were advertised only for men, as were the means-tested Donovan bursaries. Signs of progressive thinking emerge in a Mannix letter recommending that Newman scholarships, based solely on academic merit, should be open to women and to non-Catholics.

Admitting non-Catholic men to Newman was only fair: talented Catholics had been winning places at Ormond for many years. Mannix was not sure, however, how to house the women who won scholarships. He suggested giving a sum equivalent to the value of a scholarship to help pay for the lodgings of those who were not living at home. Clearly that didn't amount to equal treatment for women, and in November 1917 Mannix invited the Loreto order to take charge of a separate establishment. He paid £5000 for a house in Parkville, where, with the addition of a second property, some of Melbourne University's Catholic women students were housed until 1966.[44] It was part of Newman College but known as St Mary's Hall.

It is possible that if money had been found to carry out Marion Mahony Griffin's plans for a women's wing at Newman College, Mannix would have allowed it to be built. But funding for the college was already stretched, and it is certain that for the essential donor, Thomas Donovan, having women living on the Newman site, in accommodation designed by a woman, would have been the last straw. His model, Oxford University, did not allow women to take degrees until 1920, and until 1957 it maintained an admission quota of one woman for every four men.

St Mary's Hall was inconveniently placed, too far from the university, but under the Loreto nuns' guidance it established a religious and intellectual tradition of its own. It opened in March 1918, just after Newman College, but quietly, with none of the crowds and excitement that usually attended a Mannix day out. It had a long battle ahead for the equal status it reached in 1966 when permission from Mannix, given not long before his death, cleared the way for the present building. Co-education eventually followed in both Newman and St Mary's.

The women students of 1918 were in some ways made part of the Newman College community. They came to college tutorials; their examination results were included in the college reports; they contributed a section to the college magazine. Their numbers were low—only nine residents and ten external students in 1918—but that reflected the general inequality in women's opportunities. The total University of Melbourne enrolment in that year was only 1209. In the overall context, Newman's sum of sixty-five men was not insignificant. Trinity, Queen's, Ormond and Newman had a very strong influence on university life until their numbers were diluted by increased enrolments after the Second World War and by the establishment of more colleges for men and women.

Emerging from the Newman project, bruised and still underpaid, the Jesuits should have been wary of another Mannix deal. Yet, when it came, it looked like an apology. Mannix offered them a beautiful house in Studley Park Road, nearly opposite Raheen, in which to set up a preparatory school for Xavier.[45] The house was a gift to Mannix from businessman T. M. Burke, who had bought it from the federal government. Once the home of the Austrian consul, Carl Ludwig Pinschof, and his wife, the singer Elise Wiederman, it was a centre for art and music until 1916. War stopped the music; the Pinschofs were declared enemy aliens, and their house, confiscated, lay empty until 1920. Mannix passed it every day on his walk from Kew; he would have had time to think of many ways to use its elegant rooms and spacious grounds. Giving it to Xavier for a junior boarding school was not the obvious choice.

Mannix's commitment to the Jesuits as educators continued. When he asked them to take charge of a new seminary in 1923, they accepted readily. It was an honour to be trusted with the education of the diocesan priests. At Maynooth, Mannix's presumed model, the diocesan clergy trained their own, as they did at St Patrick's College, Manly, in Sydney. When he arrived in 1913, Mannix assumed that, as in Ireland, there would be a national college. The Manly Union was set up in 1916, with that aim. As the Australian Catholic Church became less dependent on Ireland, the Manly college could have been expanded to take in the growing numbers of men from all states. However, no agreement between Mannix and Archbishop Kelly ever stood a chance. Mannix's tolerance for Kelly's narrow vision and fussy piety was limited; they got on best when the length of the Hume Highway kept them apart. Perhaps more important, the Sydney diocese owned the immensely valuable harbourside property on which the seminary stood. If this became a national asset, Sydney risked losing control. Matters drifted until 1921, when the decision was referred to Rome.[46]

More than a year later, in October 1922, Rome replied. There was a nod of approval for the Manly Union but an endorsement of differing local needs gave Mannix the go-ahead. Within eight weeks of Rome's decision he bought the pioneering Chirnside family's mansion and pastoral estate at Werribee, outside Melbourne, and announced that a new college would open in early 1923. The Jesuits agreed to staff the college, to be named Corpus Christi, and Albert Power was transferred from Newman to be its first rector. The Archbishop of Hobart would send his future priests to Corpus Christi, as would all the Victorian bishops. This alliance added to Mannix's prestige and widened the Sydney–Melbourne divide.

Neither the conversion of the old house at Werribee for staff nor the new buildings for students engaged Mannix as Burley Griffin's Newman design had done. He was, however, proud of the seminary, which he thought was a better and happier place than his own Maynooth had been. It had the advantage over Maynooth in that staff and students mixed in a friendly way. Now and then, Albert Power had to contend with one of Mannix's impulsive money-saving ideas. One of these, 'sprung on us', Power grumbled, during a Mannix visit, was that Power's staff take over the management of the parks, orchards and vegetable garden. 'We are expected to sell flowers to make the garden to some extent self-sufficient.' It was a lot of work, and they were not trained for it.[47]

Corpus Christi, Werribee, is long since gone. Mannix never had to face today's realities of vocations in freefall and priestly training under the dark shadow of the clerical abuse scandal. He lived long enough to question clericalism and a triumphalist church but not to see their full cost.

With their two colleges, Newman and Corpus Christi, their schools, Xavier in Kew and St Patrick's in East Melbourne, and their big parishes in Richmond and Hawthorn, the Jesuits flourished. Tensions with Mannix eased, not just because the Newman project was complete, but because the usual Jesuit reshuffle replaced the head of mission, John Ryan, with William Lockington, Mannix's friend and his voice coach from early days at the Cathedral. Mannix liked to chat with Bill Moloney, who was teaching at St Patrick's College, and from the early 1920s he had Jeremiah Murphy and the Irish republican exile William Hackett permanently on call to Raheen. With these men he could be sure of stimulating company, and as close a set of friends as his high rank and his reserved nature allowed. The Jesuits would not always agree with Mannix. They put up with some unreasonable demands over the years and some ill-advised ventures. But in spite of the angst they endured over Newman College, they emerged as Mannix men. The founding of Newman was a magnificent gamble: a poker game in which Archbishop Mannix didn't have a strong hand but was able somehow to win the game without alienating his opponent.

Newman College wasn't the only important educational venture of the wartime years. Closely related to Mannix's aims for Newman was an idea of the Christian Brothers, the main providers of teaching for working-class boys. Six months after Newman was launched, Mannix spoke at the opening of St Kevin's College in East Melbourne. This was a central school alongside but separate from the Brothers' well-established Parade College. Many of the Christian Brothers' schools concentrated on preparing boys for the Intermediate examination that qualified them for entry to the public service. Those who taught the later years had small classes and often lacked the specialist training needed to bring boys to university entrance standard. So as to make the most of their best teachers and to give clever boys their chance, the Brothers consolidated their talent in the central school. Students who came mainly but not exclusively from other Christian Brothers' schools in Melbourne could qualify for university entrance at St Kevin's; soon by competing for the newly established Donovan bursaries at Newman they challenged Xavier's dominance in the college enrolment.

There were disadvantages in taking the best and brightest out of the neighbourhood schools; St Kevin's won prestige at their expense. But at a time when the state's director of education, Frank Tate, was creating new government high schools it was right for the Catholic system to look towards tertiary education. For boys who wanted to enter the professions, the lack of university entrance teaching had been a barrier. It was still a barrier for women, especially those who wanted a career in medicine. Few Catholic schools for girls offered good teaching in the sciences. Jean Grant, who graduated in medicine in 1925 and practised with her husband, John Gorman, in Bendigo for many years, had to move from a Catholic school to University High School in order to study physics and chemistry.

Mannix did not claim the credit for St Kevin's that some have given him. The idea seems to have come from the Brothers themselves, with Brother Mark McCarthy pushing his sometimes doubtful colleagues along. Asked if he had discussed the plan, Mannix said, 'No, there was no question of my being asked by Brother McCarthy. At all events, why should I be? I had always thought the idea was a good one. The Brothers knew my mind well enough.'[48]

The opening of St Kevin's was crucial for several young men whose careers were watched and shaped by Mannix. One was Frank Maher, later to become director of Catholic Action. He had left school and was working in the public service when he heard about this new way to matriculation. He enrolled at St Kevin's and went on to Arts–Law at Melbourne University with a Donovan bursary at Newman College. Other intellectuals from the early St Kevin's years were lawyer and editor Gerard Heffey and Mannix biographer, writer Niall Brennan.

Best known of all the St Kevin's entrants was Bartholomew Augustine (Bob or Bobby) Santamaria who came from Christian Brothers College, North Melbourne, in 1930 to a Leaving Honours class of sixty of the brightest boys from all the Christian Brothers schools. In his second year, still too young to go to the university,

Santamaria became dux and captain of the school. He shared a double desk with his future political opponent and latter-day friend Jim McClelland, who became a Sydney barrister and a cabinet minister in the Whitlam government. In old age, each wrote about St Kevin's and about the other. Both remembered inspired teaching. McClelland was surprisingly forbearing about a lecherous Brother whose sexual advances left him bewildered rather than angry. Santamaria stressed the huge debt of working-class boys in Depression times to their hard-working teachers. Santamaria and McClelland were friendly rivals. McClelland remembered Santamaria as 'a small, dark, vivacious boy who gave the impression of walking on the tips of his toes as though he were about to levitate'.[49]

Gifted boys from working-class homes, McClelland and Santamaria exemplified the young Catholics for whom Thomas Donovan gave the Newman bursaries. But neither one chose to leave home for college life. The extra costs—a dinner suit, tickets for the annual ball—may have been a factor for McClelland. Coming from a greengrocer's shop in Brunswick, Santamaria was better off than McClelland, who could hardly ever spare threepence for coffee in the student union. Both were powerfully influenced by the social inequities of the Depression. Over the summer before they entered the university they compared notes on their reading. McClelland was impressed by H. G. Wells and George Bernard Shaw; Santamaria by Belloc and Chesterton. For both young men, Daniel Mannix was a familiar figure, often seen walking past St Kevin's on his way to the cathedral. McClelland, then beginning to detach himself from the Catholic Church, felt only a remote interest. Mannix dazzled Santamaria, and would soon change his life. And just as the Newman project brought the Jesuits into

Mannix's inner circle, so too the order would be drawn into the tangled web of Catholic Action, in which Santamaria's problem child, the Movement, gave inspiration to some and headaches to others.

CHAPTER SIX

THE ARCHBISHOP AT RAHEEN

LATE IN 1917, for the first time in his life, Daniel Mannix was looking for a house of his own. Everyone expected him to move into the solid bluestone building, known as 'the Palace', beside St Patrick's Cathedral, where Archbishop Carr had lived for thirty years. And so he did, but not for long. Reserved and reclusive by nature, Mannix wasn't suited to the big, busy household in which Carr had been a calm, fatherly presence.

After Carr's death, the Palace was a house of mourning. Vicar-General John McCarthy had been with Carr in Ireland as a young priest; they had shared memories of the 1880s in Galway, and their friendship had grown year by year. McCarthy was named Bishop of Bendigo in mid-1917, but he was still in Melbourne and at Carr's bedside in early May, when the old man drew his last quiet breath. At the bedside too was Hubert Cooney the sacristan. Devoted to Carr, he found Mannix abrupt and tactless in his early years, though later they became friends.[1] The assistant priests in the archbishop's household had watched Carr's pain-filled decline, and some blamed Mannix for bringing worry and dissension into the last days of a tranquil life.

All the official messages of sympathy for Carr's death came direct to Mannix. As Carr's successor, Mannix had to read them and reply. Some of the words would have stung. There was a constant stress on the qualities in Carr that Mannix didn't possess, or at least had not yet shown: gentleness, tact and openness. Presbyterian leader Dr Laurence Rentoul wrote of his admiration for Archbishop Carr's 'quietude of manner and powers of self-command in circumstances where many others, perhaps, would have shown excess of temper or of language'.[2] No 'perhaps' about it: Rentoul's 'others' meant Mannix. The governor-general, Sir Ronald Munro-Ferguson, sent a conventional expression of grief. More frankly, he reported to the Colonial Office in London: 'Dr Carr is dead. That firebrand Mannix is now Archbishop of Melbourne.'[3]

His four years in Melbourne had taught Mannix that there were different ways to be an archbishop. He knew that he could never be like Carr; he could never match his warmth and social ease. Inside and outside the Palace, Carr gave the same sense of reassuring goodwill to everyone. Mannix was a man of moods and surprises, genial and witty at times, but capable of disconcerting silences, flashes of anger, even rudeness, as well as unexpected moments of gentleness. He could work magic with a crowd, but when he took Carr's place at the head of the dining-room table in 1917 he was awkward. His seemingly self-assured style masked shyness. Few felt relaxed at his table, least of all Mannix himself.

When warmth was lacking, the chilly formality of church etiquette took over. There was a universal style, much the same in any archbishop's house in Australia, as it was in Ireland.

The priests who shared the table at the midday meal took their places in order of seniority, with the youngest, who were served last, seated so far from the archbishop that anything even resembling a conversation was impossible. Like royalty, the archbishop chose the topic; the priests could only respond; they could not talk among themselves. This deadly etiquette persisted. As late as the 1950s Edmund Campion experienced the long tedium of Cardinal Gilroy's table in Sydney. The young priests used to compete with one another in asking inane questions on the chosen topic in the hope that the cardinal would tire of it and move on.[4] In Melbourne the cathedral staff had the added frustration of Archbishop Mannix's quiet voice. When told that the young men at the end of the table could hear only half of what he was saying, Mannix replied with wilful mischief, 'Indeed. Then I must try to speak even more softly.'[5]

As well as having to take his main meals every day with the same group, and feeling at best a poor substitute for Carr, Mannix felt the pressure of never being alone. In the late months of 1917 he was out and about nearly every Sunday. He had taken on much of Carr's workload as early as 1916.[6] The confirmation ceremonies and country visitations were his, and to these and other official duties he had added the stress of political involvement. When the second conscription debates began he was under constant scrutiny, even surveillance.

On weekdays Mannix had the administrative routine to deal with; he had also to think about his next public address. Although he always spoke without notes, and some flashes of mischief would have been spontaneous, there is evidence that Mannix planned his speeches carefully. This took time, and the weekly public performances were physically and emotionally exhausting. No wonder he was short-tempered with the Jesuits in the last months of 1917, when the negotiations over Newman College were stalling. And no wonder that one of his first acts as Archbishop of Melbourne was to find another place to live.

Other archbishops had a second house. In 1885 Cardinal Moran had built 'the Palace' at Manly, a splendid mansion with magnificent harbour views.[7] Archbishop James Duhig of Brisbane enthroned himself in 'the Gold Room' in his sumptuously furnished house in Brisbane. Daniel Mannix wanted distance more than splendour, and in the last months of 1917 he made his choice. Perhaps with memories of secluded Maynooth, he chose a house in Kew, which was close enough to the cathedral where his daily work would be done, but, in 1917, still semi-rural. Raheen, high on the Studley Park hill, was a square-towered, red-brick mansion, set well back from the road, with a circular carriage sweep. Seen from the gates, the house was grand enough to assert its owner's importance. Its fountain and the terraced gardens that sloped down to the Yarra River were made for pleasure and display while within its eleven acres there were quiet bushland walks, paddocks for a dairy herd, handsome stables, and a vegetable garden for provender.

Raheen was designed in the early 1870s for Edward Latham of the Carlton Brewery. By the 1880s, when its owner was in financial trouble, Knowsley, as it was then called, earned the unofficial title of 'Latham's Folly'. Latham's term of folly ended in 1888 with an auction of all the household furniture and the sale of the estate to Sir Henry Wrixon, an Irish-born barrister and politician. Wrixon renamed it Raheen, which, as the Irish word for a little fort, was apt for Mannix's mood in embattled 1917.

In the Wrixons' time, Raheen was a family house on a grand scale. Sir Henry Wrixon's wife, Charlotte, a daughter of Australia's richest man, financier Henry ('Money') Miller, liked to entertain. Raheen's lavish balls and garden parties were an expression of Marvellous Melbourne. All this splendour was for sale in 1917. But why would a solitary churchman want it? To some extent Mannix was obliged to live in style. Only a very unusual prelate would opt out of the dignity of his calling. There was an air of confidence about Bishopscourt in East Melbourne, the home of the Anglican Archbishop of Melbourne, which might have reminded Mannix of Dublin Castle, where he had dined on his last night in Ireland with Lord and Lady Aberdeen. He had no intention of ever dining at Bishopscourt, nor would he be invited for many years to come. Nevertheless, he wanted a house in which he could entertain properly. There would be formal occasions: cardinals and archbishops would come from Rome, Ireland and the United States. Mannix had to keep up, but compared with the establishments in Sydney and Brisbane, Raheen was low key.

Mannix was a minimalist by nature, attuned to Burley Griffin's austere style for Newman College, appalled by decorative excess. After Carr's death, attended by a handyman, he went round St Patrick's Cathedral, removing anything fussy. His order 'Take it down, Michael' was said so often that the handyman became known as Take-it-Down-Michael.[8] Raheen gave Mannix outward splendour and inner simplicity.

When Mannix moved to Raheen, he went alone. This was unusual. Archbishops and bishops were expected to have a priest-secretary in permanent attendance. Instead, Mannix combined the duties of administrator, vicar-general and secretary in one competent, over-worked cleric who lived at the Palace. Except for the rare grand occasion, when extra help had to be called in, the house was managed by a housekeeper and a cook, with one or two gardeners who would also do odd jobs. From the mid-1940s, the essential roles were filled by two sisters, Jean and Lena Virgona. At various times Mannix had a dog for company. When his small white dog, with black paws and nose and no pedigree, went missing in 1934, he offered a £1 reward, which was a handsome sum in those days.[9] He had no chauffeur, no car of his own. If he needed one, he sent for Carr's Motors, of Kew. On certain big occasions, he was driven in an open Rolls Royce lent by Kilkenny-born Pierce Cody, owner of the Austral Wine and Spirit Company, who lived at Rangeview in Mary Street, Kew, not far from Raheen.

Raheen had some good furniture, bought thriftily from the Wrixons, and its main rooms were impressive. At each end of the dining room, which comfortably seated twenty people, were large beautifully carved matching cedar chiffoniers, with mirrors above them that caught the light from the crystal chandeliers. Paintings lined the walls. Some, like a dimly lit view of London showing Big Ben by moonlight, had belonged to the Wrixons. Irish landscapes of variable quality would accumulate over the years as presentations to Mannix. A landscape by Arthur Streeton was a token of friendship, given by the artist. The only room downstairs that showed any intimacy was Mannix's study, where leadlight windows gave colour, and books were untidily heaped on his desk.

Mannix turned the Wrixons' ballroom into an imposing library, lined with blackwood shelves. It was not just for show. As two young priests discovered when invited to 'take any book' after Mannix's death, there were many with pencilled annotations in his distinctive hand.[10] Mannix had dinner alone, most nights: he wrote letters, dropping them on the floor for the housekeeper to pick up and post the next day. He read until the ritual hot drink was brought in at 10 p.m. and then went upstairs to his private quarters.

A young medical practitioner, Charlie McCann, called to see a priest who had been taken ill while visiting Mannix, felt the chill of the unheated rooms. In the room where he saw his patient, there was a single unshaded light bulb dangling from a cord in the ceiling. There was only one telephone, and it was high on the wall near the front door: 'you had to make calls standing up'.[11] All messages came through the housekeeper: Mannix never used the telephone.

If he wanted company, as he did about once a week, Mannix invited someone amusing and congenial. The two Jesuit 'court jesters', William Hackett and Jeremiah Murphy, came often. Father Francis Moynihan, editor of the *Advocate*, was another source of company. When the archbishops of Sydney or Brisbane came to stay, they brought their secretaries, and there were big formal dinner parties. Most of the time, however, Raheen was as quiet as a monastery.

Upstairs, there was no grandeur. Mannix's bedroom, almost as plain as a monk's cell, had a Victorian bedstead with brass knobs. It was so high that when Mannix's successor, Dr Simonds, was confronted with it he had to ring for a little set of steps.[12] There was one armchair. In extreme old age, when he could no longer manage the stairs, Mannix had a television brought up. He protested against having an air conditioner on the grounds that he would not live long enough to make the expense worthwhile.[13] The claw-footed bath in his unheated bathroom was a period piece; it had a corrugated iron canopy which, when the taps were turned on, made 'a lovely spray'.[14] From 1917 on, there were few changes made to Raheen, and they were mainly for the look of the thing, not for Mannix's comfort.

The kitchen and scullery were late Victorian in 1917, and they stayed that way for years. An 'early Kooka' gas stove was installed in the 1930s. Anyone who spent time at Raheen on a cold day would look sadly at the three-bar radiators that hardly began to heat the splendid, high-ceilinged library. Surrendering overcoats as well as hats on entering the house, they would soon wish for another layer of clothing.

For Mannix, an ascetic who did not want soft cushions any more than he wanted gilt or marble, Raheen was the right place. He could be sure of privacy; he could see people on his own terms. And he could get a good idea of how life was experienced in Melbourne by walking to work.

The four-kilometre walk to St Patrick's Cathedral took Mannix from affluent Studley Park through some of the poorest parts of the inner city. He took different routes according to whim or weather. Often, he would cross the road and walk a block or so on Studley Park Road, past Goathlands, the opulent red brick mansion of the Gibson manufacturing family, later bought by Dr John Murphy and renamed Glendalough. Today, Jesuit-owned, it is Campion College. Next he would pass the former home of the Austrian consul, Carl Ludwig Pinschof, Studley Hall, which became the Xavier preparatory school Burke Hall in 1920. Then came the white stucco mansion, Studley House. Here lived Mannix's controversial neighbour, John Wren.

It has been said that Wren paid for Raheen. There seems no evidence for that claim, and no reason to doubt that the money came from the diocese. The diocese benefited in 1957 when seven acres were sold to assist the Catholic Schools' Provident Fund. In any case, it never belonged to Mannix; it devolved on those future archbishops of Melbourne who had the stamina for its testing regime. 'Raheen was always a nightmare', said former archbishop Frank Little, who wanted to live on a smaller scale, and to have better heating.[15] That Mannix knew Wren well is not in doubt. Whether, in Wren's case, Mannix broke his rule of never making private visits is uncertain. But it makes little difference whether they talked inside the gate of Studley House or outside it. They were neighbours; they became friends and Mannix accepted many gifts from Wren on behalf of the church. One of Wren's sons recalled sitting on the archbishop's knee and counting the buttons on his soutane.[16] That sounds like a Wren visit to Raheen; Mannix wouldn't have worn his soutane if he was visiting a private house.

Mannix never walked all the way with anyone. When the talk was finished as far as he was concerned, he would stop at the next cross-street, and raise his hat. Whether it was John Wren or Robert Menzies, or some chatty stranger, that was that.

Some days he turned left, just past the Wren house, walked down Walmer Street, crossed the iron bridge and made his way through Abbotsford by Victoria Street to Victoria Parade and East Melbourne. On other days he went over the Yarra by the Johnston Street Bridge and through the Collingwood slums. Either way, he saw extreme poverty. He took a pocketful of coins, and gave them away. A sixpence from 'the toff in the topper' or a stately greeting: every day brought an encounter. He steered a blind man across busy Victoria Street to a corner pub; he bought boots for a needy boy. Astonishingly in all those long walks in the public streets no one ever threw a stone or even an apple core at that shining, tempting target, the Mannix top hat.

Historian Patrick O'Farrell defines the Mannix style as theatre:

> Daniel Mannix had all the marks of a consummate actor. He carried on to the stage, wherever it was, the commanding presence of an aristocratic self-image which he projected with all the aid of his poised physical bearing, superbly crafted lines deliberately underplayed, and a range of props: top hat or biretta, even a cape in the Victorian thespian tradition...His enormous audience relished this performance, enjoying it because of its studied excellence as a role, and because it was constructed from, and deeply relevant to, real Catholic life. Here was leadership, not merely as directional encouragement, but by projecting effortless superiority. The money given away in the legendary private walks was aristocratic largesse, distributed in royal progress.[17]

The Mannix walks roused wonder and bemusement in some; for others they became part of the landscape. When he boarded a bus in sudden heavy rain the conductress was so startled that she refused to take the fare. A Scotch College schoolboy in Walmer Street returned the prelate's greeting with, 'I'm not allowed to talk to strangers,' and ran as fast as he could.[18] Most Catholic schoolchildren took him for granted. Gina and Flora Nicoletti, on their way to the Catholic Ladies College from Raven Street, Kew, in the 1940s, were patted on their school hats, and were once given a striped candy stick each from the depth of capacious pockets. 'I remember Mannix as always very nice to me and Flora, and it was always he who initiated any interaction. We would never have addressed him first.' Decades earlier their mother Lucetta sat beside the archbishop on the cable tram and offered him a peppermint, which he accepted.[19]

John Funder, then a twelve-year-old at St Patrick's College, remembers 1952 as 'the year I knocked down the archbishop':

> On Mondays because the bread was stale, I'd be given sixpence for lunch, two meat pies from the local shop in Victoria Parade. Even at that age keenly interested in food, I devised an episodic stratagem to ensure early access: at 12.25 or so, hand up, miming acute abdominal discomfort. 'Sir, sir, please sir, I've got to go.' And so I went, and miraculously relieved, barrelled up Lansdowne Street, head down, little legs pumping. Around the corner, straight into Dr Mannix, sitting him down, knocking his top hat off, me spinning into the gutter where I lay paralysed by the dawning enormity of what I had done. He laughed uproariously, dusted himself off, patted my head and gave me two shillings. Manna from heaven, meat pies for the rest of the week. Except, of course, vegetable pasties on Friday.[20]

Year after year the Molan children from Gipps Street in East Melbourne greeted the archbishop on their way to school. As a young woman, Mary Molan felt confident enough to ask his help. Her fiancé, English-born David Dickson, who was not a Catholic, was required to take instructions in her faith. The young man was thoughtful and intelligent; he wanted dialogue. The archbishop listened and understood. More important, he arranged for Dickson to talk to the friendly and perceptive William Hackett. The marriage took place in the bride's church, St Patrick's Cathedral, after Dickson chose to become a Catholic.[21]

There were losses as well as gains in the decision to live at Raheen. It saved the emotional energy of a man who found social life hard: to be alone at the end of the day was often a relief. But Mannix did not share the twenty-four-hour cycle of the cathedral parish, its hum and buzz, its human dramas and comedies, its daily companionship. St Patrick's was far more than an administrative centre. It had its own neighbourhood, its own parishioners. Two of its priests were responsible for hospital visits; and it would be a rare night without a call to give the last rites to the dying. The lights were always on at St Vincent's Hospital, and the priests from St Patrick's were used to the sound of the ambulance sirens in the night. Those on night duty had to be ready to dress and hurry across the street whenever the call came. In old age, Mannix regretted many things that he had never done. One of these, so he said, was ministering to the dying.[22] But how could he have forgotten his nights in the Maynooth infirmary?

An archbishop would not have been on night duty, but if Mannix had lived in the cathedral presbytery he would have seen the wear and tear on those who were. St Patrick's, like its Sydney counterpart St Mary's, as described by Edmund Campion, was a place where you met the walking wounded: 'suicides, drunks, visionaries, dropouts, conmen, naggers and cranks—life's victims, all of them.'[23]

Living in Kew gave Mannix a few wealthy Catholic neighbours. When Vatican officials thought of moving the troublesome Mannix from Melbourne, he was protected by his ability to bring in donations from rich and poor alike. As well as John Wren, his friend and admirer, there was Thomas O'Loughlin, at Tara Hall, a little way down the Studley Park hill, and Dr John Murphy at Glendalough, opposite Raheen. Tara Hall and Glendalough were neo-Elizabethan mansions with spacious reception rooms and splendid staircases. Thomas O'Loughlin's house (later the home of Dr Edward Ryan) was the more resplendent of the two. O'Loughlin lived in state, with a manservant, a cook, several maids and a governess for his daughters. All this came from a legacy: that archetypal romance of the rich uncle who struck lucky on the goldfields was literal truth for the O'Loughlins. Martin Loughlin (1833–1894) born into a farming family in Kilkenny made a fortune so large that even the 1890s depression left him relatively untroubled. His nephew and heir, Thomas, passed on large sums to the Catholic Church, and was rewarded with the papal title of Count in 1911. Clerical gossips in Rome reported that 'O'Loughlin would do anything for Dr Mannix'.[24]

A piquant situation came from Mannix's decision not to change his address on the electoral roll after his move to Kew. He had made the change from St Mary's in West Melbourne to St Patrick's Cathedral, and there he stayed, still in Labor territory, state and federal.[25] Raheen is in a safe Liberal seat. Its federal member for many years was Mannix's neighbour Robert Menzies, who held Kooyong from 1934 until his retirement in 1966. It's never safe to assume anything about Mannix, but it seems almost certain that he voted Labor from 1913 until the party split in 1955. His federal member in the Melbourne seat from 1940 was his friend Arthur Calwell. After that? Did he switch to Calwell's opponent? His vote wouldn't have made any difference. Calwell was as firmly established in Melbourne as Menzies was in Kooyong. But if Calwell happened to be at the East Melbourne polling booth when Mannix made his entrance, he might have wondered, as he knelt to kiss the archbishop's ring, which square on the ballot paper the old man would choose.

Living at Raheen and walking to work: that was the pattern

of Mannix's life from early 1918 until his ninetieth birthday in March 1954. He saw the social changes as the big estates of Kew were subdivided: pioneering families moved on and were succeeded by young middle-class householders, doctors, lawyers, businessmen. Mannix's doctor, Gerald Doyle, lived only a few minutes' walk from Raheen, as did his financial adviser, Michael Chamberlin. Religious orders in Kew included the training house for a missionary order, the Pallottines, in Studley Park Road and the Carmelite monastery in Stevenson Street. Catholic shop owners seemed to have a monopoly in the Kew High Street. J. J. Murphy was everyone's grocer; Old Xaverian Ted Marsh had the butcher's shop; the Laracy family ran the newsagency; the Reens had the corner milk bar.

The sense of solidarity among Catholics in this neighbourhood owed something to Mannix's presence. The children went to the same schools, played together, met at mass on Sundays, went on errands to the same shops, which were almost always the ones owned by Catholics. It was an enclosed world. I doubt if any of my generation ever thought that an invisible fence had been built around our neighbourhood in the conscription years by the old man in the top hat whom we saw on his daily walk.

Mannix was not interested in crossing the Catholic–Protestant divide. Over the years, there were overtures from Government House. Lord Somers did his best in 1927, but, as Mannix's friend William Hackett ruefully reported, 'when it comes down to tintacks there is nothing doing'.[26] A later governor, Lord Huntingfield, tried harder but his charming invitation to 'lunch quietly *en famille*' was turned down. Mannix's refusal, awkwardly done, sounded unreasonable:

> You have made it hard for me to write this letter, for it must seem ungracious on my part to say that I never go out to lunch or dinner. But your quite unexpected and truly generous invitation almost tempts me to break my self-imposed rule of living & most of my resolutions are often broken. But I have been faithful so far to this one. Your Excellency therefore must not become the cause of my first fall from rectitude in this matter.
>
> You will believe that I truly appreciate your very exceptional kindness and that I shall always be ready to co-operate in the promotion of those interests which we value in common.[27]

Everyone had to come to Raheen, and eventually nearly everyone did. In 1957, the newly appointed Anglican archbishop of Melbourne, Frank Woods, called at Raheen and was made welcome but there was no question of a return visit. Was it shyness that kept Mannix at home? A safeguard against losing independence? A need for a quiet routine, conserving nervous energy for his public appearances? He didn't have a ghetto mentality: he wanted young Catholics to take their place in the professions and in politics. But for himself, the barriers were never lowered. As president of Maynooth he had dined at Dublin Castle; perhaps in the bitter ensuing years he made up his mind never to defer to the Crown. Whatever the reasons, Raheen suited Mannix. Catholic Kew was his village and he was its tribal chieftain.

CHAPTER SEVEN

FOR IRELAND'S FREEDOM

ST PATRICK'S DAY 1920 was pure theatre. Melbourne had seen nothing like it. With Archbishop Daniel Mannix in the lead role, and the whole performance directed by John Wren, it was a tremendous spectacle, with complex, contradictory meanings.

In Archbishop Carr's time, the feast day of Ireland's national saint was a time for unity and good spirits. At Federation in 1901, Carr offered the pleasant thought that Ireland's green made part of the newly formed Australian spectrum: the Irish spirit, he said, was like a note in music that united with others to make 'angelic harmonies'. Welcoming the governor-general, Lord Northcote, to a St Patrick's Day concert in 1904, Carr described the vice-regal role as 'a centre of unity' that harmonised the various tints in the national picture.[1] Carr was a good Irishman who believed that

England would keep faith and give the long promised Home Rule to Ireland. He was on friendly terms with the governor of Victoria as well as the governor-general, and he always invited a vice-regal representative to the St Patrick's Day festivities.

With war in Europe, the postponement of Home Rule, and the Easter Rising and its brutal aftermath, the mood altered. Carr's sunny optimism died with him. Because of an epidemic of Spanish influenza there was no celebration of St Patrick's Day in 1919. Instead, there was an discordant episode when Mannix's offer to send some of the Sisters of Charity from St Vincent's Hospital to help nurse the sick in emergency accommodation in the Exhibition Building was rudely received. The sight of the nuns, it seemed, would upset the patients. Mannix, affronted, withdrew the offer.[2]

The 1919 federal elections stirred more sectarian feeling. Mannix's open support of the Australian Labor Party was a mixed blessing. Some candidates thought that he lost them Protestant votes and blamed him for the party's poor showing. Mannix in turn blamed the Labor Party for not recognising the support that Catholics gave it. The *Australasian* commented drily that 'Dr Mannix did the [Labor] party enough harm by befriending it in public'.[3]

As the 1920 St Patrick's Day celebrations drew near there was a real risk of a demonstration against the archbishop. John Wren, whose devotion to Mannix came with an entrepreneurial flair and deep pockets, took charge. Fourteen winners of the Victoria Cross, each mounted on a white horse bought at Wren's expense, made a guard of honour for Mannix's open limousine. Wren knew that some owners in Victoria would be unwilling to sell their horses to honour Mannix, so he turned to the other states. Even in distant Queensland, the word went around that Wren's men were out looking. White horses suddenly became as scarce as unicorns, and their owners could name their price. Wren would have liked twenty VCs, but did well to get fourteen. Few of them were Catholics. Some had never ridden, but they all managed to stay in the saddle.[4]

The day was a triumph for Mannix. White horses, green flags fluttering in the breeze, the shining motor car from which he waved like royalty: it was a spectacle to rival the welcome given to the Duke and Duchess of York in 1901. An ominous sight for many non-Catholics, it roused Catholic pride. This St Patrick's Day was more than a day out for the Irish, more than an outflowing of nostalgia; it was a confident, noisy, aggressive demonstration, a perfect backdrop for Mannix's quiet, unassailable dignity.

The parade was an implicit reply to the charge of disloyalty against Mannix. Six thousand ex-servicemen, most of them in uniform, marched behind his motor car. Wounded and disabled men followed in cars, and behind them marched at least twenty thousand schoolboys. At a cost of £3000, Wren had the whole procession filmed, and released for showing as *Ireland Will Be Free.*[5]

Behind the scenes, the mood was different. By 1920 Mannix had roused widespread hostility. His speeches were remembered, not only for their anti-imperial spirit but also for sounding something like Bolshevism. 'The war, bad as it is, will not have been altogether in vain if it opens the eyes of the people to the necessity for radical change in the condition of the toilers.'[6] The language smacked of socialism; it was not what was expected from an archbishop. In the wake of the Russian Revolution it was bound to worry many Australians, Catholics included.

For the acclimatised Irish, Mannix could be an embarrassment. He was worse than that to politically committed Irish-Australians who put their faith in a constitutional progression to Home Rule. His declaration for Sinn Féin's armed struggle against the British sidelined these moderate nationalists. And now that Mannix owned the *Advocate*, they had lost the outlet that the paper's former owner Joseph Winter had given them. When the second Melbourne Catholic paper, the *Tribune*, put up some resistance to the Mannix line on Ireland it was promptly squashed. Morgan Jageurs was one of the prominent Irish-Australians who resented Mannix's takeover of the nationalist movement for Sinn Féin and his unreserved support for de Valera as leader. Writing to Irish Party MP John Dillon in Ireland, Jageurs expressed their fury. The Sinn Féiners, he said, were 'slobbering all over the [returned] soldiers in order to use them as a buffer against the sectarians who oppose the procession'.

> The d—d hypocrisy of the whole thing, however, is sickening! Anything, however to secure a Roman triumph, not for San Patricio but in pure laudation of Dr Mannix and de Valera—the Caesars for the time being...There is no doubt he is a great power throughout Australia amongst our own people—a power, unfortunately for much evil where the interests of the Irish constitutional movement are concerned.[7]

St Patrick's Day 1920 was just the beginning. When Mannix announced that he was setting off in May to pay his obligatory visit to the Pope, his admirers planned a grand farewell. John Wren pledged £5000 to start a presentation fund of £50,000 for the archbishop. Mannix refused the money, but he couldn't refuse the poem that Wren wrote to mark the occasion. It was inspired partly by Wren's awareness that Prime Minister Hughes hoped to stop Mannix from returning, perhaps by making him take an oath of loyalty. Wren's poem, set to the tune of 'Come Back to Erin', was ready for Mannix's send-off:

> Come back to Australia our prince and great leader
> Come back to Australia the land you have blessed
> Bring back the news that old Ireland has her freedom
> Australia will clasp you with love to her breast.[8]

Mannix's departure went on for days. He was given a farewell at the Exhibition Building, attended by thirty thousand people, at which 'autographed photos of His Grace sold briskly'.[9] A few days later, when Mannix left St Patrick's Cathedral to take the train to Sydney, Collins Street was lined with schoolchildren, all primed to sing Wren's 'Come Back' accompanied by a number of bands. A five-minute drive became a celebrity motorcade. The car was surrounded by devotees wanting to kiss the archbishop's ring. In spite of the efforts of mounted police to clear the road, Mannix missed his train. He returned to Raheen for a night's rest before trying again, this time taking the train at North Melbourne.[10]

It was the same in Sydney: another extravaganza. Before Mannix boarded the *Ventura* he made his way through an eager, jostling crowd. Cards and photographs were held out for him to sign. A roaring trade in Mannix lapel buttons exhausted the supply. To the strains of 'Come Back to Erin' and 'God Save Ireland' the *Ventura* moved out from Circular Quay. Above the vessel—surely a John Wren touch—a plane festooned with green streamers swooped in farewell. Mannix had chosen to avoid the usual Melbourne–London route and to travel via Honolulu to San Francisco. He planned to cross the United States by train, giving a series of lectures on the Irish question, and meeting Eamon de Valera on the way. There were other advantages in taking this route: it reduced the time at sea—Mannix was a bad sailor—and it avoided the very British atmosphere of an Orient or P&O liner. Even so, he was in trouble over national anthems. Why didn't he stand up when the *Ventura* was farewelled by the American national anthem as it left Honolulu? Was it because he was feeling seasick? Or because he mistook 'America' for 'God Save the King'? Whatever the truth of the incident, it soured his welcome in San Francisco.[11]

Soon, however, the lecture tour, organised by Sinn Féin, brought out Irish-Americans in their thousands, from San Francisco to Los Angeles and Denver. Mannix had one central point to make: it was Ireland's right to choose the government she wanted. He put Ireland's cause in the context of a war allegedly fought for the freedom of small nations like Belgium.

Crossing the continent by train, the Mannix party stopped for sightseeing at the Grand Canyon. Most of the group made the descent into the canyon on horseback, but Mannix and his cousin Bishop Daniel Foley chose to walk, although it was a hot June day. By late afternoon, they had not returned. A search party found them in the depths of the canyon. It was a strange tableau. Foley was stretched on the ground, seemingly unconscious. Nearby, Mannix was seated on a hollow log, in a fugue-like state, muttering unintelligibly to himself, unresponsive to others. Foley, who soon recovered, may have had heatstroke. Mannix's behaviour sounds like a panic attack. Somehow the two men were helped back to base, and the incident was hushed up. 'Lost in the Grand Canyon' was the official version. After Mannix's death, his biographer Father James Murtagh heard the story in Ireland, where Foley had told the Mannix family about the episode. Murtagh began to question the legend of the imperturbable Mannix, and to look for other moments of emotional fragility.[12]

The Grand Canyon incident came at what should have been a restful period, between the spectacular West Coast welcomes and the main event of the tour, the meeting with Eamon de Valera. As Mannix made his roundabout way to Rome, de Valera was always in his mind. More pressing than giving his report to the Pope was Mannix's need to get in touch with Ireland again. And for him de Valera was Ireland's future.

Rightly or wrongly, Mannix had put his faith in the austere and schoolmasterly Eamon de Valera, known as the 'Long Fellow'. They had met only once, very briefly, when de Valera first came to Maynooth as a new and under-qualified, part-time teacher.[13] Since then de Valera had made himself one of the most powerful men in Ireland, and had attained the title of President. There was, however, an alternative leader, Michael Collins. Collins was the head of the secret organisation the Irish Republican Brotherhood. A natural leader of men and loved by many women, Collins projected warmth, magnetism and recklessness. Beside Collins, de Valera appeared prim and dry. Teacher of mathematics, devoted husband and father, firm in his Catholic faith, he was totally lacking in glamour. Yet he had the special status of having faced execution as one of the leaders of the Easter Rising; his name was written in history. Both de Valera and Collins were brave; both had endured long terms of imprisonment. They would soon become rivals, but at the time of Mannix's visit they were closely allied in the cause of Irish freedom. In February 1919, Collins had organised de Valera's escape from Lincoln Prison where he had been held for nine months on suspicion of promoting collusion between Sinn Féin and Germany. The rescue was done in storybook style with a skeleton key smuggled inside a cake, an impression made with melted wax from altar candles—some say it was soap—and two failed attempts before the key worked and de Valera escaped to the waiting Collins and his other rescuers.[14]

Lincoln was only one of at least eight prisons where de Valera served time. Arrested again in 1921, 1923, 1924 and 1929, he was held first by the British, later by the Irish Free State government.[15] His wife, Sinéad, and his five young children lived miserably, with neither home nor income, dependent on relatives and the kindness of some of de Valera's colleagues, including Michael Collins. De Valera was not indifferent to his family's suffering. Loving letters to Sinéad, and her replies, show the closeness of their marriage. But the cause came first.[16]

Like Mannix, de Valera gained status from his part in opposing conscription. When the British government proposed to extend conscription to Ireland in 1918, there was outrage in church and state. The Archbishop of Dublin, Dr Walsh, was no friend to Sinn Féin, nor was Cardinal Logue of Armagh, but they and others of the Irish hierarchy agreed to see de Valera and others at Maynooth to discuss the crisis. After hearing de Valera, the bishops endorsed his argument in an official pronouncement. Forcing conscription on Ireland, they said, 'was an oppressive and inhuman law which the Irish people have every right to resist by every means that are consonant with the law of God'. Although the bishops were uneasy about seeming to endorse Sinn Féin, they hoped that 'the law of God' would prevail over armed resistance. There was a one-day national strike. One million signatures on an anti-conscription pledge drafted by de Valera showed a new level of intensity in the struggle against British rule. De Valera's performance at Maynooth was praised by William O'Brien, a veteran of the Land League, and one of the older nationalists on the delegation:

> His transparent sincerity; his gentleness and equability captured the hearts of us all. His gaunt frame and sad eyes deeply buried in their sockets had much of the Dantesque suggestion of the man who had been in hell. His was that subtle blend of virility and emotion which the Americans mean when they speak of a 'magnetic man'.[17]

In the event, conscription was not imposed on Ireland. The British government would not take the risk of a violent reaction from the Irish people. But the crisis over conscription fatally weakened the Home Rule Party. Its representatives had not been able to defend Irish interests in the Westminster parliament. The Sinn Féin party, which had always said that going to Westminster was a waste of time, was vindicated. Irish voters in the 1918 elections were offered a choice. They could trust the Home Rule Party's power of persuasion once more, and hope for an Irish parliament with limited powers. Or, they could vote Sinn Féin with its policy of withdrawing from Westminster and setting up an Irish republic in defiance of the British. Sinn Féin won by a huge majority. It then called all members of parliament to meet in Dublin's Mansion House on 21 January 1919. Home Rulers and the Unionists of the north stayed away, and some Sinn Féiners were in gaol, but twenty-seven Sinn Féin members repeated the Declaration of the Republic which had been made at the 1916 Easter Rising. De Valera's escape in February, and British prime minister Lloyd George's decision in April to release the other Sinn Féin prisoners, gave ballast to the party. The Dáil (as the new parliament was called) elected de Valera as president, and he appointed his cabinet. After a failed appeal to the Peace Conference at Versailles on behalf of Ireland, one of the small nations it was pledged to protect, de Valera decided to campaign for support in the United States.

De Valera made the voyage across the Atlantic, disguised as a seaman and hidden in a rat-infested corner of the ship. Then, shaved and respectably dressed again, he emerged at the luxurious Waldorf-Astoria Hotel, which became his New York headquarters. He then embarked on a fundraising lecture tour of the United States, appealing to Irish-Americans to help the struggle in Ireland. De Valera wanted donations but he also wanted the main political parties to recognise him as the head of the legitimate government of Ireland. The Waldorf-Astoria seems an extravagance, given the straitened means of his party. Perhaps for the boy from the mud-walled cabin in Bruree there was satisfaction in sending his demands to the world and to President Woodrow Wilson from the gilt and brocaded public rooms of the big hotel. As his biographer Tim Pat Coogan remarked: 'one could place the entire Bruree dwelling in the drawing room [of Wilson's house] and still have plenty of room to serve the coffee'.[18]

In Melbourne, Mannix had chafed at being so far away with only scant or unreliable news and without the direct access to power that the Irish bishops had. He was enmeshed in a routine of church administration far from the scenes where history was being written. His letters were censored, as they had been since the wartime period. He had listened eagerly to news from recently arrived Irish priests, and although the information they gave him was fragmentary, he was impressed by their stories of de Valera's courage and commitment. Mannix was due to make his duty visit to the Pope; he wanted to visit Ireland and see his mother and sister; and he had decided first to meet de Valera in the United States.

From first to last, Mannix's American tour was political. He was met in San Francisco by Diarmuid Fawcett, one of de Valera's entourage. The central event was the meeting between de Valera and Mannix, one to one, in Omaha, Nebraska, where both had kept time for a quiet talk at St Columba's Missionary College. Their meeting, and their subsequent appearances on the same platform, fed Mannix's anger towards British rule in Ireland, and his longing for involvement. He met other Irish radicals whose testimony would have confirmed his belief that the British government's policy in Ireland was brutal and unyielding. Hence, Mannix's most inflammatory speech, given in Cliff Haven, Plattsburgh, New York:

> There is no use mincing words. Ireland is ruled by an alien Government. I see no way out but American recognition of Mr de Valera. Some have said that England is a friendly nation. No, England never was a friend of the United States. When your fathers fought it was against England. Ireland has the same grievance against the same enemy only ten times greater. I hope Ireland will make a fight equally successful. England was your enemy; she is your enemy today; she will be your enemy for all time. England is one of the greatest hypocrites in the world. She pretended to be your friend in the war. Now the war is over she tells you to mind your own business.[19]

There was instant rapport between de Valera and Mannix. The landscape of County Cork was part of their being; the land question resonated for them both, even though there was a world of difference in their backgrounds. De Valera lacked Mannix's wit and comic sense, and Mannix was the better public performer. But they both had the *gravitas* that inspired hero-worship. They even looked alike; it was said that they could be taken for brothers.[20] Though de Valera was only thirty-eight in 1920, his face was deeply furrowed and his dark eyes, deep set, gave him the Abraham Lincoln look that was also used to describe Mannix. His sight was poor and he needed the glasses that Mannix, even in his nineties, seldom wore. De Valera's gaze had an unseeing visionary look that added to his remoteness. In old age he would be completely blind. His long black overcoat, draped on a frame as tall and spare as that of Mannix, looked clerical; a Roman collar wasn't needed to complete the resemblance. Both chose headgear that added height. De Valera's high-crowned black Homburg matched Mannix's tall purple biretta. De Valera was half-Spanish and looked it. In Shane Leslie's *Doomsland*, a semi-fictional version of Maynooth, the college president, based on Mannix, is 'Monsignor Spanish'.[21] Both men had a sense of theatre. Mounted on a white horse and wearing a flowing black cloak, de Valera led torchlight processions in Ireland with all the panache of Mannix and his cavalcade of VC winners on St Patrick's Day. An added touch, which John Wren had not thought of, was to have the manes of the horses braided in Republican colours.[22]

Some of de Valera's colleagues were intimidated by bishops and archbishops. De Valera was nonchalant. 'Oh, there's nothing in that. I have lived all my life among priests.'[23] Because of his teaching post at Maynooth he knew many church leaders, and was on friendly terms with some. He could have made his career within the church, which he seems to have considered doing. His presumed illegitimate birth was an obstacle; although the religious orders would have accepted him, the diocesan seminaries would not. For better reasons one need look no further than his family life and the fact that in old age he and Sinéad were a 'Darby and Joan' couple.[24]

Mannix's importance to de Valera is easy to understand. No other archbishop unequivocally took the republican cause. No other prelate fought so hard to make de Valera head of a free Irish government. What was it about de Valera that made Mannix so sure? Many saw de Valera as rigid, aloof, pedantic, devious as leader and politician, with an ego that made comradeship difficult; he always had to be in charge. Mannix might not have seen the ruthlessness; de Valera would have deferred to the older man. He owed Mannix his first job at Maynooth, and he knew how to value the support of an internationally famous archbishop who could work magic with crowds. Most of all, de Valera's status as a hero of the Easter Rising would have marked him out for Mannix.

Even so, there had to be something more. One consistent quality in Mannix's life was his being drawn to the outsider. His sympathies quickly went to the Germans and Italians interned in the First World War, and in the Second World War to the Jews as well. In Ireland and in Irish politics generally, de Valera's Spanish name and appearance set him apart. Just at the time of his meeting Mannix in Omaha, de Valera was accused in a Dublin Castle newssheet of having 'inducted Ireland into the murderous treachery of his race'.[25] In Australia at a later time, propaganda about 'the Black Hand of Santamaria', and comparisons with Machiavelli, fanned sectarian fires around Bartholomew Santamaria, Mannix's other protégé.

When Mannix and de Valera shared a platform at Madison Square Gardens in New York in July 1920, it must have been hard to say whose words were the churchman's and whose the politician's. An audience of fifteen thousand people heard Mannix's demand that Ireland be given the same status in postwar planning as the other small nations of Europe whose fate was being decided by President Wilson's Fourteen Point Plan. Two hundred and thirty police and ten mounted men were sent in case of trouble but that trouble was confined to 'a volley of hisses' when the president was mentioned, and 'gales of groans, boos and hisses' for Lloyd George. That night the alliance between Mannix and de Valera was made plain when the Archbishop of New York, Cardinal Hayes, offered Catholic New York's 'esteem, affection and loyalty' to the two most distinguished Irishmen on the Atlantic seaboard, Mannix and de Valera. The applause that greeted Mannix lasted fifteen minutes.[26]

The strain on Mannix the public performer was plain to see. While celebrating a solemn mass at St Patrick's Cathedral, New York, he showed signs of exhaustion and he had to withdraw from the altar and lean back on Cardinal Hayes's throne, while Hayes moved to a chair beside the other clergy.[27]

All through the remaining days of his tour, Mannix linked Ireland's cause with de Valera's name. He openly identified himself with the Easter Rising: 'I am going to Ireland soon and I am going to kneel on the graves of those men who in Easter Week gave their lives for Ireland.'[28] He also made it clear that he wanted nothing less than a republic for Ireland.

Going to Ireland? Not if the British government could stop

him. Mannix had official warning that he might not be allowed to land in Ireland. As always, he took no notice. There could be no better proof, he said, of the 'jumpy and frenzied' state of the Lloyd George government than this proposed prohibition.[29] His planned voyage from New York to the Irish port of Queenstown (Cobh) began with industrial trouble. After being farewelled by de Valera along with thousands of Irish-American fans, he boarded the White Star liner *Baltic* on 31 July. Once on board, he heard that the British cooks and stewards would go on strike rather than accept him as a passenger. 'Take him off!' they said. This provoked the Irish firemen. Remove Mannix, their leaders said, and *WE* go on strike. When the firemen were backed by the longshoremen who promised to 'deal with' the cooks and stewards, the captain of the *Baltic* had no choice but to set sail with his troublesome passenger on board.[30] Several British Secret Service agents kept watch. Mannix was almost never alone.

The *Baltic* was so close to the Irish coast on 8 August 1920 that Mannix could see the lights of Queenstown and the flames of huge bonfires of welcome on the hilltops. He could also see a 'smudge of something' which as it came closer was revealed as a British destroyer, the *Wyvern*. The *Baltic* was ordered to stop, and to lower a gangway for a naval lieutenant and two Scotland Yard detectives. The archbishop was summoned to the captain's cabin where Mannix's secretary, Father Arthur Vaughan, joined him. They were told that the British government would not permit Mannix to land in Ireland. Liverpool, Manchester and Glasgow (all of which had big Irish populations) were also off limits. The destroyer would take him to another British coastal destination.

The British cabinet had been taking legal advice as to how best to deal with Mannix. Under the Defence of the Realm Act he could be kept out of Ireland, where his presence might lead to violent demonstrations. It was also claimed that his speeches in the United States amounted to sedition, and that if he landed in England he could be arrested and deported. The idea of charging Mannix with sedition was rejected on the grounds that the archbishop would get bail and that there would be a long drawn-out trial. As a compromise it was decided to have him arrested at sea, brought to England, and kept under surveillance.

Vaughan described the drama in the captain's cabin and the ensuing scene:

> We took our time getting ready for the transhipment. When quite ready we went to the deck, where the gangplank was let down to the waiting pinnace with its crew of British Jack Tars. The Archbishop then quietly and deliberately said: 'I refuse to leave this vessel' thereupon throwing the onus for his removal entirely on the British Government. One of the Scotland Yard men then placed his hand on the Archbishop's shoulder, which amounted to a technical arrest.[31]

Rather than make an angry protest against being kept out of Ireland and denied the chance to see his mother, Mannix played it as comedy. The British government helped by landing him at Penzance on the Cornish coast. Calling himself the Pirate of Penzance, he provided a perfect line for the press, and made the government look silly. All the same, his mood was grim. That glimpse of the Irish coast stirred longings for home.

There was no one to meet him at Penzance. He was tired and hungry, having been too seasick to eat anything on the destroyer. No one was at home in the local Catholic church. Vaughan found a convent, where nuns gave them breakfast, and made some phone calls. A well-placed old friend, Bishop Timothy Cotter of Portsmouth, offered to meet the London train en route and work out the next move. One of the few Irish bishops in England, Cotter was as intransigent a nationalist as Mannix, and just as outspoken. Two years younger than Mannix, he had been to the same school in Fermoy, County Cork, and had followed him to Maynooth before being sent to parish work on the Isle of Wight.

Advised by Cotter, Mannix went on by train to London where he had the satisfaction of refusing the government's offer of a suite of rooms at the Jermyn Court Hotel. Instead he stayed at a retirement home for priests at Hammersmith, run by the Sisters of St Joseph of Nazareth. Here he amused himself by slipping in and out without being seen by the Scotland Yard men assigned to keep watch. As always he fed the press some good lines. The best of them appeared on 11 August 1921 in the London *Times*:

> Since the battle of Jutland, the British Navy has not scored any success comparable with the chasing of the *Baltic* from the Irish shores and the capture without the loss of a single British sailor of the Archbishop of Melbourne.

For more than a year, the British government had Mannix on its doorstep, refusing to go away or to accept whatever concessions they offered him. He did not need bed and board. The Hammersmith nuns, and later the Bishop of Portsmouth, were happy to look after him. Prime Minister Lloyd George tried to remove a grievance that Mannix's friends exploited: a poignant image of eighty-nine-year-old Ellen Mannix waiting in Charleville to see her son, probably for the last time. 'The Mother Who Waits in Ireland' was one emotive headline.[32] Mannix haughtily refused the government's offer to bring his mother to London.

Although it has been claimed that Ellen Mannix did come to London, the evidence is against it.[33] If known, her visit would have deprived the archbishop of a telling reason to prolong his stay. He could not afford to let Lloyd George appear magnanimous. The risks of smuggling her in were overwhelming. British intelligence would have been watching the mother as well as the son. Ellen was living in her married daughter's house near Charleville, in a small community where everyone knew everyone's business. Even a whisper from any one of Ellen's extended family, or from her neighbours, whose politics were not all on the archbishop's side, would have been heard. At eighty-nine Ellen could not be expected to dodge about London evading Scotland Yard, and though it is tempting to imagine her dressed as a nun to make the journey, Mannix family memories rule out any such enterprise.

According to Mannix's cousins, Ellen Mannix wanted to go to London. She was in excellent health and she was eager to see Dan. She would have accepted Lloyd George's offer if her son had allowed it. She felt that his isolation in England was leading him astray; he simply did not know how it was in Ireland.[34] He made his choice, with what degree of pain or regret no one can ever know. He put politics ahead of the family tie, and his mother never saw him again.

To have an archbishop in the family would have been a glory in normal times, but in 1920 there was good reason for his relatives to be afraid for Mannix's safety, and their own. Shootings and reprisals were daily events. The military barracks in the main street of Charleville was fortified with steel doors and shutters and defended to the street with sandbags and machine guns. Ellen Mannix may have longed to see her son, but she didn't like the course he had chosen. Her family, the Cagneys, were anti-republican, and she had spoken with snobbish disdain about de Valera having 'sprung from a poor class of people'.[35]

Another possible family reunion of 1920 presented quite different problems. Ellen Mannix's second son, Patrick, lived in Lancaster with his English wife, Winifred. Biographers have called Patrick the black sheep of the Mannix family, but from the viewpoint of Patrick and Winifred a visit from the Sinn Féin archbishop would have been an embarrassment.[36]

Family sources reveal Patrick Mannix's complex and romantic story. At the turn of the century, he was established in medical practice in Lancaster, where he lived in the house of his senior partner Dr William Wingate Saul. Patrick Mannix and Saul's niece Winifred Sharpe fell in love and wanted to marry.[37] Her family expected better than an Irishman, no matter how charming. The real obstacle, however, was religious. Winifred would not marry in a Catholic church, and Patrick was just as resolutely against an Anglican ceremony. Patrick's sister Mary was invited to stay with the Sauls in Lancaster. She was told that the Sharpes opposed the marriage. '*We* don't like it either,' responded Charleville's emissary. Neither Patrick nor Winifred gave way; the engagement was broken off and Winifred made a more suitable marriage.

When Wingate Saul died in 1906, Patrick set up practice in Mayo House, a handsome establishment on Castle Hill, Lancaster. Some time after that, he and Winifred met again. She was estranged from her husband, Edward Cadman, who had gambled away her money. Winifred and her two children were living in her father's house, Halton Hall. She and Patrick Mannix were photographed together at an archery match; there was gossip about an affair. Then the First World War broke out. Edward went to France with his regiment, won the DSO, and was killed in May 1918. Less than a year later—improperly soon, it was said—Winifred married Patrick Mannix in a registrar's office. He was then fifty-four, and she was forty-four.[38] The wedding allied Patrick with a very English family, steeped in military tradition. He and Winifred lived in Mayo House where in 1920 their only child, Timothy Patrick, was born.

Daniel Mannix could have seen his brother Patrick in 1920. Instead he sent a curt message with their sister Mary who had come to visit him in London: 'Tell Pat to come and see me.' 'Tell Dan to come and see *me*,' was Patrick's reply. Neither one took the few hours journey between London and Lancaster, and the brothers never met again.

Mannix hadn't intended to visit England, but he made the most of his involuntary stay. As in the United States he commanded big audiences. Banned from Manchester, Liverpool and Glasgow, he spoke at mass meetings outside the cities' limits. The arrest at sea, reported in British newspapers, only added to the excitement. Being kept out of the centres with big Irish populations was no hindrance. Wigan, within easy reach of Manchester and Liverpool, drew crowds from both, and every time another region was deleted from his itinerary ('Banned in Bootle') it made the government look ridiculous.

Irish and Irish-Australian bishops, who had mixed feelings about their colleague, came together to protest against the 'insulting treatment' to which he had been subjected.[39] Britain's primate, the Cardinal Archbishop of Westminster, Francis Bourne, felt differently; he met the embarrassment by pretending that Mannix wasn't there.

It was hard for Mannix to accept that while he was confined to Britain, Archbishops Kelly of Sydney and Clune of Perth were free to cross the Irish Sea. In late August, Kelly wrote from Enniscorthy to suggest meeting Mannix in London. Mannix's reply, 'I hope to see you in Ireland before I go to Rome', was unrealistic.[40] The two eventually met in Portsmouth, where Mannix settled in for the winter, staying with Bishop Cotter, and showing no impatience to get to Rome.[41]

Archbishop Clune was invited by Lloyd George to mediate between the British government and some Irish leaders. He was a sound choice. In background Clune was as Irish as Mannix, and his nephew, Conor Clune, had been arrested for no apparent reason, and taken to Dublin Castle where he was tortured and killed. Clune made the trip to Dublin, met de Valera, Collins and others, and narrowly escaped being shot before returning to London where an irascible Mannix waited to hear his news. The talks had failed and Clune was later accused of giving the false impression that Irish resistance was weakening. 'We have murder by the throat,' Lloyd George said in November 1920.[42] Mannix's envy was plain in his patronising comment that Clune might just as well have played with the squirrels in Hyde Park as try to make peace with the British.[43]

It was frustrating to be in London—kept in cold storage, as Mannix described it—but he was closer to the heart of things than he would have been in Melbourne. The news at least was fresh, whether he read it in the London *Times* of the day, or heard it in Irish political circles. He walked in Hyde Park with Winston Churchill's cousin Shane Leslie, an Anglo-Irish convert to Catholicism and Irish nationalism who had renounced his baronetcy and changed his first name to its Irish form, but still had

Establishment links. They had last seen one another at Maynooth. Leslie was dismayed at the change in Mannix. He saw 'an old and war-weary man':

> Instead of the spruce college President, enshrined in its success and armoured with his books, stood a battered old man, his flesh worn away, his skin shrunk upon the framework of bones which upheld his purple biretta. His hair had changed and turned a light grey, his eyes were sunk in their sockets and every year of his life in Australia seemed to have left a deep chevron across his face.
>
> But the old fire was there and his eyes darted defiance, softened as they caught sight of a friend…it might have been an Archbishop Croke returned to life and as smilingly unafraid of the British government as ever.[44]

Shane Leslie did all he could to arrange talks between Mannix and the British government, and to get Mannix to Ireland. Between them, Mannix and Leslie composed a statement to be circulated to British political leaders in Leslie's name. Some conciliatory words in the typescript were crossed out by Mannix who sharpened the tone. It concluded:

> As to going to Ireland [the archbishop] thought it would do the government less harm if he were in Ireland than in England. He would give no conditions. If the Govt gave out that he went under conditions or assurances he would decline to go. He could make no statement on Ireland unless he found himself there. He was totally opposed to putting anybody to death under any circumstances. He could only

> say that if he were a British Premier serving the interests of the Empire he would take the line of killing the Republic with kindness and giving without negotiations or conditions the largest measure of Dominion Home Rule compatible with the Empire. The Irish could at least be made to try that and see whether it worked.[45]

Shane Leslie offered to go to Brixton Prison as a hostage if the government would allow Mannix to visit Ireland, but the archbishop 'preferred not'. Another player in background diplomacy, Lord Morris, former prime minister of Newfoundland, thought Mannix could act as a moderating influence on de Valera: 'I believe [Mannix] is the man if he could be got to act,' he told Leslie.[46] Mannix interrupted his lecture tour to meet Morris in London. The meeting wasn't a success. All that Morris could say afterwards was that he had had a 'most interesting hour and a half'.[47]

Mannix's strategy was to provoke the British government. At all costs, the Irish question must be kept in the public eye. There was a cost to Mannix himself. During the months of fiery speeches and covert diplomacy he had his portrait painted by the fashionable Belfast-born portraitist Sir John Lavery, whose wife, Hazel, gathered Irish nationalists at their London house and was said to be having an affair with Michael Collins. Lavery, who usually flattered his sitters, did not show the ravages discerned by Leslie but his portrait, 'pale, austere and upright as a paschal candle', had an edge of sadness that reflected its time and place.[48] Soon after the Lavery work, the prominent Australian artist Max Meldrum was commissioned to paint a welcome home portrait of the archbishop from his Melbourne people. Its vigorous presence shows no shadow of doubt. Meldrum had to work with photographs and from his own memory, knowing that a triumphalist look was wanted for the hero's return. If he had been painting his subject from life in 1920s London he would have seen a different man.

While Mannix was in the United States, his home city Cork had been enduring dark hours. In March 1920, its Sinn Féin Lord Mayor Tomás MacCurtain was murdered in his house, in front of his wife, by men with blackened faces who were later proved to be members of the Royal Irish Constabulary acting on British orders. A verdict of 'wilful murder by David Lloyd George', was delivered by a powerless Irish jury. MacCurtain's friend, poet and playwright and Sinn Féin member for Mid-Cork, Terence MacSwiney, succeeded him as Lord Mayor in full knowledge that he too would join the death list. He had served less than six months in his post when he was arrested for possession of seditious documents and sentenced to two years gaol. He immediately went on hunger strike as a protest against the sentence and the fact that he was tried by a military court.

Visiting MacSwiney several times in Brixton Prison, Mannix saw the full human cost of suffering in Ireland's cause. 'It is not they who can inflict the most but they who suffer most who will conquer,' MacSwiney said.[49] The sight of his pain, stoically endured, left Mannix awed, and deeply angry. Refuting some Catholic churchmen who judged the hunger strike to be suicide, and therefore a grave sin, Mannix gave MacSwiney the last sacraments.

After enduring seventy-four days on hunger strike, MacSwiney died on 25 October. Fearing riots if the coffin were taken by road between Dublin and Cork, the government sent it directly from London to Cork. Mannix went as far as he could with the funeral procession. After a requiem mass in Southwark Cathedral, the procession of ten thousand mourners, with an escort of mounted troopers, moved slowly through crowded London streets to Euston Station. 'Resplendent and grim-faced, on foot, Mannix led the procession, walking at a respectful distance behind the hearse.'[50] Before the coffin, wrapped in the yellow, white and green of Sinn Féin, was placed on the train, Mannix said the *De Profundis* and other prayers for the dead. He then boarded the train to say his own final prayers, ignoring attempts to end the ceremonial farewell. The train left twenty minutes late.

MacSwiney's death intensified Mannix's anger against Britain. Like the executions of the Easter Rising leaders, and the Omaha meeting with de Valera, it was a pivotal moment. Instead of the measured statements, carefully crafted to derail government policy, or the mischief that he made from his arrest at sea, Mannix's speeches in late 1920 were naked expressions of emotion:

> If Ireland's cause is a just and holy one, as I believe it to be, then I think the Irish people have a right to look to me, Archbishop though I be, for something better than lip service. For I am bone of their bone and flesh of their flesh.[51]

As the English winter set in, Mannix quietened, perhaps from exhaustion. He spent December and January in Portsmouth, staying with Bishop Cotter. There was not much to do, except to walk by the cliffs of the seaport, watching the ships, the movements of the tides, the naval officers in gold braided jackets, the white and navy blue caps of the men. Mannix and Cotter had plenty to talk about, and not much to console them as they remembered their boyhood, their schooling at Fermoy in County Cork and all that had happened to Ireland in the intervening years. On 11 December, they had disastrous news. Cork City was burning. In a night of 'unimaginable terror and destruction' set off by British troops, large parts of the city were destroyed.[52]

News of de Valera was hard to get. The Irish leader who carried Mannix's best hopes was on the run, using a series of safe houses. When he visited his wife, he did not let the younger children see him; he waited till they were asleep before looking in at them. Michael Collins was able to slip in and out of London in Scarlet Pimpernel style but de Valera seems not to have risked being recognised. In fact, the British did not want him captured: despite the difficulty of pretending not to see him, it was more convenient to have him out of gaol and under surveillance.[53] Mannix's best means of conferring with de Valera was by way of one of the many Irish or Irish-Australian priests who were crossing and re-crossing the Irish Sea in late 1920. One direct link was the erratic Father Michael O'Flanagan, vice-president of Sinn Féin, who was in London in January 1921 for talks with Lloyd George.[54] Mannix would later welcome O'Flanagan to Melbourne. Father Arthur Vaughan carried a message from Mannix in his shoe, and delivered it to an unknown man in a Dublin park. While he was out, Vaughan's hotel room was ransacked by British intelligence, but nothing was taken.[55]

Mannix's speaking tours in England and Scotland were arranged by Art O'Briain, London-based head of the Irish Self-Determination League.[56] O'Briain, who was a conduit for intelligence from Ireland, helped Mannix to get news from Australia. Secure, but not free, with his base in the Hammersmith convent, Mannix was a man without a country. It was possible that he would not be allowed to re-enter Australia. He couldn't stay indefinitely in England. A desk job in Rome? That would be preposterous and Rome certainly didn't want him. 'God forbid!' said Cardinal Gasquet, when King Edward VII suggested it. 'At least in Australia he's ten thousand miles away.'[57] An Australian politician and a friend of Father Vaughan, Harold Glowrey, was asked to find out Billy Hughes' intentions. There was talk of Mannix's being barred from Australia, or admitted only on condition that he took an oath of loyalty. Glowrey sent back reassuring news. Reporting to Art O'Briain, which was safer than directing a letter to Mannix, Glowrey said that Hughes would not carry out the threat. Given Mannix's popularity in Australia, the cost in Catholic votes would be too high.[58]

Mannix left Portsmouth in mid-February 1921 for a three-week speaking tour of northern England and Scotland. These talks were meant to rouse British shame as well as expatriate fervour. At last, on 16 March 1921, he left for Rome, where he spent an edgy stay of about three weeks, wondering what Pope Benedict XV would say to him. He visited Propaganda College, an international community of students for the priesthood. Two young Australians, both destined to be archbishops, saw their famous visitor in quite different ways. Matthew Beovich, from Melbourne, was ecstatic. He urged the rector to allow a big celebration for his archbishop, but, perhaps because Mannix was likely to stir division among the students, Beovich was told that there should be 'no frills'. With or without frills, the occasion was pure delight for Beovich; he wrote in his diary that he would never forget it.[59]

By contrast, a student from the Sydney diocese, Norman Gilroy, was cool about Mannix. Before entering the priesthood he had served as a wireless operator with the Anzac forces at Gallipoli. Mannix had said that he loved Ireland above all nations. This, Gilroy thought, was wrong. Mannix should put Australia first.

Mannix would scarcely have noticed these two young men.

His mind was fixed on his audience with Pope Benedict. It was rumoured that the Vatican would make a pronouncement against Sinn Féin; if so the Archbishop of Melbourne would be in deep trouble. Mannix may not have known that the Pope's attitude towards the Irish struggle for independence had been softened by Archbishop Clune, whose first-hand report on the travails of his country was the more persuasive because of Clune's utter lack of the Mannix 'firebrand' reputation.[60] When Mannix finally met the Pope, there was no rebuke for his recent conduct. After two puzzling meetings, in which Benedict seemed deliberately to ignore the Irish question, Mannix brought matters to a head by saying that the Irish people believed Rome did not fully understand what they were suffering. Benedict, seemingly taken aback, said that the Irish cause did indeed have his sympathy. He asked what he could do to make it plain. Mannix made two suggestions: a donation to help the widows and children of the dead combatants, and an accompanying letter to express sympathy with the victims.

Pope Benedict readily agreed. He asked Mannix to draft the letter, and waited about ten minutes while Mannix sat at a side table and wrote. Even in its English version, which he was ill-equipped to understand, Benedict approved the draft. After its translation into Italian to give him a second look, the letter was translated into Latin and back into English, before being published on 22 May 1921. In spite of triple translations, the Mannix spirit survived. The great point of satisfaction (calculated to dismay the English) was that, in deploring the conflict, the Pope put the English and the Irish on equal terms. Rather than presenting the Irish as rebels, as the British did, he called the conflict a war. As Mannix's words, these would have been mild. But given voice by Pope Benedict, they were incandescent:

> We are most especially concerned about the condition of Ireland...we do not perceive how this bitter strife can profit either of the parties, when property and homes are being ruthlessly and disgracefully laid waste, when villages and farmsteads are being set aflame, when neither sacred places nor sacred persons are spared, when on both sides a war resulting in the deaths of unarmed peoples, even of women and children, is carried on. We exhort English as well as Irish to calmly consider...some means of mutual agreement.[61]

'This,' Mannix said later, 'was the closest I ever came to writing an Encyclical.'[62]

On his last night in Rome, Mannix dined with the influential Cardinal Cerretti. News of the death of William Walsh, Archbishop of Dublin, on 9 April, had just reached them. In 1913, when he left for Melbourne, Mannix was thought the man most likely to be Walsh's successor. Eight years on, he had wrecked his own career. A disruptive force in Australia, an anti-British agitator in the United States, and a nightmare to the British government, he must have known then that his only chance of going back to Ireland depended on peace with Britain and the ascendancy of de Valera. These were just remotely possible. Predictably, the Vatican appointed a safe man in Dublin, Walsh's coadjutor, Edward Byrne, a moderate nationalist who could be trusted not to make matters worse.

With the Vatican audience behind him, it was time for Mannix to return to Melbourne. Although he had been away from his duties for eleven months, he was in no hurry. From Rome, he went to Lourdes, and to the battlefields of France where Australian soldiers had died. Back again to England for two more weeks—did he hope to see Ireland after all? Or to be included in peace talks between de Valera and Lloyd George?

It was late May 1921 when Mannix and his secretary Arthur Vaughan at last sailed for Melbourne, and even then he took his time. Rather than take the usual route via Suez to Melbourne, Mannix chose a roundabout voyage, embarking from Marseilles on a Japanese ship, the *Kleist* (formerly German) that took him via Hong Kong, Shanghai and Yokohama to Manila where the Mannix party changed to the *Nikko Maru*. This meant more days at sea and, for Mannix, more seasickness to endure. The week in Yokahama was a respite. Mannix went to Tokyo to visit Terence MacSwiney's sister Kit, a nun who was then teaching in a girls' school. The chance to see her may have influenced Mannix's choice of homeward route. It is possible that he was honouring a promise to the dying man. Because many prelates saw a hunger strike as suicide, McSwiney's sister would have needed all the comfort and reassurance that Mannix could give her.

There were strategic advantages in avoiding what was then known as the Empire route, or Red route, with stops at Aden, Bombay and Ceylon. It would be hard for the British government to maintain surveillance. The choice of Japanese ships was a shrewd move. Japan had been an ally of Britain in the First World War, but its government wouldn't take kindly to a British intrusion on the *Kleist* or the *Nikko Mauru.* If Hughes were to carry out his threat to exclude Mannix or make him take an oath of loyalty to the Crown, he would have to do it when the archbishop first stepped onto Australian soil. And that, thanks to Mannix's ingenious travel plan, was on Thursday Island. An arrest on this little outpost would have been at least as comical as the 'Pirate of Penzance' episode.

Mannix went on by sea to Townsville and then to Brisbane, where he was welcomed on the wharf by Archbishop Duhig. Bishop McCarthy of Sandhurst and Mannix's administrator, Father Barry, came north to offer a welcome from Victoria, as did John Wren and Patrick Cody. Mannix had a few days rest before appearing in public with Archbishop Duhig. He then travelled by train from Brisbane to Sydney, where the crowds were out as they had been in 1920. Queensland and New South Wales Catholics waved green flags as Mannix's train slowed down to pass through little country stations. John Wren, who came on from Brisbane with Patrick Cody, arranged for more 'swooping planes' overhead as Mannix arrived in Sydney. The whole triumphal progress down the east coast was Catholic Australia's 'Hands off Our Dan' signal to Billy Hughes. A west coast arrival by way of Perth, whether by sea on the Great Australian Bight, or by train across the desert, would have done nothing to demonstrate the Catholic strength. Sydney put on a good show. After a *Te Deum* thanksgiving service in St Mary's Cathedral, arranged by Archbishop Kelly, Mannix was farewelled by a massive crowd at Central Station, and a forest of green ribbons and rosettes.

Mannix reached Melbourne on 11 August 1921. He had been away for fifteen months. The welcome from Catholics—or most of them—was as ecstatic as if he had brought news of peace to Ireland. Hughes and other opponents obliged him with more talk of sedition and deportation. Nothing had changed, except Mannix himself. A weary old man accepted the gift of his own portrait by Max Meldrum. He said he was glad to have a reminder that he once was better looking. It sounds like a Mannix joke, but as he stood beside the portrait of his vigorous former self, it would have been hard for anyone to laugh.

Back in Melbourne, Mannix had a great deal to think about. What had been gained from his year-long campaign for Irish freedom? The country was still torn apart. The list of men and women in English and Irish gaols was still growing. Murders and executions with minimal semblance of justice were being repaid in brutal reprisals. The Irish economy was a wreck. Although Britain was losing heart for the struggle, there was still no clear road to peace. Mannix's American tour and his arrest at sea had added to his celebrity, but what use was that? Father John Barry and the rest of the team at St Patrick's Cathedral had shown how well they could manage without him. And his hero's return, as Mannix knew very well, was in large measure a product of their organising skills.

The huge crowds that welcomed the archbishop back to Melbourne hadn't assembled on an impulse of devotion. Religious fervour, tribal loyalty and the enjoyment of a day out combined to make the whole weekend a magnificent *Mannixfest*, done to timetable. Not for the first time, the parish structure made it happen. When Mannix arrived by train from Sydney at 3 p.m. on Saturday 13 August 1921, the shops had closed, city streets were empty, and workers were free. With the precision of a military operation, Melbourne's Catholics took their places along the route from Spencer Street station to St Patrick's Cathedral, waving green flags and singing 'Come Back to Australia'. The numbers and the timing were worked out well in advance at the cathedral; the parish priests passed on instructions at Sunday masses, and in case anyone missed out on the plan of welcome, they had only to look it up in the *Advocate*. The archbishop's open motor car was followed by a procession of cars from which visiting archbishops and bishops looked out and waved, as did Mannix.[63]

The returning archbishop could take some satisfaction from the vigour of the Melbourne church. The strategic map drawn up for his welcome home showed how well the parish structure was integrated. The placing of 'Strong Posts' on Mannix's route to St Patrick's Cathedral was in effect a map of Melbourne parishes. Thirty-six posts were chosen, to which sixty-six parishes sent members. Larger parishes filled their posts single-handed. Collingwood Catholics were given the important Town Hall spot. Carlton took the high ground at the south corner of Exhibition and Collins Streets, looking across to the combined Flemington and Kensington force on the north side. At Strong Post Number 30, Glenhuntly, Caulfield, Malvern East and Oakleigh were also combined. There was a Strong Post for South Yarra, which had a substantial working-class component but none for upper-class Toorak. The old-established Jesuit parish of Richmond got a good place at the top of the hill, close to St Patrick's and opposite Kew, the parish that encompassed Raheen.

Next morning, the archbishop was on view again with all the ceremony of a Sunday High Mass at St Patrick's: music, incense, procession, flowers. And on Monday night the welcome was completed with more singing and speeches at the Exhibition Building. Again, there was a big splash of purple. The archbishops of Wellington, Sydney, Adelaide and Hobart were there, as were the bishops and monsignori of Goulburn, Armidale, Port Augusta, Ballarat, Sandhurst (Bendigo), Wagga Wagga and Wilcannia-Forbes.

When it was all over and Daniel Mannix was alone again at Raheen, what did he think it of it all? He was clear-sighted enough to know that the hero's welcome came from good teamwork, the public's need for a focus and the drama of his excursion into the wider world. There was admiration, certainly, and a kind of love for the archbishop in whose public persona Ireland and the Catholic Church were entwined. But, as he climbed the stairs to his austere quarters in his huge, empty house, was he warmed by the popular acclaim? Just as Raheen's high fences kept out intruders, Daniel Mannix held his own counsel.

CHAPTER EIGHT

HOME TIES

FROM THE TIME of his return to Melbourne, Mannix waited impatiently for reports from Ireland. Late in 1921 he received news of a truce in the war against Britain. Between October and December, a series of meetings was held in London to discuss the terms on which a treaty of independence might be reached. In a strange and controversial decision, de Valera refused to be a member of the Irish delegation. He kept himself aloof from the crucial decision: to sign or not to sign on the best terms that could be won from the formidable British government team led by Prime Minister Lloyd George, Winston Churchill, Austen Chamberlain and Lord Birkenhead. Against these were set the inexperienced and battle-worn Irish delegates Arthur Griffith, Michael Collins, George Gavan Duffy, Eamon Duggan and Robert Barton, with the austere and uncompromising republican Anglo-Irishman Erskine Childers as secretary and advisor.

The Irish delegates, divided as to what they should accept, were placed under intolerable strain. They were offered concessions: their own parliament, their own army. Rather than be called a Dominion, like Australia and Canada, their title would be Irish Free State. But on other key issues they lost. The oath of loyalty to the King of England remained. More important, the treaty in effect accepted partition and failed to safeguard Irish Catholics in the north. Griffith and Collins believed that the terms were as good as they could hope for. Collins spoke of 'stepping stones' to full independence. The oath, he said, was sugar-coating on the pill that the British would have to swallow.[1] Gavan Duffy and Duggan dissented. The casting vote went to Robert Barton, an Anglo-Irish landowner and committed republican who had been imprisoned by the British. Lloyd George turned the full force of his dramatic personality on Barton. Holding up two envelopes, both addressed to the British military commander Sir James Craig, he announced that one of them would go by special train to Holyhead and then by destroyer to Belfast. He would break the truce. 'If I send *this* letter it is war—and war within three days,' he said.[2] After hesitations and discussion with the other delegates, Barton signed, but he later retracted an agreement made under duress.

De Valera, who had expected to control the delegation in absentia, was angry. By staying in Dublin while the London talks were held, he intended to keep a statesmanlike distance, ready to give final judgment. This was control without responsibility or, as a biographer described it, 'wanting his bread buttered on both sides'.[3] Accusing the delegates of exceeding their powers, de Valera argued that without the consent of the Irish people, the treaty was not binding. He was not satisfied with the gains that had been made in the London talks, even though these included the departure of

British troops after seven hundred years of occupation. But when the treaty was referred to the Dáil, it was endorsed, though by a small majority.

For de Valera and others, the treaty was a betrayal of the living and the dead. It left Ireland within the British Empire and ceded the six counties of the north, in which Catholics would face persecution. The Free State would have no independent foreign policy; its defences would be effectively in British hands.[4] De Valera resigned as president, Arthur Griffith took his place, and Michael Collins became chairman of the new provisional government. Civil war followed. Collins took command of the Free State Army and de Valera headed the opposing side. It was warfare, with the added heartbreak of setting Irishmen against their brothers, and bitterly dividing families. The Irish Free State could arrest and execute—and it did. Sinn Féin did the same.

Quietly or openly, the overseas Irish took sides. Mannix backed de Valera with his usual single-minded vigour. Duhig, Kelly and most of the other Irish-Australian bishops saw the Free State as the legitimate authority and the best way to peace. They followed the lead of the Irish bishops who met at Maynooth in April 1922 and welcomed 'the freedom [the treaty] brings us for the first time in seven hundred years'. The bishops conceded that 'every Irishman is entitled to his own opinion' but gave the ruling that to oppose the treaty by violence was 'a grave matter of conscience'.

Membership of the anti-treaty forces was not yet grounds for excommunication but it soon would be. De Valera's excommunication in April 1923 did not lessen Mannix's support. Nor did it appear to trouble de Valera who brushed off the Pope's edict as if it were a mere formality: 'Though nominally cut away from the body of Holy Church,' he wrote, 'we are still spiritually and mystically part of it and we refuse to regard ourselves except as his children.'[5]

It was hard for Mannix to get first-hand news of de Valera or a personal view of the Irish scene. His mail was still being censored and telegrams were seized. An informal talk with Archbishop Duhig was all but ruled out by the distance from Brisbane and the opposing views of the two prelates. Yet Duhig had much to tell. He was in Ireland in August 1922 when Arthur Griffith, worn out from the strain of the treaty and the renewed warfare, died from a heart attack. Michael Collins was photographed kissing Duhig's ring at Griffith's funeral. A few days later there was another funeral. Duhig was there again with the new Archbishop of Dublin, Edward Byrne, both of them mourning the death by assassination of Michael Collins. Duhig blamed de Valera for leading a 'futile and destructive' campaign. Australia, he said, would have no sympathy for the anti-treaty forces.[6]

Mannix took the opposing view. He couldn't have known all the complexities of the negotiations. He had placed his faith in de Valera, and that was that. He may have been right, but to throw his weight behind de Valera without full knowledge of the situation looks like arrogance. As with other choices Mannix made, it put idealism before realism.[7]

Mannix's best source of insight into the condition of Ireland came by chance in March 1923. Home at Raheen at the end of the day he found a little package of papers and photographs. One of the Jesuits from Xavier College had called: a Father William Hackett. Newly arrived from Ireland, he came with an aura of mystery. No one quite knew why he had been sent to Australia. Whether it was for his own safety or for the reputation of the Jesuit order, it was certain that Hackett's politics had got him into trouble. He was close to de Valera and Erskine Childers; he had known the two dead leaders, Michael Collins and Arthur Griffith. Unusual among the Irish Jesuits of the time, Hackett took the anti-treaty side. And he left Ireland just after the Irish bishops spoke out against de Valera. Mannix read Hackett's message and wrote at once with warmth and sympathy for a fellow exile:

> I am sorry that I was out when you called. You will come another time and we shall sit by the rivers of Babylon and weep, when we remember Sion.

That was the beginning of one of Mannix's few close friendships. William Hackett, then in his forties, came from a big family in Kilkenny where his father, a doctor and friend of Parnell, had been in trouble with the Irish clergy because of his radical politics. Dr Hackett cheerfully ignored clerical disapproval and sent his six sons to Ireland's most expensive boarding school, Clongowes, where the Jesuits were charmed into educating all six for nothing.

As his journals and letters show, William Hackett was happy in his priestly life. He knew, when he joined the Jesuits in 1895, that he might spend a lifetime teaching schoolboys. Yet wherever he was posted, he found ways to connect with the wider world. His ideas about social justice brought him into contact with Ireland's political activists. He shared a platform with Pádraig Pearse, and had other friends among those who, like Pearse, were executed after the Easter Rising. Through his father, and because of his wide interests and gift for friendship, Hackett was made welcome in republican circles, both Catholic and Protestant. He was part of the inner circle at Glendalough, County Wicklow, the home of Robert Barton and his sister Da (Dulcibella). Hackett and Da

Barton became couriers for the illegal newssheet edited by the Bartons' cousin, Erskine Childers. Childers and de Valera were Hackett's heroes. He kept a dangerous rendezvous with Childers in Donegal in July 1922, and he heard the confessions of 'irregulars' who were holed up in Glenveigh Castle.

Less controversial but equally risky were Hackett's travels with a camera, recording British atrocities, and his fact-finding missions for the non-denominational relief organisation, the White Cross. His last act before accepting exile in Australia had been to seek out Michael Collins, presumably in the hope of reconciling him with de Valera. A friendly letter from Collins—the last he ever wrote—reached Hackett too late. Collins was murdered the next day.[8] Within the week Hackett was on his way to Australia, carrying the Collins letter in a trunkful of subversive papers. All this and more Hackett recounted at Raheen. He brought a record of the treaty negotiations written by Robert Barton for Mannix, smuggled out of gaol and typed hastily and in secret just before Hackett sailed.

Mannix and Hackett needed one another in these tragic times of civil war in Ireland. Mannix fretted at being so far from home—Ireland was still home to him—and cut off from the centre where history was being made. Hackett was desolate at the loss of friends, especially Erskine Childers and fellow republican leader Liam Mellows who were executed by Free State troops in November 1922. He was ashamed at being safe in Melbourne while others were dying every day in Ireland in the service of the republican ideal. He felt isolated at Xavier College where he was teaching French to bored fourteen-year-olds, and where his colleagues avoided talk of politics: 'Mum is the word about all Irish movements—no one cares.'[9] Rescue came when Mannix took up the idea of establishing a city library for the intellectually under-nourished Catholics of the time, and made Hackett its director. Transferred to the Richmond parish from Xavier, where his superior had censored his mail, Hackett was free to keep up his Irish correspondence and relay news to Mannix.

The Free State was accepted by many—perhaps most—Irish-Australians, and by most of the general public. When Mannix protested on behalf of de Valera, then in gaol, and spoke of deplorable prison conditions, there was a testy response in the *Sydney Morning Herald* correspondence columns: 'Australians really do not care what happens to de Valera. A few Sinn Féiners, in safety out of Ireland, are alone responsible for utterly misleading statements to the contrary.'[10]

As long as the Irish civil war continued, it dominated Mannix's public life. In March 1923, he welcomed two Irish republican delegates, Father Michael O'Flanagan and J. J. O'Kelly, whom Duhig refused to meet. The two were later deported, after a failed High Court appeal, partly funded by Mannix, in which a promising young barrister Herbert Evatt was the junior brief. The Irish envoys' presence in Melbourne on St Patrick's Day provided the occasion for a forthright Mannix speech. He denounced the bias in press reporting on the Irish situation. British and American newspapers, he said, had concealed the truth about the execution of Erskine Childers and Liam Mellows in Free State gaols. And he used the occasion, once again, to praise de Valera: 'a man who deserves our respect and our homage, no matter how much we differ in some things, if, indeed any of us differ from him at all'.[11]

In May 1923, de Valera ordered his followers to put down their arms. But the conflict was not over. The first general election under the Free State's constitution was shadowed by violence on both sides. Many republicans were still in gaol and de Valera, who had been on the run, was arrested while addressing an election meeting. Held for more than a year as a threat to public safety, de Valera emerged from gaol as resolute as ever, and looking for a way to bring his Sinn Féin party out of the political wilderness. As long as he and his followers refused to take the oath of allegiance to the crown and enter the Dáil, Sinn Féin would continue to win seats to no purpose. It was stalemate in Ireland, and, in Melbourne, Mannix could do nothing to help.

On tour in Tasmania in April 1923, Mannix took care to place himself as an Australian by adoption, well aware of its history. He spoke of convicts from Ireland who had been exiled to Tasmania, and he praised the Anzac heroes.[12] But he always returned to the present state of Ireland to insist that a false peace had been proclaimed by a government that served England, and that de Valera would be vindicated.

Daniel Mannix saw Ireland for the last time in 1925, after an absence of twelve years. When the Pope declared 1925 a Holy Year, the Australian bishops decided to sponsor a pilgrimage to Rome and other holy places. Generously—for he had been a trial to most of them—the bishops invited Mannix to lead it. It may have been a gesture of sympathy for his exclusion from Ireland in 1920; it is likely also to be the bishops' recognition that many pilgrims would line up to go with Mannix, who was by far the most charismatic of them all.

One hundred and seventy-two pilgrims, part of a larger group, set off from Melbourne on the *Mongolia* on Easter Monday 1925. They were led by Mannix, with Father Arthur Vaughan, the affable companion of his 1920 travels, acting again as his secretary.[13] They disembarked at Marseilles and visited Lourdes, Avignon,

Nice and Genoa. In Rome at the end of May, the Pope gave a private audience to Mannix and a public one to his group. De Valera made a quick trip to Rome. There was no chance that the Irish Free State government would let him have a passport, so, as he had often done before, he travelled in disguise. One of the Holy Ghost fathers lent his passport to de Valera, who dressed as a priest and merged into the Vatican scene.

In and out of gaol, members of de Valera's party still had support; they won votes in the Free State elections but they couldn't enter the Dáil unless they backtracked on their vow never to take the oath of allegiance to the crown. Mannix was to be the circuit-breaker: his visit to Ireland, planned in Rome, was designed to help de Valera's followers accept a new political strategy and come in out of the cold. De Valera and Mannix had not met since their American tours of 1920, and their correspondence was limited by surveillance of Mannix's mail, de Valera's stints in gaol, and his strategic sense as a politician. A surviving letter of 1921 shows de Valera more cautious than Mannix: he had 'wanted to run across to see [Mannix]' in England but knew that such a meeting would be misunderstood. Now he suggested that Mannix come to Ireland without the pilgrims, as a private individual.[14]

De Valera should have known better. Mannix took no notice.[15] He was determined to come back to Ireland as an archbishop and to bring his pilgrims with him. As in London in 1920, he hoped to play a mediating role in Irish politics, especially by opening up discussions on the oath, that stumbling block for church and state. If he had come in quietly to Ireland in 1925 he could have met the Irish bishops. By refusing discretion he made this impossible. He must have known how disastrously he was wedging the Irish hierarchy. Having excommunicated those who still waged war for the republicans, they could not publicly welcome a republican archbishop.

The pilgrimage made its leisurely way across Europe to London. Mannix went to Portsmouth to stay with Bishop Cotter, in whose company he relived the experiences of 1920. He needed a rest. As in 1920, the press commented on his haggard appearance, 'though he is only about sixty'.[16]

Mannix landed in Ireland on 29 June 1925. There was a big crowd at the railway station, where 'ten thousand throats roared and there was a blizzard of waving handkerchiefs'.[17] Romantic Ireland was there to meet him. Maud Gonne MacBride, the legendary muse of W. B. Yeats and widow of one of the 1916 martyrs, was still a dramatic figure in her black draperies. With her was Constance Gore-Booth, the Countess Markievicz, whose legend lives in the Yeats poem, 'On a Political Prisoner'. But the Archbishop of Dublin, Dr Edward Byrne, was missing, and there was no welcome from the Irish bishops as a group. A dour letter from Byrne, sent to Mannix in Rome, had spelt it out. Mannix would not be invited to stay at the Palace in Dublin unless he promised not to make any contentious speeches. Mannix's reply was to have rooms booked at Dublin's best hotel, the Shelbourne. He had already arranged for Sinn Féin to manage all his speaking engagements.[18] Having taken his depleted flock of Australian pilgrims—only ninety out of the original two hundred and forty-three—to Killarney, he left them at Cork and went on to Charleville.

Daniel Mannix paid the full price of his intransigence. Although he stayed four months in Ireland, no one invited him to Maynooth, and the only bishop to visit him—his former vice-president at Maynooth, Robert Browne, Bishop of Cloyne—came discreetly at night, unseen. A few old friends, including Browne, invited him to stay. Their invitations were alike in offering peace and quiet, and pleasant drives in the countryside. Bishop Browne, Archbishop Gilmartin of Tuam and Bishop MacRory of Down and Connor all begged Mannix to come and rest. Mannix may have interpreted these kind letters as a hint that he was welcome only if he kept quiet. He hadn't come to Ireland for a holiday, and he had no intention of being quiet. Sinn Féin was organising big meetings throughout the country. His role was to give new heart to the dispirited republicans and at the same time to chip away at their leaders' resistance to taking the oath.[19] This pragmatic approach was a new one for Mannix but he had had a long time to wait and think about the consequences of doing nothing.

Going home to Charleville was painful. He was too late to see his mother. She had died early that year, and although there had been a big crowd at her funeral, the only bishop to attend was Dr Cotter from Portsmouth. The dominant figure at the church, Eamon de Valera, stood alone, looking the embodiment of mourning in his long dark overcoat and tall black hat. The Mannix family snubbed him. When de Valera asked if he could have the honour of being one of the coffin-bearers, Timothy Mannix refused: the arrangements, he said, were already made. De Valera was not invited back to the house after the burial.[20]

Family divisions over politics could be left unspoken but they weren't forgotten. Timothy Mannix and Mary Wallis, who met their brother in Cork and drove back to Charleville with him, took different sides politically. Mary's marriage into a family with a history of radical nationalism, made her a natural ally.[21] Unexpectedly, the townspeople gave Mannix a welcome:

> It was darkening, with a light mist-like rain falling, when the people of Charleville walked out of town to greet a

> native son…[they] formed a torchlight procession, with turf dipped in kerosene, held aloft on pitchforks, leading the Archbishop to his native Charleville which he had not seen since 1912. The crowd cheered and sang as the procession moved slowly, with jostling and joking, on the way to the Church…
>
> The party was in for a nasty shock when it reached the church. While the town was aglow with bonfires and with makeshift festive lighting the church was locked and in complete darkness.[22]

The crowd hung about awkwardly for a short time and then went home. Two of the three local priests had prudently gone on retreat and the third, taking no chances of his bishop's disapproval, had locked up and taken an early night. For the rest of his stay with Mary Wallis and her family, Mannix said his morning mass at the convent of the Sisters of Mercy, where the nuns were braver.

The contrast between the torchlight procession and the closed church in Charleville symbolised for Mannix the state of Ireland. Writing some years later in response to a rebuke from the Vatican, he spelled out his thinking. He believed that if the Irish bishops could not support the full national aspirations of the people, their best course was 'to discountenance violence and then allow the Irish people to work out their own political salvation, as they were quite capable of doing'. Mannix deplored the control exercised by the bishops. He had ample evidence in his stay of 1925 that 'no priest could dare to take an independent view without the risk of displeasing his Bishop'.[23] His own policy of refusing to censor his priests in Melbourne was reinforced by this experience.

Daniel's relationship with Timothy was edgy. Before leaving for Melbourne, Daniel had paid £1000 to settle his brother's debts and save Deerpark, but the gift hadn't helped. Timothy was deep in debt again and drinking heavily. A neighbour sent the archbishop an embarrassing plea to repay money Timothy owed her.[24] There were other bills. Timothy hadn't been content to work the farm, so recently reclaimed from the landlord. Breeding racehorses, following the hunt and generally living above his means, he was close to bankruptcy. Timothy's daughter Mary, a nurse, followed by her brother Denis, had already started a chain migration of Mannixes to New York. Soon Timothy and his wife, Helena, would be living in an East Side tenement and, like Denis, Timothy would take a series of low-paid jobs.

Daniel Mannix paid for a handsome family monument in the Newton Shandrum cemetery, where his parents, his aunt Lizzie and his youngest brother, Michael, were buried. This was arranged by his nephew Jack Wallis, a Charleville doctor, who admired Uncle Dan, and shared his allegiance to the de Valera cause. The degree of Mannix's isolation from his family has been exaggerated. As well as meeting Timothy's debts more than once, he paid expenses for Timothy's eldest son Michael (later a priest) and he was ready to help Mary Wallis's younger sons Edmond and Michael. One of the nieces was invited to join the party of Australian pilgrims; others sent family news to 'dearest Uncle Dan'.[25] This younger-generation affection, however, did not outweigh some dismal facts: Deerpark was lost; Timothy would soon be a struggling middle-aged migrant in New York; Patrick had married into the English upper class; and there were only distant memories of Michael and his early death.

Mannix had the satisfaction of huge crowds as he made his

way around Ireland, but he also saw blinds drawn in disapproval. Some parish priests forbade their curates to attend any Mannix function, but a big 'night of the priests' in Dublin showed that the Irish church was not of one mind. Visiting the Anglo-Irish landowner Robert Barton in Wicklow, Mannix was greeted warmly. Barton, the reluctant signer of the treaty, wrote to William Hackett in Melbourne:

> [Dr Mannix] spent 2 or three hours chatting with us. I like him very much, character, manner, appearance, everything. He requires no armour plate of formality to preserve his dignity. The Ministers and Bishops, lacking the qualities that go with breeding, have treated him with discourtesy. His politics do not matter in the circumstances. He is a great dignitary of his church.[26]

But his politics did matter. He left Ireland after four months of political campaigning, interspersed with periods of rest with his sister's family and private meetings with de Valera and a few senior churchmen. It is likely that his presence heartened the republicans, and it seems certain that he helped with de Valera's decision that his party members should compromise on the oath and take their places in the Dáil. When Mannix sailed for Melbourne in November 1925, de Valera was his one big investment in the future of an Ireland he would never see again. Personally, the visit had been painful; the rebuff of the bishops, the closed gates at Maynooth, and the divisions within his family were much harder to take than any of the political attacks he had experienced. 'I'll not give [the bishops] a chance to insult me a second time,' he told his cousin John Cagney.[27]

Mannix did not give up his campaign to make Irish freedom an international issue, and he continued to raise money for the republicans from wealthy Australians such as the Countess Freehill, one of the 1925 pilgrim group.[28] His involvement with Ireland would be from a distance, with de Valera, the embodiment of his hopes, twelve thousand miles away, and his own family fragmented.

When Mary Wallis died in October 1930, Daniel Mannix lost his only strong emotional link with home. Her house, near Charleville, had been his fortress in 1925; in between his fiery speeches on the Sinn Féin trail he retreated there for undemanding company. If anyone knew his mind, his sister did. He had written to her every week—letters which he must have asked her to destroy—and sent her the weekly *Advocate*, in which his doings were always front-page news. While the three Mannix brothers led their separate lives, Mary was the link between them. Timothy's down-at-heel existence in New York in the midst of his struggling migrant family contrasted with Patrick's affluence in upper middle-class England with a rich wife and a cherished only son. Although—or perhaps because—Daniel Mannix had helped Timothy financially more than once, relations between the brothers were cool. 'There's always one fool in a family,' Timothy remarked when he heard that Daniel had refused John Wren's offer of a £50,000 testimonial gift in 1920. In 1928, when Timothy had followed his daughter Mary and son Denis to New York, Daniel may have decided that he had done all he could.[29] The ebullient Timothy had worked as an auctioneer in Cork. New York brought a sharp drop in status. The family had a hard time in the Depression. Denis sold rail tickets; Timothy worked as a grocery assistant. Neither he nor Patrick, the Lancaster doctor and alderman, had much in common with their brother the archbishop.

Alienated from Patrick and Timothy, Daniel did his best for his sister Mary and her family. Her six sons faced the usual problems of young Irishmen in a struggling economy. The eldest son, Patrick, joined the Holy Ghost order, and spent some years in missionary work in Africa.[30] Timothy Charles, the second son, volunteered for service in World War I, reached the rank of lieutenant, and won the Military Cross in France in 1917.[31] He did not go back to Ireland; after qualifying as an engineer he settled in Reigate, Surrey, with his wife, Cynthia, as thoroughly Anglicised as his uncle Patrick Mannix.

Next came Jack, the Charleville doctor whose surviving letters show his pride in his Uncle Dan. Ned Wallis, the fourth son, joined the archbishop on part of his 1925 tour. Like Jack and the fifth son, Michael, Ned was committed to the de Valera leadership. That allegiance, and being nephew to the archbishop, wasn't necessarily an advantage in 1920s Ireland. The youngest Wallis boy, George, whose education did not continue past primary school, went to the United States where, like one of Timothy's sons, he worked as a jockey. Their only sister, Ella, was a nurse at St Vincent's Hospital in Dublin before her marriage in 1946.

Mannix brought two of the younger Wallis boys to Australia. He took charge of Michael, who as a schoolboy in 1920 had run away from home to join the fight against British forces, and sent him to Newman College in 1925, aged nineteen, to study arts and law. The rector, Jeremiah Murphy SJ, reported to Mannix, then in Ireland, that having been homesick, unhappy and uncommunicative in his first term, Michael was learning to like his new country.[32] As soon as Michael qualified in law, Mannix bought him a partnership with one of his Newman friends, law graduate (later judge) Frank Field.

Field had his main practice in the outer suburb of Dandenong. Michael took charge of a small, well-placed city office at 100 Queen Street. Melbourne's Irish nationalist circles welcomed the archbishop's nephew, and Michael became secretary and president of the Victorian (later Australian) Irish Association.[33] He worked briefly with Arthur Calwell's wife on the *Irish Review*, established in early 1933.[34] Mannix showed his confidence in Michael in 1934 when he chose Field and Wallis to represent the Melbourne archdiocese in a big case over a disputed will. Robert Menzies KC was briefed to lead, and Michael's friend Gregory Gowans was his junior.[35] The case, which was lost on appeal at the High Court, would have kept Michael busy for two years. Living in expensive Toorak, he was seen at Newman College functions, where he was known for his beautiful voice and his affable manner.[36] Mannix must have had high expectations.

The Fields thought Michael was lonely; they often invited him to their house for their Sunday roast dinner. The Field children loved him. 'He made a great fuss of me and my sister and brought us presents,' Pamela Field said.[37] Then Frank Field discovered that money was missing from the firm's trust fund. A sad story unravelled. Michael, who was often seen at the races, had big gambling debts and was drinking heavily. Field had no choice but to tell Mannix. The archbishop repaid the firm so that no client suffered, or even suspected, the theft, which at that time was not mandatory to report.[38]

As a disgraced thirty-five year old, how did Michael face Uncle Dan? By now it was wartime. Michael joined the army as a private in June 1940. 'Archbishop's Nephew Enlists', the press reported. But after only six weeks in training camp he went absent without leave and was found drunk. This was the first of a dozen episodes that showed him unfit for service. In a series of hospital admissions, psychiatric as well as physical illnesses were diagnosed and he was discharged from the forces in 1941. He was still on the electoral roll in 1942, living in Port Fairy, perhaps on a remittance from Mannix, and he remained on the Victorian *Law List* until 1946. After that he disappeared from the public record in Australia. His scattered family heard that Michael died alone in 1968 in a bush shack, having become a hermit and a 'metho drinker'. Police identified him by papers found on his body.[39] He never asked for any help, his sister Ella said, and he never wrote home. There was, in any case, no family centre in Ireland. Jack Wallis, the only one of Mary's six sons to stay at home, had died in 1935 from pneumonia after a short career in medical practice in Charleville.

Mannix might have seen signs of Michael's unhappiness and addiction: if so, he was helpless. His own isolation from Ireland would have hit hard at this time, as would his lack of close friends in Melbourne. There was no one who could fully share his distress. Daniel Foley, Bishop of Ballarat, who had shadowed his brilliant cousin at Maynooth, was Mannix's chosen companion on the voyage out in 1913, in the United States and on the *Baltic* in 1920. The cousins had shared a holiday at Lorne in 1913, and when Mannix visited the dying Terence MacSwiney in Brixton Prison, Dan Foley was with him. But by the time Michael Wallis's story was reaching its sad climax in his army service, Dan Foley was critically ill; he died in November 1941. Jeremiah Murphy would have understood Michael Wallis's tragedy, but Mannix would have been a hard man to comfort. On Michael's side there may have been too much idealisation for closeness. As a nineteen-year-old, writing to his brother Jack from Newman College, he had called his Uncle Dan 'one of the very few bright stars in this present generation of hypocrisy and sham', 'loved and venerated' by his fellow countrymen.[40]

Ned Wallis, known as Eddie in Australia, had a happier life than his brother, though an undistinguished one. When Ned arrived in 1927, Mannix found him a job as station hand on Warwie Station, in Balranald, New South Wales. Working for the Connellan family under tough conditions, he was watched over by the parish priest, Father Killian, brother of Mannix's friend Archbishop Andrew Killian of Adelaide. Eddie kept his ill-paid job as a casually employed station hand for some years. He lived in Balranald where he joined in local activities, gave donations from his small means to local charities, fired the starter's pistol at a race meeting, and collected firewood for the hospital. A big man with a hearty laugh, Eddie Wallis was known for his friendliness.[41] He went droving in the 1930s drought years and was in court for trespass when some of his flock strayed. Having enlisted in the army in 1942, he reached the rank of sergeant after much effort: his war records show him as a plodder, struggling to attain each skill. He went back to Balranald for a few years after the war, before moving to Colac where he became a herd tester.[42] Neither in Colac nor in Balranald did he make much of his relationship to Mannix.

Mannix tried to keep track of the nephews, even visiting distant Balranald in the 1930s on the pretext of attending a school opening for Father Killian, whose diocese was Wilcannia-Forbes in New South Wales.[43] He may have blamed himself for unsettling these two wanderers, who were naïve young Sinn Féiners in 1920, the year he was debarred from entering Ireland. If either one had founded a family in Australia it would have given the archbishop the base in everyday life that he never had. Notionally he was father to his flock in Melbourne, with special paternal care for his priests. In practice, for most of them, he was a remote figure, seen on public occasions, revered by many, but too distant to be loved except by the few who had the confidence or the special need to seek him out.

CHAPTER NINE

THE PERMISSIVE AUTOCRAT

BY THE 1930s, Daniel Mannix's course was set. Melbourne was his centre. There was no going back to Ireland, and he had only distant connections with Rome. His *ad limina* visits to the Pope, due every ten years, lapsed, presumably by his own choice, after 1925. There was a big Eucharistic Congress in Dublin in 1932, to which he was not invited. That must have hurt. Even de Valera, who had formed a new party, Fianna Fáil, and won government with Labour Party support in 1932, didn't want Mannix to come and upset the precarious balance.

At home in Melbourne Mannix kept his distance from churchmen of other denominations, and from Government House. In 1919, for no special reason, he had chosen to attack the non-conformists for their 'blank and gloomy' Sunday observance, with any form of 'rational amusement' forbidden.[1] No one should be expected to pray all day, he said. An acerbic exchange with the Anglican Archbishop Head in 1934 shows no sign of ecumenism. They clashed on the question of a Sunday Eucharistic procession in Sunbury, north-west of Melbourne. Mannix seemingly paid no respect to the consciences of those who opposed Sunday travelling.[2]

Anyone brave enough to invite Mannix to dinner, whether to a presbytery or private house, got a polite refusal. He wasn't convivial; he liked to see people on his own terms, out walking, or at Raheen where anyone could get an appointment at short notice just by phoning the housekeeper. Mannix did not do visitations, the formal tours of inspection that showed an archbishop how the parishes and religious houses were doing. These were occasions to look and question, praise or rebuke, even count the altar candles or check the holy water font. Mannix thought that they were a waste of energy. When his under-employed coadjutor, Archbishop Simonds, decided to fill his empty diary with a round of visitations, Mannix waited sceptically for the results. 'They all seem to be doing very well, Your Grace,' Simonds reported. 'Good,' said Mannix. 'That's what happens when you leave them alone.'[3]

The policy of non-interference went further. Mannix never dropped in on his parish priests, or even called on them by appointment. When he came to a parish to give the sacrament of confirmation (a duty only a bishop could perform) he was greeted at the church entrance, taken to the sacristy to put on his vestments, and on to the altar. It was usually a long ceremony, and especially so when Mannix gave the adolescents his usual sermon on the dangers of alcohol. Afterwards, he would thank the parish priest and step into the shining motor that took him back to Raheen. No tea and cakes in the presbytery; no time to chat with the priest.

Those who had the best chance of observing Mannix were the priests at St Patrick's and nearby St John's, East Melbourne, who used to have lunch at the archbishop's table. Father John Brosnan, appointed by Mannix as chaplain to Pentridge Prison, was a curate at St John's in 1945 and returned there in 1956, when his chaplaincy began. Brosnan, the 'knockabout priest', friend to derelicts and criminals, a vigorous anti-hanging campaigner in the Ronald Ryan case, revered Mannix:

> Dr Mannix was the only person, man, woman or child, I have known in my life I couldn't take my eyes off. His every movement was worth watching, his every word worth hearing. I could watch Don Bradman bat or Polly Farmer move in a football field and I could watch Dr Mannix drink his soup...You realised you were in the presence of greatness.
>
> It is hard to explain, but looking at Dr Mannix and his graceful movements, I could understand how people appreciated the ballet. The old-world grace of it certainly appealed to this country lad who had his first experience as a priest in orphanages and in industrial suburbs.

Brosnan learned confidence from Mannix, and he learned not to be concerned with 'who people were'. He found Mannix a good listener, ready to learn and to be amused. 'But there was a line you never crossed with him.' His rebukes, very rare, would have 'the kick of a mule if you overstepped the mark'.[4]

Mannix was impatient with the proliferation of devotional practices. He disliked the 'Mass on nine First Fridays' with its promise of ultimate graces: the only arithmetical practice that interested him, he said, was the fifty-two Sundays. A priest who believed that Russia would be converted if everyone wore the medal of the Blue Army of Our Lady was gently deflated: '"In all events," [Mannix] said slowly, not putting down the priest or the Blue Army too much, but making his feelings perfectly clear, "the number of things in which Catholics are bound to believe is comparatively few."'[5]

It would have been impossible for Mannix to know all his parish priests, but he kept every Friday morning free in his office at the cathedral for any priest or layperson who wanted to talk to him; others sought him out at Raheen. In the mid-1950s, Father Tom Brophy, whom Mannix had ordained in 1949, went to him in desperation. He felt that he was failing as a curate; his relationship with his parish priest was bad, and the only solution he could see was a transfer to a country parish. 'Very well, you may go,' Mannix said, and a transfer to Mansfield was arranged. That done, Brophy reconsidered. He went back to Mannix. 'Very well, you needn't go.' But he wanted to see Brophy regularly to make sure that he was all right. So, every week for seven weeks, Brophy went to Raheen, where he sat in the garden with the archbishop. More than half a century later, Brophy expressed his gratitude: 'I can't remember a word he said. But he listened. He was my godfather.'[6]

Brophy wouldn't have been the only one to receive comfort from Mannix. One of the Blessed Sacrament fathers, Father Lemieux, spoke of Mannix's 'sensitivity to souls, kindness and compassion to priests…so far ahead of his time in opposing legalism in the care of souls'.[7] But some priests were shy; others hesitated to come unless they had a serious problem. Others, no doubt, had problems they wanted to hide. Because Mannix had been a parish priest only for a brief stint at West Melbourne, it would have helped to spend time in the parishes, not in formal visitation style, but talking, listening and observing. Faultlines in a parish might show themselves in a bullying older priest with a tense, unhappy curate. Drunkenness or an affair with a parishioner might come out of loneliness. Freedom and trust were well and good, but surely Mannix took non-intervention in the dioceses too far. Although the micro-managing prelates in other dioceses did no better in detecting sexual predators, Mannix's gift for listening might have been more widely exercised.

Meanwhile, Catholic Melbourne flourished. Rome couldn't complain about Mannix's prosperous diocese. As the suburbs stretched outwards, church buildings followed. There were 160 churches in the diocese when Mannix arrived in 1913. When he died in 1963 there were 300. The postwar period brought a population explosion with consequent strain on the Melbourne school system and on the parish priests.[8] The children of migrants from Catholic countries were added to the 'babyboomer' generation that began with couples who had been parted during the war, or who married when it ended. The total number of Catholic schoolchildren grew steeply, with the poorer suburbs feeling the increase most acutely. Even well-established schools in prosperous suburbs, with few migrant children, were overwhelmed. Our Lady of Victories primary school in middle-class Camberwell had 280 children enrolled in 1955. They were taught by four nuns.[9] This was easy compared with St Margaret Mary's in North Brunswick, where in 1956 one teacher, Lorraine Furlong, had 105 in her 'babies' class. 'It was the norm for the time; I didn't think anything of it,' she said years later. The next year, when 140 were enrolled, a second teacher was found, and Lorraine had only seventy children to look after.[10]

For all the pressures of the postwar years, the seminary system was still producing priests in good numbers. By putting the diocesan seminary at Werribee under the direction of the Jesuits, Mannix saved himself the trouble of giving it close supervision. It was a quite different model from that of the Manly seminary in Sydney, which was staffed by diocesan priests directly responsible to their archbishop. Different too was Mannix's reluctance to follow Sydney's habit of choosing talented seminarians to study in Rome. Comparatively few Melbourne seminarians were sent on this path. This may reflect Mannix's confidence in the Jesuit teaching at Werribee or his lack of enthusiasm for the Roman experience.

Religious orders often chose Melbourne in preference to Sydney because it was known that Mannix welcomed new initiatives and gave more freedom than other Australian prelates. If he liked your idea, he let you get on with it. Sometimes he intervened to rescue an order whose freedom was being threatened, as he did with the Carmelite nuns, whom he had established in Kew in 1928. When he heard that the nuns were in danger of a takeover by Carmelite friars, thereby losing self-determination, he stymied the friars by appealing to Rome and appointing himself as superior of the nuns' community.

The Irish Cistercian monks from Roscrea tried to set up a foundation in Sydney, but negotiations broke down because Gilroy's managerial style threatened their independence.[11] They came on to Melbourne where Walter Broderick, a businessman and friend of Mannix, found land for them at Tarrawarra in the beautiful Yarra Valley. Carmelites and Cistercians, dedicated to prayer and silence and retreat from the world, were essential to Mannix's idea of a Catholic community; he might be seen as a political activist but he also spent up to five hours a day in prayer and contemplation.[12]

Mannix brought grace and reverence, and a feeling for music to the ceremonies at St Patrick's Cathedral. His greatest gift to its musical tradition was his impulsive sponsorship in 1929 of a talented schoolboy, Percy Jones. Son of a Geelong bandmaster and music teacher, Percy knew at fifteen that he wanted to be a priest and a musician. He also dreamed of going to Rome. From his father, an unusually well-travelled survivor of an orphanage childhood, Percy knew the great names in music studies in Europe. With remarkable confidence, he persuaded his father to take him to see Mannix:

> I said to Dad…'If I'm going on for the priesthood would you see the Archbishop about the possibility of my going to Rome to do music as well as theology and philosophy?' So we went and saw the Archbishop. Archbishop Mannix and Dad did all the talking because I was only young, I was only fifteen. All that I remember was that during the conversation Archbishop Mannix said: 'Well, nothing will give me greater pleasure than that [Percy] should come back and direct the music of this diocese.'[13]

Nine years later, Percy Jones came back, having been ordained a priest in Rome, with experience in Ireland and France. He was taught by 'at least seven of the greatest scholars and lecturers [in music] the Church possessed in that period', and he had the luck to sail for Melbourne just as war broke out in September 1939.

At the same time, the Mozart Boys Choir from Vienna was stranded in Perth, just as its ship was due to sail for Europe. Mannix sent a telegram to the choirmaster, offering to take responsibility for the whole group. He paid the expenses of the twenty boys, aged between nine and fourteen, billeted them on chosen parishioners in East Melbourne and Fitzroy—no one could refuse the archbishop's request—and sent them to the Christian Brothers' school in Victoria Parade. As the angelic choristers turned into sturdy adolescents, their German accents put them at risk of meeting hostility in wartime Melbourne. Mannix arranged for one of the Christian Brothers to give the boys English lessons and he made them welcome at the cathedral, where Father (later Bishop) Patrick Lyons was primed to give them tea and biscuits whenever they called. The arrangement, which kept the group intact but also allowed some sense of family life in their foster homes, did not work equally well for all the boys but it was far better than housing them in an institution. When their choirmaster Georg Gruber was interned because of alleged Nazi connections, the archbishop became a father-figure for many of the boys. Many years later Walter Hauser, who lodged with the cathedral sacristan Hurbert Cooney and his wife, said of Mannix: 'I really loved him. He was very good to us.'[14]

When Percy Jones was appointed as director of music at St Patrick's Cathedral in 1942, the Vienna boys made up the nucleus of his choir. In a long and prodigiously creative career, Percy Jones transformed Catholic church music in Melbourne and did much for the wider community. His appointment as vice-director of the Conservatorium of Music at the University of Melbourne in 1951 was a surprise to many; it was a new thing to have a priest on the academic staff, and for some academics it was unwelcome. Mannix's response was: 'Why not?'[15] He chose to release Percy Jones from parish duties to a full-time academic post—though one somehow combined with vast responsibilities to music in the churches and schools. So, too, with the philosopher-priest Eric D'Arcy (later archbishop), whom Mannix sent to Oxford in the mid-1950s, and who became head of the Melbourne University Department of Philosophy. It looked as if the drawbridge to the secular world, or to other denominations, was being lowered, and to some extent it was.

Percy Jones's friendship with the Master of Ormond College, Davis McCaughey, was a way into the ecumenical movement of the 1950s and 1960s. Jones worked with McCaughey on the Week of Prayer for Christian Unity, held in Melbourne in 1955, presumably with the archbishop's consent. Mannix usually resisted proposals for joint statements with other churches. 'I do not like "Christian churches", though usage is against me,' he had said in 1943.[16] Catholics were not permitted to attend non-Catholic services. In special cases, small concessions were made after an appeal to the archbishop. A young Melbourne woman was told in 1951: 'In the circumstances you may attend the wedding but not as bridesmaid.'[17]

The remarkable alliance between the archbishop and the musician-priest prompts the question: why Percy Jones? Mannix's love of music is only one factor. There would be more obvious ways to remake the cathedral musical tradition than to send a sixteen-year-old away for nine years' training in Rome. One element must be the certainty of Percy Jones, his self-belief, and his audacious request. It wasn't enough to be a dreamer; you had to have a plan.

Another dreamer with an unorthodox plan that appealed to Mannix was Raymond Triado, a brilliant young law graduate of Spanish descent who founded a quasi-monastic community, Whitlands, in the Victorian countryside in 1941. This was an agrarian dream joined with a monastic way of life: the men built their own log huts; they shared the work of the land; they had daily mass; they sang an office in Gregorian chant. In its heyday Whitlands drew many visitors as well as some dedicated recruits. Mannix released one of his priests, Father Jack Heffey, to be its chaplain, and he himself travelled to Whitlands, near Mansfield, to bless the chapel. 'Your Grace, you can't bless the chapel,' the Mansfield parish priest protested. 'It's got no roof on it.' 'You can bless anything,' replied His Grace, and that ended the argument.[18] The Whitlands idea drew disapproval and suspicion. The settlement was based on the belief that only in complete separation from the secular modern city could a full Catholic life be lived. This ran counter to official papal teaching on social issues by which Catholics were exhorted to change the world by working within it. By giving his approval to Whitlands, Mannix stirred arguments among clergy and laity. A historian of the Whitlands experiment, David de Carvalho, explained their objections:

> Many priests regarded Jack Heffey's posting to Whitlands as doubly wrong, not merely because he was 'under' the authority of a layman, but primarily because they regarded the real job of the priest to be ministering to ordinary Catholics struggling to live out their faith in an alien culture, not digging up potatoes and singing songs in the bush, 'feeling superior'.[19]

Triado was a charismatic leader, a fine athlete, a good amateur actor, and very attractive to women. When young single women decided to follow him and join a community made up of single men who were vowed to celibacy, and a few family groups, the communal ideal faltered. Its immediate fate was settled by an accident. Inadvertently, Triado had chosen land outside the border of Mannix's diocese, which meant that Whitlands was under the jurisdiction of Bishop Stewart of Sandhurst (Bendigo). Stewart became agitated at 'talk' about the young women and wanted Whitlands closed. Mannix, who was also perturbed, withdrew Heffey from his post, which meant that the religious status of the community was lost. Triado led twelve members of his community on a six-day 'March on Raheen' to make a dramatic appeal to Mannix, who then said that Heffey could stay provided Bishop Stewart approved. But, as Mannix would have known, Stewart would never agree to a community that included unmarried men and women. Triado had to choose between the chaplain and the single women. He chose the chaplain and found temporary accommodation for the women while he travelled to Rome with the frail hope that the Pope would give approval for Whitlands to continue. Predictably, Rome told him to obey his bishop.

If Whitlands hadn't been on Stewart's territory, what would Mannix have done? His permissiveness certainly didn't stretch to extra-marital affairs, and the rumours (never substantiated) about 'a little Whitlander' fathered by a Sydney visitor, would have shaken him. In the event, Triado resolved the matter by renouncing his vow of celibacy to marry one of the young women, Betty Feehan. Mannix performed the marriage ceremony at St Patrick's Cathedral and the press, oblivious of Triado's lost dream, reported the event under the headline 'Athlete Weds'. As for Father Jack Heffey, Mannix listened to his request to be allowed the solitary life of prayer and contemplation to which he felt called. 'I don't understand but if that's what you feel you must do, then you had better do it.'[20]

Now and then Mannix made an unexpected sortie into an

unfamiliar place. He invited himself to Pentridge prison in 1939, where the governor, unused to visits from senior clerics, grumpily advised him to wash his hands in disinfectant after meeting the inmates.[21] Endearingly, Mannix greeted the prisoners with: 'We all make mistakes.' He would never attend a non-Catholic service but on Saturdays he often called in at the Bourke Street Synagogue, where he listened to the children's scripture lessons and talked informally to Rabbi Solomon.[22] He liked to look in at the exhibitions of the Society of Australian Artists in East Melbourne, near the cathedral. Theatres were out of bounds for clerics, but Mannix enjoyed concerts.

The Scottish singer-priest Father Sydney McEwen was invited to stay at Raheen, and to bring his mother who travelled with McEwen on the Australian tour. Women guests were almost unknown under the Raheen roof so there is something emblematic in the fact that when Mannix's chauffeur-driven car departed for the big concert with the archbishop and the tenor in the back seat, they forgot to take Mrs McEwen.[23]

The secondary schools in Melbourne, run by religious orders, were used to being left alone. The shock of a Mannix intrusion appears in a letter from the Jesuit provincial to the rector of Xavier College. The teaching orders were told suddenly in April 1944 that rather than send their students to the junior public (fourth form) examinations, they must exercise their right to determine the syllabus, set papers and do their own marking. The Jesuit provincial saw this as an abrupt reversal of received wisdom:

> The Archbishop's request is an extraordinary one, and the Brothers will be furious. And I would not do it unless I had to. But, it would seem to be the case that you have

> to do it. It is amazing how we change our points of view. Hitherto, at least in Sydney, the Catholic schools opposed the interior exam system very sternly, as, the Catholic authorities maintained, the system favoured the Class [A] schools to the detriment of the more popular schools...And now we are all for it. And, to do that without getting the advice of those concerned, is indeed a piece of totalitarianism. I have no more to say.[24]

Even more startling was Mannix's incursion into sex education in the period 1942–45. This was a new idea for the Catholic system, and it wasn't welcome. Schools used the Catechism signposts; few teachers wanted, or felt equipped, to explore the territory beyond. 'Immodest thoughts, desires or feelings,' the 1940s children learned from their Catechism, 'are not sins unless we knowingly and willingly consent to them.' Yes, but what was 'immodest', and what was 'consent'? These questions were usually dodged, and here was Mannix telling teachers to be frank and open. He told his director of education, Father Dan Conquest, that he 'wanted people to be able to talk about sex without feeling ashamed or embarrassed'.[25] And he made a serious attempt to change the culture of the Catholic schools in the matter of sex. Accompanied by Conquest and Dr John Catarinich, Victorian director of mental hygiene, he addressed about ten meetings of boys' secondary school principals, speaking for an hour or more with a disconcerting directness. Lapses in purity, Mannix said, should not be presented as the greatest of sins. He suggested that the training colleges for teaching brothers were too rigid; they caused 'the suppression of personality and frankness for the sake of conformity and obedience to rule'. This did not go down well with the brothers, but they had to listen. Resistance showed itself in silence. Mannix was disappointed not to have been asked more questions. Many of the religious must have been uncomfortable, even confused, to hear wet dreams, copulation, rhythm method, venereal disease and 'self-abuse' discussed by their dignified and remote archbishop.

Mannix then turned to the nuns. This was even harder. During 1943 he spoke to the principals of the girls' schools. His forthrightness was a shock to an audience accustomed to prim circumlocutions or total silence. 'Sexual curiosity is good and natural,' he said. 'All of us are too puritanical in matters of sex.'[26] It is most unlikely that such a radical statement was ever made in any Catholic school then or for many years to come. Most schools wanted nothing to do with sex education nor did many of the parents. Others were doubtful about the schools' capacity to teach it.[27]

Mannix's audience, Father Conquest said, 'didn't want to be informed at all'.[28] Some complained to Conquest. The campaign failed, and the schools went on much as before. Teachers' resistance was matched by parents' alarm. Because his authority did not reach those orders with headquarters outside Melbourne, Mannix depended on voluntary cooperation which was never likely to be given.

From today's perspective it's hard to know whether to praise Mannix as a brave, lone voice, or to blame him for not carrying his program through with his obdurate school principals and beyond them to the young men and women in the seminaries and novitiates. But where would the teachers come from? It wasn't easy for celibates to teach sex education, and there is no reason to think that Mannix questioned priestly celibacy. He could have found allies among the men and women of the Catholic Action movements which began in the late 1930s. Frank Maher, director of Catholic Action from 1938 and his then deputy B. A. Santamaria were responsible for the Social Justice statement of 1944—*The Family*, written by Santamaria—which recommended that sex education be given in the home but with the backup of suitable pamphlets.[29] It doesn't offer any critique of the puritanical culture which Mannix deplored. In 1947 the archbishop was still pursuing his point:

> In times past there was a tendency on the part of parents to put [children] off with some sort of white lie. It was quite wrong to tell them fantastic stories about the coming of the baby. The curiosity of the children after all comes from God. They should be told the truth.[30]

Mannix's insight into what he called the 'false consciences' and 'exaggerated gravity' regarding supposed sins of impurity came partly from his Saturday stints with the general public in the confessionals at the cathedral. Children were invited to talk about what they were learning and whether they liked their subjects. If they were being bullied, this gave them a chance to tell their story, and some may have done so; as a confessor, Mannix was unusually approachable. A bemused nineteen-year-old, who had come across a book by Marie Stopes, asked Mannix about French letters and coitus interruptus. Mannix 'gently explained so that I got a faint idea'.[31] Marie Stopes' advocacy of contraception was contrary to Catholic teaching but her book *Wise Parenthood* was on the Raheen shelves.[32] Mannix would have been strongly opposed to Stopes' thinking on birth control, and it is to his credit that he read and kept her work and didn't rebuke the boy for having read it. Other prelates of his age would have burned it.

Conquest's successor as director of Catholic Education, Monsignor John F. Kelly, took up the challenge of sex education in the schools but without the vigour of Mannix's campaign. Kelly's booklet *From Boy to Man* is an example of the direction taken: material to be read at home, preferably with parents on standby to answer questions. How well this worked depended on the parents.[33] Father Maurice Catarinich gave lectures in some schools, and according to Helga Griffin's memory of the late 1940s at the Academy of Mary Immaculate in Fitzroy, he would blush when he explained the sexual act.[34] Monsignor Kelly's Pre-Cana conferences for couples about to be married were useful initiatives.[35]

Mannix wasn't successful in his education campaign, Daniel Conquest said, 'but he did try anyway'.[36] If he had managed to create a healthier, more open attitude in the schools, the seminaries might have been more alert to the unsuitable entrants who were to go on to cause tragedy as sexual abusers.

Mannix could probably have done more in this regard in the diocesan seminary, Corpus Christi, at Werribee. His authority over the training of future secular priests, though shared with the other Victorian bishops and the Archbishop of Hobart, was stronger than his authority in the schools. It now seems obvious that seminary educators failed to help the sexually immature. More seriously, it failed to detect future clerical predators, with the results now made plain in the public inquiries and the 2014 Royal Commission into sexual abuse.

In his account of Mannix's reformist ideas on sex education, Daniel Conquest cited events in Fred Schepisi's film *The Devil's Playground* as examples of what was wrong in the system. 'There was a lot of that going on at the time,' Conquest said. What was 'going on' in the film was the inept and sometimes brutal enforcement of a rigid system administered by the brothers of a teaching order, some of whom had unresolved sexual problems of their own. Bedwetting by a troubled twelve-year-old, masturbation, bullying, hellfire sermons, and the condemnation of natural sexual curiosity as sinful made *The Devil's Playground*, set in the 1950s, a sensation when it appeared in 1972. Many Catholic viewers refused to believe that a Catholic institution could so disastrously fail its young students. Yet as Conquest's testimony shows, Mannix was concerned as early as 1942 with this climate of fear and guilt. At a time when corporal punishment in boys' schools, and in some girls' schools, was inflicted even for poor progress in learning, he was unusual in arguing for its abolition.

The Devil's Playground is set in one of the junior seminaries or 'juniorates'—boarding schools for boys from the age of twelve—which were intended to lead to the priesthood or to the Brothers. These schools were more popular in Sydney than in Melbourne, where Mannix did not encourage them. A juniorate at Springwood fed into the Manly seminary. Mannix preferred to have his future diocesan priests complete standard schooling before going to Werribee. Inconsistently, however, in 1948, he opened the Marist Brothers' juniorate at Macedon, where Schepisi spent the four years on which he based *The Devil's Playground*.

It is possible that Mannix tried to bring sex education to the seminaries as well as the schools: if so he failed. It now seems obvious that some young men who should never have been admitted went through to ordination without anyone diagnosing a range of sexual disorders. Some were simply immature and destined to be unhappy in the wrong vocation. Others were criminals in the making, and, once ordained, they had power over the young and naïve. Such was the reverence for the priesthood that the predator's victim often accepted the guilt of the situation or kept quiet about it from a fear of not being believed. Power, and the abuse of power, were at the centre of the problem.

Mannix took a special pride in Corpus Christi. The Jesuits, who accepted its management in 1923, were experienced men, with a fair sprinkling of their distinguished scholars. Mannix made the training course seven and a half years instead of six and a half as at Manly in Sydney. He often said that Corpus Christi was a better place than his own former home, Maynooth; because it was smaller, it was 'like a family', with closeness between staff and students. Certainly, compared with Maynooth and its six hundred young men, Corpus Christi had a sense of community. Its rector in the period 1930–47, Henry Johnston SJ, lacked warmth, but his successor, Charlie Mayne SJ, was well liked. Flaws in the system, evident now, were not thought of.

It was too easy to be accepted for the diocesan priesthood. A good academic record was of more interest than personality or motive. Terry O'Neill, who was at Corpus Christi for four years, remembers a brief interview with Monsignor Fox in 1956:

> I can't recall being questioned at any depth as to why I wanted to be a priest. And really it was a very impulsive decision. I didn't have any idea what I was choosing. I wasn't asked if I had thought about the celibate life. Acceptance of my application seemed almost automatic although I would probably have been found unsuitable had I been questioned at greater depth.

Moral theology was taught at Werribee with no mention of paedophilia; few had ever heard the word.[37] Textbooks were in Latin and so was much of the teaching. Some who came into the seminaries uncertain of their sexuality were ordained without any resolution of their confusion. They would have to battle for themselves. Most gained the strength to become good priests, but the records show that some sexual predators were ordained from Corpus Christi, and were able, at least in Mannix's later years, to do appalling damage in the parishes. Mannix's policy of trust and his habit of keeping his distance from his priests may have shielded him from full knowledge.

It is sometimes suggested that Vatican II and the social changes of the 1960s destabilised the priesthood. The meagre records that survive show that clerical convictions for sexual abuse increased slightly in the decade after Mannix's death but the figures aren't conclusive, nor has sufficient work been done to show whether such crimes under the *laissez faire* Mannix leadership were any more or less numerous than under the interventionist Gilroy in Sydney.[38]

One might ask, too, how much Mannix and his contemporaries understood of the lasting psychological damage to the child victims of abuse. Addiction to alcohol was imperfectly understood; sexual addiction not at all. Psychiatry in postwar Australia was underdeveloped as a specialty and regarded with suspicion by many Catholics, who saw Freud and his successors as sexual libertarians and deniers of free will. Very little was done for or about child mental health. Mannix, to his credit, asked in 1951 for a report from St Vincent's Hospital on the status of psychiatry at the hospital. The senior psychiatrist stressed the 'tremendous amount of misunderstanding about psychiatry among the public, medical men and many nurses' and proposed 'a minimum of thirty beds [at St Vincent's] for the short-term treatment of acute nervous and mental disorders'. As with his sex education campaign, Mannix was blocked in his efforts to respond to the need. He was told that the hospital lacked the space to expand into psychiatry. Nevertheless, there was space for other specialties: new inpatient beds were found for the growing fields of neurosurgery and orthopaedics. The hospital's lack of confidence in the senior psychiatrist was a factor, but a general mistrust of psychiatry among Catholics was reflected in the policy.[39]

Because too much was claimed for the institutional Church—perfect, infallible, beyond criticism—sexual predators flourished. In an Irish-Australian Catholic community with an 'us' and 'them' mentality, the urge to keep our problems to ourselves was overwhelming. The cesspit of clerical abuse of children must always have been there, though most Catholics were conditioned not to see, hear or think about anything that questioned clerical standards. 'Giving scandal' was the great fear.

In recent years, the squalid story of abusive parish priests and members of religious orders has been told. The United States, Ireland and Australia have had to face evidence of sexual abuse, and physical violence has been located in orphanages, schools, training centres and holiday camps. Often, parents refused to believe that anything was wrong, so that the victims were doubly betrayed. Even the inadequate records and a great deal of denial cannot hide the abuse, or the culture of cover-up. It goes back to Mannix's last years. It can be found in his Melbourne diocese, and elsewhere in Australia, and it would be naïve to think that it began in Mannix's time, or in Carr's time, or Goold's. Wherever there is power, the powerless will be abused by some.

In the late Mannix years, the Catholic Church in Australia

looked strong and confident. People were comfortable with their parish priests; trust was taken for granted. Idealistic young men and women were entering seminaries and novitiates in large numbers. There were notable scholars within the orders and the dioceses. After generations of being patronised, Catholics could be proud of their faith. Perhaps that made it easier for the men at the top to ignore or deny the poison in the system.

In the absence of adequate records Mannix can't be cleared of knowing about child abuse by priests in his diocese. The notorious abuser Father Kevin O'Donnell, ordained by Mannix in 1942, was reported to Monsignor Laurie Moran between 1958 and 1959, and the charge is said to have been known to Bishop Fox from that date. O'Donnell was finally tried and jailed in 1995. Was Mannix told? There is anecdotal evidence that Fox sifted the news that went to Raheen in Mannix's last years, when he had stopped going to the cathedral. A priest who had been seen with a young woman in his car was threatened by Fox: 'If this happens again I will inform the archbishop.'[40] If it is true that only about twenty per cent of the cathedral mail was taken to Raheen in the last decade of Mannix's life, it may be that Mannix was kept in the dark about many things.[41]

As early as the 1930s Mannix's responsible deputy in the Catholic Education Office, Matthew Beovich (later Archbishop of Adelaide), felt free to 'issue circulars to teachers in Mannix's name on issues where he [Beovich] was likely to face opposition'.[42] Mannix wasn't always obeyed, and his intelligence system was open to error. In 1936 he placed an absolute ban on the serving of alcohol at any Catholic function following reports of young women at the Xavier College ball for past students falling down stairs, helplessly drunk. William Hackett, then rector of Xavier, went to Raheen to put the record straight. He told Mannix that there were no stairs to fall down, that the ball had been well conducted and that Mannix's informant had not been present. As Hackett was a total abstainer as well as a close friend, his testimony should have made Mannix backtrack. Not a bit of it. Mannix's ban lasted many years. It led to a form of BYO at functions. Guests would come to Catholic balls and dances carrying bottles of wine or beer in little overnight bags. I remember a Xavier ball of the mid-1950s at which our party, headed by former captain of Xavier, Frank Hurley, was greeted jovially by Father Stephenson SJ, with 'Good evening, good evening, Frank, have you come for the weekend?'

Mannix was tough with drinking priests. He did not, however, make his priests abstainers like himself; alcohol was served at formal dinners at Raheen. He was severe, too, about gambling. His priests were banned from attending race meetings, except as chaplains in case of emergencies, and he took a mischievous pleasure in choosing as parish priests at Flemington those who were known to have no interest in the sport that defined their parish.[43]

As for the gambling games of 'housey' and 'bingo', often used as fundraisers as well as amusement, Mannix seemed not to know how pervasive these habits became in the postwar period. He retorted sharply in 1954 to an accusation of clerical gambling:

> The fact is that I expressly forbade any priest in Melbourne to have recourse to 'housey' for raising money. As far as I know that order has been obeyed. I know nothing about what you call 'Bingo'.[44]

As only Mannix could have failed to know, bingo was another name for housey; this popular gambling game, which dated from the First World War, was played all through his archdiocese. Father Brosnan explained its place in parish life:

> It wasn't TOO illegal if you know what I mean...it was simply a small-time, small-change diversion which gave a little innocent pleasure and helped the parish funds at the same time...Priests were expected to be at the housie and euchre nights. It was where you met the parents and grandparents of your schoolchildren, where you picked up the gossip and heard who was in trouble and needed help.[45]

If Mannix had known more about the daily life of the parishes he couldn't have missed their dependence, social and financial, on bingo. One consequence of his policy of 'letting them alone' was that it gave the parish priests considerable power within their sphere.[46] They were allowed to use their initiative, and this was both good and bad. The parish priest made decisions about the primary school, arranged the staffing, directed the day-to-day teaching. This left little chance for the nuns, on whose free labour the schools depended, to make decisions of their own. Some priests would listen to the nuns; others were petty tyrants. 'Letting them alone' also meant hardship for many parish priests; they had to pay the bills. The convents too were stretched, especially in the Depression. Individuality was generally discouraged or suppressed within the convents. It is almost impossible to imagine a nun with a grievance making her way to Raheen. She would not have had the time, the permission or the tram fare.

Whatever Mannix knew of the women in the religious orders in his diocese would have come from the top. Sometimes the heads of orders bypassed or disobeyed him, as did the mother rectress of

St Vincent's Hospital: when he refused to give adequate funding, she went ahead anyway, incurring a debt that he had to pay.[47] The Cabrini sisters, newly arrived from Italy to staff a hospital, were given little consideration for the cultural changes they had to make. Their balance sheets were scrutinised more carefully than their wellbeing. Making them repay all the money advanced to them by the diocese on arrival seemed to be the first priority.[48]

Mannix could be helpful to women with new ideas that fitted his social vision. He backed the emerging religious congregation the Company of Our Lady of the Blessed Sacrament, known as the Grey Sisters, whose prickly founder, Maude O'Connell, exhausted the patience of the equable William Hackett. Asked if Hackett could be allowed to continue a long stint as chaplain to the Grey Sisters, the Jesuit provincial refused, saying bluntly that 'he didn't want to kill Father Hackett'. Mannix insisted, and Hackett had to struggle on. Mannix had known Maude O'Connell since 1916 or earlier; her father was one of his many cousins in Australia. She came to prominence as a young woman in 1915 when she spoke at a big public meeting at the Melbourne Town Hall in support of state aid to Catholic schools. She was an active trade unionist and a member of the Labor Party. During the Depression she worked with the radical organiser Muriel Heagney to set up the Unemployed Girls' Relief Movement. The Grey Sisters' work began in 1930 with a group of women who went into homes to cook and clean and look after the small children of overburdened mothers.[49] Maude O'Connell's focus on family welfare, allied with her radical politics and independent spirit, appealed to Mannix. William Hackett described her as *une difficile*.

Mannix could be exacting and imperious. During the 1948 Eucharistic Congress he asked the Good Shepherd nuns to give a formal luncheon for five hundred guests at their Abbotsford convent. The nuns had to cook five courses (including choices of six desserts) and serve on a grand scale, rearrange rooms, borrow tables and chairs, get the protocol right in seating arrangements for delegates from visiting cardinals down the slopes of the hierarchical pyramid, and do all the work so tranquilly as to be invisible to the guests. Not even the Mother Superior had a place at the table.[50] The invisibility of nuns was part of the culture of the time and, like other prelates, Mannix accepted it.

Only a few women of the laity had occasion to work closely with Mannix. He admired the initiative and competence of Mrs Lena Santospirito, a leader in the Italian community, and of Dame Mary Daly, to whom he gave responsibility for the Catholic Welfare Organisation during World War II. Their friendly association was based on mutual respect and shared goals. On the other hand, Anna Brennan, a lawyer and member of the influential Brennan family, complained that Mannix was unhelpful in her work with Catholic professional women.[51] But he was unusual in looking, as early as 1935, for qualified women to found a Catholic Social Service Bureau.[52] One woman intellectual whose company Mannix enjoyed was Barbara Ward, editor of the London *Economist*, who visited Australia in the mid-1950s. 'There was a real sparkle in both sets of eyes,' Percy Jones said.[53]

All through the 1930s Mannix was stirring his fellow bishops to do something about Catholic Action. This initiative of Pius XI was designed to bring the laity into greater participation in the life of the church. Archbishop Kelly saw it as a way to piety through prayer. Mannix had a much more vigorous idea of its possibilities. Leo XIII's encyclical *Rerum Novarum* (1891) called on Catholics to work for social justice. Mannix wanted to strengthen the laity, to make leaders in the secular world. That had been his *leitmotif* in 1917 when he wrote a foreword for the short-lived nationalist magazine *Australia*:

> The war has made men and women think much and think hard…the people are just now in the temper to assert themselves politically, socially, industrially. And if they are to move along safe lines it was never more necessary than it is now that the public mind should be leavened by Catholic principles.[54]

More than a decade later, Mannix was still waiting for an active, intellectually informed laity to assert itself. He wanted leaders to emerge, not under clerical direction but with their own sense of mission. He hoped that Catholic Action would show the way for a new, independently minded laity to change the world. The sufferings of the poor in the Depression of the 1930s were to be seen each day as Mannix walked to work. He gave coins to the needy; he helped fund St Vincent's Hospital; he encouraged religious orders to undertake social rescue work. But until the laity asserted itself, he believed, nothing would really change.

CHAPTER TEN

THE VATICAN CHESS GAME

OCTOBER 1933. AN ordinary evening in inner-city Melbourne. Cathedral Hall in Brunswick is the setting for a lecture on Irish culture. There is no reason to expect fireworks from His Grace. After twenty years in Melbourne, Daniel Mannix is still a celebrity, but it seems that his years of provoking controversy have ended. Two prominent Melbourne Catholics, Benjamin Hoare and Auguste de Bavay, are regretting their 'rude behaviour' and 'intemperate language' towards Mannix at the time of the conscription issue.[1] The Irish troubles have quietened. But, even in Brunswick, a world away from the Vatican, the unpredictable Archbishop of Melbourne was still attentively watched.

Mannix was giving an expression of thanks to Monsignor English, the rector of St Leo's College at the University of Queensland, for a lecture he had given on Irish cultural history. The rector's name invited a little joke. There was nothing un-Irish about Monsignor English except the name, Mannix remarked. Then for no special reason he was moved to speak about the sort of Irishman (or un-Irishman) who was 'treated as a pet' by the British press. His example was General Eoin O'Duffy, an admirer of Mussolini and Hitler, leader of the Irish Blueshirts, who was at that time a serious threat to the first de Valera government. Sacked by de Valera as head of police, O'Duffy announced that he would head a march on Dublin. This was an obvious echo of Mussolini's March on Rome, as were the blue shirts, black berets and straight-armed salutes of O'Duffy's men.

Calling O'Duffy a 'sham Irish patriot', Mannix gave his Cathedral Hall audience a reprise of the Irish troubles, with a reminder that the Blueshirt leader had fought for Britain and the treaty in 1922:

> The latest to proclaim himself an Irish patriot was Mr O'Duffy; the Press knew nothing about him except, perhaps [that] he had been concerned in taking the Four Courts and using British guns to fire on the Irish people. Now Mr O'Duffy had put on a blue shirt and he was proclaimed a patriot by the whole British Press. He was the sort of man that England wanted to lead the Irish people.[2]

Mannix's s speech was reported in the *Advocate*, presumably with Mannix's approval, picked up by the *Argus*, and read in Ireland. Back came O'Duffy's reply, questioning Mannix's right to call himself a nationalist, given his compliance with British rule in his Maynooth days. The speech was also read in Rome, where the response came more slowly but with great effect. The apostolic delegate, Archbishop Bernadini—the Vatican's man in Australia—was instructed to deliver Rome's rebuke to Mannix for endangering the 'delicate and difficult' political situation in Ireland. Mannix was told to refrain from 'any statement whatever of a political character'. His remarks, 'jokingly directed at General O'Duffy', were hindering the 'patient and laborious work of pacification which the Holy Father has so much at heart'.[3]

Now that most versions of Irish history have dismissed General O'Duffy as a drunken buffoon, and his Blueshirts as a bad joke, it is hard to see why the Vatican came down so heavily on Mannix. Yet his seemingly impromptu speech hit three targets. It was an endorsement of de Valera for sacking O'Duffy, it was a sideswipe at Britain, and, in ridiculing the Blueshirts leader, it pointed by extension at the European fascist dictators whose style and policy O'Duffy was following. In 1933, the Vatican was treading a cautious path in cooperation with Mussolini, following the Concordat of 1929. Britain too was still conciliating Hitler. The salutation 'Hail O'Duffy' sounded ridiculous, but so did 'Heil Hitler'. With Europe in crisis, it was no time for archbishops to make jokes. In fact, Mannix wasn't joking, but it suited Rome to pretend that he was.

The O'Duffy incident was read as a signal by the Vatican. It was time to do something about the Archbishop of Melbourne. He had too much power in the Australian hierarchy. In spite of disagreements with archbishops Duhig of Brisbane and Clune of Perth, and a cool relationship with Kelly of Sydney, Mannix was the strong leader of the bishops as a whole. He had a close friendship with Archbishop Andrew Killian of Adelaide and with Coadjutor Archbishop Michael Sheehan of Sydney, whose appointment he was said to have engineered. Although Australian-born bishops were emerging, it would be an Irish hierarchy as long as Mannix ruled in Melbourne.

It took two years for Vatican strategists to work out a way to diminish Mannix's power and to make the Australian church less Irish. A new apostolic delegate was needed to replace Archbishop Filippo Bernardini, whose arrival in Australia coincided with the O'Duffy speech. Bernardini's rebuke to Mannix may have lacked the necessary vigour; at any rate he was replaced as soon as it could decently be managed. After only two years in Australia, Bernardini was posted to peaceful Switzerland, where he was left undisturbed for nearly twenty years. His successor, Archbishop Giovanni Panico, arrived in March 1936 and settled in for a ten-year stint of remodelling the Australian Catholic church.

When Panico came to Sydney, all smiles and compliments and fractured English, the *Te Deum* of thanksgiving was sung for him at St Mary's Cathedral. Some were more thankful than others for his coming, and the smiles were not for everyone. Probably exaggerating his own skill, Panico boasted to the press that he had acquired his English in one month's study before embarking for Sydney. His uncertain grasp of the language gave an advantage to the Rome-trained priests and bishops with whom he could speak in Italian. Mannix had never studied in Rome and his Italian was minimal. Communication in Panico's primitive English was limited. The alternative was to chat in Latin.

Panico soon proved to be tough and abrasive. He became known as an opportunist who lined his pockets by charging large fees for officiating at church functions. His list of fees ranged from £250 for the consecration of a bishop to £100 for receiving debutantes at a Catholic ball. Nuns were said to lock up their silver before a Panico visit in case he chose something to take home with him.[4]

There was no mistaking Panico's mission to dilute Irish influence by appointing Australian-born bishops. Cautiously watched by the six archbishops, who in 1936 were all Irish, Panico sped up the process of Australianisation which was already under way in the more remote regions—hardship posts for the most part. By 1936 there were Australian-born bishops at Townsville, Geraldton, Lismore, Wilcannia-Forbes, Rockhampton and Port Augusta. Corpus Christi seminary, founded by Mannix in 1923, and the older-established Manly seminary in the Sydney diocese guaranteed a steady flow of Australian priests, but the older generation of Irish archbishops remained. The line held in Perth and Brisbane. Archbishop Clune was succeeded by his coadjutor, Irish-born Redmond Prendiville, in 1935; Patrick O'Donnell, also Irish, would eventually take over from James Duhig in Brisbane.

When Duhig wrote to Mannix, 'if we are not vigilant anything might happen', he meant that an Australian might rise to the top level.[5] The unthinkable happened in 1937 when Justin Simonds was appointed Archbishop of Hobart. If Panico can be believed, the triumvirate of Mannix, Duhig and Killian had done their best to frustrate his appointment in favour of 'an Irish intriguer'.[6]

There was much the same reluctance in the Church of England to appoint a local man. Dr Marcus Loane, appointed archbishop in 1966, was the first Australian to reach that level.[7] Mannix's opposite number in Melbourne, English-born Archbishop Head, told his first audience in 1929: 'I love the Empire and I want to serve it and keep it Christian.' But from the conscription period on, Mannix was edging his people to move away from an Empire First position to 'put Australia first'.

In the mid-1930s Mannix, Duhig and Killian were all in their seventies. Panico had an eye on all three but especially on Mannix, who was physically fit and intellectually as sharp as ever. There was no way of moving him, nor any case for giving him a coadjutor. There was then no retirement age for the clergy; and as long as he felt fully competent Mannix wouldn't ask for a coadjutor. The next best thing for Panico was to weaken his administrative support.

Mannix was the tribal chieftain in a church that was still very Irish. As historian Oliver MacDonagh commented:

> Up to 1897, the great majority of parish clergy and religious of the archdiocese were not only Irish in the broad sense of derivation but actually Irish-born and educated. It would indeed be a nice question at what point in the twentieth century they were at last outnumbered by Australian and other outside-born priests, nuns and brothers. Still, no matter how early that date might be—and it surely must have post-dated 1914—so long as Daniel Mannix reigned, the Melbourne archdiocese continued to enjoy (or suffer, according to one's point of view) a massive Irish presence. *Ubi Mannix, ibi Hibernia*.[8]

There was not much that Panico could do with what MacDonagh calls the 'straggling mass of spiritual infantry' in the parishes. He had to start at the top. In Sydney, Archbishop Kelly was widely regarded as a tiresome, vain nonentity who fussed about small matters. He was best known for commissioning a statue of himself to stand outside St Mary's Cathedral. His coadjutor, Archbishop Michael Sheehan, was a sensitive man with an engagingly self-deprecating sense of humour. An intellectual, with a brilliant academic record, Sheehan had taught classics at Maynooth in Mannix's time and they were on the best of terms. Although he had been a friend of Professor O'Hickey, whose passion for the Irish language he shared, Michael Sheehan came to Sydney in October 1922 with Mannix's strong support. Panico complained that Sheehan had been appointed without any consultation with the then apostolic delegate.[9] In that and other appointments, Panico said, Mannix had been the '*deus ex machina*'.[10] Now, Panico would play the deciding role. He would prevent Sheehan from succeeding Kelly in Sydney, and he would keep Mannix and the rest of the hierarchy in the dark.

Panico began to unravel the Irish tangle. From his observation post in the delegation headquarters in Edward Street, North Sydney, he took in the situation at St Mary's Cathedral. Archbishop Kelly was eighty-five. Quick action was needed to prevent the automatic succession of Archbishop Sheehan, who, at sixty-five could expect to settle in for a long reign. And his friendship with Mannix would bring Melbourne and Sydney together in a formidable alliance that Panico was determined to prevent.

Perth, Adelaide and Hobart, each with its own archbishop, were not much more than country towns compared with the eastern capitals, while the country Victorian, New South Wales and Queensland bishops, in theory independent, usually fell into line with the archbishops in the state capitals of Melbourne, Sydney and Brisbane. How to dispose of Sheehan before Kelly died? Bishops were not easily removed. Sheehan was hard working, well liked and of exemplary character. He could be transferred to Ireland, if a bishopric came vacant, or perhaps given a desk job in the Vatican. Panico must have considered these options. But he had a more subtle strategy in mind.

It was known in the Vatican that Sheehan had left himself open to removal. Having served thirteen weary years under Kelly's petty tyranny, he despaired at the prospect of more. When Kelly fell ill in 1935, Sheehan began to hope. But then, as he wrote irritably to Cardinal MacRory in Armagh, 'the old archbishop is dangerously well'. Letting comic sense overcome caution, he let his old friend in Ireland know the strains of life in Sydney:

> It is not the mere fact that [Archbishop Kelly] may survive me that causes me to tremble. It is rather the thought of the panegyric which he would preach over me. He is the oddest mixture of oral piety, fatuousness and roguery. You would burst yourself with laughter if I were to tell you of the outrageous things I have heard him say in public—but I daren't commit them to paper. As it is you will admit I have trespassed a few paces into the field of indiscretion.[11]

Sheehan asked MacRory to explore the possibilities of his coming back to Ireland as a bishop.[12] It seems not to have occurred to him that the Irish bishops might see him as a radical. His commitment to the Irish language, strongly held from his Maynooth days, linked him with troublesome nationalists. Sheehan's appointment to Sydney, just before the outbreak of civil war in Ireland in 1922, meant that he had missed the faction fighting and political manoeuvres, as well as the pain and violence, of the later 1920s. It was naïve to think that he could come home as if nothing had happened. Complaints about the fussy despotism of Archbishop Kelly and a timetable crammed with tedious fêtes and communion breakfasts made Sheehan sound self-indulgent.

In another unwise moment Sheehan wrote to Cardinal Fumasoni-Biondi in Rome expressing a wish to leave Sydney for a post in Ireland. He made himself disastrously clear in February 1936: 'If [the archbishopric] of Sydney were vacant tomorrow I would not be interested in it.'[13] Fumasoni-Biondi was reassuring: he would make sure that if Sheehan were to be moved it would be in his own time and on his own terms. It would be a matter of waiting for the right place. Time passed; Sheehan missed out on several bishoprics in Ireland and he began to think that Sydney was not so bad after all. Kelly could not live for ever. But his impulsive letter to Rome was in the files for Panico to use.

In May 1936, Panico swooped. He sent for an unsuspecting Sheehan and read him a letter from the Pope accepting his resignation. He could go back to Ireland as soon as he wished. A suitable pension would be found. An appointment? No, but he would have the time for scholarly pursuits that he had always wanted.

Distraught, Sheehan wrote to Mannix. He had never wanted to retire. Apart from the incubus of Archbishop Kelly, there was much in his Sydney life that he found trying, especially its public side: 'You can fill in the items with ease,' he wrote to Mannix '… big dinners, concerts, communion breakfasts lasting 3 ½ hours etc.' But if he had to choose between Sydney and retirement, he said, 'I would stay on here working with a full heart to the end of my days.'[14]

Mannix, infuriated, leaped to the defence. He wanted to challenge Panico, but was advised by Sheehan that it would be futile: 'If you say anything in protest against the decision, you may find him all excitement and rage at the bare thought that anyone could suggest the revision of any decree of HH [His Holiness].'[15] Sheehan tried a direct appeal to the Pope by telegram but had no reply. He then conceded defeat. Time was short: Sheehan's passage home had been booked. But Mannix wasn't ready to give up. He wrote to Cardinal MacRory in Armagh and Bishop Gilmartin of Tuam asking support.[16] He may not have known that Sheehan had been unduly frank the year before in telling the cardinal how much he wanted to leave Sydney.[17] Mannix's letter, double the length of his usual brief missives, stretched the truth in saying that Sheehan and Kelly were back on good terms. He pressed the cardinal hard, ending with a plea to do anything possible 'for so old a friend'. But MacRory did not—perhaps could not—help.

As well as lobbying in Ireland, Mannix made Sheehan the unrealistic offer of a Melbourne parish. Sheehan declined: taking refuge in Mannix territory wasn't practical. He couldn't accept a parish priest's job without permission from Rome, and he was in no mood to ask Rome for anything. Besides, it would be risky for Mannix to have an archbishop assisting him at confirmations and other higher duties. It would be 'seized on as an excuse to clap a "regular" coadjutor on you without consulting you', Sheehan told Mannix.[18] Mannix took the train to Sydney to see his friend and ally sail for Ireland. An eloquent letter, signed by all the Australian bishops, deplored Sheehan's 'resignation' as a tragic loss to church and people. They all knew he had been pushed, though the mystery remained as to how Panico had managed it.

Two months later, a forlorn Sheehan, living on a meagre pension, wrote to Mannix from a convent hostel and convalescent home in Dublin. The nuns were kind, he said, but he had no space for his books. The house was an echo chamber. The nice old ladies in the next room could tell from the rattle of his beads exactly where he was in the mysteries of the Rosary.[19] He told Archbishop Killian of Adelaide that he felt like 'an emptied old tin, with a jagged lid, tossed onto a shelf to gather dust for a while before being thrown into the place of interment of derelicts'.[20] That dismal image, however, did not end Sheehan's story. He found a little seaside cottage in Ring, County Waterford, near the Ring Irish College, which he had co-founded in 1906, and devoted himself to the cause of the Irish language revival.

A few weeks after Sheehan's departure, his successor in Sydney was named. It was the Bishop of Port Augusta, Norman Gilroy. Australian-born, and only forty years old, Gilroy caught Panico's attention in November 1936 with an invitation to tour his vast and mainly empty rural diocese where eleven thousand Catholics lived in an area larger than Spain and Portugal. Gilroy was doing well in Port Augusta, visiting tiny far-flung parishes in day-long drives alone in searing heat. A smiling photograph of Gilroy astride a camel at Oodnadatta showed his adaptability.[21] He did not lose himself in the wilderness. His first post after ordination had been as secretary to an earlier apostolic delegate in Sydney; he knew how Vatican diplomatic wheels were oiled. A later stint as secretary to the Bishop of Lismore was a useful guide to the Australian episcopal scene. Even after being sent to Port Augusta, Gilroy managed to attend big events in the eastern states, and because he was young and efficient he was made secretary of the Australian Bishops' Conference. This kept him in touch with all the bishops and with Panico.[22]

Inviting Panico to Port Augusta was a shrewd diplomatic move. As Gilroy's guest, Panico toured arid spaces, saw kangaroos and spinifex, and admired the young bishop's toughness and energy. Because Gilroy had been trained in Rome, he spoke fluent Italian; a relief to Panico for whom English remained a struggle. During the visit, Panico assessed Gilroy and found him perfect for the Sydney post. He was thoroughly Australian. A latecomer to the priesthood, he had volunteered for the AIF and served as a wireless operator on a transport carrying troops and supplies to Gallipoli. Although he came through unscathed, his experience when the ship came under shellfire was formative.[23] Whatever Gilroy thought about conscription, he had seen action and Mannix had not.

Gilroy may have made his reservations about Mannix known to Panico in their talks at Port Augusta. As a student in Rome in 1920 Gilroy had heard Mannix declare a degree of loyalty to Ireland which he thought inappropriate in an Australian prelate. An entry in the young Gilroy's diary records his disapproval:

> [Mannix] said that he loved Ireland above any nation in the world, afterwards adding however that he loved Australia the land of his adoption with Ireland the land of his birth. This lowered him in my estimation (not that that counts for anything I know) because as an Archbishop of a flock he should be their father, as father he should love the country where his life & labour is destined to be spent with a love that supersedes every other love. In addition it would seem that his cry Australia first is a mere catch-cry such as is used by any politician.[24]

The fact that Gilroy was in the 'Roman mould' was an advantage in Panico's mind; so was his practical nature. Gilroy would make an efficient coadjutor for Sydney, which, in the later years of Kelly's long reign, showed signs of neglect. And there would be no Irish political nonsense from this pious, sensible, limited man.

Nevertheless, Gilroy could not have expected so quickly to reach the dizzy heights of Sydney. Summoned by Panico, who liked to read his Vatican correspondence aloud to winners and losers alike, he was astonished to hear that he was chosen for coadjutor with right of succession to Kelly. It was a huge promotion for the youngest Catholic bishop in Australia. He went back to Port Augusta, packed and said his farewells. On his return to Sydney, he was met at the railway station by a group of priests with whom he had studied. 'Welcome back, Norman! Good on you, Norman!' they called cheerfully. 'Thank you, Father,' their new leader responded to each one with his trademark smile. The priests knew better than to use his first name, ever again.[25]

Neither Sheehan nor Mannix was impressed with Sydney's new coadjutor archbishop. Hearing about the appointment in Dublin from three visiting Sydney priests who seemed 'much upset', Sheehan reported to Mannix: 'I passed the matter off by saying that at all events he is a man of zeal.'[26] Panico's coup rankled with Mannix. Instead of witty, scholarly Sheehan he faced the years ahead with Gilroy, who was intellectually mediocre and stubborn.

There was more bad news for Mannix. Panico's next move was to replace Gilroy at Port Augusta. His choice might well have fallen on someone from the Adelaide diocese who knew the terrain. It should have been a young, energetic man, fit enough to traverse vast distances as Gilroy had done. Instead, Panico snapped up Monsignor John Lonergan, Mannix's trusted deputy. Lonergan had taken charge of the diocese during Mannix's absence in 1925, and had become his friend as well as his right-hand man. Quietly and unobtrusively he managed everyday matters while Mannix was in the national and international arena.

Melbourne-born, in 1888, to a working class family, Lonergan worked in small country parishes from his ordination in 1911 until his appointment to the cathedral staff in 1916, a year before the death of Archbishop Carr. He impressed Mannix, who gave him huge responsibilities. From 1924 Lonergan filled three posts: administrator, chancellor of the archdiocese and private secretary to the archbishop. He organised big public events, including the international Eucharistic Congress in Sydney, and served on important boards and committees in Melbourne. Known for his 'genial manner and unfailing courtesy', Lonergan was said to be the best-liked man in the diocese. He was loyal to Mannix and deflected some of the hostility that followed the conscription debates with his generosity of spirit and good nature. By extending personal friendship to Protestants in Melbourne he 'help[ed] to assuage some of the bitter animosities of the war years'.[27]

In 1938, when Lonergan was posted to Port Augusta, he was not quite fifty years old but in bad health. Melbourne was his world: no one knew it better. Panico's decision to send him to the desert in order to weaken Mannix was cruel and unnecessary.

Mannix was angry on his own behalf and concerned for Lonergan. Writing to Archbishop Killian, he deplored the decision and the secrecy in which it had been made: 'The change for him will be truly drastic.'[28] He worried about Lonergan's health—and with reason. No sooner had the appointment been made than Lonergan collapsed from a heart attack. He died some months later, without having been consecrated a bishop, and without leaving Melbourne. Mannix farewelled 'the bishop that never was' with a heartfelt tribute. The requiem mass, which was sung by Mannix himself, and the panegyric, showed the affection and respect in which Lonergan was held.

It was another win for Panico. With Sheehan and Lonergan taken from him, Mannix had lost two moves in the Vatican chess game. Mannix then replaced Lonergan with another Australian priest, Patrick Lyons, who had been on the cathedral staff for three years. Lyons was thirty-five, energetic and intelligent, but he did not have Lonergan's openness and tact. Again, Mannix united the three main administrative jobs in one man. In 1938 Lyons became administrator of St Patrick's Cathedral, chancellor of the archdiocese, and private secretary to Mannix. A year later he was given the title of vicar-general.

With Sheehan gone, Mannix's main ally in the hierarchy was Irish-born Andrew Killian, who was close enough in friendship to be invited to share Mannix's summer holidays at Queenscliff. Only five letters from Mannix to Killian have survived; the rest must be presumed destroyed in accordance with Mannix's advice. Those that remain show the warmth and candour of the alliance. Mannix confided his annoyance at Panico's choice of James Hannan, a Melbourne priest, for promotion to the rank of monsignor.[29] He disliked the policy of scattering monsignori titles like confetti; the touch of purple attire that went with the title was rare in Melbourne. Disparagingly, Mannix called the Sydney diocese 'the purple east'. His irritation at Panico's incursions into Melbourne diocesan matters appeared in disparaging remarks about Hannan, whose somewhat flashy style he disliked. When the new monsignor (in church terminology a 'domestic prelate') stopped his red sports car, with a screech of brakes, at the front door of Raheen, Mannix said, 'If that's a domestic prelate, I wouldn't want to see a wild one'.

With Sheehan's downfall in mind, Mannix told Killian to be on guard:

> Lest there may be any old document from you in the archives it might be a wise precaution for you to write a letter cancelling, annulling and making utterly void any

> letter of resignation or any letter interpreted to be a letter of resignation, which may be dug up in the Roman or any other archives![30]

When Killian died, in June 1939, Mannix lost his last friend in the hierarchy. He had little in common with Duhig whose conservative politics irritated him, or with Perth's Archbishop Redmond Prendiville. Born in Ireland in 1900, Prendiville came to Australia at twenty-five with a reputation as an all-Ireland football player, and for having been expelled from All Hallows seminary for smoking the night before a retreat.[31] This robust sportsman, only thirty-five when he took over from Archbishop Clune, was a mere boy in Mannix's eyes. The Archbishop of Hobart, Australian-born Justin Simonds, represented the future. As it happened, Simonds' future and Mannix's were to be entwined, with the knot expertly tied by Giovanni Panico.

Justin Simonds was ordained by Panico as Archbishop of Hobart in February 1937. No one could complain that Panico had made a bad decision. For once, the priests of the diocese were consulted, and Simonds was their unanimous choice. Panico claimed that Mannix had tried to bring in another Irishman, and so he may have done but no evidence to that effect has been found. After Simonds had worked happily and productively in Tasmania for five years, it was probably time for Panico to move him on to a bigger and more demanding post. But rather than look to the interests of the Australian church as a whole, Panico used Simonds to cut down Mannix. Without consulting either man, he created Simonds Coadjutor Archbishop of Melbourne. It was done abruptly and in secret in September 1942. By then, Italy had entered the war; communications with Rome were disrupted, and Panico had even more liberty than before to shake up the Irish hierarchy in Australia. Luckily for him, he was classed, not as a citizen of Italy which might have meant internment, but as a citizen of the little independent and neutral state Vatican City.

In 1942, Mannix was seventy-eight. Physically fit and intellectually as capable as ever, he did not want a coadjutor. Still less did he want one chosen by Panico. The circumstances in which the new coadjutor was transferred from Hobart to Melbourne were guaranteed to enrage Mannix and embarrass Simonds. Panico had sent for Simonds without explaining anything, told him to come directly to Sydney, and on no account to stop in Melbourne on the way. Simonds' travel to Sydney was arranged before any news could get to Mannix, to whom Panico sent a perfunctory telegram announcing the appointment.

Meanwhile, in Sydney, Panico produced a letter to Pope Pius XII and asked Simonds to sign it. Simonds said that he never signed anything that he hadn't read. Panico then allowed Simonds to read the letter. It stated that Mannix had become incapable of governing the archdiocese of Melbourne. Simonds, who knew this statement was not true, refused to sign. Panico then gave Simonds lunch, and suggested a siesta before any further discussion of the letter. Rescue came just in time, when Archbishop Gilroy arrived to take Simonds to stay at the cathedral palace. Without waiting for Panico to wake from his siesta, Simonds ran from the house and jumped into Gilroy's car, saying, 'Drive, Norman, drive!'[32]

It does not seem that Mannix ever heard about this little comedy in Sydney. If he had known how honourably Simonds had behaved, he and his coadjutor might have become friends. Although Mannix never denigrated Simonds, their relationship never became close. Simonds was installed at St Mary's, West Melbourne, where Mannix had been happy to spend his own years as coadjutor. There was an essential difference. Carr had asked for Mannix and was glad to share the workload, even though Mannix's interventions in the political dramas of 1916 and 1917 were not always to his liking. Because of Sheehan, and because of Lonergan, Mannix was angry with Panico, and Justin Simonds was caught in a conflict that was none of his making.

Having put Simonds in place in Melbourne, Panico had more plans to unsettle Mannix. In November 1942, he told him that it was the wish of the Holy See that Simonds should take over as chaplain-general of the armed forces:

> In view of your advanced age the Holy See cannot expect Your Grace to perform the duties of Chaplain General... and has therefore instructed me to request you to cede to your Coadjutor Dr Simonds the jurisdiction you now have over military chaplains.[33]

Mannix had held that post since 1917, much to the disgust of political opponents in the second conscription debate. Now, in the Second World War, with Australia directly under threat, Mannix supported the war effort, and he had no intention of giving Simonds anything—certainly not when it was Panico's idea to do so. Back to Panico in Sydney went the Mannix reply: a firm No. Father Tim McCarthy, Mannix's deputy chaplain, was spending two days a week in camp visits, and doing overtime at night. Dr Simonds had 'a full time occupation in the discharge of his duties in this diocese'.[34]

Mannix conjured up a helpful statement from the army. The shared responsibility with Father Tim McCarthy was working well;

it was not advisable to make a change. Dr Simonds would need to be available at army headquarters for two days every week and at other times 'in the event of urgent decisions being necessary'.[35] The army preferred that no change be made.

Meanwhile Archbishop Simonds had no choice but to live quietly at St Mary's, while Monsignor Lyons kept the cathedral running smoothly. Patrick Lyons was efficient, hardworking, and devoted to Mannix. He was authoritarian in temperament; and it is likely that Mannix was not told all that he should have known about his diocese. By delegating too much to one man, in a diocese grown beyond recognition since 1917, Mannix was once again stretching the capacities of a deputy. The appointment of Simonds was a lost opportunity. Mannix never learned how to share power.

Panico found another way to destabilise Mannix's regime. In June 1944 he promoted Lyons, whisking him off to be Bishop of Christchurch. New Zealand was on the Vatican's administrative map as part of the same region as Australia: Oceania. The little city in New Zealand's South Island was very English—slow, decorous, conservative, with a small Catholic population. It was not the right place for Lyons, nor did the appointment fit Panico's professed policy of promoting the native-born. But—New Zealander or Australian—what did that matter so long as the new bishop wasn't Irish? Lyons would spend six years in Christchurch before being brought back to Australia as Bishop of Sale.

Mannix knew that Lyons had to be replaced quickly before Panico swooped again. He promoted another cathedral staff member, Father Arthur Fox. This meant a smooth transition, no waiting, and none of the disruption that might have come with an outside appointment. Fox gave the total devotion of an immensely hardworking man. But, just as Lyons fell short of Lonergan in warmth and breadth of vision, Fox was less intellectually able than Lyons. He was a narrow and literal-minded organisation man who was good at detail, with a precise memory and a commitment to keeping things as they had always been. The strategy of uniting three jobs in one—administrator, vicar-general and private secretary—gave Fox more discretionary powers than he was capable of exercising.

Unlike Mannix's affrays with Billy Hughes, where the moves were made in the open, his war with Panico was silent. Panico discussed nothing, gave no warnings. He simply sat by his Vatican chessboard and pounced. This put Mannix on the defensive, a strategic position to which he was not temperamentally suited. He refused to cooperate with Panico; he sidelined Simonds and he held onto his chaplain-general's office, but he didn't have the power to dislodge the Vatican's chosen representative, nor the freedom to denigrate his tactics openly. Mannix had loyalty and obedience from his deputies, Lonergan, Lyons and Fox. In return, they were given a remarkable degree of freedom to use their own initiative. 'I know of no other archbishop or bishop,' said Fox, approvingly, 'who delegated so much authority to another.'[36] Fox was allowed to interpret 'the mind of the archbishop' in ways that unduly simplified Mannix's ideas, and caused a great deal of trouble. There was a price to pay for liberalism, one which Mannix seems not to have considered. If any priest wanted to deceive him, Mannix said, there was no way to prevent him.[37] In Mannix's mind, trust was the best way to run an archdiocese: 'I trust my priests', he said regally. Was that his strength or his weakness as an archbishop? Probably both.

CHAPTER ELEVEN

THE CARDINAL'S RED HAT

BY SEPTEMBER 1939, when the Second World War broke out, the Vatican policy of ending the Irish leadership in the Australian church was close to total success. Archbishop Panico had only to topple Mannix: without him, the Archbishop of Brisbane, James Duhig, would be isolated and easier to manage. But Mannix was as popular as ever, and his diocese was thriving. It was still mainly Irish-Australian, but a sizable number of European migrants, mainly Italian, was beginning to change its character.

During the 1930s Mannix had become concerned that the Italian migrants, almost all Catholics, were not becoming part of the church in Australia. They needed priests who spoke their language. Many were from peasant backgrounds; they knew little English, and the Irish-Australian Catholic majority, rapidly rising in the world, kept its distance from this new underclass. Mannix wanted the newcomers to integrate with the community, but he could see that a bridging period with special attention to cultural differences was needed.

In 1938 Mannix invited an Italian Jesuit, Father Ugo Modotti, to come to Australia as chaplain to the Italian community. With sermons in Italian, observance of Italian feast days and pious customs, an Italian language newspaper and group activities under the Catholic umbrella, Father Modotti made a place for himself in Melbourne, and was at first on good terms with the apostolic delegate, Archbishop Panico. But the outbreak of war, and Mussolini's alliance with Hitler, changed the situation of the Italian community in Australia and sharpened the antagonism between Mannix and Panico. Conscription was not an issue as it had been in the First World War, and Mannix supported the war against Germany. But Ireland under de Valera declared itself neutral, and this made it possible for Panico to stir suspicions that Mannix was disloyal to the Allied cause. When it became clear that Modotti's prime loyalty was to Mannix, Panico saw a way to discredit them both.

As soon as Italy entered the war, in June 1940, the federal government began a hasty process of internments, and many Italian-Australian families were in distress. With wage-earners sent to spend the war behind barbed wire, the wives struggled to maintain themselves and their children. Sorting out fascists from anti-fascists and both of these groups from the politically naïve or disinterested Italian-Australians needed more discernment than a wartime government possessed. Mannix was the first to contribute to the fund set up to help the families of those who were interned. His gift of £100 set an example to the better-off Italians in the community. It enabled Modotti to send Christmas hampers filled with 'spaghetti, cheeses, black olives, garlic, toothbrushes and religious books' to the internment camps.[1]

Mannix had already come to the rescue of German Pallottine missionaries in the Kimberley, whose long record of work with Indigenous communities had not saved them from internment. He also intervened on behalf of two German priests among the 'enemy aliens', who arrived on the *Dunera* in August 1940 and were interned in Hay in New South Wales, as were two Austrian schoolboys for whom Mannix found places at Xavier College.[2]

It is thought that Archbishop Panico engineered a campaign against Father Modotti.[3] If it could be shown that Mannix's man in the Italian community was a fascist, then questions could be asked about Mannix's loyalty to Australia. Panico's hostility to Modotti is well documented. But if, in fact, he went as far as to frame Modotti, as Arthur Calwell claimed, he had only partial success.

The evidence against Father Modotti was flimsy. He *might* have been at a meeting at which supporters of Mussolini were present, and he had accepted the gift of a Fiat car from a group of Italian-Australians, some of whom were suspected of fascist sympathies. An attempted arrest in June 1940 was comically maladroit.[4] When military police arrived at Modotti's house in Power Street in Hawthorn, Modotti had time to jump into his Fiat and drive to Raheen, where he could rely on Mannix to give him shelter and advice. A quick message from Mannix—who was still the chaplain-general of the armed forces—did the trick, and Modotti was back at work in the Italian community, though under surveillance. Later, Mannix's deputy chaplain, Father Tim McCarthy, wrote to Brigadier William Simpson, director of security, to reinforce the message—no tampering with Father Modotti:

> I am telling you again, my dear Bill, that this man instead of being a hindrance to the Australian war effort is one of our closest allies...he has one object in view—to make [Italian migrants] better Christians and better Australians, and it is time his worth to the Commonwealth was publicly recognised instead of dogging every step he makes.[5]

As well as his good relations with Mannix, Modotti had a friendly association with Arthur Calwell. When Modotti made representations for the release of Italians who could be shown to be no danger to the war effort, Mannix asked for help from Calwell as a Catholic, a cabinet minister in the Labor government, and a friend to the Italian community, many of whom lived in his Melbourne electorate. Calwell, whose friendship with Mannix was unwavering, may have looked more benignly on Raheen's case list than on others; it may also be that Mannix with Modotti beside him was better informed than other church leaders. At any rate, the internment rate in Victoria was lower than in other states.[6]

Modotti's own story shows the perils of being a Mannix man. It didn't help that he was a Jesuit. Giovanni Panico must have known that his own catchy, irresistible nickname of 'Panicky Jack' was a Jesuit joke. It stemmed from an incident when Panico was accompanied to New Zealand by a group of Jesuit priests. When the ship scraped a rock as it entered Wellington Harbour late at night, the Jesuits were playing poker. Panico appeared in his nightshirt to ask what was happening. Refusing to believe that there was no danger, he rushed back to his cabin to put on his biretta, 'so as to die like a priest'. The Jesuits went on playing poker. The story went back to Mannix who would have relished the image as well as the nickname.

When the war ended, in 1945, Panico had been in Australia for nearly ten years. He was due for a new post and hoping for a better one than Australia, based on his 'de-Irishing' performance. One last manoeuvre was needed to crown his work. This was to persuade Rome that Australia should have its own cardinal. Not since the death of Cardinal Moran in 1911 had a churchman in Australia been given the high honour of the title of cardinal and the red hat that went with it. Now, having seen Norman Gilroy manage the Sydney diocese with dignity and competence, Panico could make a good case for giving Sydney the honour once again. This move had the double advantage of recognising Australia's coming of age and of delivering a final snub to the old Irishman in Melbourne.

Whatever Rome thought of Mannix—and he had caused more anxiety and rage than most prelates—he was a magisterial figure, known throughout the world. Ireland under de Valera was not free of problems, with partition a lasting evil, but there was stable democratic government in Dublin. Mannix's public statements had been thoughtful and generally liberal. People listened when he denounced the use of the atomic bomb, urged the end of capital punishment, questioned the justice of the White Australia Policy, spoke out for equality for Aborigines. Moreover, he had built his diocese to impressive heights. The future would bring painful questions about some of the priests trained on his watch; but in 1945 there was no sign of scandal within their institutions. Melbourne was looking good as the war ended, and Mannix *was* Melbourne. Cardinal Mannix sounded just right. But...Cardinal Gilroy?

The news broke on Christmas Eve, 1945. Hearing the radio announcement at home in Melbourne, Arthur Calwell was incandescent with rage. He had hero-worshipped Mannix since

Clifton Pugh's portrait
of Mannix, 1962.

Daniel's parents: Ellen Mannix, née Cagney, and Timothy Mannix.

Mannix's birthplace, Deerpark, Charleville, County Cork.

St Patrick's College, Maynooth (below); the library (above).

Mannix with Queen Alexandra and Cardinal MacRory during the royal visit, Maynooth, 1906.

Eamon de Valera (1882–1975).

Mannix on a country tour to give confirmations, Gaffneys Creek, Victoria, 1913, 'A Hundred Thousand Welcomes'.

St Patrick's Day procession, Melbourne, 1920.
Inset: the white horse guard of honour provided for Mannix by John Wren.

Pro-Ireland demonstration at Chelsea Pier,
New York, as Mannix sailed in, 1920.

Bob Santamaria, signing the role of practitioners at the Victorian Supreme Court, 1938.

Patrick Mannix (1865–1957), brother of Daniel.

The conscription debate, Prime Minister Billy Hughes v Archbishop Daniel Mannix: 'A VITAL QUESTION. Will the Favourite Fall, and let the Imported Outsider Win?'

Raheen, Kew, Mannix's home from 1917 until his death in 1963.

Newman College.

In London, 1920.

Postcards of Mannix were sold before he sailed for the US and Europe.

Mannix in the 1930s.

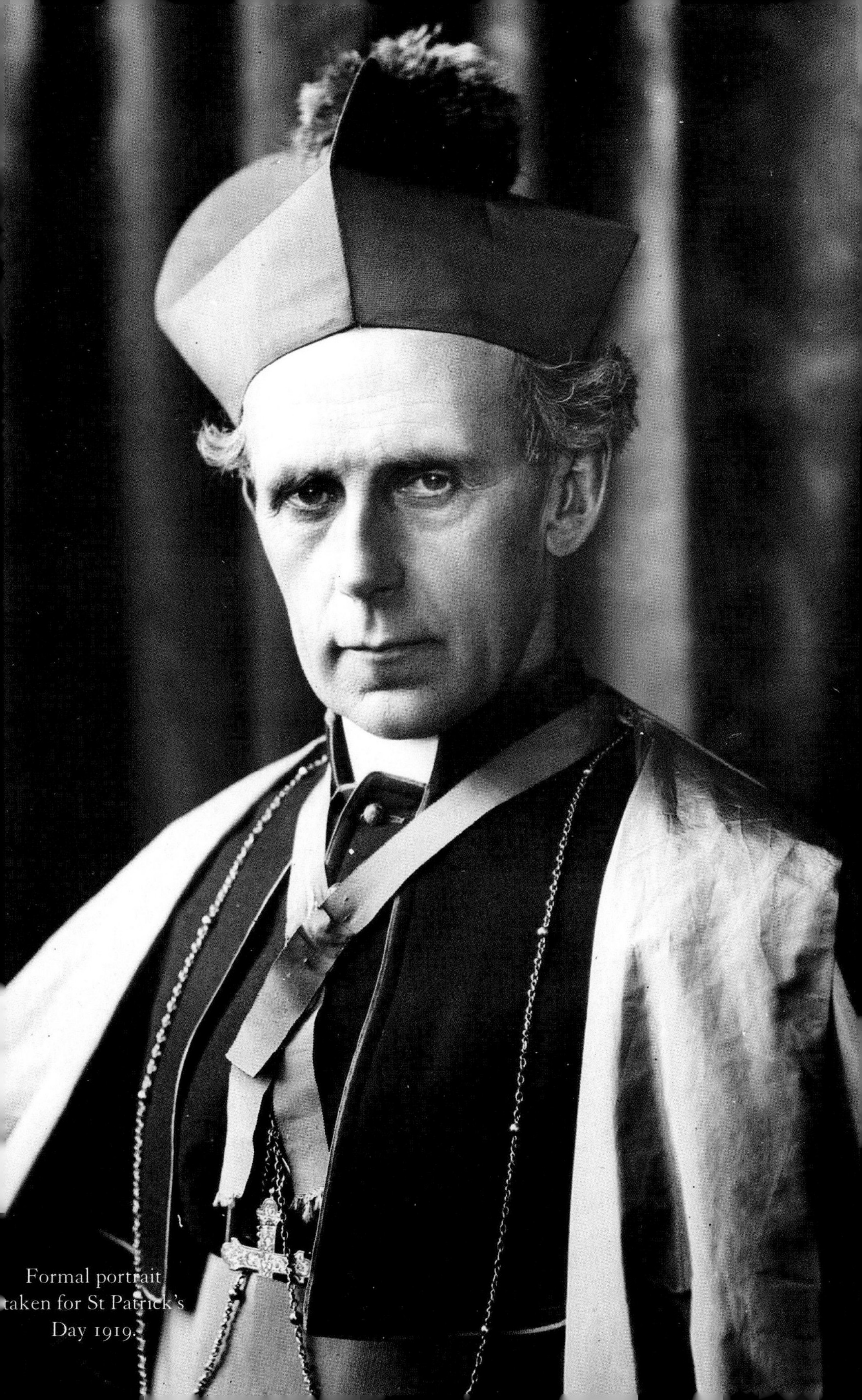

Formal portrait taken for St Patrick's Day 1919.

St Patrick's Day procession,
Melbourne, 1941.

With the Mozart Boys Choir from Vienna, 1939. Mannix took responsibility for the boys stranded in Australia at the outbreak of WWII.

Jacob Children in O'Keefe Case

Miss Ann Jacob—daughter of Mrs. Jacob, the Indonesian woman (now Mrs. John O'Keefe), whose deportation has been ordered by the Immigration Minister—is shown here chatting with Archbishop Mannix at the Sunbury Eucharistic Festival on November 7 last. Ann, aged 17, an employee of the Dutch Consulate, enjoys diplomatic immunity and cannot be deported. Neither can her brother, Peter, aged 5, who was born in Australia. But, under sentence of deportation is Tineke Jacob—also in the photograph—who with the remainder of the eight Jacob children are ordered to leave.

Mannix with Ann Jacob, daughter of Annie O'Keefe, 1949, during the controversy over Annie's refugee status.

Outside St Patrick's Cathedral,
East Melbourne, c. 1945.

Working with the Little Sisters of the Poor, c. 1949.

At the National Catholic Girls' Movement conference, Essendon, Melbourne, 1954.

Mannix at Raheen, c. 1960.

Walking sticks and cloak in the hallway, Raheen.

Walking to St Patrick's, c. 1954 (the year Mannix gave up his daily walk to the cathedral).

The burial of Archbishop Daniel Mannix, St Patrick's Cathedral, Melbourne, November 1963.

1913; and over nearly three decades he had been a close friend and a frequent visitor to Raheen. Without pausing to measure his words he called a press conference at which he made his views clear. Rome had chosen the wrong man. This, from a senior member of the Australian government, was indiscreet. Rome did not like being corrected. But Melbourne people—many of them at any rate—took their cue from Calwell and felt affronted. Sydney–Melbourne rivalries were roused. Gilroy's people were pleased. Some at least of the Australian-trained bishops and priests took Gilroy's promotion as an affirmation of a mature church, no longer dominated by Irish ways.

Once again, Archbishop Panico stirred the pot. In mid-1946, while Modotti was in Rome to recruit Italian priests for his Australian mission to the Italian community, Panico claimed that Calwell's outburst against the Pope's decision had been prompted by Modotti. This was palpably false—Calwell never needed prompting—but it contributed to Modotti's downfall. He never returned to Australia and the Jesuits closed down his mission.

In September 1946, Calwell had more to say. He was forthright about the apostolic delegate's preference for wealthy Italians. Writing to the father-general of the Jesuit order, he praised the 'distinguished' Father Modotti and spoke his mind about Panico:

> This is not the occasion for me to recite a litany of complaints against the Delegate for his tactlessness and for the embarrassment his requests concerning certain wealthy ex-internees (Prince del Drago and other known Fascists, the al Corso brothers and so on) have caused the Government of which I am a member. Suffice it to say that, if certain letters written by the Delegate are ever made

> public, the Catholic Church in Australia will be placed in a situation of great difficulty. In a word the Delegate has often represented not the interests of the Holy Father but the interests of the Italian State, and his continued interference in secular matters that are of no concern to any Delegate and are the source of much resentment, has worried and annoyed those Cabinet Ministers acquainted with his doings. My colleague Dr Evatt has told me that the late Prime Minister [John Curtin] had no time for Dr Panico which means that the Delegate was very much *non persona grata* [sic] with the head of the Australian Government.[7]

Calwell wanted to make it clear to the Jesuit father-general that Modotti had nothing to do with his own protest against the elevation of Gilroy. He had called the press conference within a few hours of hearing the announcement on the radio, and he had told no one but his wife. Calwell wrote with the same candour and indignation to the Vatican secretary of state, Archbishop Montini. With none of the polite circumlocutions with which the secretary of state was usually addressed, Calwell demanded that Panico, the author of 'a long and bitter vendetta against Archbishop Mannix', be removed from Australia.[8] Panico's predecessors, apostolic delegates Cardinal Cerretti and Archbishops Cattaneo and Bernardini were included in a vigorous attack on the standard of behaviour of the Vatican's representatives in Australia. All four were self-seeking, Calwell believed, but Panico was the worst.

Panico's vendetta against Mannix, Calwell said, had destroyed the good work done by Father Modotti ('a great priest who never spared himself') by making Modotti seem disloyal to the Pope. Nor was the claim that Modotti had manipulated Calwell over the

'Red Hat' matter the only example of Panico's malice: 'Believe me, Your Excellency, the Catholic Church is at the crossroads. Unless Rome takes heed [by removing Panico] the great work done by the pioneer bishops and priests will never be maintained'.[9]

Calwell was blunt about the Vatican's policy of Australianising the hierarchy. It had created a set of bishops and archbishops who were 'probably the most mediocre in the English-speaking world'. Except for the three Irish-born archbishops and one or two bishops, Calwell wrote, 'there is little personality and less leadership observable'.[10]

It was a splendidly vigorous, tactless letter. In Dublin and Rome, the fallout was watched with fascinated attention, and some amusement. The head of Ireland's department of external affairs, Fred Boland, was briefed by Thomas Kiernan, Ireland's first ambassador to Australia, to whom Calwell confided the full text of his letters of protest. Boland then passed it all on to his man in Rome, Joseph Walshe, head of the Irish diplomatic mission to the Vatican.

Kiernan interpreted Calwell's letters as 'a heavy shot fired for two purposes—to get rid of Panico and to make sure that his successor will not be an Italian'.[11] According to Calwell, all the delegates had amassed large private fortunes from their offices in Australia. Panico had eclipsed the others in his greedy demands for high fees for performing routine clerical duties. Free to speak his mind to his chief in Dublin, Kiernan summed up with a career diplomat's cynicism:

> All of this [the profiteering] is, however, what I should regard as the normal line which an Italian career prelate would take; and I think that underlying the whole issue is

> the seemingly insolent attitude which Monsignor Panico has adopted towards Archbishop Mannix.[12]

Kiernan noted that Mannix sent his Propagation of the Faith collection money, which was 'much bigger than that of Sydney' direct to Rome, instead of having Panico forward it. Was this a hint that Panico had his fingers in the till? Or that Mannix disdained to recognise Panico's existence? In context, the hint of corruption seems to be Kiernan's intended meaning. Kiernan also commented on the fact that on his visits to Melbourne, Panico never visited Raheen. The two men would have met on official occasions and exchanged the usual courtesies. Otherwise, it was sub-zero temperature between them.

Calwell wanted the Vatican to recall Panico and make Archbishop Simonds the new apostolic delegate. Having an Australian to represent the Pope would be a timely move, given the impending appointment of an Australian governor-general, William McKell. It would do Mannix a favour, in removing a coadjutor who wasn't needed, and it would do justice to Simonds whose abilities were being wasted. And when the Pope made his next round of appointments, Calwell said, he should make Mannix a cardinal.

Calwell spoke with the confidence of a prime minister in waiting, as he believed himself to be. He had reason to think that he, rather than Herbert Evatt, would succeed Prime Minister Ben Chifley, who was in poor health.[13] In the last months of 1946, with Gilroy's promotion still much in mind, Calwell set off for a six-week tour of Europe. Chosen by Chifley to initiate Australia's postwar migration program, Calwell had a busy program ahead of him, to which he gave his unstinting attention. But as well as his official duties, he planned to put right the wrong done to Mannix in the matter of the Red Hat, and the destruction of Modotti's work with the Italian community. He expected to visit Dublin and confer with de Valera before going to Rome for some face-to-face diplomacy. He had already prepared the way by asking Dr Evatt, then minister for external affairs, to brief the Australian high commissioner for talks with the British foreign secretary, Anthony Eden. Dr Evatt, according to Calwell, admired Mannix greatly.

Reporting all this to his chief in Dublin, Ambassador Kiernan stressed Calwell's significance. He was a major figure in Australian politics, but he was also a loose cannon:

> Mr Calwell is an extremely honest and sincere man, outspoken, and, in matters relating to Ireland, I may find him more in need of counsels of restraint than of pressure. He represents a safe Labour constituency in Melbourne and will be a power in Australian politics for very many years to come...he will go to England after Easter, via the USA so that he can see Cardinal Spellman and tell him the Panico position and get his influence with the Vatican to have him removed; and then when he goes to England, he will visit Ireland, and he is anxious to meet the Taoiseach [de Valera].[14]

As the worldly-wise Irish diplomats could have told Calwell, advice to the Vatican was bound to fail. Letters between Dublin and Rome show their scepticism. Ireland's foreign affairs secretary, Fred Boland, was uneasy about getting involved. He respected Calwell as a good friend to Ireland, and he was not about to offend someone who might well be the next Australian prime minister, but he and the Irish ambassador in the Vatican, Joseph Walshe, were relieved when Calwell's time in Europe ran out and his visit to the Vatican had to be cancelled.

There was a real possibility, Walshe believed, that because of his public attack on Gilroy's appointment as cardinal, Calwell would have been snubbed by the Pope. At the least he would have been asked to give 'some satisfactory explanation of the famous speech which was regarded here as an insult and an indirect aspersion on the Holy Father's judgment'.

Unaware of all the trouble he was causing, Calwell telephoned from London, confidently instructing the Irish ambassador to speak to the Vatican on his behalf. He wanted Archbishop Montini to be asked why he had not replied to Calwell's letter about Mannix and Panico. Montini should be told that 'Australia wanted a delegate from the English-speaking world and she also wanted Archbishop Mannix made a cardinal...' It was not really Walshe's business to act as go-between in the Vatican for an Australian politician and he probably did not carry out the instructions. He wrote back to his chief in Dublin:

> I do not wish to conceal that I am very glad that Calwell is not coming to Rome. He seems to be the Bull in China shop type and he might be quite impervious to advice. Ultimately the Vatican might think that we [the Irish Government] had something to do with his visit and our stock mightn't be raised as a consequence. I felt obliged to tell Montini that Calwell might pay a visit to Rome, and I hope, now that he is not coming, we shall get the credit for putting him off.[15]

Calwell was the most forthright critic of Gilroy's elevation, but he was not the only one. To pass over Archbishop Mannix for a much younger man who had done nothing special since his appointment was widely seen as an outrage. In Ireland, too, it was taken as a snub: even though Mannix had been a trouble in the past, that was seen as a family row which Rome had no business to enter. It roused Melbourne–Sydney rivalry. And for those in the know, Gilroy's promotion looked more like the work of Panicky Jack than any informed decision from Rome. Who knew what reports he had sent back during the war years? It was easy to guess that Panico would have put the worst possible spin on Mannix.

Other responses to Gilroy's elevation ranged from the offensively racial—'So the Dago's Pup has got it, after all'[16]—to a naïve and devious ploy devised by Archbishop Duhig of Brisbane. Duhig and Mannix had never been close: there was always an element of amused condescension in Mannix's attitude to 'James the Builder'. But they were as one in detesting Panico and in their pride in the Irish achievements in Australia.

Knowing that as an archbishop he could not openly criticise the Pope for choosing Gilroy over Mannix, Duhig wrote to Jeremiah Murphy, rector of Newman College, enclosing an article that he wanted Murphy to place in a Melbourne newspaper, preferably the *Argus*. If Murphy did not want to 'father' the article himself, he could use a pseudonym. Murphy must have gasped at Duhig's innocence. After polite remarks about the wisdom of Rome and a claim that the Melbourne diocese was pre-eminent in Australia and an inspiration to the world, Duhig made it clear that, in appointing Gilroy a cardinal, Rome had blundered:

> The Pope labours under a disadvantage common to great

> men, particularly in high places who have to see through the eyes of others and hear through their ears…it is an open secret that [Archbishop Mannix] has never had a friend at court. Sinister influences have come between him and the Holy See, to which his loyalty has been outstanding, and this more than any other circumstance may account for his being passed over in the giving of a Cardinal to Australia.[17]

Writing just two days after the announcement of Gilroy's success, Duhig signed off with a hasty postscript: 'Would prefer His Grace to know nothing at this juncture.' Nothing came of the venture. Mannix would have been touched as well as surprised at Duhig's generous impulse.

As Mannix's closest friend and ally, de Valera could have joined in the protests. He did not do so. Knowing Mannix as he did, he might have hesitated to underline the humiliation of being passed over by making a public statement. His silence may also have been a matter of prudence. De Valera had come a long way since the civil war period when the Vatican had excommunicated him and his allies for their armed resistance to the treaty with Britain. Before and after de Valera came to power in 1932, he had been mending fences with Rome and with the Irish bishops. He did, however, make it known that Panico need not think of visiting Dublin: he would not be received. As de Valera's envoy in the Vatican remarked, it was a delicate situation:

> Our own objection to the visit of Panico was almost unprecedented, though it was the right and only thing to do in the circumstances. It showed them our solidarity with our people outside Ireland. But we can't afford to let

> Calwell involve us in Australian intrigues. I hope Kiernan is learning to lie very doggo in ecclesiastical matters.[18]

Mannix could not help being affronted by the choice of Gilroy for the Red Hat. It did not in itself make Sydney more important than Melbourne—the archdioceses were all equal and independent of one another, in theory at least—but it was the highest honour that the Pope could bestow. Membership of the College of Cardinals meant having a vote for the next Pope. And it was going to a mediocrity, promoted by Panico to replace the unlucky Archbishop Michael Sheehan.

Mannix used the occasion of a High Mass at St Patrick's Cathedral to respond to the news. While seeming to celebrate Gilroy's elevation, he subverted the new cardinal's official welcome with finely tuned irony. Comparing Mannix's words with the 'vinegar' of Calwell's statement, Tom Fitzgerald of the *Nation* described it as a delicate dry white wine.[19] You had to read it slowly to understand that the apparently gentle words carried a sting:

> I am old enough and observant enough to have watched [Cardinal Gilroy's] career since he put his foot upon the first rung of the ecclesiastical Jacob's ladder that has brought him to his present exalted position. God looked after him. He protected him on the shell-raked shores of Gallipoli. He called him to the sanctuary and guided him to Propaganda College [Rome] that nursing mother of many prelates. For years the future cardinal was buried in the silent catacombs of the [Apostolic] Delegation and no doubt, too, that was providential. But there was a resurrection when he went as Bishop to Port Augusta. Perhaps people thought it was

> not a milestone on the way to the Sacred College. But God has His own way of working out His designs. Dr Gilroy soon went to Sydney, and, if there was to be an Australian Cardinal, his selection was inevitable...[20]

Mannix then offered a comparison between Gilroy and Cardinal Newman. He said that there were likenesses as well as contrasts, but attentive listeners would discern that the contrasts prevailed. Mannix set Gilroy as 'man of action' against the scholar Newman. He contrasted the years of suffering and calumny Newman had endured with Gilroy's ascent 'by pleasant ways and easy stages'. Mannix ended on a softer note with a tribute to Gilroy's 'zeal for the salvation of souls', his 'natural, unlaboured dignity' and 'gracious urbanity'. But those in the know would have taken the references to the 'silent catacombs' of the apostolic delegation as well as the meaning of the call from Port Augusta and drawn their own cynical conclusions.

The war years brought Archbishop Panico close to completing his project of Australianising the Catholic hierarchy. There were Australian-born archbishops in Sydney, Adelaide and Hobart. Australian bishops ruled in Geraldton and Townsville, Canberra, Ballarat, Bendigo. You could still hear sermons with an Irish accent in many parishes; international religious orders still brought out some Irish men and women. But the Irish were now scarcely needed to supplement the growing numbers of vocations in a time of triumphalism and Australian nationalism within the church. It was the end of the Irish mission, or very nearly. The great survivors were James Duhig of Brisbane and Daniel Mannix in Melbourne. In 1945, Duhig was seventy-four and Mannix was eighty-one. Duhig gave his coadjutor Patrick O'Donnell a hard time. Mannix continued to ignore Justin Simonds. It would have rounded off Panico's stint in Australia nicely to see the two old Irishmen end their days in retirement. But they stood their ground.

There was, however, a price to pay for Calwell's outspoken support for Mannix. Panico was due for transfer in early 1947. Rather than have Rome appear to yield to pressure from Calwell and admit a mistake, it was decided to extend Panico's term for two more years.[21] Panico was still in Australia in 1948 when the centenary of the Melbourne archdiocese was celebrated. He enlivened the official dinner, in the presence of Mannix's guests, Cardinal Spellman and Eamon de Valera, with the provocative words: 'I look forward to the day when every Bishop in Australia will be Australian.' As host, should Mannix have let the insult pass? Not when he could make such a neat riposte:

> I was most interested to hear what the Apostolic Delegate had to say, that he looked forward to the day when every bishop in Australia would be Australian. I would like to say that I look forward to the day when the Apostolic Delegate will be Australian.[22]

To this day one can find references to 'Cardinal Mannix' in text books and other printed sources, from writers who assume that a man of such prominence must have been a cardinal. Yet he was never given the honour. In Irish diplomatic circles, it was believed that the Panico's role was crucial.[23] The affair of the Red Hat poisoned relations between Mannix and Gilroy.

Giovanni Panico went on his way, with a posting to Peru in 1949. Strangely, given his condescending attitude towards Ireland as an 'intellectually backward' nation, he fished for an appointment to Dublin, but Mannix made sure that de Valera would block it.[24] In 1962, the news of Panico's retirement reached the then ninety-eight-year-old Mannix. The Vatican honoured Panico with a red hat of his own. As Cardinal Panico, he would be one of those to vote with Gilroy and the other members of the College of Cardinals when his former chief, now Cardinal Montini, was elected as Pope Paul VI, in 1963.

The rebuff from Rome must have hurt and angered Mannix, but he did not let his feelings show. To his tactless champion Arthur Calwell, he said: 'If I had ever wanted to be a Cardinal, I would certainly have charted my life quite differently.'[25]

CHAPTER TWELVE

ENTER SANTAMARIA

EVERY MONDAY NIGHT, from the 1920s until his death in 1954, William Hackett dined with the archbishop at Raheen. In later years, he was invited to stay overnight. 'I get away, if I am lucky, on Tuesday'. Five or six hours a week in Mannix's company: what did they talk about?

Of course, Ireland came first. A strong bond had been forged between Mannix and Hackett from their shared sorrow and their sense of exile from the homeland. Yet their friendship never quite became one between equals. For Mannix, who needed the companionship more than sociable Hackett ever did, the bond was almost brotherly. Mannix was the elder, quick to put the younger one in his place. Hackett's upbringing, as the fourth of six sons in a gifted and intellectually competitive Kilkenny family, had taught him resilience but he couldn't permit himself to match an archbishop's quips and put-downs. He would have liked to be given some praise, but that wasn't the Mannix style. 'Am I a snob?' Hackett asked, in a letter to his sister. 'His Grace says that I am.' In fact, his social range stretched from Lord Somers, the governor of Victoria, with whom he went bushwalking, to a friend who served a long sentence in Pentridge prison. That breadth of human sympathy, allied with an irrepressible sense of fun, enriched the friendship for Mannix.

Hackett dreaded being asked to live at Raheen, whose splendours and silences he found oppressive, but he sensed the archbishop's loneliness, and his unexpected shyness. It wasn't easy to be always the most important person in the room, as Mannix was in Melbourne. When there were guests staying at Raheen, the archbishop would send for Hackett. 'It is a curious thing that Dr Mannix does not like to be left alone with *one* visitor. He tolerates me, but then I don't count,' Hackett wrote.[1] But Hackett did count. He was diplomat, mediator, envoy, entertainer and candid friend to the archbishop, and from the 1930s he was an essential link between Mannix and a new generation of young Catholic intellectuals.

'And now, what is the news?' Mannix would ask, as he and Hackett sat down to dinner. Much of the news came from Ireland, where Hackett kept up a correspondence with members of de Valera's inner circle. Hackett's three brothers in the United States, all of whom were shrewd political observers, wrote often as did his novelist sister in Kilkenny. But in the early 1930s, the weekly dinners at Raheen found a new focus. As the director of the Central Catholic Library, established by Mannix in 1925, Hackett had a vast circle of friends and acquaintances, linked by a common interest in books and ideas. The library was centrally placed in the Orient Line building in Collins Street, a tram ride from Melbourne

University, and a few minutes walk from Parliament House and the Treasury. In between the top end of Collins Street, where medical consultants clustered, and the legal precinct, it was an inviting place for students and professional men. The latest novels were well represented, and there was a good supply of children's books. Hackett, who had two clever sisters, knew better than to ignore or patronise women members; they were made welcome, and a visit to the library was often part of a shopping trip to the city. Although he never learned to balance a budget, Hackett made the library a remarkable success. And when he spent too much on books, as he usually did, Mannix always found the money.

Mannix took a special interest in one story from the Catholic Library and followed it week after week. This was the emergence of a group of talented young men who came to the library to discuss Catholic teaching and the social order. It was a new beginning for Melbourne Catholic intellectuals. Convened by arts–law graduate Frank Maher, and named the Campion Society, the group included law students Murray McInerney and Gerard Heffey, arts students Kevin Kelly and John Merlo, and teacher and journalist Denys Jackson. Not surprisingly, given the times, the members were all men.[2] One of the youngest recruits to the Campions, Bob Santamaria, was just out of school when Frank Maher, who had taught him history at St Kevin's, invited him to a Campion discussion night in 1931.

Catholic secondary schooling hadn't given these young Campions much knowledge of papal teaching on social justice, nor were they used to debating their faith. William Hackett gave them books and a meeting place; he went to their discussion evenings only if he was invited and he never tried to control them. On Monday nights at Raheen, he kept Mannix abreast of their doings. One evening when the Campions' debate was at Newman College, Mannix invited himself to join the audience. His host, Father Jeremiah Murphy, watched anxiously to see if the archbishop would approve of these exuberant young men.[3] As usual, Mannix was inscrutable.

The first Campion member to come to Mannix's full attention was Bob Santamaria, who had graduated in arts and law in 1935. Towards the end of that year, Santamaria and law graduate Val Adami came to ask for the archbishop's permission to start a monthly newspaper, the *Catholic Worker*, which would give a voice to the Campions' ideas on social justice and current affairs. Testing their mettle, Mannix kept the two young men talking for nearly two hours about foreign policy and other matters without touching on the reason for their visit. Unless they had the enterprise to speak for themselves, he would not be interested in their proposal.

Finally, when Mannix rose to dismiss them, Santamaria came to the point. The idea of starting a monthly paper was modest—he knew that anyone could do that—but he wanted the archbishop's approval for the *Catholic Worker* title. Because the name involved the church, he expected that he and his associates would come under some form of clerical supervision. Mannix brushed this aside. They didn't need his permission. A chaplain? No, they didn't need a chaplain: 'I do not want a priest taking control of your work.' But, Santamaria said, they might make mistakes that would damage the church. The archbishop was amused: 'You will have heard that the man who makes no mistakes makes nothing.' He shook hands with them and sent them on their way.[4]

The older Campion Society men were not pleased by Santamaria's taking the newspaper idea to Mannix. His choice of Val Adami for support didn't help. Adami wasn't one of the

Campion founding members. The elders of the society, Frank Maher, Murray McInerney and Gerard Heffey, should have been consulted. Kevin Kelly, who had already asked Mannix about the newspaper, and had no response, was annoyed.[5] They all felt bypassed. But, in Santamaria's view, the group had been too slow to act.

The first issue of the *Catholic Worker* appeared on 1 February 1936. Santamaria wrote the entire content of the four-page broadsheet, used his university prize money as an advance on expenses, and organised the printing and distribution of an initial 3000 copies. These sold out within a few days, and another printing of 8000 copies was hastily organised. The banner headline was 'We Fight!' The first copy was posted to the Pope and the second to Joseph Stalin. The *Catholic Worker* declared the Campions' resolve to fight for their principles and to defend the values of the Catholic Church against communism and capitalism. Thanks to Santamaria, the paper was a *fait accompli*, which, at first, the older Campions accepted and worked with. As Murray McInerney described it:

> The *Catholic Worker* addressed itself to matters of immediate practical and political concerns, such as unemployment, working conditions, the provision of housing...slum areas in Melbourne, identifying the slum landlords who gave nothing back in the shape of amenities in return for the rents they collected.[6]

The paper was an immediate success. It confirmed Mannix's impression that Bob Santamaria had the capacity to take an idea to a practical conclusion. With Mannix's permission, the *Catholic Worker* was sold outside parish churches after Sunday mass. Parish priests, who took deliveries, knew that it had the archbishop's approval, and read it accordingly. Available also by subscription, the paper had an astonishing circulation of 70,000 by 1941. Everyone was happy except the senior Campions whom Santamaria had bypassed. So as to keep him from permanent control, an editorial committee of three was appointed, these to be responsible to a board. This attempt to contain Santamaria failed and later, after some disagreements, he withdrew from the paper he had founded and distanced himself from the Campion group. By nature Santamaria wasn't a team player. He saw what he believed should be done, and did it, quickly, effectively and on his own.

Mannix was impressed by the Campions' concern for social justice during the Depression of the 1930s. He was also impressed by their grasp of European politics and current affairs. What happened in Europe mattered to Mannix. He saw Australia in an international context and, in as far as the slow arrival by sea of overseas journals allowed, he kept up with international news and opinion. Although more wary of communism than fascism, he was well aware of the witches' cauldron of ideologies in 1930s Europe. He did not then know the full horrors of Hitler's extermination plan, but he was ahead of many church and state leaders in speaking out about the persecution of Jews in Germany and Eastern Europe.

Mannix's thoughts in the economic depression years had a double focus: social justice at home and anti-communism in Europe. Twenty years after the founding of Newman College and St Kevin's Central School, he was impatient for a show of political leadership from the fast-growing cohorts of educated Catholics. The 'Great Debate' on Spain at the University of Melbourne in 1937 brought the man and the moment together. Bob Santamaria was a child of the Depression and a natural leader in the anti-communist crusade, which for him and other Catholic intellectuals began in 1936 with the Spanish Civil War.

Anyone who was politically literate had a view on the struggle in Spain. For some—and this included most Catholics—General Franco was a hero. Although he had overthrown the elected republican government in a military coup, this was thought to be justified because of the nature of that government. Anti-clerical and pro-communist, it was persecuting Spanish Catholics. Backed by Russia, the Spanish republic threatened to take the communist program into Catholic Europe. Backed by Hitler, Franco's Spain could become part of the Nazi strategy.

Santamaria's first public moment came a few months before his twenty-second birthday. It was a hot night, just before the beginning of term at the University of Melbourne. The public lecture theatre was jam-packed with an audience of more than a thousand that filled the aisles and overflowed into the corridors.[7] Some young men perched on the roof, stamping their feet at times so loudly that the speakers couldn't be heard. This 'Great Debate' caught the imagination; it challenged everyone to take a side. Three young Catholics argued 'that the Spanish government has been the ruin of Spain'. All were in their twenties, bright-eyed, confident debaters with little knowledge of the world. All were recent graduates: Stan Ingwersen in medicine, Kevin Kelly in arts and Bob Santamaria in arts–law. All were ablaze with anger at the anti-clerical atrocities the Catholic press was reporting. They saw General Franco as the saviour of the European civilisation which Spain embodied. The years ahead would show that neither Franco nor the republicans had clean hands, but in the 1937 debate it was good versus evil in a fight to the death.

The case for the republic was put by two Communist Party

members, Gerald O'Day and John Legge, and writer Nettie Palmer, who had been living near Barcelona with her husband, novelist Vance Palmer, at the time of Franco's coup. They had age and experience on their side but lacked coherence as a team. The O'Day team lost the debate to the enthusiastic young men. When Ingwersen shouted '*Viva Cristo Rey*!' the audience was roused to frenzy: there was fighting in the aisles and outside the theatre; fire hoses were used to flood the corridors; police were called. Both sides had stacked the meeting, but the Catholics had the numbers. Historian Manning Clark described two howling mobs: 'It was like being in the outer at a match between Carlton and Collingwood.' Drawing on Clark's notes and those of other student witnesses, biographer Mark McKenna described the scene:

> Santamaria opened for the affirmative, raised his voice above the din of hecklers, and argued that 'the struggle for Spain was religious, insisting that the government must bear the responsibility for the revolt, in view of its opposition to democracy and its organised intolerance'. Becoming more and more passionate as his supporters urged him on, he declared that the republicans had denied freedom of the press, speech and worship. 'You must be a Spaniard to understand,' he exclaimed. 'The heart of my race has been torn.' With this the audience exploded.[8]

Mannix didn't go to public debates, but he had plenty of people to tell him about this one. Even in his own most impassioned speeches of the conscription period he had never faced such a violently polarised audience. Bob Santamaria, a 'miniature tornado of ideas and energy', impressed him at a crucial moment.[9] By 1938, the Campions had outgrown the friendly club-like character that had developed in the Catholic Library. Members were asked to speak in many Melbourne parishes, in country Victoria and in the other states. It wasn't easy to respond. No longer students but young professional men, some already married, they couldn't give undivided attention to their Campion work. They were needed, too, to keep the *Catholic Worker* going. Their work in Catholic adult education was in danger of losing momentum when Mannix stepped in. He persuaded the other Australian archbishops and bishops to fund a central co-ordinating organisation based on the Campions' ideas which would serve all the states. But because of Mannix's dominant role and its origins in the Campion Society, the new organisation had its major impact in Melbourne.

Funded by the church hierarchy, the Australian National Secretariat of Catholic Action, known as ANSCA, had its head office in Melbourne, and Mannix was one of the three prelates chosen to oversee it. Catholic Action could mean many things. Archbishop Kelly thought it meant an increase in pious practices. For the Campions, following French thinkers like Jacques Maritain, it meant taking their religious principles into the workplace, whatever that might be. They would bear witness to their moral and ethical beliefs, but they would not cross the line into politics. Their mission was to spread Catholic social-justice teaching. They aimed to do this through professional vocational groups—the Guild of St Luke for doctors, the St Thomas More Society for lawyers—and through groups founded on the factory floor, in the railways and any place in which Catholic workers were present. Santamaria, more pragmatic, saw some degree of political involvement as inevitable, even desirable. Mannix, with his long history of political activism, became his model.

Mannix invited the Campions to make their own choice of director and deputy-director for the new organisation. Frank Maher was the natural choice for the position of director. The Campion Society was his creation, and he was excited at the thought of developing the group's ideas on a national scale. An exceptional teacher, his great gift was in empowering others. He would quietly draw out their half-formed thoughts without making it evident how much he had inspired and shaped them. Moreover, his career in the law was not flourishing; he disliked the routine of his law firm, Adami and Maher, and spent so much time in personal counselling of his clients that he was making very little money. Santamaria, by contrast, was confident of doing well in the law, and a brilliant future as a barrister seemed assured. He wasn't an obvious choice as deputy-director of ANSCA. Arts graduate Kevin Kelly or lawyer Murray McInerney could have had the deputyship for the asking. Kelly declined because he was financially responsible for his widowed mother. McInerney was wary of being a 'professional Catholic'; he admired Mannix but wouldn't put his trust in 'episcopal princes'.[10] There was some support for Ken Mitchell, who was well read and popular but he had no academic credentials. So, almost by default, Bob Santamaria was chosen. He showed his enthusiasm and his naïveté when he left his interview with Mannix at the cathedral 'jumping for joy' at the prospect of the deputy's job.[11] He made up his mind on the spot:

> I got a phone call to go up to the cathedral to meet Archbishop Mannix…and he asked me if I'd take the second job. I'd never dreamt—so I said, I said yes because I would have said yes to anything he asked.[12]

After saying yes so impulsively, he had to break the news to his father. It says a great deal for Mannix's prestige that Giuseppe (Joe) Santamaria did not resent the sidelining of his son's career in the law. Having watched the young Bartholomew (Bob) win university exhibitions and prizes along the way, it must have been frustrating suddenly to be told about the archbishop's offer. But whatever came from Mannix was an honour; and the commitment was for only two years.

Although Joe Santamaria had very little formal education he had gained worldly knowledge in his early years. Born on the Aeolian island of Salina, near Sicily, he came to Australia at the age of twelve. He worked as a seaman, tried his luck in the United States, and re-joined his immigrant parents in Australia in 1904.[13] Peasants and fishermen on Salina, the Santamarias were part of a cluster migration from the same impoverished island background. They had some Spanish forebears—almost enough to prompt Bob's impassioned identification in the Great Debate—and Joe's political and social awareness had appeared in 1919–20 when he was on the editorial committee of *Voce Italia*, a nationalist, non-religious magazine. He founded an Italian friendly society, the *Aeolian*, and served more than once as its president.

Bob Santamaria's family values and sense of self appear in a few reticent autobiographical fragments. Born in Brunswick, an inner industrial suburb of Melbourne, in August 1915, he was the first of six children. He remembered his father's determination to be 'his own boss' and the hard work over many years that turned a small fruit shop into a thriving licensed grocery. As a six-year-old, Bob knew his father wanted him to be a lawyer. His secondary education began at the Christian Brothers' school in North Melbourne, and from there he was chosen for the St Kevin's

Central School in East Melbourne. Well taught in this powerhouse of talent and ambition, Bob Santamaria qualified for university entrance at fifteen but had to repeat his matriculation subjects while waiting to reach the minimum university entrance age of sixteen. From then on, scholarships, exhibitions and prizes eased his path and the way ahead looked bright. Living at home all through the Depression, he shared his father's strong Labor Party commitment. Prime Minister Scullin was his hero. Emotionally, Bob Santamaria belonged to Brunswick. If he wanted wider horizons, his version of self doesn't show it; his warm centre is home, family and his first friends:

> Practically all of my friends at St Ambrose Brothers' School from 1921 onwards came from low-paid working-class families...Many of them were to finish on the scrap heap of unemployment together with their fathers in the bitter depression years...When I moved from St Ambrose to 'North' and from 'North' to St Kevin's, the centre of my life was still Brunswick and my earliest friends, still the same Church near the same Town Hall outside which once a week a seemingly endless line stood immobile waiting for relief or 'sustenance'. These were not 'dead-beats' or unemployables. In the line were many of the parents of my schoolmates, the very people whom Sunday after Sunday I had seen filling the benches at the big parish Church of St Ambrose.[14]

Santamaria stood out in predominantly Irish-Australian company for being younger and smaller than most, and for his Italian name and background. Multiculturalism was then unknown in Melbourne. Those whose forebears had been called ignorant Micks and Paddys were quite ready to insult 'dirty dagoes'. St Kevin's boys might not have been so crudely racist but there is no doubt that Santamaria was seen as an outsider. His account of growing up Italian in working-class Melbourne is stubbornly upbeat; his memory of the 'cold fury' he felt at being called a 'dago' stands out because of its rarity.[15] It wasn't in his nature to admit disadvantage. His brother Joe matter-of-factly recalled being called 'darkie' by the Brunswick schoolboys with whom he played marbles.[16] But although Bob Santamaria had too strong a sense of his own value to be crushed, his not belonging to the group had its effect. Santamaria's innate competitiveness appeared when he edited one of the two class 'journals' with such dialectical vigour that he and the rival editor, Charles Sweeney, a future judge, were ordered to 'tone things down'. They took no notice, and the 'journals' (read aloud in class but not printed) were suspended for the rest of the year.

Jim McClelland, a future lawyer and Labor Party senator, shared a double desk with Santamaria and the two exchanged ideas and book recommendations over the summer holidays before they both started at university. Santamaria was reading Catholic authors Chesterton and Belloc; McClelland, more venturesome, had discovered George Bernard Shaw and H. G. Wells.[17] McClelland later thought it strange that they argued by letter rather than taking a tram from Glen Iris to Brunswick or meeting somewhere in between. The divide between these two wasn't economic—McClelland's railway-worker father was less secure than shop-owner Joe Santamaria—but neither thought of crossing the other's threshold.

At Melbourne University, Santamaria was noticed but not

assimilated. He made himself felt in class and in university politics. A brilliant debater, he easily won a place in the university team. Interstate travel to compete against teams from the other Australian universities didn't make him feel at ease with his fellow debaters. In old age, pressed by publisher Peter Ryan to give his memories of a fellow debater Chester Wilmot, he let some long-hidden anger show:

> Chester Wilmot came to Melbourne University gilded by Melbourne Grammar and an establishment background. I was an Italian fruiterer's son from Brunswick and there was not a single day that Chester let me forget it.[18]

Santamaria's sense of identity came from the secure home base of the Brunswick shop. Winter days that began in the dark when his father went to the market, Sundays when his mother made pasta for the week, church and football, four younger brothers and one sister: it was a self-contained world to which he returned from forays outside. He thought of the tiny Aeolian islands of his forebears as part of his being, and the Aeolian community in Melbourne as his source of stability:

> It was the Aeolian families that gave me the things that were most significant of all: the sense of the family, which is more important to the peasant than it is to the nobleman; the necessity of religious belief, without which life is meaningless; the importance of accumulating some modest property of one's own in order to achieve a degree of independence which always eludes the wage-earner dependent on a boss.[19]

In a rare moment of self-scrutiny, Santamaria said that more 'than with any of [his] school friends', he felt a deep personal bond with the Aeolian families in Melbourne—the Dimattinas, Bongiornos, Tesorieros, Casamentos, Fontis, Santospiritos and many more.[20] Yet when he fell in love, in 1938, he chose someone from a very different world. Helen Power was one of the young library assistants whom Father Hackett appointed to work in the Central Catholic Library. He chose them for their good manners, intelligence and love of books rather than their expertise in cataloguing. Helen was educated at Genazzano Convent in Kew, in a manner that prepared young ladies for prosperous middle-class marriages. Her family had no money, having had losses in the Depression, and she took a risk with the impetuous young man from Brunswick. 'Helen Power is marrying a young man with an Italian name', her school friends said, implying a leap into the unknown. Helen looked fragile, but without her courage, and the closeness of their marriage, Bob Santamaria could not have managed the strenuous and ultimately stormy public life that he chose. Their engagement, approved by Hackett, who liked and admired Helen, would have been a news item reported to Mannix at the Monday night dinner at Raheen.

There was an immediate rapport between Mannix and Santamaria. On the young man's side, it began in bedazzlement. The lure of closeness to a great and powerful man was impossible to resist. In one move the twenty-two-year-old leap-frogged older men of considerable talent. Murray McInerney (later Sir Murray) would become a much-admired judge of the Supreme Court of Victoria. Kevin Kelly completed a career as a diplomat with the post of Australian ambassador to Portugal. The fact that they hadn't wanted the ANSCA job was irrelevant. An Italian outsider in Irish-Australian Melbourne became an insider.

And for Mannix? One way to understand what he found in Santamaria is to look back at the de Valera alliance. There are striking parallels between the boy from Bruree and the boy from Brunswick: religious fervour, social disadvantage and an extraordinary self-belief. De Valera's Spanish name and his alleged illegitimate birth put him on the margins. Santamaria's family background was stable and supportive but in racially intolerant Irish-Australia it set him apart.

De Valera and Santamaria were devout Catholics and shrewd tacticians. They roused devotion for their leadership, wonderment at their inventive skill, exasperation at their deviousness and fury at their refusal to consult. Family men (each had eight children), they shared an idealised vision of life on the land. This appears in de Valera's much celebrated—and derided—speech of St Patrick's Day 1943, about 'the Ireland that we dreamed of': a rural idyll of 'cosy homesteads and sturdy children'.[21] Santamaria's *The Earth—Our Mother* (1945) and his work for the National Catholic Rural Movement within Catholic Action assert the moral primacy of agriculture. Daniel Mannix's passionate commitment to land ownership and his memories of rural Charleville would find echoes here.

When Prime Minister Robert Menzies first met de Valera, he found an unexpected 'wintry charm' and humour in the Irish leader. Santamaria had charm too, but it wasn't wintry. Meeting him for the first time was often a surprise; those who expected gloom and an aura of moral straitjackets had to revise their views. De Valera was tough: so was Santamaria. As leaders, both took too much on themselves. Neither was able to foster a successor. Santamaria was always rescuing square pegs from round holes and trying to carve a square hole to fit them. It never worked.

Vincent Buckley, who deplored much of Santamaria's later work and fought its influence within Melbourne University, was impressed by Santamaria's 'calm and [his] lack of obsessiveness'.[22] He was a good host, Buckley said, 'solicitous, self-effacing and above all unostentatious'; he didn't, like some great men, keep his teeth sharp on the ankles of waiters.[23] Mannix, always quick to deflate pretentiousness, responded to this unusual blend of simplicity and self-confidence.

In an unguarded moment on one public occasion, Santamaria said that he loved Mannix 'even more than [his] own father'. Later, he was appalled that he had said such a thing, not because he didn't mean it, but because Giuseppe Santamaria might hear about it and be hurt. Luckily for them both, it was reported only in a regional journal, but it found its way into the Perth diocesan archive.[24] Denys Jackson, writer and journalist for the Catholic press, recalled Mannix saying that Santamaria was the son he never had.[25] This may be emotionally true, but would Mannix ever say anything so revealing? More likely it's what Jackson believed, and in old age thought he had heard.

Another way to look at the relationship is to see Santamaria, and de Valera before him, as living the life that Mannix could never have. This takes us close to the paradox of Daniel Mannix. Michael Chamberlin called Mannix 'a monk without a monastery'.[26] He was also a political leader without a party. Strangely, within the cool and sceptical Mannix was a messianic belief in de Valera and Santamaria as 'saviours' of their people. Did he see them as possessors of gifts of oratory and leadership like his own, but with greater freedom to use them in the public sphere?

In backing Santamaria, Mannix added a dimension to his own

life. Without the energy, vision and verve of this very young man, he might never have returned to the political activism inspired by de Valera, or the impassioned crusade of the conscription years. He would have made trenchant statements on public questions, as he had always done, giving his people a lead against capital punishment and racism as well as communism, and arguing the case for state aid to church schools. But without Santamaria he couldn't have exercised the pressure needed to make social changes, nor to influence political policy. Whether he was right, or wise, to give such a free rein will always be debated. As a counterbalance, Mannix refused to suppress the *Catholic Worker* group who became Santamaria's most articulate opposition. These men found it hard to rebel against someone they greatly admired; they made a respectful visit every year to the archbishop, implicitly thanking him for his permission to publish the paper, permission he said they didn't need. When Santamaria asked that they be stopped from using the word Catholic in the title of their paper, Mannix refused to step in. He said once that he never banned anything—and that was very nearly true.

Mannix's appointment of Maher and Santamaria to ANSCA was a new departure; laymen were not usually given such independence to act within the church, and their roles were never clearly defined. Mannix was always vague about money and he did not know enough about family life to understand what he was asking from his two leaders of Catholic Action. Frank Maher started on an adequate salary of £500 a year and Santamaria on half that sum. The Mahers were to have five children, the Santamarias eight. Santamaria's salary increased when he married in 1939 but he would have had far better financial prospects as a barrister.[27] Working for the church had other drawbacks. One was the assumption that family life would somehow blend in with the job, seven days a week, and that there would be an open house for any bishop or priest who felt like a chat. Nuns in those days stayed in their convents, and Daniel Mannix kept his rule of never visiting anyone, but the Maher house, close to two trams and to the Kew parish church, was a popular rendezvous for priests and Catholic intellectuals. Mollie Maher, whose first child (christened Paul Campion) was born while Frank was giving a talk in Kilmore, said that she got used to doing the ironing in the company of the clergy, but that it cost a lot to keep them in cakes. She reported with wry amusement the advice of an affluent friend: 'Mollie, you must *pray* for a maid.' The Santamarias, living in then semi-rural North Balwyn, were less accessible to casual visitors, but Mollie Maher worried about Helen Santamaria, who had a near-fatal bout of pneumonia in 1946.[28] On the other hand, Bob had more domestic skills than Frank. Unusual in a time when most men found it a serious challenge to grill a chop, Bob Santamaria cooked with flair and enjoyment. He would check the oven and make the roast lamb more interesting by inserting some garlic, and every Sunday night he took over the kitchen and made pasta for the family, effortlessly accommodating large numbers as his sons and daughters married and brought a new generation home.[29]

His wife, Helen, their children and his home were the centre of Bob Santamaria's life. He never wanted to travel: once arrived at his destination he would be impatient to go home. During a trip to Europe he astonished his family by refusing to visit his parents' birthplace on the island of Salina when it would have been easy to do so.[30] A man of endless inventiveness, he was paradoxically resistant to change. Even the achievements of five gifted daughters scarcely touched his conviction that a woman's fulfilment was to be found solely in the domestic sphere. Mannix's view of home and hearth, formed in nineteenth-century Ireland, was much the same; so was de Valera's.

For its first two or three years, the Australian National Secretariat of Catholic Action flourished under Maher and Santamaria. By appointing Hackett as its 'ecclesiastical assistant' Mannix made sure of hearing about its progress. ANSCA comprised four distinct sections: Young Catholic Students (YCS), Young Christian Workers (YCW), National Catholic Girls' Movement (NCGM) and National Catholic Rural Movement (NCRM). The Rural Movement was Santamaria's special responsibility, although, as he said, he had never even grown a lettuce. As a result of ANSCA, study groups proliferated in city and country. Most of the bishops in the other states were welcoming; they were funding the secretariat and expecting it to spread to their regions. Sydney was always cautious and would become hostile to a Mannix-sponsored venture that was only loosely under clerical control. Inevitably, because he was a riveting public speaker, Santamaria took more of the limelight than Maher. He spoke at a Peace Rally in May 1939, on the same platform as Archbishop Mannix, Prime Minister Menzies and the premier of Victoria, Albert Dunstan.[31] Santamaria's prominence didn't seem to trouble Maher, whose quasi-paternal affection for the younger man went back to St Kevin's where Maher had taught history to the twelve year old. He saw Bob as a phenomenon: 'you couldn't hold him back'.[32]

Others felt differently. As ANSCA became bureaucratised from 1940 on, many of the Campions put their energies into the *Catholic Worker*, which Santamaria had left behind, and became a quietly enraged opposition force. Loyal to Mannix, and schooled in the 'keep it in the family' Catholic solidarity, they didn't make a public attack on Santamaria, but they strongly disapproved of a new direction in which he was taking Catholic Action. With no official name or identity, Santamaria's creation was known as 'the Movement' or 'the Show'. It was based within the industrial unions and committed to fighting the Communist Party's campaign to control them. The *Catholic Worker* group had no illusions about communism, but it disapproved of the incursion of ANSCA, a church-funded institution, into the trade unions and the union-based Australian Labor Party. The *Catholic Worker* influence waned during the war years because most of its editorial committee members were called for military service in 1942. ANSCA was less affected. Bob Santamaria already had his uniform and rifle when Mannix intervened, asking that Maher, Santamaria and the secretary of the Young Christian Workers, Ken Mitchell, be exempted to continue their essential work for the church.[33] Maher, nearly thirty-five, and Mitchell, much the same age, would probably not have had to serve, but Santamaria's exemption had a momentous effect.[34] He stayed home and waged his own war in the trade unions, with no one but Mannix to command him.

CHAPTER THIRTEEN

DIVISIONS

FOR DANIEL MANNIX, the Allied victory in the Second World War was not an ending. He looked at the map of Europe and saw persecution and displacement. Rather than join wholeheartedly in the rejoicing in May 1945, when Germany was defeated, or in September, when Japan surrendered, Mannix spoke of the victims of war on both sides. He had deplored the bombing of civilian targets in Leipzig as well as Coventry, and he was appalled by the mass destruction caused by the use of the atomic bomb in Japan, an act of war which, he said, was 'indefensible and immoral'.[1] Postwar Australia had a duty to repair some of the damage and take in as many of the homeless as it reasonably could.

Throughout the 1930s when there was little attention in Australia to the plight of the Jews in Europe, Mannix's sensitivity on questions of race had been made clear. In May 1933, he sent a message of support and sympathy to the Australian Jewish community, and he later endorsed a series of petitions on behalf of Jewish refugees.[2] In 1939 he backed a scheme for a Jewish Homeland in the Kimberley region of Western Australia. Expressing his 'horror and distress' at the suffering of the Jewish people, he said that the proposed homeland in Australia 'would remove a stain on our common humanity'.[3] In March 1939, he reminded his people that Catholics and Jews were 'all children of the One Eternal Father':

> The Jews were being hunted post and pillar, out of every country in Europe. Many of them were coming here, but some people who did not seem inclined to welcome them, had an inborn hatred of the Jews. That was not the Christian spirit. The Founder of the Christian religion was Himself a Jew, and derived his manhood from a Jewish mother. Those things should be remembered by those who were inclined to be hard upon the Jews and to be unsympathetic to their suffering.[4]

When the postwar migration program began in 1946, Mannix was emphatically inclusive. Rather than restrict his welcome to migrants from Catholic countries, he made a point of mentioning those who were then least wanted: Jews, Italians and Germans. In a gesture against the White Australia policy, he also named Indonesians as people who should be welcomed. Speaking of the anti-Semitic feeling that was then surfacing in Australia. Mannix reminded Catholics of their duty to be generous in act and word to a people in need. It had been alleged that newly arrived Jews were getting housing that was denied to Australian people, and this perception was stirring bad feeling and 'immoderate language'.

> Jews had their faults like others but they were a great people who had maintained their traditions down the ages in the face of great difficulty and great suffering…Many people could well moderate their language in speaking of the Jews, about whom they appeared to be jealous. Hard workers and more industrious and clever in many ways than others, Jews succeeded in life and credit should not be withheld from them.[5]

The Archbishop of Melbourne was an ally worth having. Mannix had learned during the time of the conscription campaign how to manage the media. He took the *Advocate*'s shorthand writer to his weekly functions in Melbourne, and later checked and corrected the text. His speeches, at communion breakfasts or the laying of foundation stones, were widely reported in the metropolitan dailies, the Catholic press and country town newspapers. Thus, his reprimand about anti-Semitism, made to a gathering in Kew, and published in the Melbourne *Argus* and the *Advocate*, was picked up by the *Western Star and Roma Advertiser* in Toowoomba, Queensland, and made the subject of an editorial in the *Catholic Weekly* in Sydney.

Mannix's interventions on behalf of Jewish refugees in the 1930s show how closely he followed foreign affairs. Although he backed the war against Germany, he had always believed that the Soviet Union was an even greater threat than the Third Reich. The betrayal of Poland at the Yalta peace conference showed the double standard of the victors. They had gone to war to save the Polish people from Hitler; now there was 'a blanket of silence' over the Soviet's annexation of Poland and other small nations.[6]

Mannix's warnings about communism were not new: they went back to the time of the Spanish Civil War. They had a closer and sharper focus in the 1940s when he became aware of communist activity in the Australian trade unions. It was in this context that he encouraged the controversial venture, to become known as 'the Movement'. It began in 1941, when Bob Santamaria was asked by an influential member of the Victorian ALP executive, Bert Cremean, to help some trade union leaders who had lost their positions to communist activists. Faced by ballot-rigging, intimidation, physical force and mass apathy, these leaders turned to Catholic unionists to help them regain power, protect the national economy in time of war, and safeguard the Labor Government. This wasn't the business of Catholic Action, but it was perfectly suited to the executive genius of Bob Santamaria, and it roused Daniel Mannix's political instinct.

All the Australian bishops, following the Pope, regularly denounced atheistic communism; priests and lay people prayed for the conversion of Russia. Mannix, who had learned some lessons of power when he backed de Valera's fight for Ireland's independence, was more than ready to take the Australian church into the trade unions. And because the Australian Labor Party was structured in such a way as to be controlled by its affiliated unions, industrial power meant political power as well. For Mannix, communism was a threat to freedom, to be resisted by every citizen. To see a contradiction between Mannix the worker's champion and Mannix the anti-communist is to miss his reasoning. He saw the destruction of freedom in Eastern Europe, fake trials after torture, oppression under Stalin, slave camps and mass murder. Australia, in his view, was vulnerable in a quite different way from the European nations, and during the 1940s he saw reason for alarm. According to one former Communist Party leader, Bernie Taft, the 1949 national coal strike was the party's 'last desperate attempt' to precipitate a crisis and supplant the ALP as the workers' party'.[7]

The Movement, which owed its existence to Mannix and Santamaria, was an informal Catholic organisation. Nameless and secret, it came to the rescue of the beleaguered trade unionists. Santamaria saw the possibilities of the parish structure, and Mannix, who controlled the diocese, gave him the power to use them. Every Catholic belonged to a parish. The local church was the central place in which the main stages of life were celebrated, from baptism to the funeral mass. Records were kept: priests knew their people, and they could identify trade unionists. Catholics were accustomed to getting together for all kinds of good causes, under the parish priest's direction. The Australian Catholic Federation, a pressure group of the early twentieth century, had failed in its attempt to win state aid for Catholic schools, but it showed the possibilities of group action.[8]

Joining 'the Movement', or 'the Show' as the new organisation was also known, was different from other parish activities in that it was secret, and it made bigger demands. Its pledge of secrecy came readily to Catholics of the time; most knew about the Masons, and their Catholic counterpart, the Knights of the Southern Cross. Anti-Catholic discrimination in the workplace was a common experience. Many job advertisements stated it bluntly: 'No Catholics Need Apply'. In 1916 the lieutenant-governor, Sir Arthur Stanley, appointed to represent all Victorians, felt free to advertise for two Protestant housemaids.[9] Job-hunting in the desperate Depression years showed many Catholics that it was best to keep quiet about their religious affiliation and to hope that their Irish surnames wouldn't count against them. And for Mannix, with his close knowledge of clandestine manoeuvres in Irish resistance to British rule, secrecy was nothing new.

Santamaria's position with ANSCA gave him a ready-made link with parishes throughout Australia. But because the Movement was designed to go beyond discussion groups and into the business of trade union elections, parish priests needed to be sure that their bishops and archbishops approved of it. As head of the Melbourne archdiocese, Daniel Mannix gave the lead. If it was His Grace's wish that parishes should join in this new venture, that was enough for the Melbourne priests. And wherever Mannix led, most of the other Australian bishops followed. Only Sydney, always suspicious of Mannix initiatives, had reservations about the Movement and gave a qualified support which would eventually turn to hostility. Funding came from the bishops, who agreed to an annual payment for the anti-communist fight, and the ANSCA office in Melbourne became the Movement's headquarters, with Santamaria in the double role of assistant national director of Catholic Action and director of the new organisation. Mannix, as usual, kept aloof from everyday matters, but by appointing William Hackett chaplain or 'clerical assistant' to both ANSCA and the Movement, he expected to be told what was being done.

Hackett's dual role, like Santamaria's, was an example of Mannix's administrative style. His appointment matched the archbishop's policy of giving the three top jobs at St Patrick's Cathedral to one man. It also helped to keep Catholic Action and the Movement relatively free of the clerical control which, Mannix believed, had hampered and even betrayed the Irish fight for freedom. Hackett, whose family background was strongly nationalist, deplored the part played by the Irish bishops, from the downfall of his father's friend Parnell in 1890 to the excommunication of de Valera in the 1920s. His own role as priest and activist in the Irish 'troubles' was never one of control, nor was he an authority figure in Catholic Action and the Movement. He had neither the wish nor the time even to attempt the impossible task of supervising Santamaria. As director of the Central Catholic Library, Hackett had more than enough to do. He was already over-committed in 1935 when the Jesuit order gave him the major post of rector of Xavier College—from which he was abruptly removed in 1940 for having performed with more élan than efficiency. Hackett's heart was in the library and his many friendships included the *Catholic Worker* circle. Unlike his successor as chaplain to the Movement, Father Eric D'Arcy, Hackett did not have an office in the ANSCA building. He came to meetings; he gave spiritual homilies; he expressed opinions, but anyone who wanted to consult him would have had to walk a few city blocks to the Central Catholic Library. Nevertheless, he was an acute observer and he would have had plenty to tell Mannix during their Monday night dinners. But although he was an enthusiast for Catholic Action and for the anti-communist crusade, Hackett had misgivings about some of 'Bob's chaps'. Mannix, caught up in the excitement of the Movement's successes in trade-union elections, heard what he wanted to hear. 'He is always infallible: I only sometimes,' Hackett said.

The Australian Communist Party didn't look to be much of a threat. Its membership was small and its parliamentary candidates regularly lost their deposits. But the wartime alliance with Russia and the friendly face of Stalin had helped to make communism respectable. Many generous-spirited Marxists, roused by the Spanish Civil War to join the party, were slow to understand, or to admit, that the Soviet experiment was a cruel failure, a betrayal of the people it claimed to serve. Within Australia, the significant communist strength was in the trade unions, where a small organised force had taken key positions without much trouble. Between 1945 and 1948, the communists controlled a formidable number of important unions: the Federated Ironworkers, the Sheet Metal Workers' Union, the Amalgamated Engineering Union, the Waterside Workers' Federation, the Seamen's Union, the Federated Clerks' Union, the Australian Railways' Union and part of the Building Trades Union.[10] After the war, the leaders of these unions used the weapon of the strike against the Labor government. In July 1949, Prime Minister Ben Chifley had to call out thirteen thousand army personnel to mine the nation's coal and prevent a total shutdown of industry. That he should be driven to such an extreme cast doubts on his ability to handle trade-union militancy and was a factor in his defeat by Robert Menzies in the 1949 election.

Gradually, after much hard work and strategic planning, Santamaria and his Catholic recruits turned back the tide. The Movement's parish groups were the model and inspiration for 'Industrial Groups' formed in communist-controlled unions by the Australian Labor Party. The 'Groupers', many of whom were not Catholics, or fully aware of the Movement, soon learned that in order to defeat the communists in their unions, they needed the Catholic votes that the Movement was able to deliver. By 1950, the ALP was back in control of key unions after a bitter and at times violent fight. By this time, Santamaria had outgrown his role in ANSCA. His prodigious energies were going into the Movement. The National Catholic Rural Movement remained under his direction, and, while remaining officially a Catholic Action body, it eventually became a front, and a source of funding, for the Movement, which, confusingly, had only unofficial status.[11]

By Santamaria's own account, the Communist power in the unions was broken by 1952. That was the time to let go, or at least to give up the policy of secrecy, and to leave it to Labor members to make their own mistakes and win their own battles. The policy of pretending the Movement didn't exist went back to its beginnings in the reluctance of non-Catholic trade union men to be seen to accept organised Catholic help. After a decade of anonymity, it would be hard for the Movement to disband, having never announced itself. Even the bishops who were most anxious to distance the church from this political adventure would have had trouble finding an exit strategy. And Santamaria wasn't one for letting go. It was hard to refute his argument that if the Movement withdrew there would be a resurgence of communist activity. Moreover, he predicted, if the Movement were allowed to continue its work, it could, within five or six years, 'completely transform the leadership of the Labor Movement' and 'implement a Christian social programme in both the State and Federal spheres'.[12] Mannix saw no reason to call a halt, and because the bishops were either compliant or helpless in the face of his dominant personality, the Movement took the fast track to the Split of 1954–55.

Without the anti-communist struggle, Santamaria would have had a very different life. Catholic Action in any of its early versions would not have satisfied him. He needed either to leave the employ of the Australian bishops, or to find bigger challenges. He chose to stay, and challenge the world. His choice was powerfully influenced by his reverence for Mannix and the freedom to act that Mannix gave him.

Frank Maher admired the work of the Movement, but never wanted to join in. That was Bob Santamaria's province. Maher's strength was in ideas, discussion, teaching and writing. But as the Campion adventure translated into a bureaucratic nightmare, he had to confront his own creation. As director of Catholic Action he was faced every day with a vast correspondence. Bishops, priests and members wrote and telephoned, often disagreeing with one another, or offering bright ideas of their own for instant attention. Newsletters and pamphlets were written, checked, sent out, under Maher's supervision. As a national organisation, ANSCA had to direct the interstate diocesan offices, as well as the Melbourne office, headed by the equable, over-worked Ken Mitchell whose sympathies were with the *Catholic Worker* group.

Maher often said that ANSCA could not have survived without the remarkable talent of Noreen Minogue, who came straight from her Richmond convent schooling as a sixteen-year-old junior typist, at £2 a week. Her intelligence, energy and command of detail created a firm centre in the Melbourne office. When Noreen Minogue eventually faced the fact that a woman couldn't make a career in Catholic Action, or anywhere in the Catholic Church, she resigned—and in a short time became the much respected deputy secretary-general of the Australian Red Cross. Later, she won the international Dunant Award for humanitarian service. But between 1939 and 1946 she was the anchorwoman at ANSCA, an achievement that none of its many chroniclers has noticed.

For ANSCA, 1946 marked the beginning of the end. It was the year of Frank Maher's failed adventure. A lover of European culture who had never seen Europe, Maher was excited by the idea of taking his Catholic Action model to England and Belgium and to the United States. Encouraged by expatriate London-based publisher Frank Sheed, he set off in February, planning eighteen months of interaction with Catholic intellectuals, which would culminate in a lecture tour in the United States. He wanted to meet Douglas Woodruff of the *Tablet*, publisher Tom Burns, and writer and translator Father Ronald Knox. Contact with the Catholic thinkers who had inspired the Campions in the 1930s would make up for the isolation of the war years. Mannix was to pay the travel expenses for the Maher family, and Frank would be on salary as usual. Australian Catholicism would be enriched by his experience.

It turned out badly for Maher. It was only a few months after the end of the war, and, impatient to get started, Maher took the first available berth, leaving his wife and four small children to follow. Mannix has been blamed for withholding Mollie Maher's passage money, but the truth seems to be that berths were scarce and she was a low priority. In war-damaged London, Frank Maher, never a practical man, had to find accommodation and look after himself in a time of shortages and food rationing. It was a harsh winter; he missed his family acutely; his English contacts proved too busy to do much for him; and he became isolated and depressed. Mollie's loving letters show the closeness of their marriage and her concern for the collapse of his dream.[13] Eventually, the passages were booked and paid for by Mannix. Margaret Maher, then seven years old, remembers the suitcases in the hall, ready packed for departure, when the telegram came from her father saying 'Coming home'.[14]

When Maher returned to Melbourne, he was too dispirited to go back to the ANSCA office. Not because Bob Santamaria had taken over his work in his absence, but because the whole Catholic Action adventure had ended. The new anti-communist campaign took first place. Maher's Campion friends—Murray McInerney, Gerard Heffey, Kevin Kelly—were back from war service. They were catching up with the lost years, starting or resuming family life and finding their way in their professions. In place of the free-wheeling Campion groups, ANSCA's four organisations—the Young Catholic Students, the Young Catholic Workers, the National Catholic Girls' Movement and the National Catholic Rural Movement—shared city office space with the Movement enterprise, but there was not much harmony between them. Santamaria controlled the Rural Movement but was unable to bring the other three organisations into line.[15]

At Mannix's request, Maher was given a room in Newman College for writing and research. The rector, Jeremiah Murphy SJ, complained that he used it only to hang his hat. This was probably true. Maher preferred to work at home—he wrote best at night—but the Newman base was handy for the Law School, where he renewed friendships with law professors Zelman Cowen and Norval Morris. He resigned from ANSCA in 1951.

There is a persistent legend that Santamaria schemed to oust Maher. I have never believed it: I saw for myself the warmth of the friendship between them. The story of a demoralised Maher, driven from his leadership post, leaves Mollie Maher out of account. Highly intelligent, loyal, shrewd and decisive, she would have ended the friendship with the Santamarias if Bob had betrayed Frank. My first meeting with Bob Santamaria was arranged by Frank Maher, who took an interest in my career—or lack of one—after my father died. Without Frank's intervention I would never have thought of working for Santamaria whom I met for the first time at the Mahers' house early in 1954. I had never heard of the Movement, nor did anyone mention it to me. I had no sense of vocation, no interest in politics. I liked Bob and Helen, and was flattered by Bob's instant offer of a job as editor of the monthly journal of the National Catholic Rural Movement, *Rural Life*. Because the job offer was sponsored by Frank Maher, I accepted without asking any questions. I thought that working for the church might be dull but I never imagined that I could be involving myself in something controversial.

Much later, I heard the story that Frank Maher had been deliberately sidelined by Bob Santamaria. But I also heard Maher's own viewpoint, as he gave it in a conversation with James Muirhead SJ:

> I'm getting it all the time. They're trying to say that Bob has control of the Archbishop as an old man and got me out of the way because Bob wanted to run everything on his own lines, and he didn't want me around...It's not true and [Bob] has my total support.[16]

Clearly Maher wanted out; and after some sad years, shadowed by Mollie's sudden death in 1957, he became a serene, productive and much admired senior academic at the University of Melbourne.[17] His exit, however, had profound consequences. It made Santamaria director of Catholic Action as well as the Movement; he could now run the two organisations as if they were one, with funds flowing between the two as he thought best. He didn't appoint a deputy. Noreen Minogue could have done the job superbly, but no one at that time would even think of giving a woman authority in an essentially male organisation. While Mannix, by force of his personality and habit, controlled the bishops and ensured funding for the Movement, he gave Santamaria free rein in its day-to-day affairs. Some bishops were nervous about the Movement; others were hostile, but as long as Mannix had the votes on the Bishops'

Committee on Catholic Action, nothing would change.

In the early 1950s, the Movement was riding high. Mannix bought a big old house in Sackville Street in Kew, and asked the Jesuits to establish a new enterprise, the Institute of Social Order, as a centre for the education of trade unionists and others. The immediate need, as seen by Santamaria, was to prepare Movement members for the union jobs that had been won for them. He recognised that some of these men were poorly equipped. Hastily chosen, intellectually unprepared, mostly (but not always) well meaning, the Movement men were gaining power they did not expect or fully understand. They needed training in administration, public speaking, financial management, writing and editing skills and an understanding of how the economy worked. Their need was dramatised in the case of a Movement man who was elected State Secretary of the Waterside Workers' Federation. He stole union funds and was jailed for embezzlement. No surprise that the communists won back the post at the next election.[18]

The new centre, known as Belloc House, was intended to be more than a training ground for Movement activists. It offered courses of lectures for anyone interested in exploring Catholic teaching on social justice. In practice, however, it was colonised by Santamaria. Austin Kelly, the Jesuit provincial, was uneasy: 'I fear that it is very difficult to separate spiritual and political work in the "Movement" and as Jesuits we cannot take part in any political activity.'[19]

Mannix provided some of the funding to extend and renovate Belloc House. When it opened in 1953, it had a full-time staff of three Jesuits: Victor Turner, a war-worn survivor of Changi prison camp, John Fahey, a quiet sceptic who always seemed amused by Movement manoeuvres, and Harold Lalor, a former radio announcer with a melodious voice and a fine sense of doom. Lalor's 'fifteen minutes to midnight' warning of a communist takeover was a great money-spinner for the Movement and a source of worry to fellow Jesuits. Mannix also sent William Hackett to live at Belloc House while keeping up his duties as director of the Catholic Library. Hackett's role as the archbishop's eyes and ears became more onerous in this new venture. The two men did not always agree about Movement activities. 'We spar a lot', Hackett wrote of his Monday dinners at Raheen.

On Hackett's sudden death from injuries in a traffic accident in July 1954, a much younger Jesuit, James Muirhead, took over the direction of Belloc House and gave weekly briefings to Mannix at Raheen. He revered Mannix and greatly admired Santamaria. On his watch, little changed at Belloc House, which was in effect an extension of Santamaria's city office as a place for meetings, lectures and an annual Christmas party for Movement and ANSCA employees. In 1956 a new provincial, Jeremiah Hogan, tried to disengage the Jesuit order from the Movement. Fresh from Sydney, where they did things differently, he told Muirhead that there would be a new deal at Belloc House: 'We're going to replace any lecturers or writers who've been in any way associated with Santamaria. We're going to ease out Santamaria but it has to be done without him knowing.' The naiveté of this proposal would have shocked or amused the other Jesuits. Turner and Fahey said it couldn't be done. Muirhead stated the obvious: what about the archbishop, the owner of Belloc House? Hogan replied: 'Well, you make these changes discreetly, and we needn't be troubling him.' As for meeting Mannix, Hogan said with remarkable bravado: 'I wouldn't go near the fellow.'[20]

How to disentangle the church from Santamaria? So long as

Mannix was archbishop it wasn't possible. Like the Jesuits, the Australian bishops were divided and helpless. By the end of 1953, the Bishops' Committee on Catholic Action was getting fractious. As the diary of Archbishop Beovich of Adelaide reveals, the tension between Mannix and his coadjutor Dr Simonds was acute:

> Dr Simonds said there should be complete separation between Catholic Action & the Movement. One was spiritual, the other was concerned in politics and party politics. Dr O'Collins [Ballarat] denied there was party politics in the Movement...Dr Mannix kept to his point saying that under our system of government if one wished to influence & help his surroundings, one must to some degree enter the field of politics. Dr Simonds strongly opposed & left the meeting.[21]

While the bishops were increasingly divided, so too were the ALP leaders. Although the Groupers' control of the big unions might look like a win for the ALP, it became obvious to those in the know that the Movement had the Groupers more or less in its pocket. The ALP has always been a battleground of factions. This battle was different because the faction was church-controlled, funded in large part by the Australian bishops, with Bob Santamaria as its strategic director, and Mannix as its patron. Traditionally, ALP funds come from affiliated trade unions and many of its parliamentarians hold safe seats within industrial areas. By 1952 the Groupers' successes in the unions would give them control of the annual ALP conferences in Victoria and New South Wales. The Left was out; the Right was in. It was a difficult time for Opposition leader Bert Evatt and his deputy Arthur Calwell. As a Catholic and a devoted admirer of Archbishop Mannix, Calwell knew what was going on, and he didn't like it. Nor did he like Santamaria. He resented being displaced as the archbishop's adviser on political matters, and he was wary of Santamaria-crafted policies coming up for consideration at party meetings. Evatt was more inclined to come to terms with the new situation, and to work on his already cordial relationship with Mannix.

Older Catholic Labor men like Arthur Calwell knew their limits. They kept their religion and their politics separate. Small favours to fellow Catholics or to the church—a grant here, a job there—were as far as they would go. No one wanted to touch the policy that meant most to Mannix: state aid for Catholic schools. Ever since his arrival in 1913, Mannix had argued for the right of Catholics to be given a subsidy from the state. Why should the taxes paid by Catholics be used to maintain the state system with no benefit for their own children? It was a huge burden on the Catholic community. For Mannix, it was a matter of religious freedom and national identity. He believed that the state system reinforced Protestantism and taught allegiance to England, much as the state schools had done in Ireland.

The success of the Movement gave Mannix reason to hope for justice in the education system. Ideas that came from Catholic social policy—decentralisation, an Asian immigration quota, closer settlement on the land, a family wage—were being presented to the Australian Labor Party. These ideas, along with a foreign policy that favoured the American alliance rather than the traditional British tie, and an absolute refusal to recognise Communist China, were put forward by Santamaria's *News Weekly* and would become orthodoxy in Movement meetings. Some flowed naturally from the Australian bishops' annual social justice statements—as they would: Bob Santamaria wrote nearly every one of them.

In 1949, the long-standing friendship between Mannix and Arthur Calwell came under strain. They disagreed about an essential part of old Labor thinking: the White Australia policy. As Minister for Immigration, Calwell was the architect of the postwar immigration policy to which Mannix gave high praise. Calwell worked hard to break down Australian xenophobia. He started cautiously with British and Northern Europeans (the blue-eyed, blond Balts were well received) and then moved south. He went slowly with Italians and Greeks: dark complexions and the 'wrong' religions meant trouble. And he explained carefully that he could not bring too many Jewish people at the same time, for fear of rousing anti-Semitism. By calling all the migrants 'New Australians', he eased the path to acceptance.[22] But, on the matter of Asian migration, Calwell was inflexible. Loyalty to the ALP's traditional White Australia policy, compounded by an obsessive fear of miscegenation, brought a kindly man to make some harsh decisions. The O'Keefe case of 1948–49 brought him to a collision course with Archbishop Mannix.

Mannix took up the case of Mrs Annie O'Keefe. She and her seven children were wartime refugees from Indonesia who had been living in Melbourne since escaping from the Japanese in 1942. After her husband, a Dutch Intelligence officer, was killed in an airline crash while serving with the Allies, she married an Australian, Jack O'Keefe, in June 1947. When served with a deportation order in 1948 she appealed to the High Court and won the right to stay. Then Calwell brought in new legislation to close the legal loophole that protected her, and she was again ordered to leave. It was not clear where she and her children were expected to go. She had lost her Dutch citizenship by marrying

O'Keefe but had not gained Australian citizenship. Because of political upheaval in Indonesia it wasn't safe to go there. 'All I can do,' Jack O'Keefe said, 'is to follow the wife of my choice with her children into exile.'[23] But where? Some island in the Pacific? How could O'Keefe support the family?

Disastrously raising the stakes, Calwell alleged that the marriage of Annie and Jack O'Keefe was a strategy to beat the law, not made in good faith. Father Fitzpatrick, parish priest of St Joseph's in Chelsea, who had performed the marriage ceremony, was outraged at being accused by implication of misusing the sacrament. He defended himself and the O'Keefes at the next Sunday mass, using the pulpit to attack Calwell's 'Godless and unChristian action'. 'Priest Denounces Deportation' was a prominent story in the Melbourne *Herald*.[24]

Was this a religious or a political question? Whichever it was, there in the midst of it all was Archbishop Mannix. The *Advocate* published a charming photograph of Mannix in a fatherly, protective pose with one of Mrs O'Keefe's pretty daughters.[25] It wasn't the first time Mannix had attacked the White Australia policy, but because of the human dimension of the O'Keefe story this stand roused more attention than his earlier statements. Calwell stuck fast. He told the House of Representatives that his decision was final:

> Mrs O'Keefe and her children are not important, it is the precedent that's important...we can have a White Australia, we can have a black Australia but a mongrel Australia is impossible and I shall not take the first steps to establish the precedents which will allow the floodgates to be opened.[26]

The phrase 'a mongrel Australia' was insulting, especially to anyone who had made an inter-racial marriage: it categorised their children as inferior and unfit for citizenship. The slur on the O'Keefes (to whom a daughter, Geraldine, would be born in April 1950) did more damage to Calwell than his tasteless and ill-judged quip: 'Two Wongs don't make a White'. Archbishop Mannix made a direct appeal to Calwell on behalf of Mrs O'Keefe, but even after the High Court's decision in her favour, the deportation order stood. It was reported as a personal decision rather than an exercise of government policy: 'Calwell Orders Out Family of Nine'.[27] Newspapers in India, Malaysia and Singapore took up the story: this wasn't an economic matter, they said, it was racism. The *Washington Post* ran an emotional headline: 'Made Outcast by White Australia: Australian Chooses Exile with his Indonesian Wife'.[28] The Sydney *Daily Telegraph* and the Melbourne *Herald* set up an O'Keefe Fund, and donations flowed freely. Many were shocked at the idea of separating Annie O'Keefe from her husband and her Australian-born five-year-old son and sending her to whichever Pacific island would take her and the other children. Public sympathy was roused by a press photograph of Annie packing a suitcase and one of Jack O'Keefe playing with his stepchildren by the sea at Bonbeach.

There is no way of knowing whether or not Mannix counted the cost to Calwell and the Australian Labor Party when he intervened publicly in the O'Keefe case. For him, racial discrimination was a moral question. He had been advocating a quota of Asian migrants for years. At the end of the Second World War, when the brutalities of the Japanese prison camps became known, Mannix urged Australians not to succumb to hatred of the Japanese race. 'We are all God's children,' he said. His indignation on behalf of the Aborigines had appeared as early as 1938, when he called for 'reparation for all the wrongs, wittingly or unwittingly' that the white settlers had inflicted on them.[29] Very few people were saying 'Sorry' in 1938.

Mannix's intervention in the O'Keefe case was carried out with his usual political expertise. Posing for a photograph with Mrs O'Keefe's daughter was an obvious set-up by an archbishop who knew the power of the visual image. It was no coincidence that brought several members of the besieged O'Keefe family from Bonbeach to Sunbury to meet Mannix at one of his big Sunday church functions.[30]

Calwell didn't yield. In order to circumvent the High Court decision, he introduced two bills to federal parliament: the Aliens Deportation Act (1948) and the Wartime Refugees Removal Act (1949). But before the O'Keefe deportation order could be carried out, the 1949 federal election was called. Undeterred by the bad press over the O'Keefe case, Calwell told an election meeting in Brunswick that he could not allow the Filipino-born Sergeant Gamboa to join his Australian wife. Gamboa had a distinguished war record and held American citizenship. 'If we let in any US citizens,' Calwell said, 'we will have to admit US Negroes. I don't think any mothers and fathers want to see that...We don't want half-castes running over our country.'[31] This crudely populist approach probably won some votes for the ALP, but it damaged Calwell as a potential party leader.[32] Prime Minister Chifley was urged to 'restrain' Calwell or lose 'very many votes at election time—especially the Catholic vote', but he backed Calwell.[33] Whatever Chifley thought of the wisdom of Calwell's public utterances, it would have been dangerous to bring the White Australia policy any further into the election debates. The ALP lost to Robert Menzies' Liberal Party for many reasons apart from the

O'Keefe case. Yet, although Mannix's long established friendship with Calwell continued, the Catholic community took note of the difference between them and applauded when Menzies allowed the O'Keefes to stay. A new generation, university-educated, was more sensitive to racism in the Australian Labor Party. Many who were hostile to Santamaria found it hard to admit that his immigration policy was more enlightened than Calwell's. One way to deal with this dilemma was to give all the credit to Mannix.

Other Asian refugees were not as lucky as the O'Keefes: several hundred were deported under Labor in the late 1940s. The new Minister for Immigration, Harold Holt, accepted Mrs O'Keefe, and others in her position, as a 'wartime legacy'. A more flexible attitude to Asian immigration developed under Menzies and his successor Holt, and the Whitlam ALP government removed the White Australia policy from the party platform. It would be unfair to suggest that Calwell was unique, or even unusual, in his attitudes on race. He was more outspoken than his colleagues, and as minister for immigration he had the most power. But widespread indifference, even fear and hostility, to refugees of another race, remains to the present day, in both major political parties and in an even more virulent form.

Defeated in the federal election of December 1949, Labor leader Ben Chifley was said to be worried about the Movement but too tired to take it on. He died in June 1951. His successor, Herbert ('the Doc') Evatt brought high intelligence and limitless ambition to the post. A former High Court judge, he had an impressive record for his work in establishing the United Nations, especially in the Human Rights Charter. He had served as attorney-general in the Chifley government. He wasn't easily bracketed as a man of the Left or the Right. Having appeared for the Federated

Ironworkers when it was communist-led, he knew the trade union movement. His close friend, High Court judge Edward McTiernan, a Catholic and a devoted ALP man who knew a good deal about the Movement and strongly disapproved of it, could have briefed Evatt on Santamaria.[34] Whether he heard it from McTiernan, or Calwell, or anyone else, Evatt knew the problem he inherited with the leadership, but like other ALP leaders he chose to keep quiet about it.

Evatt's good relationship with Mannix appears in correspondence in the late Chifley years. 'Your letter was little short of a blessing', Evatt wrote to Mannix during the industrial crisis of mid-1949, when he and Chifley were defending the arbitration system against communist manipulation of the Miners' Federation. Faced by a crippling strike, Chifley sent troops to the coalfields and gaoled some communist union leaders. Evatt's letter to Mannix supports that strategy, while adding that 'we have always to be careful against moving too far to the right while combating extremist force on the left'.[35]

In April 1950, Prime Minister Robert Menzies introduced the Communist Party Dissolution Bill, designed to make the Communist Party an illegal organisation. Writing to Mannix, Evatt deplored the bill's 'tyrannical' substitution of executive trial for judicial trial. His letter ended with a plea to Mannix the freedom fighter: 'I appeal to Your Grace for help in accord with all you have done for liberty and justice in Australia.'[36]

Mannix disliked the Menzies legislation and in the referendum that followed he voted No. His own abstention from the debate was a signal to Catholics to make up their own minds. 'Politicians are best left to themselves,' he told Archbishop Duhig, whose approval Evatt was courting.[37] His vote against banning the Communist

Party was consistent with earlier decisions: in spite of his strong temperance views, Mannix had voted No against prohibition in the referendum of 1938. The 1951 referendum on the Communist Party Dissolution Bill was one of the rare occasions on which Mannix and Santamaria disagreed. Santamaria urged a Yes vote. Mannix by pointedly giving 'no advice or direction' helped the No vote. He and Archbishop Duhig, from quite different viewpoints, kept out of the fray. A Mannix letter to Duhig suggests that Evatt had reason to hope that the traditional Catholic ALP vote was safe:

> Dr Evatt was greatly pleased that you stated publicly that you were not going to give a lead on the Referendum. I am glad, also, because I too had come to the conclusion that the politicians could best be left to fight their own battles in the matter.[38]

When Evatt faced his first federal election as leader in May 1954, he was optimistic about the Catholic vote. His relations with Mannix were good. He had never met Santamaria, but he expected to work with the Movement and the Groupers. His deputy, Arthur Calwell, was in the awkward position of being an admirer and friend of Mannix while deploring Santamaria and the Movement. Calwell had no choice but to keep quiet. The Communist Party had all the intelligence it needed to expose the existence and activities of the Movement but couldn't do so without exposing its own strategies. Neither the Movement nor the Communist Party could tell the full story of the union battles. Santamaria's *News Weekly* carried political and industrial news. It attacked Communist Party policies and tactics, promoted secret ballots and other reforms, as well as many ideas that were new to traditional ALP thinking. The fact that Santamaria controlled and wrote much of *News Weekly* was not evident. All that was on show for the general public was that it was published by 'Freedom Publishing Company'; it solicited donations for its 'Fighting Fund' and published a list of donors which included a high proportion of Anons.

As well as *News Weekly*, the Movement had the resources of the Catholic Church behind it. The bishops also supported Catholic Action, and paid the salaries of Maher, Santamaria and their ANSCA support staff. From time to time, too, Mannix invited Catholic businessmen to meetings at Raheen, where Santamaria would address them on the need to support the anti-communist fight in the unions, which, as a substantial national force, had to be directed by trained, paid organisers. Cheque books at the ready, the businessmen rallied to the archbishop's suppers. Donations were accepted without undue gratitude or fuss. One of Mannix's supporters, Wally Broderick, recalled being seen off at the Raheen front door by the archbishop: 'Well, I'll say goodnight to you now, Mr Broderick—and go in and count the spoons.'[39]

One absentee from Movement benefit nights at Raheen was Melbourne's wealthiest Catholic, John Wren, who was hostile to the Movement and would not give a penny to Santamaria's enterprises. Yet his friendship with Mannix, dating from 1917, remained strong, and it cost him a great deal more than any cheque. Frank Hardy's *Power without Glory*, a sensation when it first appeared in August 1950, was so closely based on the life of John Wren that no one could miss its intention. Readers were shocked, horrified or delighted, depending on their religious or political positions. It was a bulky novel, written with more energy than subtlety, but its fascination as a *roman à clef* carried it through. Even without the key to the major characters that was circulated at the time, it wasn't hard to match names and places. John West was readily identified with John Wren. Jackson Street, Carringbush, was Johnson Street, Collingwood, and Archbishop Daniel Malone was a stage-Irish Mannix lookalike. Wren's reputation as owner and operator of the illegal tote, and as a fixer in local and state politics, was as widely known as his vast wealth. Frank Hardy embellished the record with baseless stories of murders arranged by West and adultery committed by his allegedly neglected wife Nellie.

The irony, from Wren's viewpoint, was that the Movement he disliked so much was the real target of the novel, while he himself was collateral damage. Hardy wanted to expose poverty and corruption in various aspects of Australian life and in so doing make the case for the Communist Party. But the immediate impulse came, not from Hardy himself, but from communist leaders who were worried by the Movement's successes in the unions. According to popular legend, they gained insight into Santamaria's organisation, not only by observation of union elections, but also by a railway cleaner's random discovery in Archbishop Duhig's sleeping compartment. By this account, the absent-minded prelate, going home to Brisbane after a meeting of the bishops in Sydney in 1945, left his top-secret copy of the meeting's minutes under his pillow; this gave the Australian Communist Party material to expose the Movement in the *Guardian*.[40] But, apart from party members, hardly anyone read the *Guardian*. A novel, aimed at a popular readership, could do more damage. According to a senior Communist Party member, Cedric Ralph, the idea came from Ted Hill, a lawyer who was prominent in the Victorian branch of the party:

> It was Ted's idea from the very beginning. Ted wanted to put a dent into the activities of Catholic Action, and he thought that an attack on Wren was really hitting at the core of the whole thing. He believed that Wren was responsible for much of the Movement's finances...but at what point Frank [Hardy] was brought into it I don't know.[41]

After several years' research and a great deal of help from party members, Frank Hardy produced his novel. An interview he gave at the time of publication suggests that he wanted to be sued for libel: 'Our man John West was ready made. I could not have invented him.'[42] The libel suit was undertaken but not on behalf of Wren himself. An ill-advised action taken by Wren's sons was intended to defend Nellie Wren against the allegation of an affair by 'Nellie West' with a builder's labourer by whom she had a child. The lawsuit backfired. Counsel for Hardy took the line that no reasonable person would identify Mrs Wren, a woman of blameless virtue, with passionate, seductive Mrs West, suburban Melbourne's Lady Chatterley. Hardy was acquitted; and generations of readers have taken *Power without Glory* far more seriously, as an historical account and as a literary work, than it deserved.

The effect on Wren's reputation was profound and lasting. John Wren had been content to live quietly, scarcely known outside the world of money, politics and sport. William Hackett, who knew the Wrens better than most, was one of very few invited to dinner at their house. Hackett's letters, written to his sister in Ireland, describe the Wren household as simple to the point of austerity. The big white house was impressive from the outside, but the Wrens had no servants and no car. Hackett found Wren dull (more interested in power than in books or ideas) but liked his wife. 'She and I are excellent friends', he wrote, and he often called to see her. Mrs Wren took the book and the court case calmly. Hackett and Mannix were angry on her behalf.[43]

It has been said that Mannix considered a lawsuit against Hardy. This seems unlikely. He would have been annoyed at Hardy's presentation of a bustling, garrulous Archbishop Malone who 'chuckles slyly', says 'That will be fine, Mr West. We're sure doing things in style',[44] and scatters exclamations of 'musha' for emphasis. But Mannix would have known better than to initiate a court appearance. He would have been asked about the scene in which Archbishop Malone takes the tall sinister Mr Parelli, who stands in for small, cherubic Santamaria, and 'fish-eyed' Cregan, Bert Cremean's fictional counterpart, to ask Wren for money. Aided by these creepy henchmen (Parelli defined by thin cruel lips and a pink cigarette holder, and Cregan by fat boneless hands and thick sensual lips) Malone puts on the pressure and West gives in. Fear of hellfire triumphs over resentment at being the 'mug who puts up the money' against his own political interests, and the Movement gets £50,000.[45]

Mannix could not have denied in court that he had ever asked Wren for money for the Movement; and it is possible that Wren did give a small sum in the early days of the anti-communist campaign.[46] By 1946, however, relations between Wren and Santamaria were hostile. A request to Wren for a donation to the Archbishop Mannix Institute of Christian Studies (Belloc House) was made indirectly, with Archbishop Duhig as go-between.[47] It suited Hardy to ignore these complexities. *Power without Glory* was more effective as propaganda if Wren, Mannix and Santamaria were all tied together in one unholy package. According to Santamaria,

Wren's antagonism stemmed from local politics, where Stan Keon challenged Wren's control of the Richmond city council. With Keon marked for success in federal politics as the Movement's most promising candidate for prime minister, Wren had reason to resent Santamaria's influence.

Somehow, Mannix was exempt from Wren's anger. Their friendship continued and Mannix's causes, except for the Movement, could still count on Wren. He gave generously to Caritas Christi, the hospice established on land that adjoined Raheen. Now and then, Mannix was able to give something back. In 1947 Wren's daughter Margaret, separated from her husband, Paul Andreas, was stranded in Germany where she and her two children had endured a hard war. Wren asked Mannix's help to get Irish visas for them all. This was done through a direct request from Mannix to de Valera, and the Andreas family made a new life in Dublin.[48]

When John Wren died in November 1953, Mannix was 'much moved'. 'I have lost one who was a loyal supporter for forty years,' he said to William Hackett.[49] It has been claimed that Mannix tried to distance himself from Wren after reading *Power without Glory*. On the contrary; he presided at Wren's funeral mass at St Patrick's Cathedral, where he was joined by Archbishop Simonds. Arthur Calwell was a pall bearer.[50]

Mannix's friendship, once given, was lasting. His commitment to Santamaria did not mean withdrawing friendship from Santamaria's antagonists—Wren and Calwell included. And he gave some of the key jobs in the archdiocese to anti-Movement men. Monsignor John F. Kelly could have been replaced as director of Catholic Education and sent to some hot and dusty rural outpost. Charlie Mayne, SJ, rector of the Corpus Christi seminary, refused to listen to a rousing talk by Santamaria to newly ordained priests.

Mayne made his point by ostentatiously reading a newspaper until the talk ended.[51] Jerry Golden SJ, who was openly hostile to the Movement, wasn't moved from his influential post as chaplain to Catholic students at the University of Melbourne. Santamaria complained that Golden was creating a damaging anti-Movement force: 'I think you are leading us, and your own policy, to a great deal of trouble.' He wanted Mannix to impose unity, but the archbishop 'became quite impatient at that sort of remark'.[52]

The *Catholic Worker* men made a permanent opposition for the Movement. Mannix let them be. More than that, he asked for, and obtained, Gerard Heffey's early release from the army in order to edit the *Catholic Worker*, the journal that gave Santamaria consistent, reasoned opposition.[53] Heffey, a *Catholic Worker* man from the beginning, was also given the editorship of *Twentieth Century*, a quarterly funded by Mannix. Murray McInerney recalled a friendly relationship, unaffected by McInerney's *Catholic Worker* commitments. In April 1955, Mannix showed his displeasure at the *Catholic Worker*'s first open criticism of the Movement by withdrawing permission for the paper to be sold at the cathedral door. Other parish priests followed his lead, with disastrous effect on sales. But in other dealings between Mannix and the *Catholic Worker* men, nothing changed. In October 1956, Mannix briefed Murray McInerney to appear for the Victorian bishops in a dispute with the builders of the new diocesan seminary. Another *Catholic Worker* member Xavier Connor was part of the legal team. McInerney's account shows Mannix, then ninety-two, forthright, dominating and alert:

> [Mannix] seemed to me to have a very sound instinct for the law and I suspect that he had read the appropriate chapters

> on building contracts which appeared in Halsbury's *Laws of England*, a copy of which was in his study…Nevertheless he was not guilty of the fault of trying to overrule his legal advisers, and I remember on one occasion when we were engaged in dealing with a point that had been raised by the Bishops and one of the Bishops interrupted our explanation [he] was promptly rounded on by Archbishop Mannix who said in imperious and very plain terms: 'Oh, shut up!'[54]

Mannix reassured some dissident priests who had been warned by a Movement-inclined colleague that their careers were at risk. There would be no repercussions. 'In my diocese no priest should be afraid to say what he thinks…I do not agree with you but I respect your right to take that position.'[55] As with the Movement, so with other matters of contention. Public criticism of Mannix from his priests was rare to non-existent, but Mannix was remarkably forbearing with fiery Father Billy Mangan. In spite of having made scathing attacks on Mannix in 1941 for allegedly having misdirected money from a legacy to the church, Mangan wasn't moved from his Balaclava parish. A severe tongue-lashing was enough to vent Mannix's fury; and when seniority gave Mangan a place as consultor to the archdiocese, in 1956, the two old men sat down together.[56]

In 1950, as a tribute to Mannix, the Archbishop Mannix Travelling Scholarships were set up to help Catholic academics to get overseas degrees. Two of the first winners, Max Charlesworth and Vincent Buckley, were vigorous and articulate opponents of the Movement. Granted that it would have been improper for Mannix to play any part in directing these awards, a less intellectually liberal archbishop might have tried.

A senior *Catholic Worker* man, academic and ALP candidate, John Ryan was asked by the Pentridge chaplain Father Brosnan to sum up Mannix in one word for Gough Whitlam. The scene was the launching of a book by Barry Jones for the Anti-Hanging Council. Ryan responded:

> I said 'Permissive'. [Brosnan] turned to Gough and said: 'There you are. What did I tell you?' Gough said: 'Oh no, no…' I had to point out to Gough that this was a considered judgment on my part—the very opposite of what people would have thought. I put it to him, given the years in which Dr Mannix lived, in what other diocese in Australia could you possibly imagine the *Catholic Worker* and *News Weekly* growing up side by side?…He would pat Bob Santamaria on the back but he wouldn't squash the *Catholic Worker*.[57]

At the end of 1953, there was an uneasy peace within the Australian Labor Party. Evatt, who needed the Catholic vote, probably believed that as prime minister he could manage Santamaria. Calwell could see more clearly than Evatt that the Movement men, who were coming up in the unions and the ALP branches, were reshaping the party. He was caught. He couldn't denounce the Movement without seeming 'soft on communism'. The Catholic vote wasn't automatically Labor as it had once been: Robert Menzies, demonstrably anti-communist, could scoop up votes from newly prosperous Catholics. Calwell's loyalty to Mannix and the Catholic Church was as strong as ever. The *Catholic Worker* men were caught too. They couldn't attack Santamaria without exposing the bishops for funding the Movement, and that would mean challenging Mannix for leading the bishops astray. They respected Mannix for his liberal views on nearly everything. The Movement was the only sticking point. Tribal loyalty kept them quiet. As Mannix's ninetieth birthday came close, they wouldn't rock the boat. Time was not on Santamaria's side—or so they thought.

CHAPTER FOURTEEN

THE LAST HURRAH

'I HOPE VERY much to be able to see Your Grace on your hundredth birthday,' said the reporter. Mannix was ready for him: 'I don't see why you shouldn't, young man. You look quite healthy to me.'[1] Daniel Mannix's ninetieth birthday, on 6 March 1954, was a time for the old man to look back, and for his people to pay homage. After forty-one years in Melbourne he seemed to have grown past censure; the storms over conscription were half-forgotten, as were the passions of Ireland's years of crisis.

His birthday came within his summer holidays which, for many years, he had spent by the sea at the little coastal town of Queenscliff, and later just across the bay at Portsea, a holiday resort of great natural beauty where for many decades wealthy Victorians had built holiday houses.

Mannix's holidays, like his walks from Raheen, followed the same pattern. In mid-January every year, his housekeeper packed bed linen, tablecloths and napkins, silver and crystal to send ahead of the archbishop's arrival. Next day, with everything in readiness, Mannix left Raheen for his usual absence: four weeks in his prime, stretching to six or seven weeks in old age. Carr's Motors of Kew sent the usual black Humber with the owner's son, Dick Carr, at the wheel. Beside Mannix in the back seat was William Hackett, whose charm and good spirits had enlivened Mannix's summers for nearly twenty years. Hackett was never sure that friendship with such a high dignitary was possible, and he had to tell himself that it was a great honour to be chosen for the summer holiday—'though no one else wants it'. Meals were trying. Mannix 'only picks at things', never asks for anything at table and never passes anything to Hackett.[2] Yet Mannix depended on Hackett, and although the holiday weeks passed slowly for the self-styled 'court jester', a mutual trust and Hackett's sometimes exasperated affection grew over the years.

One of the frustrations for William Hackett was the stillness in which Mannix spent the long summer days. Mannix had never wanted to swim or take a boat out on the bay, as the restless Hackett always longed to do, but in earlier years the two men had walked on the beach together, Mannix wearing a Panama hat and Hackett in a 'tiger-hunting topee' that made him look like a retired Indian Army colonel. Sometimes when there was no one else on the beach Mannix would sing softly: Irish songs that belonged to their shared past. In their black suits and white hats, Hackett said: 'His Grace and I look like two penguins on an ice floe.'[3]

The Portsea house, Mandalay, belonged to the Sisters of the Good Shepherd, whose school for deaf children was on the same property. Mannix spent hours every day on a swing chair on the back veranda. Neither reading nor talking, he looked out over the bay as the big ships passed, ocean-going or making for the port at Melbourne. If he wanted to change the subject or to end a conversation he would say 'ships passing'. There was no possible response except a 'Yes, Your Grace', which led nowhere.

English writer Christopher Hollis found Mannix disconcerting. The archbishop replied to questions but didn't elaborate or try to keep a conversation going. But there was a tang about his quips, an irrepressibly Irish quality, like a 'Bernard Shaw in Holy Orders'. The long pause and the punch line were characteristic: 'I never get headaches...but I frequently give them to others.'[4] It was rare for anyone but Mannix to deliver the punch line. The Jesuits treasured a story told by their provincial, John Fahy, who protested against Mannix's expulsion of a Corpus Christi student for smoking. It was a first offence, Fahy said. 'Adam and Eve's was a first offence,' Mannix retorted. Fahy got the last word: 'But, Your Grace, that was God.' Mannix laughed and relented.

As at Raheen, so at Portsea: visitors came to see Mannix. Priests on their own summer holidays drove down the bay road to Mandalay. Bob Santamaria came from his Mornington holiday house, usually leaving Helen and the children to have a swim on the nearby beach while he and the archbishop talked. He was nearly always late. 'Where is he? Where is that man?' Mannix would ask, always impatient for the news and for the energy and buoyant spirits of Santamaria's presence.[5] After their talk, he would welcome Bob's family. Even if he was vague about which of the children was which and didn't have much idea of what to say to them, they felt that he really liked to see them.[6]

One of the paradoxes of Bob Santamaria was his way of presenting a dire situation—the threat of communism, the financial plight of the Catholic school system—with irrepressible optimism;

in desperate straits there was always something that could be done. Mannix responded to that quality.

In 1954 the usual trickle of visitors became a stream; everyone wanted to congratulate the old man on his ninetieth birthday. Some thought it might be the last time they would see him. Political leaders made the most of the occasion; this was an election year and, thanks to Santamaria's Movement, the Catholic vote was being carefully assessed by both parties. Menzies announced that he would come for a visit. Evatt and Calwell sent telegrams.[7]

After the birthday celebrations, William Hackett noticed a change in Mannix. He was not as independent as before, and he had decided that the daily walks would have to end. He even delayed going back to Raheen; the six weeks planned that year stretched to seven. Mannix had always relied on Hackett to help receive and amuse his guests at Raheen and Portsea: now he expected attendance on public occasions as well. 'The poodle goes too,' Hackett said in a rare angry moment.[8]

The two men had always argued, and it must have made the friendship precious to Mannix that Hackett was not in awe of him. Nonetheless, on the 1954 holiday, Mannix was irritable—so much so that Hackett even wondered if his weekly dinners and overnight stays at Raheen could continue. 'It is sad when autocratic people argue,' Hackett wrote from Portsea. He and Mannix were 'very good friends' but they differed on some points.[9] They would not have differed on matters of faith or morals. Differences about politics seem the most likely cause of arguments. For all his bonhomie, Hackett could be tough and stubborn.

Mannix had offered friendship and understanding in 1923 when, newly arrived in Melbourne, Hackett had been finding exile hard to bear. The Central Catholic Library, Hackett's creation and the centre of his working life, owed everything to the archbishop's backing. In turn, by appointing Hackett chaplain to the Movement, Mannix gained a direct line to whatever was happening in industrial and political affairs. When Santamaria wanted Hackett replaced by someone more useful in fundraising, or more pliable in matters of policy, Mannix refused to allow the move and Santamaria had to put up with Hackett, who sometimes asked awkward questions.[10]

As Mannix knew very well, this birthday had many meanings. Most of his people were pleased that 'the old man made it to ninety'. His coadjutor, the permanently sidelined Archbishop Simonds, must have sighed. There were the usual little jokes at Simonds' expense: 'Long time no see' was one of them. Simonds wasn't widely known among Melbourne Catholics, but he had friends and admirers who deplored the waste of talent in his long wait. Living as Mannix had done in 1913 to 1917 at beautiful St Mary's, West Melbourne, and given ample leave for overseas travel in Europe and as a delegate to the United Nations, Simonds' life had compensations. But by 1954 his health was declining: a combination of failing eyesight and heart trouble made him a bad risk for ever being able to rule the Melbourne diocese.[11] In Rome, where complaints about Santamaria's Movement had been circulating for some time, Daniel Mannix's birthday was a date to remember: when the old man died it would be easy to deal with Santamaria.

Soon after Mannix's return from Portsea, Bob Santamaria called at Raheen with exciting news. That morning, during his weekly staff meeting at Belloc House, he had taken a phone call from Dr Evatt's secretary, with an invitation to meet the leader at the Windsor Hotel in Melbourne and talk about election policy. Santamaria's identity as director of the Movement was still a secret; it had to be, because the existence of the Movement itself was a secret. Most of the ALP rank and file knew no more than the general public but, as leader, Evatt was well aware of Catholic involvement in the unions, and Santamaria's consequent power within the ALP. He knew how the Movement worked, as did his deputy Arthur Calwell. As former ALP senator Jim McClelland said:

> I, like most politically literate people, knew [about the Movement] by no later than 1952, and Evatt was unfit to be leader of the ALP if he did not know it...There was ample documentation, accessible to the most elementary research, to disclose the philosophical motivation and even the strategic plans of Santamaria's Movement.[12]

Quoting Evatt's later claim, that he had not the slightest idea that Santamaria was the head of a secret Movement, McClelland added: 'Tut, tut, Bert.'[13] A meeting between Evatt and Santamaria before the 1954 election was not surprising; in fact it was overdue. Hungry in Opposition, Evatt had been eyeing the Catholic vote for years, and Mannix's refusal to back Menzies' attempts to ban the Communist Party had made him hopeful.

Santamaria asked Mannix's approval before confirming an appointment with the ALP leader. Mannix, never one for caution, could see no reason to refuse, and in a series of three meetings Evatt made promises about clean ballot legislation, compulsory unionism, migration and state aid to Catholic and other independent schools. And Santamaria's close associate of that time Stan Keon, federal member for Yarra, would have a place in an Evatt cabinet.[14]

Santamaria was shocked by Evatt's opportunism. Telling his wife, Helen, about the meeting he spoke of Evatt as 'a man without a soul'. He refused to go to Canberra to discuss election policy; this annoyed Evatt but, in a later phone call, Evatt said, 'Santa, things are going very well. If your people "stick", we are past the post.'[15]

A telegram from Evatt to Mannix, sent just two weeks before the election, shows how eager Evatt was to demonstrate his close association with the Catholic Church. Having been described in a newspaper report as a Catholic, he tried, without success, to take advantage of the mistake:

> It has occurred to me that it might be proper and fitting for Your Lordship to issue a public statement to the *Age* alone to the effect that although I am not a Catholic I had the general support of good Catholic men and women for my continuous fight against communism... The political campaign seems to be going in the correct direction.[16]

Santamaria was not keen on an Evatt government, although he thought that Evatt's 'power at all costs' opportunism made him more amenable than Calwell, whose principled, stubbornly anti-Movement stance could cause trouble. It would be better if Evatt lost and a reshuffle brought a Movement-dominated front bench to the next parliament. 'Bob wants more time to reform the chaps on his side of the fence', Hackett was told.[17] Evatt, however, seemed likely to win. After six years of a Menzies Liberal government, it was time for a change. Santamaria wasn't so sure. The 'new men' who were associated with the Movement were not yet sufficiently established. If Evatt lost, there would be a chance to bring them forward.

As the election of May 1954 came near, Mannix was in a very pro-Evatt mood. There is reason to believe that Evatt visited

Raheen.[18] Mannix was tempted by Evatt's promises of almost unlimited sums for Catholic schools. Now that the communist threat to the unions had been checked, he could see the possibilities of righting an ancient wrong. For Mannix, the schools question was not just about money, although the struggles to build and staff new primary schools were financially crippling. It was about equality. After half a century in Melbourne, he was no closer to winning state aid, which he saw as an acknowledgment of full citizenship for Catholics.

It seems likely that the arguments between Hackett and Mannix reflected their disagreements about the election as well as Hackett's disapproval of some Movement activities. Hackett was worried about its use of power in the Cain State Government. This was exemplified in the fate of his friend Dr John Garvan Hurley, one of three members of the Hospitals and Charities Board. In June 1953 as a result of a Movement decision, Bill Barry, Minister for Health in the Cain Labor Government, sacked the Hospitals and Charities chief Cecil McVilly who was judged to be unsympathetic to Catholic hospitals. Collateral damage: Hurley was dismissed along with McVilly.[19]

Evatt should have won the 1954 federal election, even though Santamaria, through *News Weekly*, gave only muted support, and Evatt's campaign style was unimpressive. Fate intervened with an unwelcome surprise for the ALP less than two months before the election. Vladimir Petrov, third secretary of the Soviet Embassy in Canberra, defected. In asking for asylum, Petrov offered evidence that he and other embassy officials had been spying for Moscow. A hasty attempt by Soviet embassy officials to get Petrov's wife back to Moscow dramatised the whole affair. Australian newspapers carried photographs of a distraught, dishevelled Evdokia Petrov, one shoe missing, being rescued by customs men in Darwin. This sensational event brought Cold War fears to the surface just as the election campaign began. Coming so soon after Evatt's success in campaigning against his attempt to ban the Australian Communist Party, Petrov's defection was electoral gold for Menzies. There is no evidence that Menzies stage-managed the defection but he was guilty of failing to warn Evatt before announcing it in the House of Representatives.

Labor was narrowly defeated in the federal election in May 1954. Evatt's leadership of the Australian Labor Party was weakened by poor electoral performance. Further damage was done when the Royal Commission, set up to investigate Petrov's revelations of Soviet spying in Canberra, was given the names of three of Evatt's staff members. Challenges to Evatt's leadership were inevitable. Calwell, who had the support of the right wing, was the most likely winner. Evatt then looked to the left wing for support. In October 1954, he made his bid for survival as leader by denouncing Movement members and supporters for disloyalty, and by indirectly exposing the still unknown Santamaria's role in undermining Labor Party independence. Another Labor Split—the third in Mannix's time in Australia—brought back much of the sectarian bitterness of the conscription period.

Santamaria went to Raheen to ask how he should respond to Evatt's attack. Mannix gave his usual advice: decisions on strategy were not his business. But when Santamaria said that the Movement would fight back, Mannix showed his approval. Expelled from the Labor Party, the Movement men and their associates in the federal government formed the Australian Labor Party (Anti-Communist). They lost their seats in the federal election of December 1955, which was called by Menzies to take advantage of Labor chaos.

The overall result was a disaster for Evatt. The fall of the state Labor government of Victoria in 1955, and that of Queensland in 1957, compounded the damage. The Movement men and their allies in the Industrial Groups, directed by Santamaria, created the Democratic Labor Party. This new party was not expected to win more than a few seats at best. Its role was to make the ALP negotiate. But like most civil wars, this one brought bitterness and entrenched loyalties. Labor seemed unable to renew itself. Evatt showed serious symptoms of dementia and was given a cynical, face-saving appointment to the Supreme Court of New South Wales. Calwell's moment had passed; elected as leader in 1960, he lost the next three elections. With the benefit of DLP preferences, Menzies sailed serenely on to a series of victories.

The Catholic Church had its own Split. The bishops did not publicly quarrel about the Movement, and many continued to support Mannix and Santamaria. The most significant division was between Melbourne and Sydney. It took time for Gilroy to work out his tactics, but the strategic sense of his auxiliary bishop, James Carroll, would eventually win the day, with a successful appeal to Rome, in 1957, against the Movement's claim to be a form of Catholic Action. Mannix, however, would not admit defeat.

For reasons that had nothing to do with the political storms, the mid-1950s were hard years for Mannix. One cold, wet night in July, William Hackett, crossing Cotham Road in Kew in his usual impetuous style, was struck by a taxi. Fatally injured, he survived for ten days in St Vincent's Hospital, where he quipped: 'I never thought I'd have a taxi to take me to heaven.' Mannix spoke at Hackett's requiem mass. His age and loneliness showed in the tone and words of his 'fond, proud and sad farewell' to his friend of thirty years. The panegyric, Gerard Heffey wrote in the *Catholic Worker*, was 'nearer to music than anything could be without actually being music…[like] the slow movement of a sad and stately sonata—a *pathétique*'.[20]

The emotional and physical effort of speaking at Hackett's requiem mass was too much for Mannix, and he had to cancel his engagements for the next few days. But that night he wanted company. He asked his other 'court jester', Father Jeremiah Murphy, to have dinner with him, as Hackett had done every week for nearly twenty years.

Jeremiah Murphy in his prime was as amusing as Hackett; and as rector of Newman College for thirty years he had gained an unrivalled view of events and personalities inside and outside the Church. But at the time of Hackett's death, when Mannix needed his support, Murphy was depressed and in failing health. The Newman rectorship had become too much for him, and he was devastated when the Jesuit provincial transferred him from Newman to Xavier College, a retirement post with no responsibilities. In his diary he marked the transfer with 'Entered the desert'.[21] Within a year, he too was dead, at the age of seventy-one. In another exhausting public ceremony Mannix mourned the loss of Murphy, the 'bright star'. Without these two witty companions, Mannix was lost. His Irish past seemed remote. By the 1950s de Valera was an elder statesman. Secure in power, he wrote cordially to Mannix, but he no longer needed the archbishop's support. Mannix now depended more than ever on Santamaria; and Australian politics became as absorbing an interest as it had been in the conscription years.

At the time of the Split, I had been working in the official Catholic Action office for several months, editing the National Catholic Rural Movement's monthly *Rural Life*, and acting as a one-person press-cutting agency for Bob Santamaria, who subscribed to all the Australian daily papers and the airmail edition of the London *Times*. I knew that whatever Santamaria did, it was with Mannix's approval; and in our clerically dominated church that seemed a guarantee that it was right. I had joined an outfit I didn't understand, and I began to learn the elements of journalism. I changed the dull newsletter look of *Rural Life*, putting a bush scene with gum trees on the cover, wrote an article on country kitchens, recycled press cuttings and typed handouts of speeches from Rural Movement meetings. I can't remember when I took on the books page of *News Weekly*, the anti-communist paper which, although it wasn't a Catholic Action publication, had its editorial headquarters within the ANSCA office. Ted Madden, a gentle film buff, who sighed over Bob's last-minute interventions in the paper's content, was a benign supervisor. I liked the taste of journalism, the choice of heads and subheads, the layout and the photos on the books page, and above all I liked unpacking the parcels of new books which I had all to myself. Bob occasionally asked me to commission a review of a particular book but no one queried the space I gave to P. G. Wodehouse or Agatha Christie—neither of which had much to offer the anti-communist cause. So it went on until one day soon after the 1954 federal election when my press-cutting duty suddenly became much more interesting.

Evatt's attack on the ALP men who were associated with the Movement wasn't a complete surprise. I had read two articles by Sydney journalist Alan Reid which explained the link. And I'd been aware of an atmosphere of excitement around the office: more visitors than usual, men in suits looking preoccupied, Bob's door closed for long meetings. I wasn't invited to meetings, nor were any of the other women. Bob's secretaries, Beulah Carter (Movement) and Dorothy Jensen (Rural Movement), must have known a good deal, but they were unfailingly discreet. There was never a word about politics, and the conversation was so bland that I usually went out for the lunch hour. The women had a separate lunch room and we all took turns to wash the men's plates and tea cups as well as our own. That's how it was in the 1950s. Politics was men's business, as I'd found it at Melbourne University where the Catholic intellectuals of the Newman Society excluded women from their senior discussion group until 1957. In those days, bishops were bishops; one assumed that they all agreed with one another, and Dr Mannix was no more to be questioned than the Pope.

For some time there had been moves to separate Catholic Action from the Movement. Santamaria could see the risks of their connection becoming known, and he offered to resign his Catholic Action post. William Hackett had told members in early 1953 that they should distinguish Movement policy from matters of faith. Obedience to a Movement directive was not a matter of conscience; members were bound only by the pledge they took.[22] The fact that this needed to be said was a sign that things were getting out of hand. But Mannix saw no reason to separate Catholic Action from the political and industrial activities of the Movement. Back in 1917 he had claimed the right to speak on political matters while wearing his archbishop's biretta. He didn't see why running the Movement need exclude Santamaria from holding office as director of Catholic Action. He was accustomed to getting his own way, and the increasing uneasiness among the bishops didn't make him pause.

Because of the Movement's policy of secrecy, many Catholics were hit hard by Evatt's attack. Some who had worked with the Industrial Groups without knowing about the Movement were suddenly confronted with a painful choice. It was 'bloody Commos' versus 'bloody Groupers'. After a lifetime of an almost automatic dual loyalty to the Catholic Church and the Australian Labor Party, Catholics were being asked to take sides. Careers suffered. Families quarrelled and divided. The Labor Party tore itself apart. The Industrial Groups were disbanded. The federal members associated with the Movement were expelled, and would later lose their seats. For Daniel Mannix, this damage might have seemed a minor echo of the Irish civil war in which his own family had been divided, and many lives had been lost. And because neither he nor Santamaria had any emotional link to the Australian Labor Party, they probably underestimated the pain that would be caused by the Split.

Throughout 1954, Mannix was still making public appearances. Although he spoke more slowly than before, his voice was still clear and his seemingly unscripted words were telling. He replied to Evatt at a communion breakfast for postal workers in late October:

> If the Labor Party is brought down in ruins the fault will not be mine. I have done what I could to prevent political folly and disruptive sectarianism. I notice that reference has been made to Catholic Action groups within the unions. They are not Catholic Action groups; they are industrial groups. There has been a lot of talk also about 'action from outside'. These groups are not acting from outside, they are acting from within, as the communists are working from within.[23]

Mannix broke with his customary tolerance by moving against

the *Catholic Worker* when, in April 1955, it openly criticised the Movement. For once, Mannix was cornered. 'I abhor censorship,' he said.[24] Yet he knew that the *Catholic Worker*'s attack would weaken Santamaria's chances of holding his forces together. The survival of the Movement's federal and state parliamentarians depended on perceptions within the Labor Party that the Catholic vote was solid. There was a risk, too, that some Movement members or associates, unhappy with Santamaria's leadership, might make a separate peace with Evatt and Calwell. The *Catholic Worker* article revealed divisions in the Catholic community that could be exploited by the Labor Party. Accordingly, Mannix withdrew permission for the paper to be sold outside the cathedral. When this was made known, and its message of disapproval reinforced more bluntly by Bishop Fox, parish priests followed their leader, and sales dropped from 35,000 to less than 15,000 in a few weeks. Many of the *Catholic Worker* men were angry. It was not that they were pro-communist: far from it. Most of them came from Irish backgrounds; their parents would have been Mannix's strong supporters in the early years. The *Catholic Worker* objected to the Movement's controlling style, and its divisiveness. They felt typecast as inferior, even disloyal Catholics.

Mannix would have known that some priests were giving quasi-political sermons, directly or indirectly supporting the Movement. There were echoes of the Parnell split of Mannix's youth, except that the Irish bishops, almost all anti-Parnell, had exercised direct control over priests and pulpits. Mannix let things work themselves out. It was widely known that Calwell was cold-shouldered among Catholics of the Movement persuasion, and that he felt a pariah in his own parish church. Calwell went to mass elsewhere, and let it be known how angry he felt. Santamaria reacted differently. His indignation with the *Catholic Worker* men—and theirs with him—didn't show at their frequent meetings at church or school events. Unlike Calwell, Santamaria was in friendly parish territory during the turmoil of the mid-1950s. A few years later, he moved from North Balwyn to Deepdene where Irish-born Father Lawrence Godwin preached pro-Movement sermons, angering some in the congregation. The mood changed with the appointment of Monsignor John Kelly who was vigorously anti-Movement, but civilities were maintained on both sides.[25]

Santamaria had plenty of adulation and the support of many, perhaps most, of the parish clergy. His daughters, from an early age, heard at their school, Genazzano, that their father was a saint: a doubtful blessing because it justifiably provoked some classmates whose fathers, *Catholic Worker* men, were by implication seen as less worthy Catholics. The Heffey and McInerney girls felt aggrieved at the open partisanship of nearly all the nuns. Marilyn Heffey, spirited and (for the times) audacious, spoke her mind on behalf of her father and his friends and was expelled from the social studies class.[26] Santamaria's daughters, who knew that the nuns weren't charging them fees—a big concession for five girls—felt the pressure to be unnaturally good at school.[27] If the *Catholic Worker* parents heard about this special arrangement, which was probably prompted by Mannix, it would have added to their indignation; they too had big families to educate. Bob Santamaria was sent hate mail, and even a bomb threat. More than once a family outing was disrupted by an angry stranger who felt impelled to speak his mind.[28] Bob was more resilient than Helen. Soon after the Evatt attack, she made a painful effort to appear at her school reunion where, pale and tense, she tried to act as though everything was normal, for the sake of her children.

Poet Vincent Buckley puzzled over the paradox of Santamaria. How could so able a man be content to walk in the 'spindly shadows' of the Australian bishops? Only because of Mannix, Buckley concluded, could Santamaria accept a badly paid and obscure post, exercising his remarkable talents among men of lesser powers. He admired Santamaria's courage and his 'great charm based on courtesy',[29] but deplored the uniformity of thought that the Movement demanded. The Catholic climate in Melbourne in the Movement years was 'suffocating'.[30] Ruminating on the situation in 1955, Gerard Heffey, as Irish in background and sympathy as most Australian Catholics of the time, saw Mannix and Santamaria as anachronisms in modern Australia:

> We do not concede that Bob Santamaria or Dr Mannix has a monopoly of political wisdom...We admire the [Movement] blokes who have worked hard tremendously. I have a great personal affection for Bob. I act [as lawyer] for his father and all his brothers. We grew up together...The error—I think—lies in secrecy...Bob and Dan do not really understand British democracy—both are racially associated with a kind of democracy which means plots and secret societies. Dr Mannix was in fact 47 years of age before manhood suffrage was introduced into the British Isles.[31]

Another senior *Catholic Worker* man, Murray McInerney, regretted a narrowing of focus: 'the whole thrust of Catholic lay activity in the postwar years seems to have been political and the church seems to have been in danger of becoming solely an anti-communist club.'[32]

Although many bishops had become doubtful and some hostile

towards the Movement, a pastoral letter issued in April 1955, and read in every parish, held the line for Santamaria. Written by Cardinal Gilroy, and signed by all the archbishops and bishops, the letter deplored the action taken against the industrial groups, and came close to urging Catholics to vote for the men who had been expelled from the ALP. Some bishops thought better of having signed, but Mannix would not let them forget it. Menzies won the federal election of December 1955, which he called ostensibly to reconcile the dates of the Senate and House of Representatives, but in fact to make the most of Labor's disaster.

There were two main dramas from the mid 1950s to the 1960s. One was the unravelling of the Australian Labor Party. Evatt's mental instability became apparent when he decided to appear before the Royal Commission set up by Menzies to investigate the claims made by Vladimir Petrov. To settle the claims of Soviet espionage—so Evatt announced to the House of Representatives—he had written to Molotov. When a denial from Moscow was read to the House, members were shocked, amused or saddened, depending on their feeling for a fine mind in disarray. In a cynical ploy to manage a change of leadership with some appearance of dignity, a place was found for Evatt in February 1960 as a judge of the Supreme Court of New South Wales. Calwell became ALP leader, with the new man Gough Whitlam as his talented deputy. Asked by a TV interviewer in 1960 about the ALP's election prospects under his leadership, Calwell replied with disastrous frankness: 'It depends in part on the Angel of Death.'[33] If the angel called at Raheen, he implied, the ALP would have a better chance.

The other drama began in Sydney, moved to Rome, and then back to Sydney. Pushed by his tough-minded auxiliary bishop,

James Carroll, Gilroy tried to finish the Movement off and with it the Democratic Labor Party so that the Australian Labor Party could unite and rule again in New South Wales. He called a mass meeting at the Sacred Heart Monastery, Kensington, in September 1956 and made a direct appeal to obedience and loyalty. This, as historian Patrick O'Farrell commented, was 'the last anachronistic but powerful throw of the Irish clerical church in Australia'.[34] In October 1956, Gilroy arranged to lead a delegation to Rome, requesting a ruling on the Movement.[35] Was it or was it not Catholic Action? Mannix was sceptical about the outcome; he hadn't been impressed in the past about Rome's grasp of Irish politics, and he didn't expect better when the question was about Australia. 'Rome has blundered again,' Mannix said, when Gilroy's appeal won the day.[36] He had to accept Rome's ruling that the Movement wasn't Catholic Action, but that did not mean he was silenced. The fact that Gilroy was giving support to the ALP in New South Wales strengthened Mannix's resolve to have his own say.

Without Mannix's backing, Santamaria's survival as a power in the politics of church and state would almost certainly have come to an end in 1956. Even his remarkable courage and charisma might not have been enough to get him through the transition from a church employee to the independent director of a new secular body set up to replace the Movement, the National Civic Council. By the end of 1957, Santamaria was on his own—or very nearly. The bishops closed down ANSCA, and Santamaria moved from its office in central Melbourne into a terrace house in Gertrude Street in Fitzroy, somehow contriving to take the National Catholic Rural Movement with him, even though it was an official Catholic Action body.

I was still working there at the time and I didn't see any difference between the two offices or the work that they did. Santamaria seemed imperturbably cheerful and energetic; he kept his worries well hidden. The Fitzroy office had a backyard where the men played cricket at lunchtime, and the atmosphere was less formal in its blokey way than it had been in the city. And it was quicker and easier for Santamaria to drive home to North Balwyn by way of Raheen, as he did several times a week.

In December 1958, Mannix issued an election-eve statement that adroitly combined blunt statement with delicate suggestion. He began with one of his old favourites: whatever my enemy wants is wrong. 'Every communist and every communist sympathiser in Australia wants a victory for the Evatt party. That is alarming…' It wasn't really an argument—of course the communists put Evatt before Menzies—but replacing the ALP with 'Evatt party' was a deft touch.

Mannix's best line in the 1958 statement came in a quietly reflective paragraph about the 1955 pastoral letter, written in the wake of the Evatt attack and showing unity among the bishops. Mannix reminded his readers that this publicly distributed letter, which 'the cardinal wrote, and all the bishops signed', was still relevant. In the heat of the present contest, Mannix felt it was timely to recall Gilroy's 'calm and weighty words' about the communist threat to the security of the people. With eight words and that well-placed comma ('the cardinal wrote, and all the bishops signed') Mannix tied Gilroy embarrassingly to the pastoral letter.

One can imagine the reactions at political and episcopal breakfast tables: helpless fury, admiration, relief and astonishment that the old man could still stop his opponents in their tracks. The *Nation* (Sydney) correspondent was enthralled by the performance:

> Connoisseurs of the long career of Archbishop Daniel Mannix threw up their hands in appreciation the other day at the vintage quality of the election-eve statement made by the 94-year-old prelate to spike the hopes of the Australian Labor Party. There could be no imitation of the real thing. It made 1917 seem only yesterday; the seemingly controlled scorn, the deadly timing and above all that special blend of bluntness bordering on crudity of argument with a daring astuteness of presentation that forestalls the possibility of even senior prelates expressing public disagreement lest their Church should become a battlefield.[37]

Much was said and written about Mannix's age; how long could he live, and what would happen after his death? 'Many people think that I have lived too long,' he remarked. 'I am inclined to agree with them.' A hoax at St Vincent's Hospital in the summer of 1955 showed what a dramatic event his death would be. A young doctor, John Brenan, celebrated his last night of internship by phoning the night superintendent with grave news from Raheen. Assuming an Irish accent as an imaginary Father Casey, Brenan said that Archbishop Mannix had fallen down the stairs at Raheen and broken his fibula. Or was it his femur? Father Casey was too agitated to be sure. At any rate, it was serious. The night superintendent phoned the Mother Rectress, and John Brenan and his delighted fellow conspirators watched from a window as the lights went on in the convent and the whole hospital sprang to attention. Nuns, roused from their beds, prayed in the chapel. Nurses prepared a room for Dr Mannix, and an unsuspecting senior intern, Maurice Willis, was dispatched by taxi to Raheen to bring the patient in by ambulance. Meanwhile, another young doctor played a newspaper reporter, telephoning the hospital at ten-minute intervals for news of His Grace's condition. For the St Vincent's nuns, there was an element of triumph in the emergency. It had always been thought that when Mannix's time came, he would be taken to the Mercy Hospital, which was more comfortable than St Vincent's. Of course, no one wanted the archbishop to die, but it would be an honour to have so distinguished a patient. That dream collapsed with the arrival of Maurice Willis at Raheen, where the drive gates were locked and all the lights were out. Next morning, the conspirators were summoned and castigated for 'insulting a prince of the church', but because it was the last night of their year as interns there was no punishment.[38]

In 1959 when Rome sent an emissary, Cardinal Agagianian, to check on his capacity to carry out his duties, Mannix relished the challenge. He set out to tire the traveller by giving a big dinner party at Raheen and taking him to the Sunday afternoon opening of the new Corpus Christi seminary at Glen Waverley. He even went to Essendon Airport to meet and farewell Agagianian. 'Look, he's waving!' exclaimed the cardinal's secretary as the visitors came down the aircraft stairs.[39]

The Australian bishops and clergy often speculated about the likely effect of Mannix's death. Some of his supporters were worried. One day at Raheen bishops Lyons and O'Collins discussed the prospect of a new regime, while Mannix listened quietly. Bishop O'Collins was optimistic: 'I say that Mannix dead will be more powerful than Mannix alive.' Only then did the archbishop speak. 'That may console you,' he said, 'but I don't see what it does for me.'[40]

Mannix's public appearances diminished after 1954. He went to Newman College where he reminded his audience of the trouble he had taken to get Burley Griffin's design which 'wasn't much liked' at the time. The big public mass at Como Park for the opening of the Olympic Games in Melbourne in November 1956 was an effort. The future Archbishop of Melbourne, Frank Little, watched Cardinal Gilroy get out of his car and march ahead of Mannix at a brisk pace. 'You could see how Dan had failed. It was not kind.'[41]

The Portsea summer holidays continued after Hackett's death. A young priest on the cathedral staff was dismayed to be chosen for an honour he couldn't refuse. Leo Clarke was cheerful (a chatterbox, his mother said) and attentive to Mannix's comfort. He managed the flow of day-visitors to Portsea, which increased with every birthday. Seeing Mannix became a cultural experience for some people, and for others almost a pilgrimage.

Visitors could always rely on Mannix to say something provocative. He was master of the subtle put-down—slow, seemingly gentle, but a put-down none the less. John Challis, then a student for the Dominican priesthood, was determined to meet the old Irish legend: he made his way to Portsea and was given his audience. 'The Dominican Fathers…yes. I gave them a parish some years ago. It was at—ah—Camberwell. I think they are there still.' Challis went home with his story. The Dominicans were not amused.[42]

A young priest reported on Bishop Fox's overseas travels. Fox had been given the privilege of sleeping in a bed that the Pope had once slept in. Mannix took in the news gravely: 'Well now, Father, I think that you should make it your business to sleep in a bed that Bishop Fox has slept in. That would make you some kind of relation to the Holy Father.'[43]

No one went home without an anecdote and a sense of having met history. Manning Clark, who had asked priest-historian James

Murtagh to take him to Portsea, made a finely detailed study in his diary for February 1957:

> Dr Mannix walked on to the veranda [at Portsea] wearing a beautiful light purple biretta, a cape edged with red, a cassock with flannel underwear visible underneath black stockings and shoes with golden buckles. His face was heavily lined, [his] cheeks sagging though not flabby, the eyes moist, tinged with a faded yellow, a thin line of red along the edge of both eye-lids. The general effect, in repose, was impressive—solemn dignity which often collapsed into an impish twinkle or chuckle. He coughed a lot. His voice still bears an Irish accent though not often—pitch, generally a mumble at low pitch. We talked at first about Cork and I muffed my first compliment. Later, much later, when with more confidence I told him the people of Cork looked on him as one of their proudest sons, he said scornfully, though with that impish twinkle, 'They must be short of people to admire.'
>
> When we left, Murtagh genuflected & kissed the ring of the Archbishop. I shook him by the hand—at the door of the car I turned & it looked as though he was blessing me, & I was doubly moved. Also, he looked like a man for whom it all happened years ago, and like a man who has been stunned, knocked down by a great force, but had the courage, the faith, to stand up to his oppressors & not to whine in the gutter—supine—and a sadness deep down because he could not understand why it had happened to him and Ireland. [Mannix was] too lovable to make people afraid or angry...These men, these Catholic Bishops, are spiritual men.[44]

The combination of dignity, impish humour and sadness that captivated Manning Clark was on show for Mannix's biggest-ever audience in December 1961, when he was persuaded by Santamaria to give an interview on the ABC television program *People*. Although Mannix had virtually ignored the invention of the telephone, he had been captivated by television since its arrival in Australia in 1956. At Portsea he timed his evening meal so as to watch an enchanting young interviewer and news presenter Mary Parker whom he had seen in a school play at Genazzano Convent a few years before.[45] He had appeared briefly on TV at Portsea on his ninety-fifth birthday, but the *People* interview was a much bigger commitment. A camera crew took possession of his study for one long, hot day. There was no air-conditioning. The cameras kept overheating; they could run for only ten minutes at a time. Waiting between takes with the interviewer Gerald Lyons, Mannix might have recalled his first day in Australia, when he had doubted he could survive in a place where the sun shone so fiercely. Now, at ninety-seven, he endured the five-hour stretch without even a cup of tea.

A skilled, well-prepared interviewer, Lyons took Mannix down the years, from conscription to the Movement and the Split. All the tricky questions about the church in politics were asked; Mannix spoke slowly but firmly in reply. He spoke of Santamaria as 'the saviour of Australia'; it seems likely that he agreed to the interview because it gave an opportunity to show solidarity in the little time he had left. Ninety-eight years, ninety-nine...did Mannix ever think beyond the century? He was still in control, but, when he was gone, Archbishop Simonds was expected to make short work of Bob Santamaria.

On the matter of the Movement's secrecy, Mannix was

nonchalant. The ALP, he said, had known about it all the time: 'I think all this talk of secrecy is an afterthought.' He astonished some of his audience by taking a very mild tone on the Split. When Lyons asked if it was a sin to vote for the ALP, Mannix replied that 'every man has a right to follow his own conscience'. This wasn't the impression that Bishop Fox and many other priests and religious had been giving, and Mannix had not restrained them.

Mannix complained afterwards that 'when the lights were off they had drinks and all the time no one asked me, the victim of it all, to have a drink.'[46] He worried that his voice would not be strong enough. But the program, which ran for one hour, did all that he wanted. It showed that he was as alert as ever and that in the controversies of the 1960s he was as insistent on his right to speak his mind as he had been in the conscription debates of 1917.

I watched the interview with mixed feelings. At the time, I was belatedly extricating myself from Santamaria's office. My main interest had been the research for Santamaria's biography of Mannix, which now seemed to have been put on hold indefinitely. Although nothing had been said, I was aware that the book couldn't be published in the old man's lifetime. My doubts about the Movement were increasing, and I was uncomfortable with Santamaria's certainties. I was looking for a Movement-free zone, a chance to think without pressure from anyone on either side of the Split. Or, better still, just to forget about the whole tangle. Mannix's bravura performance was no help: he seemed wilfully to ignore the bitterness and pain felt on both sides of the ideological divide. All very well for him, I thought, switching off the television.

CHAPTER FIFTEEN

THE FINAL ACT

ON THE MORNING of 11 October 1962, Daniel Mannix was up early. For some months he hadn't been able to say his private mass in the little chapel beside his bedroom at Raheen: it was hard for him to stand, and his hands were not always steady. Instead, he had one of the Jesuits come across the road every day from Campion Hall and say it for him while he sat in an armchair, making the responses. This morning was different. Noel Ryan SJ was astonished to find the archbishop up and vested, ready to say his own mass. That day, as Ryan knew, marked the opening of the Second Vatican Council in Rome but he had not expected that Mannix would make such an effort for the occasion. 'I'll be saying mass myself today, Father,' Mannix said. 'I believe in Councils.'[1]

It wasn't an impulsive decision. Mannix wanted to celebrate with due ceremony. For the first and only time, he put on the shamrock-embroidered vestments sent to him from Maynooth to celebrate the golden jubilee of his consecration as a bishop in October 1912. A replica of those given to Maynooth by the Empress of Austria in 1880, they had significance beyond their beauty and historic meaning. The college that had rebuffed him in his unhappy 1925 visit to Ireland was trying to make amends with an imaginative gift. For the first time, too, Mannix used Eamon de Valera's jubilee gift of an exquisite gold chalice, a replica of the fifteenth-century De Burghe chalice. To match the special meaning of these remembrances from Ireland, Mannix wanted an occasion. There were others he could have chosen: the Feast of Christ the King was only two weeks away, with All Saints Day just after it. Was the ninety-eight-year-old Mannix, who had seen so much and had so few illusions, so hopeful that this Vatican Council could—or should—open new windows to the world? If so, he was out of step with most of the Australian bishops, and with his closest friend and associate of the time, Bob Santamaria.

The mass at Raheen on the opening day of the Council was a poignant moment that Mannix chose to celebrate quietly. But within hours it would have been known all over clerical Melbourne that the archbishop had said his own mass on that significant day. It would perplex some of his admirers that he welcomed the Council. There is a strangely oblique reference to it in Santamaria's biography of Mannix, written many years later. The narrative opens with an account of the Hapsburg vestments but makes no special point except that their replica came as a gift in 1962. It is as if Santamaria had a connection in mind but swerved away from it. So too with another biographer: Walter Ebsworth reports that Mannix wore the vestments on 11 October, but muffles the significance by saying that the date marked the feast of the Divine Motherhood of Mary as well as the opening of the Council. Ebsworth believed that the

Council caused 'hopeless confusion' which would have left Mannix 'saddened and heavy-laden', had he lived to see its effect.[2]

Archbishop James Duhig who, like Mannix, was too old to travel, thought the Council was unnecessary and likely to bring chaos. Cardinal Gilroy expected it to be over in a few weeks. No one imagined that it would take four years, outlive its instigator Pope John XXIII, and bring immense changes. Some members of the Australian hierarchy, setting off for Rome, called at Raheen. Archbishop O'Donnell, Duhig's coadjutor, reported that Mannix was as alert as ever. Just how alert he was to the forthcoming proceedings, none of them suspected. Nor did they fully take in the fact that Mannix was doing some serious reading; there was always a pile of books on his desk, but these were new and they were the latest in theology.

In the preliminary stages of the Council, a number of discussion papers, or *Schema*, were sent from Rome for consideration. Because there was only a short lead time for their being returned with comments, none of the Australian archbishops and bishops responded. Busy packing up, some of them grumbled about having to attend a massive conference that would tell them what they already knew. Pope John XXIII, elected in 1958 at the age of seventy-six to follow the long-serving Pius XII, wasn't expected to do anything new. He was loved for his warmth and openness to the world, and for the sturdy frame and peasant earthiness that contrasted with the austerity of his predecessor. Pope John seemed the last man to light a match under the dry tinder of the Vatican administration.

Left behind in Australia, Daniel Mannix read all that he could about the Council. Its preliminary papers had arrived in a tsunami of ecclesiastical Latin, sent to St Patrick's and brought out to

Raheen. Mannix found signs of hope in what was up for discussion and plenty to annoy him in the way it was being prepared. He hadn't been to Rome since 1925. It had seemed then that he could still help the Irish republican cause. But now, nearly four decades later, he was irrelevant to modern Ireland. Even though the golden jubilee gifts pleased him because of their beauty and the friendship they represented, Mannix knew that at ninety-eight he had been consigned to history. The Council, however, presented a new challenge. Even from Melbourne he might be able to play a part. Unlike some of the other Australian bishops, who expected no more than to rubberstamp Roman wisdom, he had plenty to say.

Mannix completed his mass, and sent Noel Ryan home to Campion Hall where the young Jesuits were told at morning tea about the archbishop's unexpected decision to celebrate the Vatican Council. Meanwhile in his private chapel Mannix went on with his usual hours of prayer and meditation. He took off the Maynooth vestments and put aside the gold chalice. After the huge physical and emotional effort of that morning, he knew he would never wear those vestments again, nor say another mass. For the remains of the day he had time to visit in imagination the scenes in St Peter's Square as the Council began. As it grew dark outside Raheen he could visualise the early morning light in Rome. By 10 p.m., when his housekeeper came upstairs with his bedtime Ovaltine, the opening ceremonies had concluded with Pope John's address to the delegates. By then, Mannix was ready for bed, but unlikely to sleep while Rome was stirred by an unparalleled historical happening. As one correspondent described it:

> Some 2500 council fathers, fully vested in flowing white garments with white mitres atop their heads, descended the great staircase of the palace next to the church, and seemed to flow from it through the piazza into St Peter's... At the very end of the procession, which took more than an hour to complete, came Pope John XXIII, carried on the *sedia gestatoria*, the famous chair borne on the shoulders of attendants... The basilica was filled not only with the council fathers, the theologians, the non-Catholic observers, and many others who had somehow managed to gain admission, but also with heads of state like Prince Albert of Belgium and President Antonio Segni of Italy. At the altar, under the presumed burial place of St Peter, crowned by Bernini's magnificent canopy in bronze, the Pope got down from the *sedia* and knelt at the altar, where he intoned the hymn *Veni, Creator Spiritus*, 'Come Holy Spirit'. The Council had begun.[3]

From mid-October to December, the Council Fathers met and debated, sometimes passionately, even angrily, the issues facing the Catholic Church. They soon knew that Pope John had much more in mind than a re-affirmation of past teaching. It was harder for Mannix in distant Melbourne to discern the mood of the meetings. A strict censorship prevented the description of factions and votes. Newspapers gave contradictory slants on the same speeches. The *Osservatore Romano* reported the Pope's opening address under the headline 'Chief Aim of the Council to Defend and Promote Doctrine', while for *Le Monde* the keynote was 'Pope Approves Research Methods in Modern Thought'. There were leaks, of course, and Mannix would not have missed the lively bulletins published under the pseudonym 'Xavier Rynne' in the *New Yorker*. But for the inside story—who said what, and the ways in which significant alliances were being shaped within the Council and outside it—Mannix had to wait until the Australian members came home. Even then, the degree of enlightenment they brought would vary.

Pope John was open to changes that shocked some of the bishops. The liturgy was one of these. The seemingly immutable Latin mass was challenged. With that challenge came the related question of the universality (Catholicity) of the church. If Latin ceased to be the universal language of the church, then the church's claim to be Catholic, which means universal, and the same everywhere, might be undermined. There were dramatic moments, as when Maximos IV, the Melchite patriarch of Antioch, spoke in French instead of Latin and confronted the Council with his view that the 'almost absolute value assigned to Latin in the liturgy, in teaching and in the administration of the Latin church' was a mistake. 'The Latin language is dead, but the Church is living and its language… must always be living because it is intended for us human beings, not for angels.'[4] The American cardinals, Spellman and McIntyre, were cautious about the use of the vernacular and believed above all that the mass 'should remain as it is'.[5] Döpfner of Munich, one of the younger cardinals, disagreed; he urged that the vernacular should be used even in the mass.[6] And so it went on, all through November. Pope John noted in his diary that the division was between those who had never been outside their own countries and those who had experience elsewhere. He himself, though Italian-born, had represented the Vatican in Bulgaria, Turkey, Greece and France, and was by no means quelled by the culture of the Roman Curia.

Mannix focused on the Schema *De Ecclesia*. It examined questions about authority and church–state relations, which had been central to his life and work; and the more he studied it the less he liked it. He had no means of knowing how it would be received by the Council. Would anyone want the thoughts of the ninety-eight-year-old Archbishop of Melbourne? Probably not, but he was determined to try. He had been sent the official papers. It was up to him to cast his vote, and give his reasons. Like the other members of the Australian hierarchy he was given only a few weeks to reply to the official Schema for *De Ecclesia*. He bided his time until he knew how it had been received. It was not discussed until November 1962. It ran into trouble and was sent back for revision. Knowing that it would be discussed at the second session gave an impetus for Mannix's reply.

Mannix didn't need anyone's help to decide against the draft of *De Ecclesia*. But it seems likely that he was briefed by the youngest and most progressive member of the Australian hierarchy, Archbishop Guilford Young of Hobart. Young came back from Rome in December, stopping in Melbourne on the way. He would have described the inner workings of the Council and encouraged Mannix to make his views felt before the Council resumed in 1963.

Mannix's response was brief and trenchant. He attacked legalism and clericalism in the Roman document. The draft, he said, 'smacks more of a legal document than a spiritual proclamation of a religious faith'. He disliked its tone and language. It was too much preoccupied with the rules and rights of a church desiring power and authority. Its tone suggested 'a certain hardness and perhaps even pride'.[7]

Mannix deplored the fact that the only image used to express the nature of the church was that of the Mystical Body of Christ which (although he did not say so in his response) had never had much resonance for him.[8] He asked why the document did not look to the Old and New Testaments for ways to convey meaning. Better images would be the house, or the people, of God, holy people, kingdom of Christ, bride of Christ, branches of the vine.

The method of proceeding seemed to Mannix 'derived from formal logic rather than biblical theology'. It was full of neo-scholastic concepts. Its abstractions were 'very alien to the Anglo-Saxon, African and Asian mind, and especially to Sacred Scripture itself'.

The document assumed that the clergy were in charge. What about the laity? 'No other function seems allotted to the laity of the church than carrying out the commands of the hierarchy.' The church must affirm, Mannix said, that its mandate is 'humble service and ministry to all', as Christ showed when he washed the feet of the apostles. Its lay helpers were not mere instruments: all adult Christians were required to show initiative and exercise due prudence and responsibility.

The doctrine on the union of church and state was 'very inopportunely proposed', Mannix said. He reminded the Council that although in Australia and New Zealand, North America and Ireland and much of Northern Europe there was theoretical separation, there was in practice 'harmony and equilibrium between the spiritual and temporal powers'.

Mannix was disappointed that the document had nothing to say about the obligation of the church to provide religious liberty to all people of good will. He spoke unequivocally of religious liberty as a 'strict right', which was 'most closely connected with the obligation of each and every one of us to follow faithfully the dictates of our own conscience, formed in good faith; but it is more deeply founded on respect for the human person, created in the image of God, which God Himself holds in respect and embraces in love, even if the gift of faith is no longer evident in it.'[9] At a time when the mantra 'error has no rights' was still bluntly expressed in church teaching, Mannix's words would have been disturbing both in themselves and as evidence of his being too much at home with the progressives in the Council. There was, however, nothing new in the stress on conscience: John Henry Newman, whom Mannix had revered since his Maynooth years, had spoken memorably of his belief in its primacy.

As Sydney scholar-priest Edmund Campion said of the Mannix document, it was 'a stunning performance by a very old man at the end of his life'.[10] For a sense of its advanced thinking, it is almost enough to set it against the words of Mannix's much younger colleague, Cardinal Gilroy, who gave the Council a version of religious liberty and conscience that sounded like Pope Gregory XVI in an early nineteenth-century conclave. Pope Gregory had spoken of the 'shameful font of indifferentism that claims freedom of conscience must be maintained for everyone'. 'Is it really possible,' Gilroy asked, 'for an ecumenical council to say that any heretic has the right to draw the faithful away from Christ, the Supreme Pastor, and to lead them to pasture in their poisoned fields?'[11]

Mannix's initiative was something more than an old man's resolve to put his thoughts on record. As well as sending his critical analysis to the president of the Coordinating Committee, Cardinal Cicognini, he made a purposeful attempt to have his voice heard by the more progressive cardinals of the Council, on whom, evidently, his hopes rested. He sent copies to six cardinals. At least three, Suenens of Malines, Liénart of Lille and Döpfner of Munich, had emerged as movers and shakers at the first sessions of the Council.

Cardinal Bea, the German Jesuit president of the Secretariat for Christian Unity, was another significant choice. He is credited with winning acceptance, against strenuous minority objections, of the texts on the Jews and on Religious Liberty.[12]

Letters to Cardinal Gracias of Bombay and Cardinal Doi of Tokyo signal Mannix's awareness that the Catholic Church in Asia had its own needs and that Rome had not always understood them. Mannix's public condemnation of the 'immoral' use of the atomic bomb in 1945 resonated with his feeling for the suffering of the Japanese people. He knew Gracias, who had visited Melbourne in 1952. By endorsing the Council's ecumenism, as expressed by Gracias, Mannix showed what a long way he himself had moved in twenty years. 'I cannot conceive the Pope signing a joint allocution with the Archbishop of Canterbury,' he had written to Gilroy in 1943, adding in a PS, 'I do not like "Christian Churches" though usage is against me.'[13] Now, Mannix saw Pope John's initiative as good and necessary. Bea's work towards reconciliation with the Jews was something Mannix had long believed in: his public statements on the 'stain' of anti-Semitism were on record. The Council was finally to dispose of the charge of Jewish guilt in the death of Christ, along with other offensive phrases in the liturgy.

Mannix had a compliment for each of his six chosen cardinals. He claimed Suenens as a 'kindred spirit', and congratulated him on relaxing the rule which had obliged Belgian priests to wear the soutane in public. Suenens' 'apostolate of the coffee bar' was commended along with his '*monde ouvrier*' pioneering. If the class barriers were going down in Belgium, Mannix said, it would be largely due to Suenens. The Mannix letter to seventy-nine-year old Achille Liénart of Lille ('from one old man to another') praised his interventions in the Council's first sittings. These had included comments on the 'frigid' language of the Sacred Scripture schema. '*Non Placet*': back for revision, Liénart had said.

It was often said that Mannix was incapable of flattering. His letter to Cardinal Döpfner of Munich, whom he greeted as one of the youngest and most articulate members of the Council, shows what he could do when he tried:

> It seems astonishing that the Church in West Germany should have risen so swiftly from oppression to her present buoyant life. Your own qualities help to explain the mystery; and I pray that you, in your own lifetime, may see the wonder extended to the whole of your Fatherland.[14]

Mannix's *De Ecclesia* response, and the charming, individually crafted letters that went out to the six cardinals were lost to sight for many years. In the mid-1990s, Jeffrey Murphy, a young doctoral student in Queensland, acted on a hint from his thesis supervisor, Father Tom Boland. Boland, the author of the splendidly astute biography of James Duhig, knew that Mannix had tried to reach some Council members, and he gave Murphy several likely names, including that of Suenens. Murphy then had the triumph of retrieving Mannix's text from the Suenens archive, which also held Mannix's covering letter, and a copy of Suenens' engagingly friendly reply. These were published in 1999, but because Boland did not know Mannix's full list of cardinals Murphy did not find the other letters.

That Mannix greeted Cardinal Suenens as a kindred spirit is significant. Suenens was well known for his radical views. With his reply to Mannix he sent a copy of his new book *The Nun in the World*, a work that attacked the traditional training of novices. Writer and former nun Karen Armstrong recalled that her novice mistress hid it under her cape, 'as if she were carrying a high explosive, as if we could be contaminated by the mere sight of the book'.[15]

Murphy's publication of Mannix's text caused a stir. But some doubted that the response to *De Ecclesia*—several pages of close argument, in Latin—could have been the work of a ninety-eight-year-old. The belief grew that Melbourne priest and philosopher Father Eric D'Arcy (later Archbishop of Hobart) was mainly responsible. D'Arcy, however, did not claim authorship, either when questioned by Murphy or by his former secretary, the present Bishop of Bathurst, Michael McKenna. Nor did he deny involvement. He died in 2005, and being of one mind with Mannix in the matter of papers, he left none behind.

In August 2013 the debate took a new turn. I was in the Melbourne Diocesan archives one day when archivist Rachel Naughton went looking for another Mannix document I had asked about. She tried the safe, where past archivists have placed important items. She had no luck with my request but in a magical moment of happenstance she discovered typescript drafts of the other, hitherto unknown Mannix letters and of the response itself. Only the day before, I had been in touch with Jeffrey Murphy, so there was an extraordinary synchronicity in the find. Now there is a new piece in the Mannix puzzle.

It would be hard to prove whose words make up the response. They are in excellent Latin.[16] That might point to Mannix rather than D'Arcy. Thirty years of learning and lecturing in Latin at Maynooth would have given him a bilingual fluency that D'Arcy would not have had. On the other hand, D'Arcy's book *Conscience and Its Right to Freedom* (1961) based on his Master's thesis at the

University of Melbourne, involved reading Aquinas and other sources in Latin. Its radical argument chimes well with the section of the response that deals with 'the strict right' of all people to follow the dictates of conscience.

On the whole, though, it seems that a D'Arcy initiative can be ruled out. As a youngish priest of Mannix's diocese (ordained in 1949) he would not presume to put such radical ideas—indeed, any ideas—to the old man at Raheen. That D'Arcy was involved is proved by the drafts, in which his distinctive handwriting appears in a few small corrections and a heading.[17] The Mannix signature, with its wobbly capital D, shows that it would have taken Mannix a very long time to write out the whole document. Dictation to D'Arcy from notes made by Mannix seems likely, with how much discussion between them, or contribution from the younger one, we will probably never know.

Mannix told his chosen cardinals that he had been 'persuaded' to put down his thoughts, and encouraged by what he had heard from those returning from the first session Council. The most likely persuader would have been Guilford Young, Archbishop of Hobart. Mannix would have found the bishops of Bendigo, Ballarat and Sale rather doubtful, even downcast, after the first sessions in Rome. But Young was already in tune with Council reform on the liturgy, and on other matters he would have applauded the European group with which Suenens, Liénart, Bea and Döpfner were associated. If Mannix had a mole in the Council, Guilford Young would have been his man. An interview with the Irish Jesuit Patrick Stephenson confirms Young's involvement:

> Dr Young of Hobart told me that he was to represent Dr Mannix's views at the Vatican Council and Dr Young

> called at Raheen on his way to Rome to get the [Vatican] documents and read them with him and he said, 'Look he's thirty years ahead of the lot of us.'[18]

For me, the authorship of the response to *De Ecclesia* comes down to a question of tone and context. D'Arcy might have composed it under a general instruction, though even there I find the tone too assured for someone of his then limited experience of authority within the church. In the accompanying letters, Mannix addresses the six cardinals with the ease and certainty of age and experience. Using the formal ceremonials of an earlier age, he speaks as a prince to other princes of the church. There is even a touch of *de haut en bas*, a 'Well done, young Döpfner' tone in the letter. It's much easier to believe that the documents are all essentially Mannix than that Eric D'Arcy had the effrontery as well as the dramatising skill to assume the Mannix *persona* in the six distinctive letters.

The response to Rome and the letters to the six cardinals show a new Mannix. Or perhaps a Mannix who had been obscured in the confusion of the ALP Split. His steadfast support for the embattled Santamaria has tended to categorise him. At a time of absolutes in the federal elections that followed the Split, Mannix was counted as the most powerful No-sayer to the Australian Labor Party, as indeed he was. But his characteristic response when asked by one of his priests if a vote for Labor was permissible was: 'Father, you are always free to be unwise.' Others, like Bishop Fox, made it a conscientious imperative to vote against the ALP. Mannix's statements, on political questions at least, left room for dissent. It might be an uncomfortable space, but the 'unwise' could inhabit it if they thought it right.

Mannix's reply to Rome endorsed freedom in more than one way. It stressed the right of members of the laity to act freely in the secular order. They were subject to papal and episcopal authority in matters of faith and morals, 'but in all other aspects of their temporal activity, whether concerning the practical policies to be chosen or the strategic and tactical methods to be preferred, the laity acts on its own responsibility and rejoices in full freedom, in both obedience and action'.[19]

That sounds like an endorsement of the Movement. It fits well with Mannix's record, ever since the 1940s, of tacitly or openly supporting Santamaria's judgment in practical policy, strategy and tactics. The friendship between the two men had strengthened with the years. From the mid-1950s, when William Hackett and Jeremiah Murphy died, Mannix depended more than before on the ebullient Santamaria. When the walks to the cathedral had to stop, Santamaria's frequent calls at Raheen gave an infusion of energy at the end of the day. On his side, the demonisation of Santamaria after the Evatt attack won Mannix's sympathy. If anyone knew how it felt to be attacked, caricatured, misrepresented, Mannix did. Regretting some sharp words he himself had used in the conscription period, he counselled Santamaria never to ridicule his attackers. 'You will be provoked,' he said, 'but do not reply in kind.'[20] On the whole, Santamaria restrained his anger; his style was the rueful shrug rather than any explosion of feelings. He expected alignments to be made and tightly held; no compromise, no straying from the policies he had laid down. But he did try to separate the personal from the political and in old age he was able to make peace with some former adversaries on the left of the Labor Party.

There was never a hope of making peace with Arthur Calwell.

On a chance encounter in a bookshop in 1948, soon after the death of Calwell's eleven-year-old son, Santamaria had held out his hand. Calwell's response, 'I don't want any sympathy from *you*', shows the depth of his pain. In 1948 the Movement wasn't as powerful within the ALP as it would later become, but Calwell had reason to resent it. After speaking critically of its 'anti-communist obsession' at the 1948 State Labor Conference, Calwell lost his place on the Victorian central executive.[21]

The threat to Calwell's political power wasn't the whole story. There was a Jacob and Esau rivalry between Calwell and Santamaria, with Mannix, a father-figure to both men, favouring the younger son. In the *Genesis* story, Jacob tricks his old, blind father, Isaac, into giving the blessing that should have been Esau's. Calwell liked to think that Mannix was blind to Santamaria's activities, but there is plenty of evidence that the old man kept himself informed to the end.

Strangely, Calwell never turned against Mannix, and on the day of Mannix's death he spoke poignantly of his distress at feeling 'a stranger' at Raheen. His rage was reserved for Santamaria. There were opportunities in the 1950s when a degree of compromise from Calwell might have avoided the wrecking of the Labor Party. 'Bob would kiss and make up any time; he's a pragmatist. It's Arthur who just can't move an inch,' said the Movement chaplain, Father (later Archbishop) Eric D'Arcy.[22]

Close as the two men were, Mannix and Santamaria were at odds over the Vatican Council. In a 1969 interview Santamaria recalled having seen the archbishop 'working on' his response to *De Ecclesia* during his last Portsea holiday.[23] Yet Santamaria's Mannix biography states with absolute certainty that there was nothing to interest the archbishop in the first session of the Council, and that therefore he had nothing to learn from the other Australian bishops on their return.[24] Clearly this was not so: Mannix was very interested indeed. Perhaps Santamaria did not know about the letters of encouragement that Mannix sent to the six radical cardinals. Or perhaps, by the time he came to write his life of Mannix, in the 1980s, Santamaria wanted to forget that his hero had made common cause with these radicals.

A traditionalist in matters of faith, Santamaria used to say that Sheehan's *Apologetics and Catholic Doctrine* was all he needed. He thought that Pope John's openness to the world—which included giving an audience to Khruschev's son-in-law—was dangerous.[25] The last thing he would have wanted in 1963 was *aggiornamento* at Raheen. He would have been shocked to think of Suenens as a 'kindred spirit' for Mannix.

Mannix spoke freely and often about his admiration for Pope John.[26] He felt that he himself had failed in the qualities the new Pope had in abundance. Several of the young priests who came to Raheen in 1962 and 1963 heard Mannix regret that, unlike Pope John, he hadn't been a father to his people. Perhaps for the first time in his stormy relationship with the Vatican, Mannix felt an emotional closeness to the head of the church. Santamaria wouldn't have it. Talking to Bishop Fox some years later, he recalled a disagreement with Mannix over Pope John:

> It was a Sunday afternoon—it was in the middle of the Vatican Council and [Mannix] had been greatly impressed by John XXIII and how the whole world seemed to regard him as a great figure and he said to me: 'I think the whole of my policy has been mistaken, of standing up to—I don't know whether he used the word 'standing' or 'facing

> unpopularity'—whereas, he said, 'this Pope shows that if you are ready to embrace the whole world you can have a much greater influence.'[27]

Sounding quite snappish, Santamaria said: 'I thought it was a completely wrong analysis.' His own strategy was one of confrontation. Strongly opposed to any form of dialogue with communists, he would have been horrified by signs of Mannix's throwing the windows open. But by thinking only in terms of a right or wrong analysis of policy, Santamaria was missing one point, which was at least as much emotional as tactical. In his ninety-ninth year, waiting to die, Mannix wanted to give and be given the warmth with which Pope John was surrounded. Moreover, he could see the need for change in the church, as his remarkable response to *De Ecclesia* had shown. Some of the Australian bishops experienced drastic changes while at the Council, but the old archbishop who stayed home was way ahead of them.

Santamaria's interest in contributing to the Council appeared late, and for the rest of his life he deplored the changes brought about by the progressives whom Mannix had most admired. Months after Mannix sent off his salvo on *De Ecclesia*, he backed Santamaria's request to be admitted as a lay observer. His letter to Rome, dated 23 September 1963, was unmistakably written by Santamaria himself on Mannix's behalf.[28] In his characteristic point-by-point style the letter sets out his formidable qualifications and achievements in the lay apostolate. Mannix's death intervened and Santamaria was not invited. His viewpoint on political intervention against communism was put by Bishop Stewart of Sandhurst (Bendigo).

Even many years after his death, Mannix's claims for religious liberty and the rights of conscience would still be too radical for the Vatican. When the Australian bishops gathered in Rome in 1998 for a discussion on the situation of their church they were given a list of their failings in pastoral work. These included 'an extreme individualism, seen especially in a concept of conscience that elevates the individual conscience to the level of an absolute.'[29]

The *De Ecclesia* document to which Mannix responded was not concerned with sexual matters, but if such questions had been raised the archbishop would probably have reiterated the view he had expressed in 1942: that 'all of us are too puritanical in matters of sex', that sexual curiosity was 'good and natural' and that too great a weight was being placed on sins of impurity.[30] This anticipates Pope Francis in 2013, deploring the church's obsession with preaching about divorce, contraception, homosexuality, gay marriage and abortion: 'It is not necessary to talk about these things all the time.'[31]

On clerical sex abuse, so much in the minds of Catholics of the twenty-first century, Mannix seems to have had nothing to say. Without adequate church records from his time, or from that of his successors Simonds, Knox and Little, about criminal sexual exploitation, we cannot even guess how much Mannix knew or understood. The worst period, as far as can now be known, was well after his death but some of the criminal priests were ordained during his last decade.[32]

Pope John died in June 1963, leaving the Council's work to be continued by his successor. Confined to his upstairs bedroom at Raheen and wearing his old green dressing-gown, Mannix watched the news on television: the puff of white smoke, the *Habemus Papam*, the crowds in St Peter's Square. He had lived through seven papacies. Joe Broderick, a young priest home on sick leave at his parents' house, was visiting Mannix the day after the election of Paul VI was announced:

> [Mannix] still had yesterday's papers lying around on the floor, with their photos of a few fat old cardinals who had been hoping to get the job. When I asked what he thought of the new Pope, he gestured towards the pictures and said: 'Well, at least he's the best-looking of the candidates.' Of course as well as being typical of his irony, it was his way of not committing himself to something one could quote as a serious opinion. He was always cagey. About Paul, he went on: 'I believe he remembers me. I can't say I remember him. But that's not surprising. After all, in Rome at the head of the Australian pilgrimage in the Holy Year, I was the Archbishop of Melbourne and he was just another monsignor around the place. (longish pause) Now he's come unto his own. And I'm still here, sittin' on the shelf.' That was the sort of thing he would say with a haunting mixture of good humour and pathos. I can't really describe it. I can never quite catch the tone. But there was always a feeling of melancholy and disillusionment in the air. It's a very Irish thing, I think. A profound and basic disbelief in everything.[33]

Broderick saw sadness, humour and loneliness in Mannix's last months. He felt welcome to drop in at Raheen, to talk, listen and observe. He thought of Mannix as a consummate performer, a master of the pause before the devastating punch line, the reversal of expectation. But as well as 'Mannix the thespian', conscious of the persona he presented to the world, there was the patient old man who had listened hour after hour to penitents every Saturday, tried to stay awake at endless school concerts and prize givings, and kept his door open for anyone who wanted to talk. When Broderick sought permission to accept a post with the Columban Fathers' mission in Lima, he went to Raheen, doubtful as to how this adventurous plan would be received. First came the expected rebuke:

> 'It doesn't seem to occur to you to settle down here in Melbourne and do the work you were ordained for in the archdiocese'...I can still see him reflecting, chewing his cud, as 'twere, and I can still hear the clock ticking on the wall of his room. Then came the wonderful voice: 'You may go, and you have my blessing.' (pause) 'And if I were any younger, I might even be going with you.'[34]

Broderick, who left the priesthood, married and now lives in Bogotá, counts himself lucky to have had those afternoons at Raheen: 'I felt drawn to the Old Man for the warmth of his nature, his mellowness, I guess, and his sense of fun and of his sometimes gentle (and sometimes gently bitter) expressions of debunkery...' Broderick believes that Mannix knew intuitively that he would leave the priesthood. He even treasures Mannix's ambiguous farewell. First, the qualified praise, gently spoken to Broderick's mother: '"After all (pause) he hasn't bin (pause) a complete (longer pause) failure..." And then, after the longest pause ever, the lethal qualifier "yet". He raised his high purple biretta most graciously and waved us off.' In South America, a few weeks later, Broderick heard of Mannix's death. He felt that their friendship had already been completed 'with that wonderful farewell'.[35]

Another priest of the diocese who was struggling to find meaning in his parish work was Michael Parer. Mannix neither reproached this young man for his restlessness nor tried to constrain him. Instead of the rebuke Parer might have expected, Mannix made him chaplain to the Catholic Evidence Guild, a dedicated group of 'soapbox' orators who spoke to all comers on the Yarra Bank. The archbishop, then ninety-seven, listened to ideas about using the mass media, including television, admired and chuckled over a poster that Parer had designed, and made him feel 'ten feet tall'. Parer, who left the priesthood and married after the Second Vatican Council remembered Mannix with affection:

> I saw him on seven occasions...he understood that I was a priest completely dedicated to the cause of God and yet unsure of my future. I now wonder if he was certain that I would move out beyond the established ministry...he appreciated my personal and sexual battles, and immediately went to the deeper issue that caused them, namely my own uneasiness as a priest living within the confines of a parish structure.[36]

A sterner Mannix presented himself to the administrator of St Patrick's Cathedral, Monsignor Laurie Moran. Just because Mannix was ninety-eight didn't mean he would let control slip through his fingers. Moran had to present himself at Raheen once a week with a thorough report. Normally confident, Moran dreaded the sessions. Hilton Deakin (now a bishop, then a young priest on the cathedral staff) noticed that Moran was 'terrified, sweating' and asked why. 'You don't understand. He grills you,' Moran replied.[37]

Broderick and Parer felt Mannix's understanding. Moran felt his authority. Painter Clifton Pugh had a rare chance to show these complexities when the *Bulletin* commissioned a cover sketch to accompany a profile of the ninety-eight-year-old prelate written by his television interviewer Gerald Lyons. Pugh went to Raheen for an hour-long sitting. Pugh's biographer, Sally Morrison, described the meeting:

> When Clif entered the room where Mannix was expecting him he found 'the power of his presence' overwhelming. He'd never been so impressed before, feeling that Mannix embodied 'dignity, power and compassion' and that he was a person secure within himself. 'I was not aware of the age of the man as I had expected to be. Ninety-eight years! He was no age.'[38]

Mannix's last portrait shows him in a characteristic pose: seated, meditative but alert, his left hand just touching his cheek, and the frail fingers of the right hand lightly holding an open book. The dark eyes, though hooded, see everything. Pugh asked permission to develop the sketch into a full portrait. Again, Mannix's expressive calm dominates the canvas. The jewel colours in the space behind the head suggest a stained glass window, and on the left appears the solid black shape of a heavy Celtic cross, partly obscured behind the soft folds of Mannix's voluminous black cloak. This haunting study of the archbishop now hangs in Newman College, but in the last year of Mannix's life it was at Raheen, because its subject liked it best of all his portraits. To place it beside Max Meldrum's combative Mannix of 1920 is to see how time had changed him. Even more than the fragility of the hands and the deep lines of the face, Pugh has caught the gentleness and acceptance that had so impressed Manning Clark a few years earlier. All passion spent? Not quite. The fire is there still.

CHAPTER SIXTEEN

DEATH COMES FOR THE ARCHBISHOP

IN EARLY 1963 Daniel Mannix had seemed certain to reach his hundredth birthday. His people were waiting for the day. There would be a celebratory High Mass at St Patrick's Cathedral, with Australian archbishops and bishops coming by invitation, and some chosen priests on the altar; there would be flowers and incense and triumphant music. There would be prime ministers, past and present, judges, senior public servants, reporters, photographers, radio and TV.

In those last months the archbishop's daily routine was much the same. His days were long, now that he was confined to his bedroom. Sometimes, he would allow himself to be helped downstairs; more often he received visitors in his room. As always, he read widely: new books, journals and newspapers. He had seldom, if ever, been in a cinema but he developed a taste for 1950s westerns like *Gunsmoke*, and on Saturday afternoons when Bob Santamaria called at Raheen on his way home from the football, he would find the old man ready to discuss the match of the day. Santamaria followed Carlton. Mannix's choice, predictably, was Collingwood, the team of the underdogs, his neighbours across the river from Raheen.[1]

Even in his late nineties, Mannix found it hard to admit decrepitude. He seldom wore his hearing aid, and it was a rare photographer who caught him with his reading glasses on. He had always cut his own hair, not well or very often, leaving straggling grey-white locks to emerge from below the top hat of his famous walks, or from under the tall, embroidered mitre he wore for church ceremonies. Mannix disliked 'ecclesiastical millinery' as he called it, and kept his own as simple as he could. Indoors, whether upstairs or downstairs, his purple biretta gave height and dignity, and, in its familiarity, disguised the look of age. He was never seen bareheaded and rather than allow someone else to shave him, he bought an electric razor at the age of ninety-seven. This was seen as his defiance of time: how long did he expect to live? It was quite simple, Santamaria remarked: he just did not like to be touched.[2] Of course it wasn't simple; for whatever reason, it was his last line of defence.

On 4 November 1963, the eve of the Melbourne Cup Day holiday, Mannix seemed much as usual. One of the Jesuits from Campion Hall, across the road from Raheen, came in to say mass, and left him to pray, as always, for some hours. Mannix took a ticket in the Cup sweep arranged by his staff, glanced at the newspapers, had his lunch on a tray, and dozed. Late in the afternoon he was alert for Santamaria's quick, light step on the stairs. On his last visit, three days earlier, he had brought the good news that Prime

Minister Menzies had devised an uncontroversial way of giving federal aid to independent schools, in the form of grants for science blocks. This time, the two men talked about plans for a Catholic residential college in the newly opened Monash University. Mannix wanted quick action: it had to be decided in his lifetime, he said, or it would never be done. Santamaria left with his last order from Mannix, and it was done.

Next morning, the housekeeper Jean Virgona thought that the archbishop seemed not quite well. He refused lunch, and in the early afternoon he collapsed. It was Melbourne Cup Day; the horses were running at Flemington, and Mannix's physician Dr John Cahill, a keen racegoer, was watching the big race. Agitated, Jean Virgona telephoned Mannix's eye specialist, Hugh Ryan, to ask for another name.[3] A surgeon, Fred Colahan, was summoned. There was nothing complicated in the diagnosis: a strangulated hernia.[4] Mannix had known the risk of his condition for some years but had resisted a routine operation. It was now too late and his death was certain. Colahan, and Cahill who arrived late in the afternoon, had no real choice. Mannix was dying. It was a matter of hours, both doctors said.

Somehow the news travelled round Melbourne. People gathered at the gates of Raheen; those who came to the door were admitted and taken upstairs. Those who knelt at the bedside or stood in the big, sparsely furnished bedroom made up a varied group. Mother Chrysostom from Caritas Christi Hospice next door to Raheen, held Mannix's hand, stilling a tremor. Several priests came from the Jesuit house across the road. Bishop Arthur Fox arrived from Bendigo; Monsignor Moran came from the cathedral. Jean Virgona and her sister Lena knelt and prayed. Arthur Calwell found himself in the same room as Bob Santamaria. They hadn't spoken to one another for years, nor did they break that silence. They had more to think about than one another. There were others who simply wandered in: an eccentric who used to tell Mannix about his visions, and a pious woman who brought a picture of Padre Pio to put on the bedroom mantelpiece.

The light of the summer day faded into evening. The Cup Day crowds came home. And as if in a final coup de théatre, the darkening sky was lit by fireworks.

No one has written about fireworks around Raheen that night and I can't be sure how brilliantly they sparkled while Daniel Mannix lay dying. Guy Fawkes Night was as much a ritual as the Melbourne Cup and, as I remember it, more fun for children. That year, the two festivals fell on the same day. The fireworks display had long since lost its sectarian meaning; and in backyards of the houses around Raheen, whether Catholic or Protestant, most children were allowed to let off the crackers they'd bought at the newsagent's shop. I remember the sparklers, the banging and crackling, the sputtering of the cheap devices that failed, the bright colours—purple and silver, red and green—and the occasional glory of a Catherine wheel. The most expensive and exciting were the Roman candles that released a small galaxy of stars. Did any of the Kew children have Roman candles on Guy Fawkes Night, 1963? For Daniel Mannix the imagery seems apt, except for the fact that fireworks, even Roman candles, burn out fast. The archbishop lived through Cup Day and Guy Fawkes Night. He died just after midday on 6 November, four months short of his hundredth birthday, on another day that seems chosen for him: the Feast of All the Saints of Ireland.

Mannix's people were in shock as they began to plan the last ceremonies. According to custom the body would lie in state in an open coffin so that mourners could file past and pay their respects. While Archbishop Justin Simonds was on his way home from Rome, it was for Bishop Fox and Monsignor Moran to make decisions. Even after death the *noli me tangere* of Mannix's lifetime remained. For Bishop Fox, there was no question of allowing the archbishop's body to go to a funeral parlour; the embalming had to be done 'most inconveniently' at Raheen.[5]

When his staff set about planning the funeral, they were confronted with Mannix's own clearly stated wishes. In June 1958, he had sent for Monsignor Moran and dictated his instructions. The service was to be 'as simple as the liturgy allows'. He did not want a panegyric, and there was to be no procession through the streets.[6] This would have been a startling departure from custom. How could Mannix, who had given hundreds of panegyrics and headed many processions, want or expect such a quiet exit?

Two of Mannix's last orders were disregarded. His body lay in state in St Patrick's Cathedral for five days, from 8 to 12 November. During this time an estimated 200,000 people queued in the streets to enter the cathedral and walk in line past the open coffin. Catholic school children were sent in to view the body; for some, this first glimpse of death was a shock. The requiem mass itself had all the ceremonial grandeur the cathedral could provide. The new Archbishop of Melbourne, Justin Simonds, made a huge effort to deliver the panegyric that Mannix hadn't wanted.[7] Frail and nearly blind, Simonds had to be helped into and out of the pulpit; he read with the help of strong spotlights, and he missed a whole page of his text 'without noticing the alarming discrepancy'.[8] Flags flew at half-mast over Parliament House, and there was a thirteen-gun salute in the Domain for the maverick Chaplain General of the Australian Military Forces.

One order was obeyed. There was no procession through the streets. The coffin was carried only a short distance along the Cathedral aisle before being lowered into the vault in the cathedral floor. Standing round it, gazing down, were the archbishops, bishops and priests and other notables. Not a woman in sight, not even the Virgona sisters, who had devoted themselves for nearly twenty years to their '*nonno*' [grandfather] as they would sometimes speak of the archbishop.

Back at Raheen, Jean Virgona had been in charge during the days between the death and the burial. Neither she nor Bishop Fox knew what to do with Mannix's possessions. Archbishop Simonds would not want them. Anyone who called in was given something. Priests were invited to take a book from the library, or some small devotional object. An ivory-handled walking stick, from the collection beside the front door, was given away. The famous biretta was too intimate to be passed on but somehow—then or at a later date—the military cap of a Chaplain General, which Mannix never wore but would not relinquish, went to the Dominican priory. Father Michael Parer, then working in the media, was commissioned to make a documentary for the ABC, *The Passing of a Prince*. He filmed the austere bedroom with its ancient brass bedstead; he noted the perilously high claw-foot bath—how did Mannix get in and out of it? At the end of filming, Jean Virgona offered Parer a choice of memento: a finely wrought jewelled brooch in the shape of a harp, worn by Mannix on his lapel on St Patrick's Day, or a kitsch painted-china cottage that played *Danny Boy* when you opened the door. Parer chose the harp.

Bob Santamaria, as the authorised biographer, moved fast to

take some of the Mannix papers from Raheen, thereby saving them from the incinerator or the new archbishop. There was no knowing what Archbishop Simonds would have done with the papers but he wouldn't have passed them over to Santamaria, whom he summarily dismissed from his regular spot on the weekly Catholic TV program. Simonds' successor Cardinal Knox, a brisk new broom from Rome, chose the historian-priest James Murtagh as Mannix's official biographer in 1968. By the time Santamaria published his Mannix biography in 1984, Simonds was dead, Knox had returned to Rome and Murtagh had died with his biography unwritten but having left an impressive deposit of papers.[9]

In a revealing act of possessiveness Santamaria held on to the Mannix papers that he had snatched from the burning in November 1963, leaving his sons and daughters to give them back to the diocese after his own death in 1998. His biography keeps a formal distance from its subject until, in the final chapter, feeling breaks through with a sense of the personal loss that Santamaria felt.

Mannix's Raheen was quickly dismantled. Plumbers worked overtime to create a modern bathroom, with a shower for Simonds in place of that perilous bath. The library was broken up. Much of it went to the diocesan seminary: some of the Irish collection found its way to Newman College. An exquisite Streeton landscape, a gift to Mannix from the artist, remained at Raheen, only to be casually given away by Cardinal Knox to a visiting American prelate. Faded sepia photographs of Mannix's father and mother were taken down from their places on the staircase; these went to the cathedral archives, along with the replica of the Empress Elizabeth of Austria's gift of vestments to Maynooth and the golden chalice sent from de Valera to Mannix, that was used just once in that final private mass. Whatever Mannix's people would have liked, there was no chance of keeping Raheen as a shrine. Nearly fifty years of solitary occupation ended in fragments. Although three more archbishops would live at Raheen, none would make it his own.

And none would capture the imagination of the people as Daniel Mannix had done.

Afterword

BIOGRAPHERS BEGIN with facts and opinions, find enlightenment along the way if we're lucky, and end with questions. We would delude ourselves if we thought the full truth could ever be found, or that any volume would be big enough to contain it. I keep in mind Henry James's warning: 'Never say you know the truth about any human heart.' I remember too that Mannix was so wary of biographers that he ordered the destruction of his private papers. Total destruction, of course, wasn't possible; his decision only made his biographers work harder. He made it more likely, too, that he would be misunderstood, even caricatured, as he has often been in popular accounts.

There have been eight biographies of Mannix. I have learned from them all, as I have learned from a huge mass of commentary in various forms. What today seems an excess of idealisation was taken for granted in an earlier period. Idealisation and aggression are two sides of the same coin. Pope Francis has protested against being depicted as a sort of Superman, a star. For his own people, or many of them, Mannix was a star. His opponents demonised him. In the triumphalist church of his time it was hard for him to be, in Pope Francis's terms, 'a man who laughs, cries, sleeps calmly and has friends like anyone else'.[1]

Some questions that seem obvious to me in 2015 would not have occurred to a biographer in the 1960s or the 1980s, not because I can claim to be more perceptive but because the world has changed, and will keep changing. This won't be the last word on Daniel Mannix.

For me, one of the most interesting decades in Mannix's life is the final one, when he was looking back at all that he had done and not done. He was listening then to young men who brought their perplexities to Raheen, and he was forming the views that emerged in the remarkable document he sent to the Second Vatican Council. I think of the old man in the green dressing-gown, confined to his room but travelling widely in thought and memory. When Mannix gave orders in 1958 for a simple funeral, no procession and no panegyric, was he remembering that distant day in 1917 when he walked behind Archbishop Carr's coffin and felt the people's love for that fatherly figure? His wish for a simple, even humble, farewell matches his later reflections for the Vatican Council on the 'hardness, even pride' that he disliked in the *De Ecclesia* statement. He was casting his final vote against the clericalism that has proved so destructive.

I don't think that Daniel Mannix can be seen in gloom or in rosy glow. More than most, he is a man for light and shade. We don't have to choose a single focus or look for consistency: that would deprive Mannix of all that made him human. He was a man for the big occasion; he took the spotlight with apparent ease. Interviews, portraits, photographs, sketches and cartoons exposed him to the world. Yet he lived as a recluse. In his top hat and frock coat and his indifference to the telephone and the motor car, he presented himself as a man of the past but his thinking was advanced enough, in 1938, to insist on the need to make reparation to the Aborigines.

There are records of hundreds of thousands of words spoken by the church leader and the political interventionist, but the man who spent up to five hours each day in prayer left no spiritual journal or private diary.

He made it hard for biographers to find his private self but the patterns are there to be discerned in the choices he made and the people and the causes that aroused his sympathies.

Notes

Introduction

1 Envelopes held in Mannix College Collection, Monash University.
2 William Hackett SJ has described the urgency with which Robert Barton prepared his statement and the difficulty in getting it typed in Dublin. Knowing he was under surveillance, he asked Hackett (who was sent to Australia in September 1922) to deliver it by hand to Mannix. Hackett Papers.
3 Michael Wallis to Jack Wallis, 20 August 1925. Mannix Papers.
4 The story of the burning was confirmed by Father T. P. Boland, biographer of Archbishop Duhig, who questioned May Saunders. 'It took her three days to do it.' Boland to Brenda Niall, February 2009.
5 Australian Archives Series A8911, nos. 236, 240.
6 Noted by Vera Orschel, 'Papers of John Hagan, Irish College Rome', Archival Catalogue, 2008, p. vii.
7 B. A. Santamaria, interview with Robin Hughes, recorded 23 April 1997. Australian Biography: 'Bob Santamaria', p. 11, http://www.australianbiography.gov.au/subjects/santamaria/intertext1html
8 Fr Morley Coyne, interview with the author, 1959.
9 Paul Duffy SJ helped Santamaria to pack the papers. Duffy, pers. comm., 2010.

Chapter One: THE BIG HOUSE

1 Interview with Sr Carmela Cagney, Murtagh Papers.
2 An *Advocate* galley proof of the 1955 speech, corrected in Mannix's hand, strikes out the reference to peasantry. Parer Papers.
3 In the Irish Census of 1901 Ellen Mannix is the only family member listed as Irish-speaking.
4 T. P. Boland, *Thomas Carr*, p. 3.
5 Tim Pat Coogan, *De Valera*, p.10.
6 T. Ryle Dwyer, *Big Fellow, Long Fellow*, p. 248.
7 Mark Bence-Jones, *Burke's Guide to Irish Country Houses*, vol. 1, p. 82.
8 Dr Patrick Cagney, interview with James Murtagh, Murtagh Papers.
9 Paul Bew, *Ireland: The Politics of Enmity*, p. 264.
10 Rev Dr Croke to Thomas Sanders, 17 December 1868, quoted in Ebsworth, *Archbishop Mannix*, p. 34.
11 Irish Census 1901 and 1911.
12 Barry Coldrey, *Faith and Fatherland*, p. 92. Coldrey shows that Latin was being taught in some Christian Brothers schools in the 1860s, but that it was not at that time a priority.
13 Walter A. Ebsworth, p. 28.
14 Transcribed by James Murtagh from English translation of Peadar O'Laoghaire, *Mo Scéal Féin*, *My Own Story*, chapter 23, Murtagh Papers.
15 University College, Cork, Records, courtesy Professor Dermot Keogh.
16 Colm Kiernan, *Daniel Mannix and Ireland*, p. 6.
17 Bernard H. Becker (ed.), *Disturbed Ireland: Letters Written during the Winter of 1880–81*, quoted in Buckland Estate History: www.bucklandsurrey.net
18 Patricia Wallis-McCombe to Danny Cusack, 2013.
19 Sister Carmela Cagney, interview with James Murtagh, Murtagh Papers.
20 *Cork Examiner*, 4 January 1881, quoted in Kiernan, *Daniel Mannix and Ireland*, p. 8.
21 Kiernan, *Daniel Mannix and Ireland*, pp. 8–9.
22 Published Dublin, Hodges Figgis, 1903.
23 Bob Mannix, grandson of Patrick Mannix, interview, Melbourne, 14 April 2013, and subsequent correspondence.

Chapter Two: MAYNOOTH

1 I have drawn on T. P. Boland's description of Maynooth in *Thomas Carr*, pp. 15–53 and *passim*.

2 John Healy, *Maynooth College*, p. 455. (It is not clear whether the author is quoting McHale or paraphrasing him.)
3 Figures (1552 women in convents in 1851 rose to 8031 in 1901) taken from Irish Census, quoted by Margaret MacCurtain, 'Godly Burden: Catholic Sisterhoods in 20th-Century Ireland', in Anthony Bradley and M. G. Valiulis (eds.), *Gender and Sexuality in Modern Ireland*, p. 245.
4 Patrick J. Corish, *Maynooth College 1795–1995*, p. 238.
5 *Ibid*, p. 236.
6 Francis Hackett, *The Green Lion*, p. 234. Younger brother of Mannix's Jesuit friend William Hackett, Francis Hackett was describing the Clongowes schoolboy intake, but the sense of difference would apply at Maynooth too.
7 Healy, pp. 466–67 and *passim*.
8 Corish, p. 229.
9 See Walter McDonald, *Reminiscences of a Maynooth Professor*, pp. 81–82, re bringing in religious women to take charge in kitchen and refectory; this was resisted for many years while the use of untrained male servants had led to disorder and low standards.
10 Recalled by Dean Goidenich, quoted in Michael Gilchrist, *Daniel Mannix: Wit and Wisdom*, p. 6.
11 Boland, *Thomas Carr*, p. 39.
12 *Ibid*, pp. 37–38.
13 *Ibid*, p. 41.
14 Father Brian Quillinan CSSR, pers. comm., 2013.
15 Corish, p. 199.
16 F. S. L. Lyons, *The Fall of Parnell*, pp. 116–17.
17 *Ibid*, p. 116.
18 *Ibid*, pp. 76–77.
19 *Ibid*, p. 279.
20 Thomas J. Morrissey. *Bishop Edward O'Dwyer of Limerick*, pp. 135, 137.
21 Healy, p. 512.
22 'Joe O Connor' pseud., in a Maynooth past students' publication *Vexilla Regis*, 1915, quoted in Ebsworth, p. 63.
23 Kiernan, *Daniel Mannix and Ireland*, p. 25.
24 Record of the Maynooth Union, 1901–02, pp. 56–68.
25 Ebsworth, p. 57.
26 Corish, p. 276.

27 Corish, p. 26, cites Dean Cornelius Mulcahy, 'Reminiscences', *Irish Ecclesiastical Review*, September 1945, p. 11.
28 Mannix to Walsh, 12 March 1903, quoted in Kiernan, *Daniel Mannix and Ireland*, pp. 55–56.
29 B. A. Santamaria, *Daniel Mannix*, p. 24.
30 Corish, p. 287.
31 *The Times* (London), 25 July 1903, refers to rooms decorated for the use of the royal couple.
32 Kiernan confuses George V with his father, Edward VII. If the racing colours were displayed it would have to be 1903.
33 The Irish Census of 1911 shows that a large proportion of Maynooth students were Irish speakers.
34 Kiernan, *Daniel Mannix and Ireland*, p. 42.
35 Corish, p. 292.
36 Kiernan, *Daniel Mannix and Ireland*, p. 47.
37 McDonald, *Reminiscences of a Maynooth Professor*, p. 248.
38 Mannix to Mgr O'Riordan, Irish College, Rome, 29 June 1911, and Archbishop John Healy to Mannix, 23 March 1911. Transcribed from the Maynooth archives by James Murtagh, Murtagh Papers.
39 Pádraig Pearse, *Dr Mannix and the Coiste Grothe*, quoted in McMahon, *Grand Opportunity*, p. 23.
40 Corish, p. 299.
41 Ebsworth, p. 86, gives the date of decision as July 1912, but Corish, p. 296, and Kiernan, *Daniel Mannix and Ireland*, p. 51, suggest a longer process.
42 Mgr O'Riordan to Archbishop Carr, 15 April 1912, Mannix Papers.
43 Mannix to Canon O'Callaghan, August 1912, quoted in Ebsworth, p. 94.
44 Cardinal Logue's phrase for Mannix, quoted in Ebsworth, p. 74.
45 Mannix to Eamon de Valera, 2 October 1912, photocopy of original, Mannix Papers.

Chapter Three: MANNIX IN MELBOURNE

1 Ebsworth, p. 114.
2 *North Melbourne Courier & West Melbourne Advertiser*, 28 March 1913, p. 2.
3 Ebsworth, p. 114.
4 Ebsworth, p. 115.
5 *Argus* (Melbourne), 24 March 1913.
6 Boland, *Thomas Carr*, p. 99.

7 John Rickard, *An Assemblage of Decent Men and Women*, p. 45.
8 Patrick Morgan, *Melbourne before Mannix*, p. 33.
9 *Ibid*, pp. 152–53.
10 *Argus* (Melbourne), 9 June 1919, p. 8.
11 See Morgan, *Melbourne before Mannix*, for an authoritative account of lay initiatives in Carr's time.
12 Hugh Mahon to T. J. Ryan, 3 September 1910, Hugh Mahon Papers.
13 Thomas Carr to Hugh Mahon, 14 March 1915, Hugh Mahon Papers.
14 *Argus* (Melbourne), 15 February 1916, p. 8.
15 Chris McConville, 'Nicholas O'Donnell (1862–1920)', *ADB*, vol. 11, 1988, pp. 60–61.
16 Morgan, *Melbourne before Mannix*, p. 47.
17 Charles Townshend, *Easter 1916*, p. xx.
18 *Ibid*, p. 317.
19 *Argus* (Melbourne), 1 May 1916, p. 7.
20 Declan Kiberd, 'Thomas MacDonagh 1878–1916', in Anthony Roche (ed.), *The UCD Aesthetic: Celebrating 150 Years of UCD Writers*, New Island, Dublin, 2003, pp. 34–35.
21 O'Dwyer to Maxwell, quoted in Townshend, *Easter 1916*, p. 305.
22 Patrick J. Mannix, *The Belligerent Prelate*, p. 42.

Chapter Four: DUELLING WITH THE PRIME MINISTER

1 Mark McKenna, *An Eye for Eternity*, p. 751n.
2 John Doyle, Melbourne surgeon, heard the story from Kenny's daughter, Dr Elizabeth Kenny, an anaesthetist, in the course of an operation, pers. comm.
3 L. F. Fitzhardinge, *William Morris Hughes*, vol. 1, pp. 14–15.
4 Aneurin Hughes, *Billy Hughes*, pp. 11–15, gives a detailed account of these first years in Australia but is careful also to point out that much of it depends on Hughes' own unreliable memoirs. No marriage record has been found and the births of the Hughes children appear not to have been registered.
5 Fitzhardinge, vol. 1, p. 154.
6 *Advocate* (Melbourne), 10 June 1916. I am indebted to Patrick Morgan for drawing attention to Mannix's 'beginning to link the Easter Rising with the conduct of the war', *Melbourne before Mannix*, p. 170.
7 Michael McKernan, *Australian Churches at War*, p. 81; McKernan, *The Australian People and the Great War*, pp. 18–20, *passim*.

8 *Argus* (Melbourne), 18 September 1916, p. 6.

9 J. M. Main, *Conscription*, pp. 73, 105.

10 Fitzhardinge, vol. 2, p. 216.

11 *Ibid*, p. 227.

12 Hughes to Lloyd George, 17 August 1917, quoted in Fitzhardinge, vol. 2, p. 276.

13 *Kalgoorlie Miner*, 30 November 1917, p. 7.

14 Hughes to Murdoch, cable quoted in Fitzhardinge, vol. 2, p. 286n.

15 Michael McKernan, *Victoria at War, 1914–1918*, p. 164, notes that working-class Richmond with its substantial Catholic population had a higher recruitment level than any other suburb: 2000 men, compared with middle-class Camberwell's 255.

16 James Griffin 'Mannix, Daniel, 1864–1963', *ADB*, vol. 10, 1986, pp. 398–404.

17 Fitzhardinge, vol. 2, p. 293.

18 'Mrs Winter had to sell her valuable property at Mannix's own price to avoid the introduction of a new paper by him.' Jageurs to Dillon, 6 February 1919. Dillon Papers, MS 6848/9/220. David Winter Gorman (grandson) confirms this, pers. comm., 2014.

19 Vincent Nolan to Thomas Carr, 14 February 1917, and reply by Thomas Carr, 15 February 1917, Mannix Papers.

20 Daniel Mannix to Michael Kelly, 13 April 1917, Kelly Papers.

21 Tom Hazell, pers. comm., 2011, had this account from Hubert Cooney.

22 Boland, *Thomas Carr*, foreword and pp. 423–26.

23 Ebsworth, pp. 163–73.

24 Brian Lewis, *Our War*, pp. 273–74.

25 *Argus* (Melbourne), 22 March 1918; and Gilchrist, *Daniel Mannix*, pp. 67–68.

26 Alex Leeper, *Spectator* (London), 23 March 1918, p. 314, quoted in Santamaria, *Daniel Mannix*, p. 103.

27 *Argus* (Melbourne), 19 November 1917, p. 6.

28 *Courier* (Brisbane), 21 November 1917, p. 8; *Argus* (Melbourne), 23 November 1917, p. 9.

29 Patrick O'Farrell, *The Irish in Australia*, p. 272.

30 Complaining to John Dillon of the *Advocate*'s retreat from 'the bold policy' of Joseph Winter, Morgan Jageurs blamed 'the timidity of Joe Winter's widow. She is afraid of giving offence to Dr Mannix who is regarded as the head of the Sinn Féin Movement in Australia.' Jageurs to Dillon, 24 November 1918, Dillon Papers.

31 M. E. Collins, *Ireland 1868–1966*, p. 239.

32 Morgan Jageurs to John Dillon, 5 November 1919, Dillon Papers.

33 *Ibid*, 8 December 1919.

34 'Exhibition Hospital: Ministry and Dr Mannix; Charges of Sectarianism', *Argus* (Melbourne), 22 February 1919, p. 18.

35 *Argus* (Melbourne), 9 June 1919, p. 8.

36 Mannix 'made no apology for putting Australia first and the Empire second, for Australia has first claim on him', speech at St Joseph's Church, Wonthaggi, 4 December 1915, *Age* (Melbourne), 5 December 1915, p. 10.

37 Worsley, one of Brookes' supporters, referred to Mannix as 'the Rasputin of Australia'. Worsley to Brookes, 2 April 1918, Herbert Brookes Papers.

38 Patrick O'Farrell, *The Irish in Australia*, p. 272.

39 *Daily News* (Perth), 11 January 1937.

40 For Martin Vaughan's research, see 'Billy Hughes' Family Secret', *Rewind*, ABCTV, screened 8 August 2004 (www.abc.net.au/tv/rewind/text/s1168547.htm).

41 See Aneurin Hughes, *Billy Hughes*, for an account of Helen Hughes' death, pp. 131–36, and the visit to Raheen, pp. 136–37.

42 Hughes to Mannix, [c. March 1952] Mannix Papers; Mannix to Dame Mary Hughes, 5 November 1952, Hughes Papers.

Chapter Five: PLAYING POKER WITH THE JESUITS

1 Enrolments under Father Barry rose from an abysmal five to an unimpressive seventeen. Philip Ayres, *Prince of the Church*, p. 134–35.

2 Moran to Archbishop Walsh of Dublin, 2 September 1886, quoted in Ayres, p. 135.

3 *Freeman's Journal* (Sydney), 27 March 1913, p. 15.

4 *Argus* (Melbourne), 19 May 1913.

5 James Griffin, *John Wren*, p. 27–28.

6 *Newman Magazine*, 1919, pp. 16, 19.

7 Fr Moyley Coyne, interview with the author, 1959.

8 Jageurs to John Dillon, 16 March 1920, Dillon Papers.

9 James O'Dwyer SJ to John Ryan SJ, 2 June 1915, Newman College Papers.

10 Quoted in B. J. Fleming SJ, 'The Jesuits and Newman College', p. 3, Newman College Papers.

11 John Ryan SJ, 27 August 1915, John Ryan Papers.

12 John Ryan SJ, Diaries, 2 October 1917, John Ryan Papers.

13 Bishop Phelan to Mannix, 26 October 1917, quoted in Fleming, p. 10.

14 John Ryan SJ to Edward Pigott SJ, 20 October 1917, Newman College Papers.

15 John Ryan SJ, Diaries, 2 October 1917.

16 'I, as the senior of the suffragan bishops, have never been asked for an opinion', Bishop Phelan of Sale to John Ryan SJ, 27 October 1917, quoted in Fleming, p. 10.

17 *Ibid*.

18 James O'Dwyer SJ to John Ryan SJ, 2 June 1915, John Ryan Papers.

19 Greg Dening, *Xavier*, p. 106.

20 *Ibid*, p. 102.

21 The phrase 'an ordinary trade war' appeared in the *Advocate*, 3 February 1917, but the *Argus* report of Mannix's speech, given on 28 January, had 'a sordid trade war'. It is possible that Mannix thought better of the word 'sordid' and deleted it from the *Advocate* version.

22 Wilfred Ryan SJ to John Ryan SJ, 14 October 1917, John Ryan Papers.

23 Alasdair McGregor, *Grand Obsessions*, p. 290.

24 *Ibid*, p. 294.

25 *Ibid*, p. 293.

26 *Ibid*, p. 307.

27 Daniel Mannix to Hugh Mahon, 6 April 1916, Mahon Papers.

28 George O'Neill SJ, 'History of the Jesuits in Australia', chapter 34, p. 4.

29 *Argus* (Melbourne), 25 March 1918, p. 9.

30 'Opening of Newman College', *Tribune* (Melbourne), 28 March 1918.

31 'My connection with Xavier would ensure the confidence of a good number of boys & parents', James O'Dwyer SJ to John Ryan SJ, 2 June 1915, Newman College Papers.

32 Newman College Register, 1918, has 65 entries. The 60 students listed in the 1919 *Newman Magazine* must allow for some dropouts.

33 *Argus*, 26 September 1912, p. 8.

34 Albert Power SJ, 24 September 1919, notes, Power Papers.

35 Albert Power SJ to Father Superior (Dublin), 3 February 1920, Power Papers.

36 B. J. Fleming SJ, 'Father James O'Dwyer', p. 4, Newman College Papers.

37 According to Murray McInerney, who came to Newman in 1928 and knew many of the first college members, Power was on collision course with the Students' Club 'on the matter of club colours and the like' when Murphy

was brought in to replace him as rector in 1923, McInerney, 'Memoirs', vol. 1 [Chapter 3], 'The University', p. 25.

38 E. J. Stormon SJ, 'The Aims of a Catholic College', [c.1960], Newman College Papers.

39 J. M. Murphy SJ to Daniel Mannix, 14 September 1925, Murphy Papers.

40 *Ibid.*

41 Memo by Albert Power SJ, 4 August 1920, Newman College Papers.

42 Five women students came to German tutorials, three to French. Handwritten note, n.d., c. 1918, Newman College Papers. Early issues of the *Newman Magazine* included items written by and about women students. Rooms were set aside at the southern end of the cloister for female external students in the Griffin plan. Jeffrey Turnbull, 'The Architecture of Newman College', p. 84.

43 James O'Dwyer SJ to Albert Power SJ, 7 November 1919, Newman College Papers.

44 Mary Ryllis Clark, *Loreto in Australia*, pp. 123–25.

45 Dening, p. 207.

46 Ursula M. L. Bygott, *With Pen and Tongue*, pp. 197–99.

47 Albert Power SJ to Provincial William Lockington SJ, 19 May 1926, Corpus Christi Papers.

48 W. A. Greening, 'The Origins of St Kevin's Central College, Melbourne 1918', Greening Papers, cites a 1962 interview with Mannix and suggests that the college was an expression of 'the Mannix thesis'. For a discussion of Mannix's role, see Chris McConville, *St Kevin's College*, pp. 17–21.

49 James McClelland, *Stirring the Possum*, p. 20.

Chapter Six: THE ARCHBISHOP AT RAHEEN

1 Tom Hazell, interview with the author, 2012.

2 Boland, *Thomas Carr*, p. 425.

3 Munro-Ferguson to Colonial Office, 8 May 1917, quoted in Boland, *Thomas Carr*, p. 425.

4 Edmund Campion, *A Place in the City*, p. 7.

5 Kiernan, *Daniel Mannix and Ireland*, p. 159.

6 Boland, *Thomas Carr*, p. 421.

7 Ayres, p. 137, gives an estimated cost of £11,000 in 1885.

8 Tom Hazell, interview with the author, 2012.

9 *Argus* (Melbourne), 23 October 1934.

10 Paul Duffy SJ, interview with the author, 2012.

11 Dr Charles McCann, interview with the author, 28 September 2010.
12 Maria Santospirito Triaca, 'Jean Virgona, Archbishop Mannix's Italian Housekeeper', *Italian Historical Society Journal*, vol. 4, no. 1, Jan–June 1996, p. 19.
13 Santamaria, *Daniel Mannix*, p. 253.
14 Triaca, p. 19.
15 Archbishop Sir Frank Little, interview with the author, 2007.
16 See Griffin, *John Wren*, p. 346. Griffin sees this detail as proof that Mannix visited the Wren house. I am indebted to Father Quillinan, CSSR, for pointing out that the soutane would not be worn on a visit.
17 Patrick O'Farrell, *Vanished Kingdoms*, p. 246.
18 Leonie (Gibson) Kramer lived in Raven Street as a child. Kramer, *Broomstick*, p. 15.
19 Gina Nicoletti, pers. comm., 11 August 2013.
20 John Funder, 'Melbourne Millefeuilles', in Brenda Niall and Ian Britain (eds), *The Oxford Book of Australian Schooldays*, pp. 288–89.
21 Anna Sturgess, daughter of David Dickson, pers. comm., 2014.
22 Peter Hastings, 'And I Never Owned a Motor-Car', *Bulletin* (Sydney), 16 November 1963.
23 Campion, *A Place in the City*, p. 7.
24 M. J. Curran to Father Hagan, 12 November 1928.
25 Victorian Electoral Rolls, 1914, 1919, 1949, 1963.
26 William Hackett SJ to David Robinson, 11 October 1927, Hackett Papers.
27 Mannix to Lord Huntingfield, 15 December 1936, Mannix Papers.

Chapter Seven: FOR IRELAND'S FREEDOM

1 Boland, *Thomas Carr*, p. 284.
2 *Argus* (Melbourne), 22 February 1919, p. 18.
3 *Australasian* (Melbourne), 14 February 1920, quoted in Jageurs to Dillon, 18 February 1920, Dillon Papers.
4 Griffin, *John Wren,* pp. 241–42.
5 *Ibid*, pp. 240–41.
6 *Tribune* (Melbourne), 22 July 1917, quoted in Chris McConville, *Croppies Celts & Catholics*, p. 120.
7 Morgan Jageurs to John Dillon, 16 March 1920, Dillon Papers.
8 Griffin, *John Wren*, p. 241.
9 Gilchrist, *Daniel Mannix*, p. 86.

10 Ebsworth, p. 222.

11 *Oamaru Mail*, 28 May 1920, p. 8.

12 Bishop Hilton Deakin (interview with the author, 26 April 2013), who as a young priest in the Glen Iris parish used to listen to Murtagh's accounts of the Mannix work in progress, remembers the Grand Canyon incident as a mysterious but inescapable element in the Mannix story, as was a later nervous collapse in the 1930s recounted to him by Murtagh who said that Mannix recovered at a house in the Dandenongs owned by T. M. Burke. No written record of the Grand Canyon episode has been found in the Murtagh papers.

13 'President de Valera's recollections of Archbishop Mannix', 6 November 1963, Radio Éireann, Parer Papers.

14 Coogan, *De Valera*, pp. 124–26.

15 *Ibid*, pp. 79, 81, 87, 112–29, *passim*.

16 *Ibid*, pp. 92–93.

17 *Ibid*, pp. 107–08.

18 *Ibid*, p. 140.

19 *The Times* (London), 16 July 1920, quoted in Kiernan, *Daniel Mannix and Ireland*, p. 148.

20 'Mannix and De Valera: They Might Be Brothers', *Sydney Morning Herald*, 21 August 1920, p. 13.

21 Shane Leslie, *Doomsland*, p. 187.

22 Coogan, *De Valera*, p. 432.

23 *Ibid*, p. 108.

24 *Ibid*, p. 689.

25 *Ibid*, p. 220.

26 '15,000 Cheer Archbishop Mannix', *New York Times*, 19 July 1920.

27 'Two Prelates at Mass', *New York Times*, 19 July 1920.

28 Kiernan, *Daniel Mannix and Ireland*, p. 150.

29 Patrick Mannix, *The Belligerent Prelate*, p. 82.

30 *New York Times*, 31 July 1920.

31 Arthur Vaughan to Vaughan family, published in *Footprints* (Melbourne), October 1972.

32 *Cork Examiner*, 20 September 1920.

33 Griffin, p. 26, and Patrick J. Mannix, p. 89, make this claim.

34 Mannix family members, interviews with James Murtagh, Murtagh Papers.

35 Dr Patrick Cagney, interview with James Murtagh, Murtagh Papers.

36 Bob Mannix, interview with the author, 2013.
37 Murtagh Papers.
38 Bob Mannix, 2013; *Kelly's Directory*, Lancaster, 1895.
39 'Irish Bishops Act', *Evening Telegraph* (Dublin), 16 August 1920.
40 Mannix to Kelly, 21 August 1920, Kelly Papers.
41 Mannix to Kelly, 4 October 1920, Kelly Papers.
42 Dwyer, p. 133.
43 Ebsworth, p. 250–51.
44 Shane Leslie, quoted in Gilchrist, *Daniel Mannix*, p. 98.
45 Typescript by Shane Leslie, edited and amended in Mannix's handwriting, 7 September 1920, Leslie Papers.
46 Edward Morris to Shane Leslie, 14 October 1920, Leslie Papers.
47 *Ibid*, 29 October 1920.
48 Arthur A. Ryan, *Daniel Mannix, Archbishop of Melbourne*, p. 8.
49 Dwyer, p. 122, quoting MacSwiney's inaugural address as Lord Mayor, 1920.
50 Kiernan, *Daniel Mannix and Ireland*, p. 157.
51 *Catholic Bulletin* (Dublin), November 1920, p. 679, from Mannix's speech at the Cannon Street Hotel, London, 23 September 1920.
52 Gerry White and Brendan O'Shea, *The Burning of Cork*, p. 9.
53 Coogan, *De Valera*, p. 216.
54 Dwyer, p. 150.
55 Dr Gerard Vaughan, nephew of Father Arthur Vaughan, interview with the author, May 2013.
56 'Irish Bishops Act', *Evening Telegraph* (Dublin), 16 August 1920.
57 Shane Leslie, *Cardinal Gasquet*, p. 16.
58 Harold Glowrey (1893–1974), Victorian MLA for Ouyen 1927–32, Country Progressive Party, www.parliament.vic.gov.au accessed 26 March 2014.
59 Matthew Beovich, Diaries, March 1921, Beovich Papers.
60 Sean O'Ceallaigh to Eamon de Valera, 29 January 1921 (Documents on Irish Foreign Policy, no. 58, NAI DFA, Paris, 1921, (difp.ie).
61 Quoted in Coogan, *De Valera*, pp. 219–20.
62 Santamaria, *Daniel Mannix*, p. 122.
63 Ticket of Car Number 2 is inscribed: 'His Grace Archbishop Kelly', Kelly Papers.

Chapter Eight: HOME TIES

1 Charles Townshend, *The Republic*, p. 348.

2 Dwyer, p. 224.

3 *Ibid*, p. 188.

4 See Townshend, pp. 347 *et seq*. for a full discussion of the complexities of the treaty negotiations.

5 De Valera to Monsignor Luzio, 30 April 1923, quoted in David W. Miller, *Church, State and Nation in Ireland, 1898–1921*, pp. 492–93.

6 Boland, *James Duhig*, pp. 159–60.

7 See Townshend, p. 353, who puts the treaty choice in these terms.

8 Michael Collins to William Hackett SJ, 21 August 1922, Hackett Papers.

9 William Hackett SJ to Edward Carroll SJ, n.d. [c. December 1923], Carroll Papers.

10 *Sydney Morning Herald*, 28 November 1922.

11 *Advocate* (Melbourne), 23 March 1923, p. 13.

12 *Catholic Press* (Sydney), 3 May 1923.

13 Other pilgrims, including some New Zealanders, travelled on the *Oronsay* and joined Mannix and his group at Toulon, bringing the total number to 243. Ebsworth, p. 275.

14 Kiernan, *Daniel Mannix and Ireland*, p. 187.

15 W. J. (Joe) Broderick, 'De Valera and Archbishop Mannix', *History Ireland*, Issue 3, Autumn 1994, (www.historyireland.com).

16 Kiernan, *Daniel Mannix and Ireland*, p. 187.

17 *Advocate* (Melbourne), 6 August 1925, quoted in Gilchrist, *Daniel Mannix*, p. 122.

18 Eamon Donnelly to Mannix, 26 September 1925, Mannix Papers.

19 Dermot Keogh, 'Mannix, Memory and Irish Independence', in Val Noone and Rachel Naughton (eds.), *Daniel Mannix: His Legacy*.

20 Dr Patrick Cagney, interview with James Murtagh, Murtagh Papers.

21 An obituary for Mannix's nephew, Dr John (Jack) Wallis, tells the grisly story of 'Staker Wallis', executed by the British in 1770. His head was mounted on a stake and exhibited in Kilfinane market. *Irish Review* (Melbourne), vol. 3, no. 27, 1 April 1935.

22 Kiernan, *Daniel Mannix and Ireland*, p. 192.

23 Mannix to Philip Bernardini, Apostolic Delegate to Oceania, 21 January 1934, handwritten draft, with corrections, Mannix Papers.

24 Margaret Hutch-O'Reilly to Daniel Mannix, 30 July 1925, Mannix Papers.

25 Nellie Mannix to Daniel Mannix, 10 February 1925, Mannix Papers.
26 Robert Barton to William Hackett SJ, n.d. [1925], Hackett Papers.
27 John Cagney, interview with James Murtagh, Murtagh Papers.
28 Thanking Mannix for a gift of £500 from the Countess Freehill, de Valera said that in return she would get shares in his newspaper the *Irish Press*. De Valera to Mannix, 13 June 1933, Mannix Papers.
29 Mary Mannix emigrated to New York in September 1924 and Denis followed in November 1925.
30 *Catholic Press* (Sydney), 20 November 1930, p. 22.
31 *Irish Independent* (Dublin), 9 August 1920.
32 Jeremiah Murphy SJ to Mannix, 14 September 1925, Murphy Papers.
33 *Argus* (Melbourne), 11 February 1935, p. 8; 7 February 1940, p. 1.
34 M. E. Calwell, *I Am Bound to Be True*, p. 18.
35 *Argus* (Melbourne), 7 March 1934, p. 5.
36 *Newman Magazine* reports on Michael Wallis's doings from 1925 to 1941.
37 Pamela (Field) Sublet, pers. comm., 2013.
38 Ella (Wallis) Reilly, interview with James Murtagh, Murtagh Papers.
39 *Ibid*.
40 Michael Wallis to Jack Wallis, 20 August 1925, Mannix Papers.
41 Gerard Mahony, Euroa, pers. comm., 2014.
42 Victorian Electoral Rolls.
43 Adrian Gorman, Balranald, remembers the surprise in the district when Mannix appeared, so far from his own diocese, pers. comm., 2014.

Chapter Nine: THE PERMISSIVE AUTOCRAT

1 'A Rational Sunday: Comments by Dr Mannix', *Freeman's Journal* (Sydney), 19 June 1919, p. 17.
2 *Argus* (Melbourne), 10, 14, 16 January 1934; 12, 13, 18 June 1934.
3 P. J. Stephenson SJ, interview with Michael Parer [n.d.], Parer Papers.
4 Tom Prior, *A Knockabout Priest*, pp. 43–44.
5 *Ibid*, p. 46.
6 Fr Tom Brophy, interview with the author, Hastings, Victoria, 5 February 2014.
7 Fr Lemieux, interview with James Murtagh, Murtagh Papers.
8 The number of students in primary schools grew from 21,792 to 73,695. There was an even more significant rise in the number in secondary schools, from 3216 to 28,395. Santamaria, *Daniel Mannix*, p. 150.

9 Robert Pascoe, *The Feasts & Seasons of John F. Kelly*, p. 180. Kelly was Director of Catholic Education in Victoria from 1955 to 1969.

10 Lorraine (Furlong) Barr, pers. comm., 1 February 2014.

11 Dom Camillus Claffey, interview with James Murtagh, Roscrea, Ireland, 29 June 1970, Murtagh Papers.

12 Both William Hackett and Leo Clarke describe Mannix's long sessions of prayer during his summer holidays.

13 Donald Cave, *Percy Jones*, p. 11.

14 Keith Dunstan, 'Walter Joseph Hauser, Chorister, Industrial Chemist, 15.1.1928–5.2.2012', *Age* (Melbourne), 1 March 2012.

15 Cave, p. 69.

16 Mannix to Gilroy, 15 June 1943, Mannix Papers.

17 Mannix to Miss Moffat, 14 December 1951, Mannix Papers.

18 Cave, p. 112, quoting Jones.

19 David de Carvalho, 'Whitlands 1941–1951: An Australian Experiment in Utopian Catholicism', *Australasian Catholic Record* (Sydney), vol. 80, no. 2, April 2003, pp. 145–63.

20 Marilyn (Heffey) Puglisi, pers. comm., 2013.

21 Frank Murphy to James Murtagh, 27 June 1970, and 14 July 1970, Murtagh Papers.

22 Gilchrist, *Daniel Mannix*, p. 127.

23 Tom Hazell, pers. comm., 2012.

24 John Meagher SJ to Thomas Costelloe SJ, 12 April 1944, Provincials' Correspondence.

25 Gilchrist, *Daniel Mannix*, p. 182 *et seq.*, draws on an interview with Fr Daniel Conquest.

26 *Ibid.*

27 Frank Maher, Director of Catholic Action, thought that the FCJ nuns at Genazzano, where his daughters were at school, showed Jansenist prudishness, pers. comm., c. 1953.

28 Gilchrist, *Daniel Mannix*, p. 183.

29 *The Family: Social Justice Statement*, 1944, published by the Australian National Secretariat of Catholic Action, had been written, like almost all of the Social Justice Statements in Mannix's time, by B. A. Santamaria, with the approval of the Australian bishops. It is much more cautious than Mannix in its attitude to sex education, which is seen as solely the province of the parents. It endorses an unnamed 'medical authority' who said that

'no more knowledge should be imparted than is necessary to overcome current difficulties'.

30 Speech at the first Pre-Cana Conference, 14 July 1947, Murtagh Papers.

31 Noel Tobin, interview, in Gilchrist, *Daniel Mannix*, p. 13.

32 *Wise Parenthood: A Book for Married People* was first published in 1918.

33 *From Boy to Man*, see Pascoe, p. 126.

34 Griffin, *Daniel Mannix*, p. 252.

35 Pascoe, p. 126.

36 Gilchrist, *Daniel Mannix*, p. 183.

37 Rev. Dr Ian Waters, pers. comm., 17 January 2014.

38 Patrick Parkinson, 'Suffer the Teenage Children: Child Sexual Abuse in Church Communities', February 2013, Sydney Law School Legal Studies Research paper, no. 13/09; Nicholas Tonti-Filippini, 'The Catholic Church and Paedophilia: Learning from Failures', *ABC Religion and Ethics*, 4 June 2013, reports Professor Des Cahill's evidence to the Victorian Parliamentary Enquiry into Child Abuse suggesting that 14 of 378 priests graduating from Corpus Christi Seminary, Werribee, between 1940 and 1966 were convicted of child sexual abuse. Church authorities have admitted that another four who had died were also abusers, making a rate of 4.76%.

39 Bryan Egan, *Ways of a Hospital*, p. 161.

40 Rev. Dr Waters remembers hearing this story, which was widely told as an example of Bishop Fox's style.

41 The 'twenty per cent' of mail is a figure that Dr Waters heard as a young priest.

42 Josephine Laffin, *Matthew Beovich*, p. 76.

43 Pascoe, p. 114.

44 Mannix to Mr Mann, 9 August 1954, Mannix Papers.

45 Prior, p. 41.

46 Anne O'Brien, *Blazing a Trail*, p. 10.

47 Egan, pp. 73–85, *passim*.

48 Gwynedd Hunter-Payne, *Cabrini: A Hospital's Journey, 1948–1998*, p. 74–75.

49 Kathleen Dunlop Kane, 'O'Connell, Cecily Maude (1884–1965)', *ADB*, vol. 11, 1988, pp. 49–50.

50 Catherine Kovesi, *Pitch Your Tents on Distant Shores*, p. 249.

51 Sally Kennedy, *Faith and Feminism*, p. 36.

52 Catholic Social Service Bureau (later Catholic Family Welfare Bureau) was founded in 1935 with the appointment of professionally trained social

workers Norma Parker and Constance Moffit. A priest from the diocese was nominally in charge. D. J. Gleeson, 'The Origins of Melbourne's Social Services Bureau (Centacare)', *Footprints* (Melbourne), vol. 8, no. 1, June 2002, pp. 25–48.

53 Cave, p. 110.

54 Daniel Mannix, Foreword to *Australia* (Melbourne), vol. 1, no. 1, 7 November 1917, p. 1.

Chapter Ten: THE VATICAN CHESS GAME

1 Hoare to Mannix, 15 October 1931; de Bavay to Mannix, 29 November 1933, Mannix Papers.

2 Santamaria, *Daniel Mannix*, pp. 142–45, *passim*.

3 *Ibid*, p. 143.

4 John B. O'Brien, 'The Australianisation of the Australian Catholic Church: Panico—Culprit or Victim?', in Phillip Bull, Frances Devlin-Glass and Helen Doyle (eds.), *Ireland and Australia 1798–1998*, p. 177.

5 Boland, *James Duhig*, p. 289.

6 Panico, quoted in Santamaria, *Daniel Mannix*, p. 183.

7 The first Australian-born archbishop in the Anglican Church was Dr Marcus Loane, appointed in 1966, *Canberra Times*, 5 August 1966, p. 3.

8 Oliver MacDonagh, 'The Sharing of the Green', Inaugural lecture commemorating the centenary of the consecration of St Patrick's Cathedral, 18 March 1997, typescript, courtesy Dr Kathleen McCarthy.

9 Santamaria, *Daniel Mannix*, p. 183.

10 *Ibid*.

11 Sheehan to Cardinal MacRory, 16 April 1936, MacRory Papers.

12 *Ibid*, 17 March 1936.

13 Sheehan to Mannix, 14 June 1937, quoting his own letter to Fumasoni-Biondi, Mannix Papers.

14 Sheehan to Mannix, 14 June 1937, Mannix Papers.

15 *Ibid*, 18 June 1937.

16 Mannix to MacRory, 27 June 1937; a postscript states: 'I am writing to Dr Gilmartin also', MacRory Papers.

17 Sheehan to MacRory, 17 March 1936 and 12 May 1936; Sheehan asked for the diocese of Kildare, adding that he had once thought that only the sees of Dublin or Cashel, to which he was linked by birth and education, would be suitable, MacRory Papers.

18 Sheehan to Mannix, 12 August 1937, Mannix Papers.
19 *Ibid*.
20 Sheehan to Killian, 5 February 1938, Killian Papers.
21 John Luttrell, 'Bishop Gilroy and the Diocese of Port Augusta', *Australasian Catholic Record* (Sydney), vol. 80, no. 2, April 2003, p. 192.
22 *Ibid*, p. 196.
23 T. P. Boland, 'Gilroy, Sir Norman Thomas (1896–1977)', *ADB*, vol. 14, 1996, pp. 275–78.
24 Norman Gilroy, Roman Student Diary, 27 March 1921, quoted in John Anthony de Luca, 'A Vision Found and Lost: The Promotion and Evolving Interpretation of the Movement for Liturgical Musical Reform within the Sydney Catholic Church during the Twentieth Century', PhD thesis, School of Music and Music Education, University of New South Wales, 2001, p. 149, copy courtesy Edmund Campion.
25 Edmund Campion, pers. comm., October 2011.
26 Sheehan to Mannix, 12 August 1937, Mannix Papers.
27 Chris McConville, 'Lonergan, John Joseph (1999–1938)', *ADB*, vol. 10, 1986, pp. 132–33.
28 Mannix to Killian, 27 January 1938, Killian Papers.
29 *Ibid*.
30 *Ibid*, 24 October 1937.
31 Katherine Massam, 'Prendiville, Redmond (1900–1968)', *ADB*, vol. 16, 2002, pp. 26–27.
32 Leo M. Clarke, 'Archbishops Simonds and Knox: Some Personal Reminiscences', *Footprints*, vol. 21, no. 2, December 2004, p. 46.
33 Panico to Mannix, 3 November 1942, Mannix Papers.
34 Mannix to Panico, 8 November 1942, Mannix Papers.
35 Major-General [illegible] to Mannix, 20 November 1942, Mannix Papers.
36 Bishop Fox, 27 November 1977, Ebsworth Papers.
37 Santamaria, *Daniel Mannix*, p. 148.

Chapter Eleven: THE CARDINAL'S RED HAT

1 Antony Cappello, 'Italian Australians, the Church, War and Fascism in Melbourne, 1919–1945', MA Thesis, Victoria University, 2006, pp. 55–56.
2 Oswald and Christopher Von Wolkenstein. The latter was still in friendly correspondence with Mannix in 1954. Mannix Papers.
3 Cappello, pp. 54–56.

4 *Ibid*, pp. 55–56.

5 Fr Tim McCarthy to Brigadier Simpson, Director of Security, 7 May 1943, Mannix Papers.

6 Gilchrist, *Daniel Mannix*, p. 204.

7 Arthur Calwell to the Vicar-General, Society of Jesus, Rome, 2 September 1946, NAI.

8 Arthur Calwell to the Secretary of State, Vatican City, 23 October 1946, NAI.

9 *Ibid*.

10 *Ibid*.

11 Thomas Kiernan to F. H. Boland, Secretary, Department of External Affairs, Dublin, 5 December 1946, NAI.

12 *Ibid*.

13 Three years later Calwell was still optimistic about his own prospects. He told Irish Ambassador Thomas Kiernan that if the ALP won the 1949 election he expected Chifley to retire halfway through the next term of Parliament, and that he himself was most likely to succeed: 'The only other candidate is Dr Evatt who has, [Calwell] said, lost support on account of his pusillanimous attitudes towards the Soviet, the official Labour attitude here having hardened against the Soviet…', Kiernan to Boland, 1 July 1949, NAI DFA, p. 125. The ALP lost the election and Evatt became leader of the Opposition.

14 *Ibid*.

15 J. P. Walshe, Irish Ambassador to the Vatican, to F. H. Boland, 9 August 1947, NAI DFA, p. 125.

16 Niall Brennan, *Dr Mannix*, p. 316.

17 'Why Melbourne Did Not Get a Cardinal', by 'Scrutator' [James Duhig], unpublished typescript, accompanied by a letter from Duhig to Jeremiah Murphy SJ, 27 December 1945, Jeremiah Murphy Papers.

18 Walshe to Boland, 16 July 1947.

19 'Old Irish: Dr Mannix's Excursions into Politics', *Nation* (Sydney), 6 December 1958, p. 6.

20 *Advocate* (Melbourne), 30 May 1946.

21 'The view held here is that [Panico] would not have been sent back [to Australia] but for Calwell's campaign'. Walshe to Boland, 9 August 1947, NAI DFA, p. 125.

22 Santamaria, *Daniel Mannix*, p. 189.

23 Walshe saw the Panico affair as crucial in the Vatican's denying Mannix the honour of being made a cardinal: 'If they don't make Dr Mannix a Cardinal this time [1949] we may assume that they will have been moved solely by the desire to maintain the prestige of the Italian element, in the person of the egregious Mgr Panico', Walshe to Boland, 8 August 1959, NAI DFA.
24 Dermot Keogh, *Ireland and the Vatican*, p. 212.
25 Gilchrist, *Daniel Mannix*, p. 191.

Chapter Twelve: ENTER SANTAMARIA

1 William Hackett SJ to Florence Hackett, 14 January 1951, Hackett Papers.
2 A women's group, the Margaret Clitherow Society, was of minor importance.
3 McInerney, 'Memoirs', vol. 1 [Chapter 5], 'The Campion Society and the Catholic Action Secretariat', p. 22.
4 Santamaria, *Against the Tide*, pp.18–19.
5 Duncan, *Crusade or Conspiracy*, p. 19.
6 McInerney, 'Memoirs', vol. 1 [Chapter 5], 'The Campion Society and the Catholic Action Secretariat', pp. 20–21.
7 McKenna, p. 105.
8 *Ibid*, p. 106.
9 James Murtagh, quoted in Duncan, p. 14.
10 McInerney, 'Memoirs', vol. 1 [Chapter 5], 'The Campion Society and the Catholic Action Secretariat', p. 13.
11 B. A. Santamaria to William Keane SJ, 6 January 1938, in Patrick Morgan (ed.), *B. A. Santamaria: Your Most Obedient Servant*, p. 4.
12 Santamaria, interview with Robin Hughes, 23 April 1997, http://www.australianbiography.gov.au/subjects/santamaria/intertext1html
13 Santamaria, *Against the Tide*, p. 4.
14 Santamaria, 'Early Years', in Patrick Morgan (ed.), *B. A. Santamaria: Running the Show*, pp. 5–6.
15 Duncan, p. 16.
16 Joseph Santamaria, *The Education of Doctor Joe*, pp. 18–19.
17 McClelland, p. 22.
18 Peter Ryan, 'Long Shadow Cast by Lay Prince', review of Morgan (ed.), *B. A. Santamaria: Your Most Obedient Servant*, *Australian*, 21–22 January, 2007.
19 Santamaria, 'Reflections after a Visit to Salina and the Lipari Islands off Sicily', c. 1992, in Morgan (ed.), *B. A. Santamaria: Running the Show*, p. 14.

20 *Ibid*.
21 Eamon de Valera, 'That Ireland which We Dreamed of', in Richard Aldous (ed.), *Great Irish Speeches*, p. 91.
22 Vincent Buckley, *Cutting Green Hay*, p. 132.
23 *Ibid*, p. 127.
24 Back in Melbourne after making this comment, Santamaria, anxious and upset, asked me to look in the Sydney press in case it had been reported. He was relieved that I couldn't find it. Recently I found a cutting in the Mannix Scrapbook assembled by Fr John Senan Moynihan, and held in the Perth Diocesan Archives. It had been reported in the *St Joseph's Messenger* (Orange, NSW) August 1960, p. 203.
25 Duncan, p. 389.
26 Michael Chamberlin, interview with James Murtagh, 6 June 1970, Mannix Papers.
27 Duncan, p. 23.
28 Mollie Maher to Frank Maher, 17 [? 1946], during his absence in London.
29 Cristina (Santamaria) Shannon, interview with the author, 2014.
30 Mary Helen (Santamaria) Woods, interview with the author, 2014.
31 Santamaria, *Against the Tide*, p. 41.
32 Frank Maher, pers. comm., c. 1955.
33 Mannix to E. J. Ward, Minister for Labour and National Service, 4 June 1942, Mannix Papers. Men under thirty-six became eligible for service in 1942. 'These three gentlemen are the sole lay persons in Australia thus employed full time for the religious work of the church.'
34 Duncan, p. 45.

Chapter Thirteen: DIVISIONS

1 *Advocate*, 12 September 1945.
2 'Persecution of German Jews', *Hebrew Standard of Australasia* (Sydney), 5 May 1933. Mannix endorsed a petition on behalf of Jewish refugees from the Zionist National Federation of Australia and New Zealand. *Hebrew Standard of Australasia*, 1 July 1943.
3 *Western Mail* (Perth), 28 December 1939. See also Leon Gettler, *An Unpromised Land*, pp. 76–77.
4 *Argus* (Melbourne), 27 March 1939, p. 8.
5 'The Jews, Says Dr Mannix', *Argus* (Melbourne), 17 February 1947. The *Western Star and Roma Advertiser* (Toowoomba) reported the same speech

on 28 February 1947, and it prompted an editorial in the Sydney *Catholic Weekly*, also on 28 February 1947.

6 *Advocate*, 31 January 1945.

7 Bernie Taft, *Crossing the Party Line*, p. 63.

8 Patrick Morgan, *Melbourne before Mannix*, pp. 212–214, discusses the pre-WWI Australian Catholic Federation and the Catholic Workers' Association of 1915 as possible forerunners to the Movement and well known to Mannix, who may have had 'a more crucial input into the Movement's inception and tactics than has been previously realised'.

9 *Tribune* (Melbourne), 23 November 1916, p. 4.

10 John Douglas Pringle, *Australian Accent*, p. 75; see Robin Gollan, *Revolutionaries and Reformists*, p. 130, for the extent of communist control or influence in unions by 1945.

11 Kevin Peoples, *Santamaria's Salesman* gives an insider's account of Rural Movement history.

12 Santamaria to Mannix, 11 December 1962, in Patrick Morgan (ed.), *B. A. Santamaria, Your Most Obedient Servant*, p. 75.

13 Letters between Mollie Maher and Frank Maher, courtesy Margaret Maher, eldest daughter of Frank and Mollie Maher.

14 Letters from Mollie Maher to Frank Maher in 1946 confirm my own memories of the time when both my parents, close friends of the Mahers, were involved in Mollie Maher's predicament and later in Frank's unwillingness to go back to the ANSCA office. See also Santamaria to William Hackett, 11 February 1952, Santamaria Papers, which indicates Santamaria took active steps on behalf of Maher when the latter's university appointment was temporarily suspended.

15 'The Movement' was more formally known as the Catholic Social Studies Movement or CSSM.

16 James Muirhead SJ, interview with Paul Duffy SJ, 24 June 1998, Duffy Papers.

17 Reader in Law, University of Melbourne, and co-author of several major texts, Maher was awarded an honorary LLD. Invited to stay on after retirement he was a mentor to law students until his eightieth year.

18 Paul Duffy SJ, 'The Institute of Social Order: a History', p. 4, typescript, Duffy Papers.

19 *Ibid*, p.1

20 James Muirhead SJ, interview with Paul Duffy SJ, Duffy Papers.

21 Matthew Beovich, Diary, 17 November 1953, Beovich Papers.

22 Mary Elizabeth Calwell, pp. 58–66.

23 *Washington Post*, 10 February 1949.

24 *Herald* (Melbourne), 31 January 1949.

25 *Advocate* (Melbourne), 17 February 1949.

26 *Argus* (Melbourne), 12 February 1949, p. 7.

27 *Daily News* (Perth), 28 January, 1949, p. 1.

28 *Washington Post*, 10 February 1949.

29 *Argus* (Melbourne), 24 January 1938, p. 4; Mannix added that Aborigines 'should be encouraged to live according to their own culture'. He kept himself informed by his close association with the German missionary order, the Pallotine Fathers, for whom he established a house of studies opposite Raheen. The Pallotines had a good record of respect for Aboriginal culture. They were committed to learning the languages spoken within the Kimberley area, and one of their members, Ernest Worms, had outstanding success in that enterprise.

30 *Advocate* (Melbourne), 17 February 1949, p. 4.

31 *Sydney Morning Herald*, 23 November 1949, p. 4.

32 Kiernan, *Calwell*, p. 163.

33 M. Chester, of Bentleigh Vic., to PM Chifley, 15 February 1949, Personal Papers of PM Chifley, Corres, M14555/365, Australian Archives: 'Chifley backed him up, even as the issue reverberated around the newly independent nations of Asia, provoking a strong backlash against Australia.' Quoted in David Day, *Chifley*, p. 494.

34 When I stayed with the McTiernans in Sydney, just after the Split, Lady McTiernan asked me not to mention Bob Santamaria, 'because it upsets Edward'. It was clear to me that Sir Edward had known about the Movement for years.

35 Evatt to Mannix, 13 July 1949, Mannix Papers.

36 Evatt to Mannix, 15 August [1950], Mannix Papers.

37 Evatt to Duhig, 3 November [1949], reassures Duhig that the ALP is not a socialist party, and is 'bitterly attacked as much by the Communists as by reactionary Tories on the extreme right', Mannix Papers.

38 Gilchrist, *Daniel Mannix*, p. 208.

39 Thecla Broderick Xipell, pers. comm., 2011, recalling her father's account.

40 Robert Murray, *The Split*, p. 52, refers to 'a certain bishop'.

41 Pauline Armstrong, *Frank Hardy and the Making of* Power without Glory, p. 32.
42 *Ibid*, p. 79.
43 William Hackett to Florence Hackett, n.d. [1953], Hackett Papers.
44 Hardy, *Power without Glory*, p. 359.
45 *Ibid*, pp. 626–28.
46 Griffin, *John Wren*, p. 360, names the sum of £5000.
47 Santamaria to Duhig, 20 August 1946, Santamaria Papers.
48 Mannix to de Valera, telegram, 31 December 1947. In a handwritten letter of 9 January 1948, Mannix explained the predicament of Margaret Andreas, 'daughter of a friend of mine, Mr John Wren', De Valera Papers.
49 William Hackett to Florence Hackett, 19 November 1953, Hackett Papers.
50 *Argus* (Melbourne), 29 October 1953, p. 6, and 28 October 1953, p. 3.
51 Val Noone, 'Santamaria Years: A YCW View', *Táin* (Melbourne), no. 31, June–July 2004, pp. 18–19.
52 M. Gilchrist, 'A Portrait of Archbishop Mannix: Religious Leader in a Pluralist Society', p. 120, Mannix Papers.
53 McInerney, 'Memoirs', vol. 1 [Chapter 5], 'The Campion Society and the Catholic Action Secretariat', p. 27; Service Record for C. G. Heffey, Series B883 VX139338, Australian Archives.
54 McInerney, 'Memoirs', vol. 2 [Chapter 5], 'Senior Junior Days', p. 48.
55 Noone, 'Santamaria Years: A YCW View', p. 19.
56 Mangan denounced Mannix in 1941 for allegedly flouting the will of Benjamin Backhaus, who left money for the care of 'sick and infirm priests', by diverting it to fund Corpus Christi College (Gilchrist, *Daniel Mannix*, pp. 172–74). It has been suggested that Mannix's failure to give the funeral panegyric for Mangan in October 1960 indicated lingering ill will (Griffin, *Daniel Mannix*, p. 244), but as Mannix, by then ninety-six, made very few public appearances, his frailty seems sufficient reason.
57 Gilchrist, 'A Portrait of Archbishop Mannix', pp. 115–16.

Chapter Fourteen: THE LAST HURRAH

1 Christopher Hollis, *Universe* (London), 17 May 1963.
2 William Hackett to Florence Hackett, 28 February 1949, Hackett Papers.
3 *Ibid*.
4 Hollis, *op. cit*.

5 Leo M. Clarke, 'Archbishop Mannix: What Was He Like?', *Footprints* (Melbourne), June 2003, p. 45.
6 Cristina (Santamaria) Shannon, pers. comm., 2014.
7 Telegrams, 4 March 1954, Mannix Papers.
8 William Hackett to Florence Hackett, 19 April 1954. Hackett Papers
9 William Hackett to Florence Hackett, 28 February 1954, Hackett Papers.
10 Minutes of Meeting 29 April 1949, Jesuit Provincial Consults, 1947–1979, Jesuit Archives.
11 My father, Frank Niall, a cardiologist, had been attending Simonds from the late 1940s, as had ophthalmologist Hugh Ryan. By 1962 Simonds was nearly blind and unable to read the Vatican Council's preparatory documents. Max Vodola, *Simonds*, p. 85.
12 McClelland, p. 104–05.
13 *Ibid*, p. 103.
14 Duncan, *Crusade or Conspiracy*, pp. 213–17.
15 Santamaria, *Against the Tide*, p. 142.
16 Evatt to Mannix, 14 May 1954, Mannix Papers.
17 Robert Jackson to William Hackett, 12 March 1954, Hackett Papers.
18 Robert Murray, *The Split*, p. 148.
19 Morgan (ed.), *B. A. Santamaria: Running the Show*, pp. 185–86; *Argus* (Melbourne), 22 June 1953.
20 'Father Hackett R.I.P.', *Catholic Worker*, August 1954, p. 2.
21 Jeremiah Murphy Papers.
22 Minutes of a meeting at Belloc House, 14 January 1943, in Morgan (ed.), *B. A. Santamaria: Running the Show*, pp. 196–97, 206.
23 Ebsworth, p. 394.
24 Duncan, p. 251.
25 Pascoe, *The Feasts & Seasons of John F. Kelly*, p. 207, cites comment by parishioner Ann Woodruff that Santamaria's presence at mass was 'an irritation'.
26 Marilyn (Heffey) Puglisi, pers. comm., 2013.
27 Cristina Shannon, the eldest daughter, remembers being made uncomfortably aware of the nuns' generosity.
28 Joseph Santamaria and Bernadette (Santamaria) Tobin have recalled separate incidents of this kind.
29 Buckley, *Cutting Green Hay*, p. 126.
30 *Ibid*, p. 124.

31 Gerard Heffey to 'Moll' (his sister, Sr Mary Winifred Heffey), Holy Thursday [7 April 1955], quoted in Duncan, p. 252.
32 McInerney, 'Memoirs', vol. 1 [Chapter 5], 'The Campion Society and the Catholic Action Secretariat', p. 52.
33 *Age* (Melbourne), 5 September 1960.
34 O'Farrell, *Vanished Kingdoms*, p. 278.
35 Gerard Henderson, *Mr Santamaria and the Bishops*, p. 12.
36 Griffin, 'Daniel Mannix (1864–1963)', *ADB*, p. 400.
37 'Old Irish: Dr Mannix's Excursions into Politics', *Nation* (Sydney), 6 December 1958, p. 6.
38 Egan, pp. 122–23, and John Brenan, interview with the author, 2014.
39 Tom Hazell, pers. comm., 2011.
40 B. A. Santamaria, 'The Death of Archbishop Mannix', *Sunday Magazine* telecast, Channel 9, 10 November 1963.
41 Archbishop Frank Little, interview with the author, 2007.
42 John Challis, pers. comm., 2011.
43 Paul Duffy SJ, pers. comm., 2010.
44 Quoted in McKenna, pp. 389–90.
45 Clarke, 'Archbishop Mannix; What Was He Like?', p. 33.
46 Gilchrist, *Daniel Mannix*, p. 257.

Chapter Fifteen: THE FINAL ACT

1 Brendan Byrne SJ, pers. comm., August 2013.
2 Santamaria, *Daniel Mannix*, p. 1; Ebsworth, p. 422.
3 John W. O'Malley, *What Happened at Vatican II*, pp. 93–94.
4 *Ibid*, p. 136.
5 *Ibid*, p. 134.
6 *Ibid*, pp. 134–35.
7 For the full text of Mannix's response, see Jeffrey J. Murphy, 'The Lost (and Last) Animadversions of Daniel Mannix', *Australasian Catholic Record*, January 1999, pp. 54–73.
8 Henry Johnston SJ, interview with James Murtagh, 30 December 1969, Murtagh Papers.
9 Murphy, p. 73.
10 Edmund Campion, 'I Believe in Councils', *Madonna* (Melbourne), July–August 2012, p. 35.
11 O'Malley, p. 218.

12 *Ibid*, p. 116.
13 Mannix to Gilroy, 15 June 1943, Mannix Papers.
14 Mannix to Julius, Cardinal Dopfner, draft copy. n.d., Mannix Papers.
15 Karen Armstrong, *Through the Narrow Gate*, p. 161.
16 Bill Uren SJ so described the Latin, pers. comm., 2013.
17 Handwriting verified by Bishop Michael McKenna, formerly secretary to Bishop D'Arcy.
18 P. J. Stephenson SJ, interview with Michael Parer, c. 1969, Parer Papers.
19 Murphy, pp. 70–73.
20 B. A. Santamaria, interview with Michael Parer, for a two-part ABC program, broadcast in April 1969. Original of the tape in Dr Parer's possession.
21 Graham Freudenberg, 'Calwell, Arthur Augustus (1896–1973)', *ADB*, vol 13, 1993, pp. 341–45.
22 Fr Eric D'Arcy, pers. comm., c. 1956.
23 Santamaria, interview with Michael Parer, 1969.
24 Santamaria, *Daniel Mannix*, p. 246.
25 *Canberra Times*, 11 March 1963, p. 19.
26 Paul Duffy SJ, pers. comm., 2010.
27 Bishop Fox, interview with B. A. Santamaria, n.d., Santamaria Papers.
28 Morgan (ed.), *B. A. Santamaria: Your Most Obedient Servant*, pp. 522–27.
29 http//www.vatican.va/roman.curia.congregations/ccdds/documents/rc.con.ccdds.doc.200006.d-vescovi-australiani%20.It.html
30 Gilchrist, *Daniel Mannix*, p. 182; Gilchrist, 'A Portrait of Archbishop Mannix', pp. 102–04.
31 Antonio Spadaro SJ, 'A Big Heart Open to God: A Conversation with Pope Francis', *America* (New York), 30 September 2013, pp. 15–38 (26).
32 With permission from the present archbishop of Melbourne, Dr Hart, I trawled through the minutes of the archdiocesan consultors' meetings from 1938 up to Mannix's death and through the first Simonds years. These meetings of six or seven senior priests, chaired by the archbishop, were held twice a year, usually at Raheen, to deal with appointments, promotions and transfers of Melbourne diocesan priests. Decisions are minuted but these haphazard handwritten pages (some in pencil) don't record discussion. It is impossible to know why (for example) Dean O'Sullivan was asked to 'take on trial' a priest whose shortcomings are not stated (Meeting, 9 August 1938). Anything from rudeness and insubordination to drunkenness and sexual

offences might have led to the transfer. I found only one case of alleged serious criminal misconduct. At the meeting of 7 May 1951, Archbishop Mannix summarily de-frocked Father Denis Roche, who had been an assistant priest at Mansfield for a little over a year. As far as can be made out from newspaper reports, Roche, an Irishman working in the Rockhampton diocese until 1949 under Mannix's friend Bishop Sheil, had been charged with attempted rape of a nursing sister, but the case was dismissed for lack of evidence. Roche had been drinking brandy and had bought two bottles of beer at a Yeppoon hotel where the alleged crime took place. *Morning Bulletin* (Rockhampton), 24 May 1947, p. 6; *Courier-Mail* (Brisbane), 31 May 1947, p. 3; *Northern Miner* (Charters Towers), 4 June 1947, p. 3. Roche had then been given leave for two years, during which it seems likely that there was an attempt to rehabilitate him. His transfer to Mannix's archdiocese in 1951 probably ended in his lapsing in some way after only a few months. *Australasian Catholic Directory* 1940–1951 lists Roche's postings.

33 W. J. [Joe] Broderick, pers. comm., 20 March 2010.

34 *Ibid*, 23 March 2010.

35 *Ibid*.

36 Michael Parer, *Dreamer by Day*, pp. 26–27.

37 Bishop Hilton Deakin, interview with the author, 2013.

38 Sally Morrison, *After Fire*, p. 220.

Chapter Sixteen: DEATH COMES FOR THE ARCHBISHOP

1 Santamaria, interview with Michael Parer, 1969.

2 Santamaria, *Daniel Mannix*, p. 256.

3 Father Paul Ryan, brother of Dr Hugh Ryan, pers. comm., 2010.

4 Biographer Ebsworth gave the diagnosis as cerebral haemorrhage, p. 425. Bishop Fox, reporting to de Valera, gave it as strangulated hernia, as did Santamaria, *Daniel Mannix*, p. 255, who said that Mannix had refused surgery some years before.

5 Des Tobin, interview 2011. Des Tobin, son of Phonse Tobin of Tobin Brothers, Funeral Directors, was at Raheen at the time of the embalming.

6 Memorandum, 5 June 1958, Mannix Papers.

7 *Advocate* (Melbourne), 14 November 1963.

8 Michael Head and Gerard Healy, *More than a School*, pp. 141–42.

9 The Murtagh Papers were passed on to Father Walter Ebsworth, chosen by

Cardinal Knox to carry on his work, which with minimal acknowledgment to Murtagh's immense labours, appeared in 1977 as *Archbishop Mannix*.

Afterword

1 *Age* (Melbourne), 6 March 2014.

Select Bibliography

PRIMARY SOURCES

Archives and Libraries

ASJASL (Jesuit Archives, Hawthorn, Victoria)

- Consultors' Minutes.
- Corpus Christi College Papers.
- George O'Neill Papers.
- Henry Johnston Papers.
- Jeremiah Murphy Papers.
- John Ryan Papers.
- Newman College Papers.
- Paul Duffy Papers.
- Provincials' Correspondence.
- William Hackett Papers.

Australian Archives

- Series A8911, Nos. 236, 240; Series B741, No. V/159.

Catholic Diocesan Archives, Adelaide
Beovich Papers.
Catholic Diocesan Archives, Brisbane
Duhig Papers.
Catholic Diocesan Archives, Perth
Clune Papers.
Senan Moynihan Papers.
Catholic Diocesan Archives, Sydney
Kelly Papers.
Christian Brothers Archive, Melbourne
Greening Papers.
Georgetown University
Shane Leslie Papers.
Irish College, Rome
Hagan Papers.
Jesuit Archives, Dublin
Carroll Papers.
Mannix College, Monash University
Mannix Collection.
Melbourne Diocesan Historical Commission
Mannix Papers.
Mannix (Murtagh) Papers.
Mannix (Santamaria) Papers.
Catholic Action Papers.
Diocesan Consultors' Minutes, 1938–69.
Episcopal Committee on Catholic Action, Minutes, 1938–54.
Mitchell Library, Sydney
Esmonde Higgins Papers.
National Archives of Ireland (NAI)
Department of Foreign Affairs Papers.
National Library of Australia, Canberra
Enid Lyons Papers.
Herbert Brookes Papers.
W. M. Hughes Papers.
Hugh Mahon Papers.
James Scullin Papers.
Joseph Lyons Papers.

Paul McGuire Papers.
Robert Menzies Papers.
National Library of Ireland, Dublin
Edward Lysaght Papers.
Newman College Archives
Donovan Papers.
St Patrick's College
Maynooth Records.
State Library of Victoria
Santamaria Papers.
Trinity College Library, Dublin
Childers Papers.
University College, Cork Records.
University College, Dublin
De Valera Papers.
Private Collections
Tom Hazell Papers.
Gerard Heffey Papers.
Maher Family Papers.
Murray McInerney Papers.
Michael Parer Papers.
Maurice Ryan Papers.

SECONDARY SOURCES

BOOKS

Akenson, Donald Harman, *Half the World from Home: Perspectives on the Irish in New Zealand, 1860–1950*, Oxford University Press, Wellington, 1990.

Aldous, Richard (ed.), with a foreword by Colm Toíbín, *Great Irish Speeches*, Quercus, London, 2007.

Armstrong, Karen, *Through the Narrow Gate: A Nun's Story*, Pan Books in association with Macmillan, London, 1982.

Armstrong, Pauline, *Frank Hardy and the Making of* Power without Glory, Melbourne University Press, Melbourne, 2000.

Ayres, Philip, *Prince of the Church: Patrick Francis Moran, 1830–1911*, The Miegunyah Press, Melbourne, 2007.

Beaumont, Joan, *Broken Nation: Australians in the Great War*, Allen & Unwin, Sydney, 2013.

Bence-Jones, Mark, *Burke's Guide to Irish Country Houses*, vol. 1, Ireland, Burke's Peerage, London, 1978.

Bew, Paul, *Ireland: The Politics of Enmity*, Oxford University Press, Oxford, 2007.

Boland, T. P., *James Duhig*, University of Queensland Press, Brisbane, 1986.

Boland, T. P., *St Patrick's Cathedral: A Life*, Polding Press, East Melbourne, 1997.

Boland, T. P., *Thomas Carr: Archbishop of Melbourne*, University of Queensland Press, Brisbane, 1997.

Bongiorno, Frank, *The Sex Lives of Australians*, Black Inc., Melbourne, 2012.

Booker, Malcolm, *The Great Professional: A Study of W. M. Hughes*, McGraw Hill, New York, 1980.

Bourke, D. F., *A History of the Catholic Church in Victoria*, Catholic Bishops of Australia, Melbourne, 1967.

Bradley, Anthony and M. G. Valiulis (eds.), *Gender and Sexuality in Modern Ireland*, University of Massachusetts, Amherst, 1997.

Brady, E. J., *Doctor Mannix: Archbishop of Melbourne*, Library of National Biography, Melbourne, 1934.

Brennan, Frank, *Acting on Conscience: How Can We Responsibly Mix Law, Religion and Politics?*, University of Queensland Press, Brisbane, 2007.

Brennan, Niall, *Dr Mannix*, Rigby, Adelaide, 1964.

Bryan, Cyril, *Archbishop Mannix: Champion of Democracy*, Advocate Press, Melbourne, 1918.

Buckley, Ken, Barbara Dale &Wayne Reynolds, *Doc Evatt: Patriot, Internationalist, Fighter and Scholar*, Longman Cheshire, Melbourne, 1994.

Buckley, Vincent, *Cutting Green Hay: Friendships, Movements and Cultural Conflicts in Australia's Great Decades*, Penguin Books, Melbourne, 1983.

Buggy, Hugh, *The Real John Wren*, Widescope, Melbourne, 1977.

Bygott, Ursula M. L., *With Pen and Tongue: the Jesuits in Australia, 1865–1939*, Melbourne University Press, Melbourne, 1980.

Caine, Frank, *The Origins of Political Surveillance in Australia*, Angus & Robertson, Sydney, 1983.

Calwell, A. A., *Be Just and Fear Not*, Lloyd O'Neil in association with Rigby, Melbourne, 1972.

Calwell, Mary Elizabeth, *I Am Bound to Be True: The Life and Legacy of Arthur A. Calwell, 1896–1973*, Mosaic Press, Melbourne, 2012.

Campion, Edmund, *A Place in the City*, Penguin Books, Melbourne, 1994.

Campion, Edmund, *Rockchoppers: Growing Up Catholic in Australia*, Penguin Books, Melbourne, 1982.

Caterson, Simon, *The Fox and the Hedgehog: John Monash and Daniel Mannix, Parallel Lives*, Mannix College, Melbourne, 2008.

Cave, Donald, *Percy Jones: Priest, Musician, Teacher*, Melbourne University Press, Melbourne, 1988.

Clark, C. M. H., *A History of Australia*, Melbourne University Press, Melbourne, 1987.

Clark, Mary Ryllis, *Loreto in Australia*, University of NSW Press, Sydney, 2009.

Coldrey, Barry M., *Faith and Fatherland: The Contribution of the Christian Brothers to the Development of Irish Nationalism, 1838–1921*, Gill and Macmillan, London, 1988.

Collins, M. E., *Ireland, 1868–1966*, Educational Company of Ireland, Dublin, 1993.

Coogan, Tim Pat, *De Valera: Long Fellow, Long Shadow*, Hutchinson, London, 1993.

Coogan, Tim Pat, *Michael Collins: A Biography*, Macmillan, London, 1990.

Coogan, Tim Pat and George Morrison, *The Irish Civil War*, Weidenfeld & Nicolson, London, 1999.

Corish, Patrick J., *Maynooth College 1795–1995*, Gill & Macmillan, Dublin, 1995.

Costar, Brian, Peter Love & Paul Strangio, *The Great Labor Schism: A Retrospective*, Scribe Publications, Melbourne, 2005.

Day, David, *Chifley*, Harper Collins, Sydney, 2001.

Day, David, *Andrew Fisher: Prime Minister of Australia*, Harper Collins, Sydney, 2009.

Dening, Greg, *Xavier: A Centenary Portrait*, Old Xaverians' Association, Melbourne, 1978.

Duncan, Bruce, *Crusade or Conspiracy? Catholics and the Anti-Communist Struggle in Australia*, University of NSW Press, Sydney, 2001.

Dwyer, T. Ryle, *Big Fellow, Long Fellow: A Joint Biography of Collins and de Valera*, Gill & Macmillan, Dublin, 2006 (first published 1998).

Ebsworth, Walter A., *Archbishop Mannix*, H. H. Stephenson, Melbourne, 1977.

Egan, Bryan, *Ways of a Hospital: St Vincent's Melbourne, 1890s–1990s*, Allen & Unwin, Sydney, 1993.

Elkner, Cate *et al*, *Enemy Aliens: The Internment of Italian Migrants in Australia during the Second World War*, Connor Court, Bacchus Marsh, Vic., 2005.

Ervine, St John, *Parnell*, Ernest Benn, London, 1925.

Fitzhardinge, L. F., *William Morris Hughes: A Political Biography*, Angus & Robertson, Sydney, 1964, 1979, 2 vols.

Fogarty, Ronald, *Catholic Education in Australia, 1806–1950*, Melbourne University Press, Melbourne, 1959, 2 vols.

Gettler, Leon, *An Unpromised Land*, Fremantle Arts Centre Press, Fremantle, 1993.

Gilchrist, Michael, *Daniel Mannix: Wit and Wisdom*, 2nd ed., Freedom Publishing, Melbourne, 2004.

Gollan, Robin, *Revolutionaries and Reformists: Communism and the Australian Labour Movement, 1920–1955*, Allen & Unwin, Sydney, 1985.

Griffin, James, *John Wren: A Life Reconsidered*, Scribe Publications, Melbourne, 2004.

Griffin, James, completed by Paul Ormonde, *Daniel Mannix: Beyond the Myths*, Garran Publishing, Melbourne, 2012.

Hackett, Francis, *The Green Lion: A Novel of Youth*, Doubleday, Doran, New York, 1936.

Hardy, Frank, *Power without Glory*, Random House, Sydney, 2000 (first published 1950).

Hart, Peter, *Mick: The Real Michael Collins*, Pan Books, London, 2006 (first published by Macmillan, London, 2005).

Head, Michael and Gerard Healy, *More than a School: A History of St Patrick's College 1854–1968*, Eldon Hogan Trust and Jesuit Publications, Melbourne, 1999.

Healy, John, *Maynooth College: Its Centenary History*, Browne & Nolan, Dublin, 1895.

Henderson, Gerard, *Mr Santamaria and the Bishops* (Studies in the Christian Movement), St Patrick's College, Sydney, 1982.

Horne, Donald, *In Search of Billy Hughes*, Macmillan, Melbourne, 1979.

Hughes, Aneurin, *Billy Hughes: Prime Minister and Controversial Founding Father of the Australian Labor Party*, Wiley, Brisbane, 2005.

Hunter-Payne, Gwynedd, *Cabrini: A Hospital's Journey, 1948–1998*, Helicon Press, Sydney, 1998.

Jory, Colin H, *The Campion Society and Catholic Social Militancy in Australia, 1929–1939*, Harpham, Sydney, 1986.

Kane, Kathleen Dunlop, *The History of the Grey Sisters*, Grey Sisters, Melbourne, 1980.

Kennedy, Sally, *Faith and Feminism: Catholic Women's Struggles for Self-expression* (Studies in the Christian Movement, no. 9), St Patrick's College, Sydney, 1985.

Keogh, Dermot, *Ireland and the Vatican: The Politics and Diplomacy of Church–State Relations, 1922–1960*, Cork University Press, Cork, 1995.

Keogh, Dermot, *The Vatican, the Bishops and Irish Politics, 1919–1939*, Cambridge University Press, New York, 1986.

Kiernan, Colm, *Calwell: A Personal and Political Biography*, Thomas Nelson (Australia), Melbourne, 1978.

Kiernan, Colm, *Daniel Mannix and Ireland*, Allela Books, Morwell, Vic., 1984.

Kovesi, Catherine, *Pitch Your Tents on Distant Shores: A History of the Sisters of the Good Shepherd in Australia, Aotearoa, New Zealand and Tahiti*, Playwright Publishing, Sydney, 2006.

Kramer, Leonie, *Broomstick: Personal Reflections*, Australian Scholarly Publishing, Melbourne, 2012.

Laffin, Josephine, *Matthew Beovich: A Biography*, Wakefield Press, Adelaide, 2008.

Leslie, Shane, *Cardinal Gasquet*, Burns Oates, London, 1953.

Leslie, Shane, *Doomsland*, Charles Scribner's Sons, New York, 1924.

Lewis, Brian, *Our War: Australia During World War I*, Melbourne University Press, Melbourne, 1980.

The Life & Times of a Cathedral, 1858–1997: An Exhibition Presenting the Story of St Patrick's Cathedral… catalogue researched and written by John P. Rogan, Catholic Archdiocese of Melbourne, Melbourne, 1997.

Lyons, F. S. L., *The Fall of Parnell, 1890–91*, Routledge & Kegan Paul, London, 1960.

Main, J. M. (ed.), *Conscription: The Australian Debate, 1901–1970*, Cassell Australia, Melbourne, 1970.

Mannix, Daniel, *Speeches of His Grace Most Rev. Dr Mannix, Archbishop of Melbourne in the Rotunda, Dublin, October 22nd and 29th 1925*, Mellifont Press, Dublin, 1925.

Mannix, Patrick J., *The Belligerent Prelate: An Alliance between Archbishop Daniel Mannix and Eamon de Valera*, Cambridge Scholars Publisher, Newcastle upon Tyne, 2013.

Martin, A. W. and Patsy Hardy (eds.), *Dark and Hurrying Days: Menzies' 1941 Diaries*, National Library of Australia, Canberra, 1993.

Martin, A. W., *Robert Menzies: A Life*, vol 1, 1894–1944, Melbourne University Press, Melbourne, 1993.

McCalman, Janet, *Journeyings: The Biography of a Middle-Class Generation, 1920–1990*, Melbourne University Press, Melbourne, 1993.

McCalman, Janet, *Struggletown: Public and Private Life in Richmond, 1900–1965*, Melbourne University Press, Melbourne, 1984.

McClelland, James, *Stirring the Possum: A Political Autobiography*, Viking, Melbourne, 1988.

McConville, Chris, *Croppies, Celts & Catholics: The Irish in Australia*, Edward Arnold Australia, Melbourne, 1982.

McConville, Chris, *St Kevin's College, 1918–1993*, Melbourne University Press, Melbourne, 1993.

McDonald, Walter, *Reminiscences of a Maynooth Professor*, Mercier Press, Cork, 1967.

McGregor, Alasdair, *Grand Obsessions: The Life and Work of Walter Burley Griffin and Marion Mahony Griffin*, Penguin Books Australia, Melbourne, 2009.

McKenna, Mark, *An Eye for Eternity: The Life of Manning Clark*, The Miegunyah Press, Melbourne, 2011.

McKernan, Michael, *Australian Churches at War*, Catholic Theological Faculty and Australian War Memorial, Sydney, 1980.

McKernan, Michael, *The Australian People and the Great War*, new edn., Collins, Sydney, 1984 (first published 1980).

McKernan, Michael, *Victoria at War, 1914–1918*, New South Publishing, Sydney, 1994.

McLaren, Margaret, *Dr Daniel Mannix, Archbishop of Melbourne, 1917–1963: A Guide to the Literature*, the Author, Melbourne, 1983.

McMahon, Timothy G., *Grand Opportunity: The Gaelic Revival and Irish Society, 1893–1910*, Syracuse University Press, Syracuse, N.Y., 2008.

Menzies, Robert, *Afternoon Light: Some Memories of Men and Events*, Cassell, London, 1967.

Miller, David W., *Church, State and Nation in Ireland, 1898–1921*, Gill and Macmillan, Dublin, 1973.

Molony, John N., *The Roman Mould of the Australian Catholic Church*, Melbourne University Press, Melbourne, 1969.

Morgan, Patrick (ed.), *B. A. Santamaria: Running the Show: Selected Documents, 1939–1996*, The Miegunyah Press and the State Library of Victoria, Melbourne, 2008.

Morgan, Patrick (ed.), *B. A. Santamaria: Your Most Obedient Servant: Selected Letters, 1938–1996*, The Miegunyah Press and the State Library of Victoria, Melbourne, 2007.

Morgan, Patrick, *Melbourne before Mannix: Catholics in Public Life, 1880–1920*, Connor Court, Ballan, Vic., 2012.

Morrison, Sally, *After Fire: A Biography of Clifton Pugh*, Hardie Grant Books, Melbourne, 2009.

Morrissey, Thomas J., *Bishop Edward O'Dwyer of Limerick, 1842–1917*, Four Courts Press, Dublin, 2003.

Murphy, Frank, *Daniel Mannix: Archbishop of Melbourne*, Advocate Press, Melbourne, 1948.

Murphy, Frank, *Daniel Mannix: Archbishop of Melbourne, 1917–1963*, Polding Press, Melbourne, 1972.

Murray, Robert, *The Split: Australian Labor in the Fifties*, Hale & Iremonger, Sydney, 1984 (first published by F. W. Cheshire, Melbourne, 1970).

Murtagh, James, *Australia, the Catholic Chapter*, rev. edn., Polding Press, Melbourne, 1969 (first published 1946).

Neeson, Eoin, *The Life and Death of Michael Collins*, Mercier Press, Cork, 1968.

Niall, Brenda, *The Riddle of Father Hackett: A Life in Ireland and Australia*, National Library of Australia, Canberra, 2009.

Noone, Val, *Hidden Ireland in Victoria*, Ballarat Heritage Services, Ballarat, 2012.

Noone, Val and Rachel Naughton, (eds.), *Daniel Mannix: His Legacy*,

Melbourne Diocesan Historical Commission, Catholic Archdiocese of Melbourne, Melbourne, 2014.

O'Brien, Anne, *Blazing a Trail: Catholic Education in Victoria 1963–1980*, David Lovell Publishing, Melbourne, 1999.

O'Brien, Anne, *God's Willing Workers: Women and Religion in Australia*, University of NSW Press, Sydney, 2005.

O'Brien, Conor Cruise, (ed.), *The Shaping of Modern Ireland*, Routledge & Kegan Paul, London, 1960.

O'Donoghue, K. K., *Brother P. A. Treacy and the Christian Brothers in Australia and New Zealand*, University of NSW Press, Sydney, 1986.

O'Faolain, Sean, *The Irish*, Penguin Books, West Drayton, Middlesex, 1947.

O'Farrell, Patrick, *The Catholic Church and Community: An Australian History* (3rd revised edition with afterword), Nelson, Melbourne, 1977.

O'Farrell, Patrick, *The Irish in Australia*, University of NSW Press, Sydney, 1987.

O'Farrell, Patrick, *Vanished Kingdoms: The Irish in Australia and New Zealand—A Personal Excursion*, University of NSW Press, Sydney, 1990.

O'Malley, John W., *What Happened at Vatican II*, Harvard University Press, Cambridge, Mass., 2010.

Ormonde, Paul (ed.), *Santamaria: the Politics of Fear: Critical Reflections by Xavier Connor [et al.]*, Spectrum Publications, Melbourne, 2000.

Parer, Michael, *Dreamer by Day: A Priest Returns to Life*, Angus and Robertson, Sydney, 1971.

Pascoe, Robert, *The Feasts & Seasons of John F. Kelly*, Allen & Unwin [for] Catholic Education Office, Melbourne, 2006.

Pearl, Cyril, *The Dunera Scandal: Deported by Mistake*, Angus & Robertson, London, 1983.

Peoples, Kevin, *Santamaria's Salesman: Working for the National Catholic Rural Movement 1959–1961*, John Garratt Publishing, Melbourne, 2012.

Priestley, Susan, *Melbourne's Mercy: A History of Mercy Private Hospital*, Hyland House, Melbourne, 1990.

Pringle, John Douglas, *Australian Accent*, Chatto and Windus, 1958.

Prior, Tom, *A Knockabout Priest: The Story of Father John Brosnan*, Hargreen Publishing Company, Melbourne, 1985.

Reid, Nicholas, *James Michael Liston: A Life*, Victoria University Press, Wellington, 2006.

Rickard, John, *An Assemblage of Decent Men and Women: A History of the Anglican Parish of St Mary's North Melbourne*, St Mary's Anglican Church, Melbourne, 2008.

Rivett, Rohan, *Australian Citizen: Herbert Brookes 1897–1963*, Melbourne University Press, Melbourne, 1965.

Roche, Anthony, (ed.), *The UCD Aesthetic: Celebrating 150 years of UCD Writers*, New Island, Dublin, 2003.

Ryan, Arthur A. *Daniel Mannix, Archbishop of Melbourne*, Advocate Press, Melbourne, 1949.

Rynne, Xavier, pseud., *Letters from Vatican City: Vatican Council II (First Session), Background and Debates*, Farrar, Strauss, New York, 1963.

Sanders, Robert, *A Practical Guide to the Irish Land Act*, Hodges Figgis, Dublin, 1903.

Santamaria, B. A., *Against the Tide*, Oxford University Press, Melbourne, 1981.

Santamaria, B. A., *Archbishop Mannix: His Contribution to the Art of Public Leadership in Australia*, Melbourne University Press, Melbourne, 1978.

Santamaria, B. A., *Daniel Mannix: The Quality of Leadership*, Melbourne University Press, Melbourne, 1984.

Santamaria, B. A., *The Price of Freedom: The Movement—After Ten Years*, Campion Press, Melbourne, 1964.

Santamaria, Joseph, *The Education of Dr Joe*, Connor Court, Ballan, Vic., 2006.

Sheehan, Mary, *Victories in Camberwell: A History of Catholics in Camberwell*, Pakenham Gazette, Melbourne, [1989].

Statement on the Present Condition of Their Country, issued by the Bishops of Ireland, 26 April 1922, Brown and Nolan, Dublin, 1922.

Strong, David, *The Australian Dictionary of Jesuit Biography, 1848–1998*, Halstead Press, Sydney, 1999.

Sturrock, Morna, *Women of Strength, Women of Gentleness: Brigidine Sisters, Victorian Province*, David Lovell Publishing, Melbourne, 1995.

Taft, Bernie, *Crossing the Party Line*, Scribe, Newham, Vic., 1994.

Townshend, Charles, *Easter 1916: The Irish Rebellion*, Allen Lane, London, 2005.

Townshend, Charles, *The Republic: The Fight for Irish Independence, 1918–1923*, Allen Lane, London, 2013.

Trevor, William, *Excursions in the Real World*, Penguin Books, London, 1994.

Vodola, Max, *Simonds: A Rewarding Life*, Catholic Education Office, Melbourne, 1997.

White, Gerry, and Brendan O'Shea, *The Burning of Cork*, Mercier Press, Cork, 2005.

ARTICLES

'An Australian Roman Catholic', 'The Mad Dog from Maynooth', *National Review* January 1921, pp. 644–59.

Boland, T. P., 'Gilroy, Sir Norman Thomas, 1896–1977', *Australian Dictionary of Biography*, vol. 14, Melbourne University Press, Melbourne, 1996, pp. 275–78.

Brendain, C., 'Impressions and Memories of Monsignor Mannix', *Austral Light*, vol. 8, no. 9, Melbourne, September 1912, pp. 707–19.

Broderick, W. J., 'De Valera and Archbishop Mannix', *History Ireland*, Issue 3, Autumn 1994 (www.historyireland.com).

Campion, Edmund, 'Troublesome Cleric', *Australian Book Review*, Melbourne, May 2004, p. 64 (Review (repr.) of Michael Gilchrist, *Daniel Mannix Wit and Wisdom*, originally subtitled *Priest and Patriot*).

Campion, Edmund, 'I Believe in Councils', *Madonna*, Melbourne, July–August 2012, p. 35.

Cappello, Anthony, 'Mannix, Modotti and the Italian POWs', *Quadrant*, Sydney, vol. 48, no. 7–8, July–August 2004, pp. 38–41.

Charlesworth, Max, 'Australian Catholic Intellectuals: The Catholic Worker and the Movement', in Brian Head and James Walter (eds.), *Intellectual Movements and Australian Society*, Oxford University Press, Melbourne, 1988, pp. 274–88.

Clarke, Leo M., 'Archbishop Mannix: What Was He Like?', *Footprints: Journal of the Melbourne Diocesan Historical Commission*, Melbourne, June 2003, pp. 28–48.

Clarke, Leo M., 'Archbishops Simonds and Knox: Some Personal Reminiscences', *Footprints: Journal of the Melbourne Diocesan Historical Commission*, vol. 21, no. 2, Melbourne, December 2004, pp. 43–55.

Culhane, T. F., 'Rev. William Hackett SJ, (1879–1954)', *Advocate*, Melbourne, 19 August 1954, p. 11.

De Carvalho, David, 'Whitlands 1941–1951: An Australian Experiment in Utopian Catholicism', *Australasian Catholic Record*, vol. 80, no. 2, Sydney, April 2003, pp. 145–163.

Dening, Greg, 'Beside the Seaside', *Eureka Street*, vol. 7, no. 8, Melbourne, 1997, p. 39.

Foster, Roy, 'Eroded by Rain: Lessons from the General Post Office, Sackville Street, Dublin', *TLS*, London, 21 October 2005, pp. 3–4 [review of Charles Townshend, *Easter 1916: The Irish Rebellion*].

Freudenberg, Graham, 'Calwell, Arthur Augustus (1896–1973)', *Australian Dictionary of Biography*, vol. 13, Melbourne University Press, Melbourne, 1993, pp. 341–45.

Funder, John, 'Melbourne Millefeuilles', in Brenda Niall and Ian Britain (eds.) *The Oxford Book of Australian Schooldays*, Oxford University Press, Melbourne, 1997, pp. 288–89.

Gleeson, D. J., 'The Origins of Melbourne's Catholic Social Services Bureau (Centacare)', *Footprints: Journal of the Melbourne Diocesan Historical Commission*, vol. 18, no. 1, Melbourne, June 2002, pp. 25–48.

Griffin, James, 'Daniel Mannix (1864–1963)', *Australian Dictionary of Biography*, vol. 10, Melbourne University Press, Melbourne, 1986, pp. 398–404.

Griffin, James, 'Daniel Mannix and the Cult of Personality', in Oliver MacDonough and W. F. Mandle (eds.), *Ireland and Irish-Australia: Studies in Cultural and Political History*, Croom Helm, London, 1986, pp. 95–118.

Griffin, James, 'Revisionism or Reality: Daniel Mannix in ADB10', in Richard Davis [*et al*], (eds.), *Irish Australian Studies: Papers Delivered at the Eighth Irish–Australian Conference, Hobart, July 1995*, Currency Press, Sydney, 1996, pp. 133–45.

Griffin, James, 'William Philip Hackett (1878–1954)', *Australian Dictionary of Biography*, vol. 9. Melbourne University Press, Melbourne, 1983, pp. 153–154.

Hastings, Peter. 'And I Never Owned a Motor-Car', *Bulletin*, Sydney, 16 November 1963.

Hurley, Francis, 'Father William Hackett SJ', *Xaverian*, Melbourne, 1954, pp. 104–107.

Kathleen Dunlop Kane, 'O'Connell, Cecily Maude 1884–1965', *Australian Dictionary of Biography*, vol. 11, Melbourne University Press, Melbourne, 1988, pp. 49–50.

Kiberd, Declan, 'Thomas MacDonagh 1878–1916', in Anthony Roche (ed.), *The UCD Aesthetic: Celebrating 150 years of UCD Writers*, New Island, Dublin, 2003, pp. 34–35.

Luttrell, John, 'Bishop Gilroy and the Diocese of Port Augusta', *Australasian Catholic Record*, vol. 80, no. 2, Sydney, April 2003, p. 192.

McConville, Chris, 'John Joseph Lonergan', *Australian Dictionary of Biography*, vol. 10, Melbourne University Press, Melbourne, 1986, pp. 132–33.

Mannix, Daniel, Foreword to *Australia*, vol. 1, no. 1, Melbourne, 7 November 1917, p. 1.

Mannix, Daniel, 'Father William Hackett SJ: Archbishop Mannix's Tribute', *Xaverian*, Melbourne, 1954, p. 104.

Martin, F. X., 'The Evolution of a Myth—The Easter Rising, Dublin, 1916', in Eugene Kamenka (ed.), *Nationalism: The Nature and Evolution of an Idea*, Australian National University Press, Canberra, 1973, pp. 56–80.

Massam, Katherine, 'Prendiville, Redmond (1900–1968)', *Australian Dictionary of Biography*, vol 16, Melbourne University Press, Melbourne, 2002, pp. 26–27.

Morgan, Patrick, 'Bob Santamaria Talks to the World', *Sydney Papers*, Autumn 2007, pp. 89–95.

Murphy, Jeffrey J., 'The Lost (and Last) Animadversions of Daniel Mannix', *Australasian Catholic Record*, Sydney, January 1999, pp. 54–73.

Niall, Mary Constance, 'A Boarder in Wartime', in Sister Maria Bell (ed.), *And the Spirit Lingers*, Genazzano College History Committee, Melbourne, 1988, pp. 101–107.

Noone, Val, 'Archbishop Daniel Mannix in West Melbourne 1913–1917', *Footprints: Journal of the Melbourne Diocesan Historical Commission*, vol. 27, no. 2, Melbourne, December 2012, pp. 6–14.

Noone, Val, 'Class Factors in the Radicalisation of Archbishop Daniel Mannix, 1913–17', in Frank Bongiorno, Raelene Frances and Bruce Scales (eds.), *Labour and the Great War: The Australian Working Class and the Making of Anzac*, Australian Society for the Study of Labour History, Sydney, 2014, pp. 189–204.

Noone, Val, 'Irish in the Australian Labour Movement 1945–1954: de Valera, the Queen and Eureka', *Footprints: Journal of the Melbourne Diocesan Historical Commission*, vol, 13, no. 1, Melbourne, June 1996, pp. 8–32.

Noone, Val, 'Santamaria Years: A YCW View', *Tain*, no. 31, Melbourne, June–July 2004, pp. 18–19.

O'Brien, John B., 'The Australianisation of the Australian Catholic Church: Panico—Culprit or Victim?', in Philip Bull, Frances Devlin-Glass and Helen Doyle (eds.), *Ireland and Australia 1798–1998: Studies in Culture, Identity and Migration*, Crossing Press, Sydney, 2000, pp. 177–85.

Parkinson, Patrick, 'Suffer the Teenage Children: Child Sexual Abuse in Church Communities', Sydney Law School Legal Studies Research Paper no. 13/09, February 2013 (http://ssrn.com/abstract=2216264).

Richmond, Mark, 'Lewis Charles Burne, (1898–1972)', *Australian Dictionary of Biography*, vol. 13, Melbourne University Press, Melbourne, 1993, pp. 309–10.

Robertson, J. R., 'James Henry Scullin (1876–1953)', *Australian Dictionary of Biography*, vol. 11, Melbourne University Press, Melbourne, 1988, p. 554.

Ryan, Peter, 'Long Shadow Cast by Lay Prince', review of Morgan (ed.), *B. A. Santamaria: Your Most Obedient Servant*, *Weekend Australian*, 21–22 January 2007.

Spadaro, Antonio SJ, 'A Big Heart Open to God: A Conversation with Pope Francis', *America*, New York, 30 September 2013, pp. 15–38.

Trait, Ruth, 'Fr William Bernard Mangan, 1879–1960', *Footprints: Journal of the Melbourne Diocesan Historical Commission*, vol. 18, no. 3, Melbourne, December 2001, pp. 13–17.

Virgona, Crina, 'Jean and Lena Virgona, Housekeepers to Dr Mannix, 1944–1963', *Footprints: Journal of the Melbourne Diocesan Historical Commission*, vol. 28, no. 1, Melbourne, June 2013, pp. 4–10.

Vodola, Max, 'As the Record Stands: The Biographies of Daniel Mannix and James Duhig and their Contributions to Australian Catholic History', *Footprints: Journal of the Melbourne Diocesan Historical Commission*, vol. 12, no. 2, Melbourne, December 1995, pp. 3–19.

Williams, Caroline, 'Moran, Mannix and St Patrick's Day', in Philip Bull, Frances Devlin-Glass and Helen Doyle (eds.), *Ireland and Australia 1798–1998: Studies in Culture, Identity and Migration*, Crossing Press, Sydney, 2000, pp. 143–51.

THESES

Cappello, Anthony, 'Italian Australians, the Church, War and Fascism in Melbourne, 1919–1945', MA Thesis, Victoria University, 2006.

De Luca, Anthony, 'A Vision Found and Lost: The Promotion and Evolving Interpretation of the Movement for Liturgical Musical Reform within the Sydney Church during the Twentieth Century', PhD Thesis, School of Music and Music Education, University of NSW, 2001.

Francis, Michael Philip, 'Catholics and Conscription: A Problem of Loyalty', BA (Hons) Thesis, University of Melbourne, 2013.

Mathews, Race, 'Manning's Children: Responses to *Rerum Novarum* in Victoria 1891–1996', Doctor of Theology Thesis, Melbourne College of Divinity, University of Divinity, Melbourne, 2014.

Turnbull, Jeffrey, 'The Architecture of Newman College', PhD Thesis, Faculty of Architecture, University of Melbourne, 2004.

INTERVIEWS

B. A. Santamaria interviewed by Robin Hughes, 23 April 1997, Australian Biography Project, National Library of Australia, http://www.australianbiography.gov.au/subjects/santamaria/interview1html

Father Harold Craig SJ interviewed by Father Liam O'Connell SJ, Summer 1978, transcript, (ASJASL).

MISCELLANEOUS

'Billy Hughes' Family Secret', *Rewind*, ABCTV, screened 8 August 2004 (www.abc.net.au/tv/rewind/txt/s1168547.htm).

Coldrey, Barry M. (comp.), 'Religious Life without Integrity: The Sexual Abuse Crisis in the Catholic Church' (BishopAccountability.org).

Tonti-Filippini, Nicholas, 'The Catholic Church and Paedophilia: Learning from Failures', *ABC Religion and Ethics*, 4 June 2013.

Acknowledgments

I thank Archbishop Denis Hart for giving me access to the Mannix Papers and other records in the Melbourne diocesan archives and for his kind interest in this project. Dr Ian Waters, then chair of the Melbourne Diocesan Historical Commission, and Rachel Naughton, the commission's archivist and manager, gave invaluable support. I am grateful also to diocesan archivists Stephania di Maria (Perth), Pru Francis (Hobart), Jo Robertson (Sydney), Suzanne Ryan (Adelaide) and Michael Taffe (Ballarat), all of whom searched for elusive Mannix material. Dr Helen Frank enabled me to draw on the resources of the Dominican order's library at Camberwell (Vic). Michael Head SJ and Liz Parker were welcoming and helpful at the archives of the Jesuit order in Hawthorn (Vic) as was Gerard Hayes at the State Library of Victoria. Mary Jones of the New York Public Library gave her time most generously. In Ireland, Danny Cusack, who gave skilled research assistance throughout the project, explored the de Valera Papers (University College, Dublin) and the archives of a number of Mannix's correspondents in the Irish hierarchy. My debt to Professor Dermot Keogh includes his searches on my behalf in the records of University College, Cork, and St Patrick's College, Maynooth. I thank him also for his advice and encouragement.

I wish that space allowed me to spell out the ways in which a wide range of people have helped in this project. I list them with much gratitude to all. The late Father Tom Boland, Dr John Brenan, Joe Broderick, Father Tom Brophy, Sean Burke, Brendan Byrne SJ, Dr Simon Caterson, Father Ed Campion, John Challis, Catherine and Bill Clancy, Mary Ryllis Clark, the late Professor Max Charlesworth, Kay Cole, Dr Michael Costigan, Bishop Hilton Deakin, Christopher Dowd OP, John Doyle, the late Paul Duffy SJ, the late Father Leonard Egan, Helen Elliott, Dr John Funder, Angela Gehrig, Dr Michael Gilchrist, Adrian Gorman, Sir James Gobbo, the late Mary Ward Haldun, Tom Hazell, the late Father Lou Heriot, Douglas Kennedy, Frank Kissane, Margaret Le Mire, Bob Mannix, Patrick Mannix, Dr Kathleen McCarthy, Dr Mark McKenna, Bishop Michael McKenna, Peter Maloney, Margaret Maher, Dr Paul Maher, Dr Race Matthews, Patsy Millett, Patrick Morgan, Dr Jeffrey Murphy, Dr Hugh Niall, Gina Nicoletti, Dr Sybil Nolan, Dr Val Noone, Michael O'Grady, Tony O'Grady, Brother John O'Halloran, Terry O'Neill, Dr Michael Parer, Marilyn Puglisi, Mother Prioress, Carmelite Monastery, Kew, Father Brian Quillinan CSSR, Dr John Rickard, Brenda Rush, the late Father Paul Ryan, Philippa Ryan, Bob Santamaria jnr, Justice Joseph Santamaria, Paul Santamaria QC, Cristina Shannon, Sister Mary of Christ, O.Carm., Anna Sturgess, Pamela Sublet, Dr Bernadette Tobin, Des Tobin, Dr Jeffrey Turnbull, William

Uren SJ, Father Max Vodola, James Walder, Robert Walder, Patricia Wallis-McCombe, Father Michael Walsh, Mary Helen Woods and Thecla Broderick Xipell.

I have several special debts to acknowledge. Peter Walsh persuaded me that it was time for a new biography of Daniel Mannix and gave the project generous funding for research and travel from the Eldon Hogan Trust. I thank him for his confidence in my work. My sister, historian Frances O'Neill, had an essential role in the enterprise. I gained a great deal from her ideas, her astute questions and close readings of my text, as well as significant discoveries in her archival research. I am grateful to Andrew Hamilton SJ for reading the first draft of the text, and giving encouraging and constructive comments. As the biography became a bigger and more complex task than I had imagined, I was lucky enough to have Jane Pearson as editor. I have benefited from her sense of style and structure, and she has helped me to keep in mind the twenty-first-century readership of the Mannix story. I thank Jane and the team at Text Publishing for bringing this work to completion.

Index

D